CLARK GRIFFITH

BASEBALL'S STATESMAN

Brian McKenna

Copyright © 2010 by Brian McKenna

Cover design by Kevin Swink

All rights reserved.

No part of this book may be reproduced in any form or by any electronic or mechanical means including information storage and retrieval systems, without permission in writing from the author. The only exception is by a reviewer, who may quote short excerpts in a review.

Brian McKenna

Visit my website at www.Baseballhistoryblog.com

Printed in the United States of America

First Printing: May 2010

ISBN 978-0-557-47295-6

To Brian and Rachel, my daily inspirations

Clark Griffith is one of those men whose unswerving faith in baseball has made possible some of its most pronounced successes. While Griffith has never been heralded with as much publicity as has Mack or McGraw, he has probably done as much as either toward the development of the National Game. He was a famous player, one of the founders of the American League, a manager of proved capacity, and is now a brand new magnate whose influence in the big show is already being felt.

F. C. Lane, Editor-in-Chief, *Baseball Magazine*, 1912

CONTENTS

Chapter Topic Highlights

Preface		i
Prologue	One Cold Day, Two Old Men	iv
Chapter One	Coons, Possums and Polecats	1
Chapter Two	Bloomington to the Barbary Coast	15
Chapter Three	Old Fox	60
Chapter Four	Bucking the System	87
Chapter Five	The American League	100
Chapter Six	Big Apple	115
Chapter Seven	Back in the National League	151
Chapter Eight	That Baseball Graveyard	162
Chapter Nine	Senators, Nationals or Nats	167

Chapter Ten	National Treasure	182
Chapter Eleven	Gaining Control	188
Chapter Twelve	Family Man	192
Chapter Thirteen	Politics of the Game	204
Chapter Fourteen	Riding High in the Nation's Capital	212
Chapter Fifteen	Relief Pitching	223
Chapter Sixteen	Great Depression	226
Chapter Seventeen	One Last Pennant	233
Chapter Eighteen	Farm System	242
Chapter Nineteen	Fertile Cuban Sandlots	251
Chapter Twenty	Role in Integration	258
Chapter Twenty-One	Financing on a Shoestring	270
Chapter Twenty-Two	…Last in the American League	278
Chapter Twenty-Three	Statesman	291
Chapter Twenty-Four	Challenge at the Top	313
Chapter Twenty-Five	Changing of the Guard	319

Appendix	Chronology of Selected Events	328
Bibliography		332
Select Index		344

CHAPTER TOPIC HIGHLIGHTS

Chapter One   Coons, Possums and Polecats

Birth family - Early life – Pop Dillon – high school baseball – Bloomington semi-pro baseball to 1887

Chapter Two   Bloomington to the Barbary Coast

Baseball 1888 to 1893 - Bloomington Reds – Pacer Smith – Hoss Radbourn – Milwaukee Brewers – James Hart - Monte Ward – Cap Anson – St. Louis Browns – Charles Comiskey – Chris von de Ahe – Dummy Hoy – Deaf Players – Tip O'Neill – Boston Reds – Arthur Irwin – Tacoma Daisies – Bill Works – Missoula, Montana – Charles Kilpatrick – Ambidextrous Pitchers – Tony Mullane – Earl Griffith – California baseball – California League – Oakland Colonels – pitching distances – Joe Cantillon – Norris O'Neill – Chicago Colts – Al Spalding – Ed Delahanty – winter ball in Oakland – Petaluma – Sacramento – Edgar McNabb – Barbary Coast

Chapter Three   Old Fox

Baseball 1894 to 1900 - Chicago Colts – Bill Lange – Bill Dahlen – Cap Anson – James Hart – beginnings of labor unrest – pitchers of the era – Clark Griffith's pitching style and techniques – shutout superstition – John Brush – horse racing – Rube Waddell

Chapter Four   Bucking the System

Arthur Soden – the blacklist – reserve clause – unionizing – American Federation of Labor – Cap Anson – Ban Johnson – wage ceiling – Protective Association of Professional Baseball Players – Chief Zimmer – Western League – American League – Charles Comiskey – Clark Griffith Company – Clark Griffith baseball – American Association – Honus Wagner – recruiting for American League

Chapter Five   The American League

Baseball 1901 to 1902 – Charles Comiskey – Chicago White Sox – soccer – John McGraw – Charlie Grant – Jimmy Callahan – Ban Johnson – 1901 pennant – Griffiths baseball club – Clark Griffith's Chicago Maroons

Chapter Six   Big Apple

Baseball 1903 to 1908 – Ban Johnson – Tammany Hall – Boss Tweed – Andrew Freedman – Amos Rusie – Hilltop Park – Baltimore Orioles relocation – John McGraw – New York Highlanders – Willie Keeler – Ty Cobb – Harry Howell – Jack O'Connor – Napoleon Lajoie – Dave Fultz – Addie Griffith – peace between American and National Leagues – Frank Farrell – Kid Elberfeld – John Brush – Montreal baseball – 1904 pennant race – Hal Chase – Jack Chesbro – relief pitching – Fred Glade – Garry Herrmann – Cincinnati Reds

Chapter Seven   Back in the National League

Baseball 1909 to 1911 – Cincinnati Reds – Garry Herrmann – Bob Bescher – pitching and batting machines – Cuba – Cuban baseball – Frank Bancroft – Armando Marsans – Rafael Almeida

Chapter Eight   That Baseball Graveyard

Washington baseball – Thomas Noyes – Benjamin Minor – Edward Walsh – Washington Nationals

Chapter Nine   Senators, Nationals or Nats

1910s baseball – Washington Nationals – Clyde Milan – Walter Johnson – Nick Altrock – Mike Martin – Washington nickname – Thomas Noyes – Joe Engel – Ty Cobb – Frank Navin – Federal League – Sam Rice – emery ball – Dover Hall Club – Billy Sunday

Chapter Ten   National Treasure

Walter Johnson – Federal League – Ben Minor – Washington Nationals

Chapter Eleven   Gaining Control

Purchasing the Senators – William Richardson

Chapter Twelve   Family Man

Marriage and birth family – Addie Griffith – Robertson family – Jim Robertson – Thelma Griffith – Calvin Griffith – Sherry Robertson – Billy Smith – Joe Engel – Edward Eynon – Clark Griffith's office

Chapter Thirteen   Politics of the Game

National Commission – Ban Johnson – Charles Comiskey – World War I – Baseball economics - Black Sox Scandal – game-fixing – gambling and gamblers – Judge Landis – Federal league – weakening of Ban Johnson's powers

Chapter Fourteen   Riding High in the Nation's Capital

1920s baseball – Washington Senators – George McBride – Ozzie Bluege – Goose Goslin – Firpo Marberry – Bucky Harris – 1924 pennant and

World Series – Jimmy O'Connell – Ban Johnson – Ty Cobb – Tris Speaker – Judge Landis – Joe Cronin – Jack Dunn – farm system

Chapter Fifteen   Relief Pitching

Pioneering relief pitching – Jack Chesbro – Jack Powell – New York Highlanders – John McGraw – Washington Senators – Allan Russell – Firpo Marberry -

Chapter Sixteen   Great Depression

Baseball economics – Judge Landis – attendance – minor leagues – Negro leagues – All-Star Game – Sunday Blue Laws - National Baseball Hall of Fame – radio broadcasting – night baseball

Chapter Seventeen   One Last Pennant

1930s baseball – Washington Senators – Joe Cronin – Sam Rice – 1933 pennant and World Series – House of David – Tom Yawkey – Babe Ruth – football – Washington Redskins – black baseball – Washington Grays

Chapter Eighteen   Farm System

National Agreement – National Association – farming rules – minor league structure – networking for talent - farming – working agreements – Chicago White Sox – player acquisitions and costs – Washington Senators – Joe Cantillon – Senators' farm system – minor league draft – Branch Rickey – Joe Engel

Chapter Nineteen   Fertile Cuban Sandlots

Cuban baseball – Cuban ballplayers – Esteban Bellan – Joe Cambria – scouting in Cuba - Washington Senators – Senators' farm system

Chapter Twenty   Role in Integration

Negro leagues – black baseball – Branch Rickey – Cuban ballplayers – Washington Grays – racism – interracial contests – Jake Powell – Griffith Stadium – Cum Posey – Washington Senators – black ballplayers – black press – Sam Lacy – Judge Landis – Jackie Robinson – Larry MacPhail -

Chapter Twenty-One   Financing on a Shoestring

Washington Senators' economics – Washington D.C. - Washington Senators – Senators' farm system – Babe Ruth – Griffith Stadium – Washington Redskins – Washington Grays – dividends

Chapter Twenty-Two   …Last in the American League

1940s and '50s baseball – Washington Senators – farm system – Executive of the Year – World War II – Elmer Gedeon – Cecil Travis – Bert Shepard – Happy Chandler – returning G.I.s – Mexican League – Danny Gardella – Cuba visit – American Baseball Guild – Robert Murphy – Bob Feller – Clark Griffith's Hall of Fame induction – Harmon Killebrew – Ozzie Bluege – Major League Baseball monopoly hearings

Chapter Twenty-Three   Statesman

Pancho Villa – Ban Johnson – military drill plan – World War I fundraising efforts – Bat and Ball Fund – Woodrow Wilson – Clark Griffith Days – Secretary of War Newton D. Baker – Eddie Ainsmith – General Enoch Crowder – World War I and baseball – World War II fundraising efforts – Baseball Equipment Fund – night baseball – Franklin Roosevelt – "Green Light" Letter – Judge Landis – World War II and baseball – Clark Griffith and D.C. – Clark Griffith's relationship with U.S. Presidents and other politicos – Robert E. Hannegan – war travel restrictions – Joseph B. Eastman – Negro league travel – Washington Senators – Teddy Roosevelt – Warren Harding – Calvin and Grace Coolidge – Herbert Hoover – Harry Truman – Dwight Eisenhower

Chapter Twenty-Four   Challenge at the Top

William Richardson – George Richardson – Washington Senators – John Jachym - H. Gabriel Murphy

Chapter Twenty-Five   Changing of the Guard

Calvin Griffith – Washington Senators – Clark Griffith's legacy – Clark Griffith's health – Clark Griffith's death and funeral – reorganization of Washington Senators – Washington Senators' economics – Clark Griffith's estate and will – Addie Griffith

PREFACE

Writing a brief introduction about the baseball career of Clark C. Griffith seems like an impossible task considering that it lasted nearly seventy years, over sixty of those in the majors. Perhaps therein lies the theme, the fact that his career spanned so many different eras and that his position in the game progressed from bush league pitcher to major league star to respected manager and finally to one of the most influential magnates in the business. To me, a biography of this caliber is one of the most interesting subjects baseball history can provide. A study of such a diverse career, one that spanned eight different decades, is actually a study of the history of the game itself.

So what exactly is so interesting about his life and career?

For one, Griffith pitched all over the country, in the northeast, the northwest, on the west coast, in the south and in a few places in between in an era when few Americans saw much of the country. His career began before the pitching distance was expanded to the current sixty feet and six inches. He pitched from 55'6" both in the minors and at the major league level. In fact, he didn't land a permanent job in the majors until the very season the distance was extended, 1893. Secondly, Griffith was one of the wiliest, brainiest in contemporary vernacular, pitchers in the history of the game. He had to be; like Greg Maddux, he didn't possess a blazing fastball like most of his successful contemporaries. Also like Maddux, he was among the top tier of his generation, effectively utilizing and controlling many more pitches than his contemporaries. Some reading this will be surprised to learn that the man they know inducted into the Hall of Fame as an executive actually won 237 games and that many rank him only behind contemporaries Kid Nichols, Cy Young and Amos Rusie, all possessors of a blazing fastball, during what has been described as the top offensive era in the game's history. I was particularly surprised at his on-the-field combativeness and his effectiveness in the batter's box. In fact, much of his career was actually new to me as I grew up knowing of him only as the kindly old gentleman who ran the Senators.

As one of the marquee pitchers in the National League, Griff, as he was called within the industry, was at the forefront of the unionizing movement that led to the rise of the American League, history's only long-term successful challenger to the National League's monopoly. In truth, the unionizing movement at the turn of the century actually grew out of Griffith's salary disputes with Chicago from as early as 1897. Given lesser credit today for the American League's success, Griffith's contributions were as essential as Ban Johnson's administration, Charles Somers' financial backing and Charles Comiskey's support. In fact, would the American League exist today if Griffith hadn't incited the players' revolt and recruited top talent for the upstart league? Along these lines it could be argued that he directly and indirectly stocked nearly every American League roster with established major league talent.

As a manager, Griffith pioneered the use of relief pitching. It should be noted that he was the one taking the mound as well. It's no exaggeration to say that Griffith was the first manager to extensively utilize a bullpen and to gain fuller use of all his personnel, both on offense and defense, on a daily basis. He was also responsible, as both a manager and club owner, for diversifying the game by extensively recruiting Cuban talent for his clubs. He became revered on the island for his efforts. It can be said, and has by Branch Rickey himself, that Clark Griffith integrated the game long before Jackie Robinson took the field for the Brooklyn Dodgers in 1947. Through a contrasting point of view, he was at times seen as an impediment to racial integration during the 1940s. This wasn't based on any personal prejudice rather in the politics of doing business in a segregated city and spurred by the fact that he made a lot of money renting his ballpark to Negro league clubs. As the American League owner with the smallest fan base, he relied heavily on rental income from the Homestead Grays and Washington Redskins.

Confused in this perception is the fact that Griffith was the major league's leading conscience in respect to the Negro leagues and attended more Negro league games than perhaps all other major league executives combined.¹ He had a close relationship with Cum Posey and others within black baseball. As such, he was the liaison between the two entities. This placed him at odds with Branch Rickey's unilateral decision to raid Negro league rosters and otherwise threatened the Negro league's very survival.

Few realize today that Griffith was the first organizer of the club now known as the New York Yankees. He began scouting locations for a ballpark in the city even before the 1902 season and John McGraw's desertion from the Baltimore franchise which prompted relocation to New York City in 1903. Griffith raided the strongest club in the major leagues, the Pittsburgh Pirates coming off a 103-36 season, to stock the new American League marquee franchise. He also ran the club almost single-handedly for years.

He was one of the fiercest and most intense competitors of his time, a trait he borrowed from his manager Cap Anson. Little known today, Griffith was the premier umpire baiter of his time whose last name wasn't McGraw. Many today see Griffith as the tight-fisted, penny-wise owner who ran the Washington Senators. In contrast, nearly no one inside or outside the game had a sour word to say about the man, save some particular bitterness, perhaps justifiable, by umpires and some of his players at negotiation time. He was befriended by all. Of note, the premier local sportswriters revered him in his two major career stops, Hugh Fullerton in Chicago and Shirley Povich in D.C.

More than that, Griffith was the game's statesman. He was an icon in the nation's capital, roundly respected by the nation's leaders and elite as perhaps no other American sports figure. It stemmed from the fact that he completely and immediately turned around the hapless Senators' franchise, making it the third strongest club in the American League during the 1910s after he took over in 1912. The club then won two pennants and a world's championship during the 1920s before flopping during the Depression after copping another pennant in 1933. An everlasting myth often repeated by baseball fans is that Walter Johnson pitched on perennially bad ball clubs; the truth is that after age 24 when Griffith took over Johnson pitched for winners. More so, it had to do with the fact that Griffith was the face of the game to the nation's leaders. He routinely visited the White House and called many in government, military and big business by their first name. Baseball was the king of sports and if the kings of politics and industry wanted into the

---

¹ Pittsburgh Pirates' owner William E. Benswanger was also an enthusiastic fan of black baseball. He attended many Homestead Grays and Pittsburgh Crawfords games at Forbes Field.

game, they called Mr. Griffith. He called them as well when baseball needed a favor.

Nearly fifty by the time America became involved in World War I, Griffith couldn't take up arms. Instead, he took to the pulpit, becoming one of the nation's leading private fundraisers via his Bat and Ball Fund and through war bond drives. He continued his efforts during the Second World War. His relationship with a succession of United States Presidents put him in a unique position to garner favorable rulings for the game. This was never more visible then during World War II. When it looked like the game would be closed down, Griffith maneuvered the *Green Light* letter from President Franklin Roosevelt that expressed the nation's need for the entertainment of a ball game. Significantly, no one else in the game could have gained such favorable status for the sport, certainly not the staunchly conservative and outspoken commissioner Judge Landis who was persona non grata around the White House. Amusingly, Griffith used his relationship with Roosevelt to make an end-run around Landis as well, to gain a desired increase in the number of allotted night games.

As mentioned, many remember Griffith as the parsimonious old owner of the Washington Senators. In actuality he was an accomplished businessman, continually making money in a tough town as one of the few owners solely dependent on his club for income. He did this as a master of public relations by first building goodwill and becoming intimately involved in the community. He then built a contender the city could be proud of with a less than ideal fan base and support, being that D.C. was in large part a transient city. After the Depression crippled his franchise, Griffith adapted and actually made the most money of his career by renting out his ballpark to the football Redskins and Negro league Grays.

As much as he was a dedicated baseball man, Griffith was as committed to his family. He was the sole financial support from the early days of his marriage for his wife and mother-in-law. He also found a job within the game for his brother-in-law, James Robertson. When Robertson, a father of seven, passed away, the Griffiths took in the whole family. They moved two of the children into their home and purchased a separate house for their mother and other five siblings. Eventually, all the Robertson children worked for the Senators' organization. Later, they inherited the franchise. He held just as close a relationship with the players, Griffith Stadium employees and countless others within the industry.

In all, Griffith lived many lives in the game. He was intimately involved in every major development during the game's evolution from the late 1880s until the mid 1950s. In the beginning he was just another bush leaguer trying to rise from the amateur fields of Illinois. He soon became the leading star and spokesman for the players in the game's second largest city, Chicago. He then jumped leagues and guided his club to the American League's first major league pennant. Griffith then took over the American League's franchise in the game's largest city, New York, and sparked the controversy that eventually mandated that a World Series be played on a yearly basis. In Washington he brought the franchise out of the cellar and built a perennial contender. In his later years, Griffith was recognized as one of the foremost members of the old guard ruling the game. His presence was so crucial to baseball in D.C. that the franchise that was long-since synonymous with his name would cut and run for Minnesota not long after his death.

PROLOGUE

ONE COLD DAY, TWO OLD MEN

April 15, 1954 was overcast and sprinkling in Baltimore but the half million fans lined up from Mt. Royal Station to Memorial Stadium to greet their new ball club didn't seem to mind. Schools closed and city workers, among others, took a half-day; there was a new team to root on. Major League Baseball had come back to Charm City after more than fifty years. Nothing could dampen their spirits. Two of the oldest and most-respected names in the game were there to welcome this latest version of the Orioles.[2]

    Connie Mack from Philadelphia was 91 years old and only retired from the dugout a mere four springs ago. It was a full seventy years since he first cashed a check from a professional baseball club.[3] Beside Mack that day was his longtime friend and on-the-field nemesis from Washington D.C. Clark Griffith. Similarly, Griffith at 84 years old had first signed a minor league contract back in 1887. The two were the elder statesmen of the game, a dying breed; the last of the owners who grew out

---

[2] At the major league level Baltimore fielded teams in the American Association from 1882-89 and another from August 1890 through '91, Union Association in 1884, National league 1892-99, American League 1901-01 and Federal League 1914-15. The latter was called the Terrapins because the name Orioles was reserved by Jack Dunn's minor league franchise in the International League.

[3] Mack first signed with Meriden in the Connecticut League in 1884. His real name was Cornelius McGillicuddy; it had to be shortened to fit in box scores.

of the player ranks to derive their sole income through their passion, their baseball franchise. They were the embodiment of the game, living symbols of a rich and colorful history.

Nearly a century and a half of baseball knowledge and experience sat in those two chairs. Their careers began long before anyone ever thought of classifying the minor leagues. Each played in a major league that few today know existed, Mack in the Players League and Griffith in the American Association. Both participated in labor movements two decades before Marvin Miller was even born. These men managed American League pennant winners before World Series competition began.[4] Each had been running ball clubs since the turn of the century.

For these veterans of many summers the game was about to change. Actually, it already had. The Braves, which resided in Boston since the inaugural National League season of 1876, moved west to Milwaukee the previous summer. Today marked the first home game of the new American League Baltimore Orioles, which relocated from St. Louis where they were known as the Browns.[5] These were the first relocations since 1903 but many more were to come. The expansion era soon followed.

The trend eastward was fleeting. Soon, the franchises that Mack and Griffith spent a lifetime building moved west. Mack saw his family sell to Kansas City interests by the next season's opener and the Senators soon uprooted to Minnesota. Both patriarchs would die within two years, four months apart. This Opening Day, 1954, was a celebration though.

On hand were two old National League Orioles from the heralded 1890s, Jack Doyle and Boileryard Clarke. Both were old foes from Mack and Griffith's playing days. Clarke was also a Griffith ally in the players union. Together, they bucked the system. Pushed around for years by National League executives, the players stood in unison to negotiate a better deal. When the magnates refused their requests, Griffith led the insurrection that in the end was partially responsible for the success of the upstart American League by stocking its rosters with experienced major league talent.

A bigger foe lurked nearby, well almost. Mrs. John McGraw, widow of the most famous Oriole of them all, came to cheer for the city her husband called home for many years. Few present realized that John

---

[4] Griffith won the American League flag in 1901, Mack the following year.

[5] When the American League became a major league in 1901 the franchise originally resided in Milwaukee, moved to St. Louis in 1902 and then Baltimore in 1954.

McGraw single-handedly destroyed the previous Baltimore major league franchise, back in 1902 when he uprooted the club's best players and led them to the National League. Mack and McGraw's on-the-field battles are well documented. Some would be surprised to know that Mack got the better of their head-to-head World Series competitions, 2 to 1. Griffith's sole World Series glory came at the expense of McGraw's Giants.

Like McGraw, Mack and Griffith were two of the most hard-nosed competitors of the 1890s. McGraw, a New York native, embraced that image and retold it over and over again to the sportswriters. It was the reason he left the American League; he couldn't abide by Ban Johnson's rules and the emerging role of the umpire. Mack and Griffith moved past it and ultimately presented a more regal image: Mack, the Tall Tactician, wearing a suit and quietly positioning his boys on the field from the dugout by waving a scorecard; Griffith, the Old Fox, diligently running his club on a shoestring budget, working behind the scenes to solve league problems and courting politicians and diplomats for the betterment of his Senators and all of baseball.

Vice President Richard M. Nixon was also in attendance. A big sports fan, Nixon was one of many of Washington's elite to hold a long friendship with the Senators' owner. Griffith's business manager Edward "Eddie" B. Eynon Jr. made a career out of catering to the government's select and judiciously seating and administering to all factions without complaint. Mr. Griffith was the game's link, its statesman. He negotiated and otherwise work behind the scenes to ensure the sport's future through two world wars and numerous political and legal battles.

He hosted every United States President from Taft to Eisenhower and even rubbed elbows with the first Roosevelt and some upstarts who would themselves be President one day. Every spring Griffith and Eynon trekked to the White House to present the Chief Executive and the First Lady with their season passes and to invite them to Opening Day and ask the President to toss out the ceremonial first pitch. Franklin Roosevelt regularly called the Senators' owner for inside dope so he could have a leg up in his daily, friendly baseball wagers with White House staffers.

By design, one man wasn't in attendance in Baltimore and his absence highlights other facets of baseball's personality and business acumen. Bill Veeck was a rebel; he irked the establishment and he could care less. Veeck didn't wear a tie nor did he act like *The Man in the Gray Flannel Suit*. He took chances and was openly amused by those that didn't. He later stood by Curt Flood in his challenge of the reserve system when no one else in the industry would. Griffith, later in life, was conservative in his affairs and he in essence was the establishment. He fought many challenges to the reserve clause after becoming an executive; like many in the business, he often referred to the reserve clause as "the backbone of baseball." The two couldn't, would never see eye to eye.

Under the surface, Griffith and Veeck were a lot more alike than either knew or dared to admit. Griffith bucked the establishment at every opportunity in both the minors and the majors when he was a younger man and pushed the game at times as he grew older. He also was a bit of a showman but on smaller scale than Veeck. Both were outgunned financially when dealing with their peers. And, both were among the most social of all the owners, mixing freely with colleagues, fans, players, reporters and each making his mark in black baseball.

The previous March, in 1953, Veeck sought to transfer his St. Louis Browns, a perpetually struggling franchise, to Baltimore. At an owners meeting in Tampa Veeck walked in the door believing he had secured the league's approval. Baltimore's National Brewery owner Jerold Hoffberger even promised the nearby Senators $350,000 to cover the loss of television revenue. Griffith was quoted as saying, "It will be great for baseball."

The deal fell through after St. Louis' mayor threatened a lawsuit and both Mack and Griffith reversed themselves. The final vote was 6 to 2 against the move. It was more a vote against Veeck than anything else. He regularly battled the commissioner and antagonized his fellow owners. Obviously, the Browns relocated but they would do so after Veeck was removed from the picture. In the end the wily Griffith negotiated a better deal. National Brewery would continue to advertise with the Senators through 1955 plus pay $300,000 as compensation to the club for Baltimore's encroachment.

Griffith believed a new club up the road in Baltimore would only strengthen his by sparking a fierce rivalry. Even in the leanest years in the standings and the box office, he usually found a way to turn a dividend for his stockholders. Soon it wouldn't be enough. Only once did the ball club draw over a million fans; the support just wasn't there in D.C., the sparsest populated American League city. Once the Old Fox passed away, the weaknesses of the franchise were exposed. His successor and adopted son, Calvin Robertson Griffith, sought greener pastures in the twin cities of Minneapolis and St. Paul.

CHAPTER ONE

COONS, POSSUMS AND POLECATS

Shortly after the Civil War, Isaiah and a pregnant Sarah Griffith packed up their three children and all their earthly possessions into a covered wagon, popularly called a prairie schooner, and left Boynton, Illinois for a brighter future in the Oklahoma Panhandle.[6] At the time, the area, the current three northwestern-most counties of Oklahoma, was administered by no formal government and wouldn't be so until 1890. Land could be had cheaply.

The burgeoning west attracted many who thought they could trade hard work and sacrifice for greater financial rewards and a brighter future for their family. A tremendous population shift occurred during the 1850s and '60s as eastern families moved to western territories. Rumors abound of rich soil, quick financial advancement and potentially easy fortunes to be had. Poor eastern families, barely living above the starvation level, found in this a possibility for escape and financial stability.

The Griffiths departed with Sarah's relatives, Jessie and Emily Dillon and Aaron and Sarah Dillon, and families and Isaiah's relatives, Joseph and Mary F. Griffith.[7] A total caravan of around twenty families in

---

[6] Census documents show the Griffiths in Illinois in 1860 and in Missouri in 1870 and 1880. Clark filled in many details during interviews with Shirley Povich of the *Washington Post* during the 1930s and '40s.

[7] Per a perusal of the 1870 U.S. Census for Vernon Country

prairie schooners left in the spring of 1867, prime-grazing time for the livestock.[8] The caravan traveled en masse for security reasons, as the open range could be a dangerous place. Many men, fresh from the training and savagery of war, roamed the countryside looking for potential victims and an easy payday. Even more so, people feared Indian attacks; in actuality, they were much more likely to die from drowning and disease.

The plan was to be established with land and shelter by the onset of winter. They followed well-worn traveling and cattle trails along and through the Missouri River, Missouri Valley and the Shawnee Trail. Such a route yielded approximately twenty miles per day barring weather-related or mechanical difficulties.[9] The group traveled by day and rested at night.

The trip, exponentially more difficult and dangerous in previous decades, was still arduous in the 1860s, especially with a large family in tow. U.S. Census records show that the oldest Griffith child, Mary, born circa 1855, was about twelve years old. She was accompanied by her eight-year-old sister, Angeline (Angela), born circa 1859, two-year-old brother, Earl H., born circa 1865, and soon-to-be-born sister, Minnie.[10] Considering all the supplies, furniture, house ware items, personal effects and dried foods that occupied space, the family had little room for movement in the schooner, especially distressing to the active young children. The bed of a typical wagon was only four feet by 10 or 12 feet. Typically, the entire party, except tired children, walked along with the wagons to avoid the heavy jostling.

Along the path, the Griffith caravan met another group that was originally headed to Texas but turned back due to hardship. They told the Griffiths, Dillons and the others of the troubles and difficulties that lie ahead.[11] Dismayed, the families considered cutting their trip short or even returning to Illinois. The Griffiths decided to discontinue their voyage and search for their new home.

After 500 or 600 miles, depending on their route, the Griffiths and Dillons waved goodbye to their fellow travelers, staked claims and settled in the township of Clear Creek, Missouri. Clear Creek, located in Vernon County, lies in southwestern Missouri about twelve miles from the Kansas border and not that much farther from the closest

---

[8] Grass wouldn't turn the proper green for the livestock until April.

[9] Oxen, the sturdiest choice to lead the wagons, traveled only about two miles per hour with their load.

[10] Ages are taken from the 1870 U.S. Census. Minnie may have actually been born in January 1867.

[11] A major hardship in traveling out west was crossing water.

contemporary outpost, Fort Scott. Their new home was just off the Shawnee Trail that initially was an Indian hunting and raiding route. It became the earliest and easternmost of the trails which Texas longhorn cattle were driven by the thousands northward to railway stations. The trail lapsed into disuse during the war and was just beginning to make a comeback in 1867.

Vernon County was originally in the middle of Osage Indian territory. The first white settlers in western Missouri were missionaries who set up stakes in 1821. By that time, the Indians were being driven out. Within four years, the remaining Osage had been ousted, finally settling on a Kansas reservation. Vernon County itself was formally established in 1855, named after War of 1812 veteran, Colonel Miles Standish Vernon. Nevada, about twelve miles from Clear Creek, with its iron mines was set as the county's seat. It was also the trading center for the area.

Leading up to the Civil War, violence spilled over from eastern Kansas into Vernon County as antislavery forces, stationed in and around Fort Scott, were beginning to exert their control and influence over the territory. Federal forces combined with the guerrilla tactics of Jayhawkers, organized local troops of radical abolitionists, had Vernon residents in a panic, fearing for their life and safety of their families.

Not one vote was cast for Abraham Lincoln in the proslavery Vernon County. The brazen of federal troops and Jayhawkers only increased after his election. Perhaps the most famous Jayhawker, John Brown led a midnight raid in December 1858 into Vernon County. He carried off a dozen slaves and a good deal of property and left a local farmer slain. Brown did the same at Harper's Ferry, Virginia a year later but was then captured and hung before he could flee the area.

Secession flags flew in Vernon in 1861 and the war was on. Actually, Missouri, as a whole, was torn and very active during the war, about 110,000 men fought for the Union Army and 90,000 or so for the Confederate Army. In all, about nine hundred battles took place in Missouri, at least four in Clear Creek itself. Of particular trouble to local residents were the intermittent battles between federal troops and the Bushwhackers. So called by the federal troops, Bushwhackers were Confederate soldiers who initially left the army to return home to protect their families, for the most part, from rape, pillage and murder by the Jayhawkers. Since Vernon County was mainly under the control of federal forces, continual skirmishes erupted throughout the area as the wondering Bushwhackers conducted guerrilla warfare tactics against the government troops in an effort to loosen their grip and will.

Eventually, the Bushwhackers became less and less honorable as they began to attract seedier members. Soon, local residents feared the Bushwhackers more than any other faction. These nomads continued for years roaming and abusing families. Part of Clark's childhood was spent staring up at Bushwhackers or other thieves who were captured by local residents and hung for current or past misdeeds. It was part of his morning ritual to run outside and see if a new corpse was swinging from the hanging tree. Understandably, he quickly learned the value of living a clean, honest life.

By the end of the war, Vernon County was in shambles. Local businesses were all destroyed and fewer than one hundred families remained in the area. The Jayhawkers and Bushwhackers absconded with virtually everything, even the fence rails. Slowly, the area was rebuilt as confederate soldiers en masse returned home and former Union soldiers relocated to the county. Surprisingly, this brought little trouble; there was just too much work to be done.

Shirley Povich of the *Washington Post* traced the Griffith family leaving Wales for America in the late seventeenth century. Isaiah was sired from sturdy Colonial Virginia stock and was the paternal grandson of John Ward Griffith who fought with George Washington during the Revolutionary War.[12]

Isaiah E. Griffith was born in Illinois in either 1832 or '33. There is an indication that his marriage to Sarah may have been his second, since his daughter Mary was born three years before their wedding ceremony; there is also the possibility that Mary may have been an adopted niece or cousin. Years later, Clark identified Angela as his oldest sibling; in fact, he never even mentioned Mary in the interview about his family.[13]

Sarah and Isaiah were married on July 7, 1858 in Logan County, Illinois. The 1860 Census places the Griffiths living in Boynton, Illinois in Tazewell County. Isaiah was listed as a farmer with an estate value of $250. A database search shows 125 Griffiths serving in the Civil War from Illinois, all in the Union Army. No Isaiah is listed but the Wright, Griffith and Dillon families all sympathized with the Union's cause. After all, they were from Abraham Lincoln's home state.

---

[12] Povich wrote a 33-part series on Griffith's life titled "Clark Griffith: 50 Years in Baseball" for the *Washington Post* in January and February 1938.

[13] *The Sporting News*, July 30, 1952, page 12

Sarah's family is much easier to trace. Mrs. Griffith, born Sarah Ann Wright on September 18, 1836 in Randolph County, Indiana, was the seventh child of James M. Wright, born November 29, 1796 in Tennessee (died July 24, 1851), and Abigail Starbuck Wright, born January 24, 1800 in New Garden, North Carolina (died November 30, 1863). They were married on October 2, 1817 in Ohio and had ten children between 1818 and 1844.

The Starbuck family first fled to the New World with the Pilgrims to escape religious persecution. Edward Starbuck, a distant relative, was one of the original purchasers of Nantucket Island in 1659. In fact, Sarah's maternal grandfather Gayer Starbuck was born on Nantucket in 1777.

James and Abigail Wright and family moved to Indiana by 1820. When James passed away in 1851, the younger children and Abigail relocated to Tazewell County, Illinois to be with Abigail's mother's family the Dillons who moved to Tazewell in 1826 from Ohio.

Gayer Starbuck joined the Dillon family in 1799 when he married Susanna Dillon, daughter of Jesse Dillon and Hannah Ruckman. The United States portion of the Dillon family developed when Luke Dillon and his wife Susanna Garrett immigrated to the country from Ireland in the early years of the eighteenth century.

By late summer 1867, the Griffiths, Isaiah and Sarah, staked a claim on a forty-acre lot for $1,500 in Clear Creek and set out to build a two-story log cabin. They initially meant to develop the land for farming to support not only their family but to provide excess to sell at the market at Fort Scott or perhaps in Nevada. The Dillon families, perhaps a little wealthier, staked larger claims. Aaron's spread cost $1,800 and Jessie's a whopping $6,000. Joseph Griffith was working as a farmhand, possibly for Isaiah or for one the Dillons.[14]

Soon, Isaiah realized that the grain crop wasn't taking hold in the Missouri soil. There would be no large commercial production, hence, no riches for the Griffith family, just work and plenty of it. The farm itself barely sustained the family. Isaiah, a frontiersman, trapped and hunted small and large animals to keep his family fed and healthy. Sarah tended to vegetable gardens and her growing family.

On November 20, 1869 at the family's log cabin, Sarah gave birth to her fourth child and second son, Clark Calvin. The new brown-eyed

---

[14] The 1870 Census listed the value of real estate.

boy represented another mouth to feed for the struggling parents. Fortunately, the Katy (Missouri-Kansas-Texas) Railroad, a branch of the newly completed transcontinental railroad, ran its first lines through Nevada in October 1870. Sparking hope for the future, the area was becoming linked to larger markets. Isaiah abandoned farming altogether to hunt and trap deer, turkey and other game, for the most part, to sell to the railroad companies to feed their laborers. He and other hunters took their catches to the market at Fort Scott and sold their goods to the waiting railroad officials.

This proved to be a bit of a windfall for the family until February 1872 when a neighbor, 17-year-old Leonard Batts, mistook Isaiah for a deer and shot and killed the 39-year-old father of five in a cornfield[15] The Griffiths were expecting their sixth child. Isaiah never met his daughter Isa.[16] The family's prospects seemed bleak. The hardship was only beginning; a pregnant Sarah and her brood took to the fields with eight-year-old Earl now expected to catch the day's meals. Sarah slaved for the family from morning until nightfall. Clark later said that he learned from her never to take anything for granted and that family and success comes from hard work and sacrifice.

Luckily, Sarah and daughters Mary, now seventeen, and Angela received a good deal of help as neighbors banded together to assist the fatherless family. Clark recalled many years later how his house seemed like the focal point of the community, friends always coming and going. Neighbors helped plow the fields, make cornmeal and cut and stack firewood. Then, to the youngster's enjoyment there would be dinner and entertainment well into the evening. Story telling, fiddle playing and dancing were some of his favorite memories.

Eventually, the help fizzled out and the family was left, more or less, to fend for itself. Earl inherited his father's muzzle-loading musket with powder bag and ramrod and was getting to be a pretty good shot. Little Clark proved to be an asset as well. Each morning, he caught the family's breakfast. He first checked his preset traps but if they were empty, he had some early morning work to do.

Still, there was no money to be had. As Clark described decades later, the medium for exchange throughout the countryside was cornmeal, apple butter, venison and pig. The Panic of 1873 added more burdens and

---

[15] The Griffiths and the Batts were neighbors and friends; the incident was just an unfortunate accident.

[16] I never actually found documentation on Clark's younger sister just reference through his interviews with Shirley Povich.

further inhibited the area's growth. Throughout their life in Missouri the Griffiths didn't see the population of Nevada, the largest nearby town, rise above 2,000.

By age ten, Clark was trapping and hunting nearly as well as Earl; however, the musket was especially daunting and difficult to load. Clark snared coons, possums and skunks, which they called polecats. Occasionally, the youngster tripped upon a red fox or other creature. Clark and Earl would trek the skins to the market twelve miles away in Nevada. If Clark's memory served him well in the 1930s, he was paid 25 cents for a possum skin, a dollar for raccoon and $1.25 for the prized skunk. Red fox hides were worthless at market but were never wasted at home. The boys had to first soak their clothes in kerosene after skinning a skunk or they found themselves unwelcome at the dinner table.

Clark later explained to Shirley Povich how he was able to hunt at such a young age. He had his favorite dog Major, half bulldog and half hound, chase the prey up a tree. Clark then climbed the tree and either shook the animal loose or club it. When it fell, Major was there waiting to put an end to the hunt. One of Clark's favorite stories involved a chase at dusk that proved particularly tiresome. After Clark clubbed the animal down, Major seemed to be having a hard time subduing the creature. The young Clark scurried down the tree and entered the fight. At one point Clark whacked Major by mistake and knocked the dog cold. Eventually, they subdued the creature. Carrying the dead animal home, Clark passed a neighbor and relayed the story. Upon examination in the light, it was discovered that Clark was carrying a sixty-pound wildcat. The youngster was forever proud of the day he licked a beast as heavy as himself.

Despite the arduous labor, Clark fondly remembered his frontier lifestyle and looked upon it romantically and for its life's lessons. From his mother, Clark learned the value of hard work and sacrifice for family. Also seared into his memory was the high value attached to honesty and the fear of never straying from the law, especially for theft – as punishments were swiftly and stiffly meted out. Much later in life Clark identified an idol as the Lone Ranger, the man who embodied life's virtues.

Clark often nostalgically recounted the time Frank and Jesse James, acquaintances of his father, spent the night at the family house. Young Clark saddled and watered Jesse James' horse; though, at the time he was unaware of the identity of the visitors. The Jameses, recalled Clark, weren't that bad until the law bombed their house, causing their mother to lose an arm. Romantically, he viewed the Jameses as the Robin Hoods of the American West.[17]

Age eleven was a turning point in young Clark's life. The Griffiths raised their children to be good Protestants and to be devoted to education; hence, the children attended public grade school in Stringtown, three miles from the Griffith home.[18] Clark forever recalled his duties as stove tender at the little red schoolhouse in the Missouri countryside.

To ease her burden, Sarah Griffith often sent her kids to temporarily live with friends and family. For example, the 1880 U.S. Census shows Clark and his sister, Minnie, living with their oldest sister Mary and her husband John Dungan, a farmer, and their two-year-old son Henry in the Dover Township.[19] Clark spent that summer working at a neighboring farm helping in the fields by chopping corn stalks and performing other odd jobs. At the end of the summer he received his pay, two small pigs. Clark later boasted of the day that summer that he bought his first pair of boots. Years later he still remembered what he referred to as his "first crush." Her name was Emma, the daughter of Clark's father's friend Ed Williams.

It was also around this time that he landed his first job in baseball as a batboy/mascot for a Stringtown team[20] of Civil War veterans who latched onto the New York version of the game, the style that is played today. Decades later Clark vividly recalled the July 4, 1876 game celebrating the 100th anniversary of the birth of the nation. First, the players cut the tall grass in a prairie and laid out a diamond. Then, just prior to the game, they passed a hat through the crowd to gain the dollar or so needed for the purchase of a new National League-style baseball. One spectator volunteered to trek the six miles to purchase the item in Montevallo. Many feared he would never return with the ball or the cash. Relief spread through the gallery when the man returned with a shiny new ball. The game began but the ball quickly became lopsided and the cover tore. The scoundrel purchased a cheap 20¢ model and pocketed the rest.

---

[17] The specific quote, "To Mr. Griffith, they were like Robin Hood," was made by Joe Cronin in article: Bob Broeg, "Griffith made Cronin part of Family affair in Baseball," *St. Louis Post-Dispatch*, November 3, 1968, p. B2

[18] Stringtown may have simply been the name of the school building, not the name of a community.

[19] The main family's residence was actually listed in the township of Montevallo in the 1870 Census. It was still the same property as the original purchase, though.

[20] They played on a field adjoining the Stringtown School.

By that time, he was nowhere to be found. One day four years later, Clark heard guns popping and dogs barking so he ran to check out the ruckus. The culprit returned to the area. He was quickly recognized and hung like a common thief.

As noted, baseballs were prized possessions; the National League didn't even require that two game balls be on hand until 1887. If one became lost, the game was held up while all searched for it. In small communities this meant that the spectators helped as well. Nearly every ball was found; after all, dozens were scouring the brush for it.

Clark played 'one old cat' and 'town ball,' precursors of the modern game, as a small child. This was during the infancy of organized baseball in the Midwest. The Civil War and westward expansion brought men together from every point of the country, exposing all to the New York rules. Groups like the Stringtown nine are seldom recognized as the grassroots of organized baseball. They established the outposts, so to speak, that were later tied together like the railroad system to form the game's future network. Later in life, Clark claimed that his thoughts were monopolized by baseball in all its forms, since he was seven years old – except for the time of course that he spent thinking of Emma.

The New York version of the game became popular in the east. Amateur clubs were formed in the 1840s in New York City that eventually led to an effort to establish a national fraternity of ball clubs. Officials met for the first time in January 1857 in an effort to form the National Association of Base Ball Players. In 1860, the first club outside New York City, the Liberty club of New Brunswick, New Jersey, joined the association. As men from other cities and communities adopted the New York rules, they, in essence, became eligible to join the national movement. Naturally, all games have to have to common set of rules to establish a fair and even set of standards. By 1867, the National Association of Base Ball Players included over two hundred clubs from seventeen different states plus the District of Columbia.

Highly publicized and successful exhibition tours by the Excelsior club of Brooklyn in 1860 and the Nationals of Washington, D.C. in the middle of the decade sparked community leaders throughout the country to develop competitive nines and focus on the New York version of the game. The Nationals, in particular, incited the western states with contests in Columbus, Ohio, Cincinnati, Louisville, Indianapolis and Chicago and with a stop in St. Louis, into Griffith's birth state.

The western tour of the Nationals in 1867 also featured a sound defeat of the Red Stockings of Cincinnati. This defeat led Cincinnati backers to hire Harry Wright as their manager with the direction to amass the sport's first acknowledged all-professional team. The result was an undefeated exhibition tour from 1869-1870 that changed the game forever. It also provided the western states with their first great team. The Reds toured from coast to coast, helping to solidify the game's hold on the country.

Around 1880, Clark began to experience periodic episodes of chills and fever. The boy was always frail looking anyway. In fact, he only grew to be about 5'6" and 160 pounds, never a hint of a gut. Alarmingly, he became bedridden for long periods of time. After two years of sporadic illness, a neighbor, Mr. R. A. Batts, father of the boy that accidentally killed Isaiah, convinced Sarah that Clark had malaria and needed to be relocated or death was sure to come. Malaria was known as the plague among Missouri lowlanders. Such a warning was sure to be taken seriously.

So with sickly 13-year-old Clark and her younger children in tow, Sarah sold the family farm and hopped a train in 1882 headed for her family in Bloomington.[21] They were returning to Illinois. Clark was sent to live on the ranch of his well-to-do uncle, Levi Dillon who married Sarah's sister Mary. The change of scenery proved to be just the tonic for the youngster. Pretty soon, he was as active as all the other children and there were a great many Wright and Dillon offspring to pal around with in Tazewell County. Virtually from the first day, Clark spent nearly his entire free time in Illinois on a ball field.

Sarah eventually opened a boardinghouse in the adjacent town of Normal. Normal was located at the intersection of the Illinois Central and the Chicago & Alton Railroads. Business was booming by the 1880s, as the town became a hub for the canning and shipping of berries, small fruits and vegetables. A boardinghouse would do well in this environment and it certainly had to bestow a better lifestyle than trying to survive in the Missouri countryside amid disease and a daily struggle for sustenance. There was also plenty of family around in Normal to provide aid and comfort for a widow and her children.

The Dillons moved to Tazewell Country in the late 1850s, first landing in Boynton and then in Normal. The family operated a profitable horse-rearing business that they brought to the area shortly after the Civil War.

---

[21] Mary remained in Missouri with her husband. Angela passed away while the family lived in Missouri.

Isaiah Dillon, born in 1834, and his younger brother by two years Levi began breeding horses in the 1850s, becoming well known throughout the country. They lucratively imported, breed and sold the animals, as one of the nation's first importers of Norman Draft horses.

Clark's younger cousin from Normal, Frank 'Pop' Dillon, born in 1873 to Levi and Mary Wright Dillon, followed him into pro ball with a seven-year lag after attending and playing ball at Illinois State Normal University and the University of Wisconsin-Madison. He eventually reached the majors as a first baseman for Pittsburgh in 1899. Dillon became a prominent baseball figure on the west coast. During the first season of the revamped independent Pacific Coast League in 1903, he was the manager and leading hitter for one of the top minor league clubs of all-time, the Los Angeles Angels. The club finished with a 133-78-record winning the pennant by 27.5 games. In 190 games, Dillon clubbed a league-leading 274 hits and posted a .364 batting average. He led the Angels to three more pennants in 1905 and from 1907-1908. In twenty-two minor league campaigns Dillon placed 2,316 hits for a sound .295-batting average.

In February 1906, Dillon passed on a young fireballer from Humboldt, Kansas named Walter Johnson because of he lacked experience, couldn't hold runners on and "telegraphed everything he throws."[22] Johnson was set to meet with Dillon again the following year but the pitcher was too timid to approach the manager while he was playing a game of billiards. Dillon finished his game and left without knowing that Johnson was even in town. The pitcher ended up playing ball for a few dollars in Idaho. Eventually, the big, shy country boy had to be virtually dragged to the east coast to join the Washington Nationals of the American League to begin his storied major league career.

The Griffith children enrolled in a public school in Normal but Earl soon departed to cattle-punch in Montana. No longer fending for his family's daily meals, Clark turned his attention, almost exclusively, to baseball. He quickly gained a reputation as a fine sandlot catcher. However, the spindly athlete was so small that he couldn't find a slot on the Normal High School team. Clark and friends often snuck into Normal University to watch ballgames. These were the first contests Clark saw that actually played under formalized, structured rules.

---

[22] Henry W. Thomas. *Walter Johnson*. 1995, p. 15

Illinois State Normal University, the present-day Illinois State University, was founded in 1857, the first publicly funded institution of higher education in Illinois. Normal, then called North Bloomington, won the right to house the facility when it outbid all other communities in the state. A Springfield lawyer named Abraham Lincoln drew up the bond committing the community to their financial backing.

By age 16, Clark converted to pitching and was something of a local celebrity for both his skills in the pitcher's box and at the plate. At the time a pitcher could freely roam in a box, much like the rules in today's fast-pitch softball. However, by this time, baseball pitchers were throwing overhand. The front of the box was fifty feet from home plate. Griffith practiced his craft by tacking a handkerchief to a fence to help improve his control. He finally made the high school team after converting to the mound.[23] He started pitching for local semi-pro clubs. The following spring he was offered $10 to pitch for a semi-pro Hoopeston team against their rival Danville. The 17-year-old won and couldn't believe his newfound fortune and for playing baseball to boot. He was quickly offered a regular slot on the club. It didn't take long for word to spread about the skinny, little pitcher who was regularly beating Danville and other foes. His full-time battery mate was Fatty Sharp, a switchman for the Chicago & Alton Railroad. Sharp was a heavy drinker, which caused him to eventually lose his catcher's job. James Kitchen, a local brick mason's apprentice, later replaced Sharp.[24]

Griffith soon joined the Bloomington squad, owned by local theatrical operators Tillotson and Fell, in 1887 in the Illinois State League. Griff, as everyone in the baseball industry always called him, brought his new catcher, Bill Graser, with him.[25] The season opened on May 24 with Bloomington in Decatur. After a parade and brass band kicked off the festivities, Clark started in right field and was called to the mound after the starting pitcher was shelled. Bloomington was ultimately crushed 21-4 on 23 errors and 25 hits. The rules at the time permitted five balls and four strikes.[26] Griff pitched and won the opening game at Bloomington's new ballpark on June 14.

---

[23] Despite the reference, mounds weren't introduced until much later. The rubber was inserted when the pitching distance was pushed back to 60'6" in 1893.

[24] "Kitchen, Griffith's Old Catcher, Dead," *Washington Post*, August 4, 1937, p. 19

[25] Fred Young, "Griff's Rival all but beat Him," *The Pantagraph*, Bloomington, Illinois newspaper, May 5, 1940, page unknown

[26] "An easy Victory," *Decatur Daily Review*, May 25, 1887, p. 4

Griffith topped Decatur on August 13, 9-4. On the 20th, Clark was on the mound as Bloomington trounced the Chicago Reserves 23-4. On September 5, he won again, 7-6 with seven strikeouts over Decatur.[27] The next day Clark played left field and first base, placing a double. On the 8th Bloomington and Decatur battled to a 6-6 tie. Griff pitched a complete game, striking out six. The game was called for darkness by mutual agreement at the end of the ninth inning. Two delays took place during the game. The first occurred at the onset as Clark took a hop every time he made a delivery to the plate. Decatur protested but the umpire ignored their pleas. After Bloomington tied the game in the 8th, they argued that the game should be called due to darkness. The ten-minute dispute was enough to force the truncation of the game the following inning. On September 9, Decatur pulled out a 12-10 victory over Bloomington. Clark played left field and added a double and a stolen base. Griffith showed a great deal of promise in 1887, enough so that he was referred to as the "Bloomington Phenomenon" by a *Sporting News* correspondent.[28] Despite the praise, Griffith spent the winter in Normal officially unsigned as club directors focused on revamping the league.

On October 30, league executives met in Decatur to reorganize the league. They would compete within the framework of Organized Baseball in 1888 in the Central Interstate League. Griffith[29] once again signed with the local Bloomington Reds. His professional career began; he was officially in Organized Baseball. First, he had to contend with his mother who didn't approve of her son playing ball for a living. Sarah soon relented after hearing about his economic potential and after gaining Clark's promise to attend college. True to his word, Clark attended Illinois Wesleyan University from 1888-1889. He also studied at law school during the winters in the late 1890s at Northwestern University in Chicago.

Clark was too much into baseball to ever concentrate on his studies for long. In a 1913 interview, Griffith's former Wesleyan roommate Rev. Dr. George H. Bradford, chancellor of Oklahoma Methodist University recalled, "It was utterly impossible for Griffith to study when springtime brought on baseball fever." Clark hid the studious Bradford's books, so he would be forced to take time out to play catch. Griffith then pitched to him until Bradford could stand it no longer. At

---

[27] Per "World of Sports," *Milwaukee Sentinel*, March 25, 1889, p. 8, Griffith also pitched for Decatur, Illinois squad in 1887.

[28] *The Sporting News*, January 14, 1888

[29] At age 19, Griffith weighed 156 lbs. and stood 5'6.5" tall. "World of Sports," *Milwaukee Sentinel*, March 25, 1889, p. 8

times the pair studied Latin but Clark wasn't focused on a career outside of baseball. He quit school before graduation to pursue his life's dream.[30]

---

[30] "Griffith Liked Baseball More Than his Books," *Washington Post*, June 15, 1913, p. S4

CHAPTER TWO

BLOOMINGTON TO THE BARBARY COAST

Clark pitched for the Bloomington Reds of the Central Interstate League for a salary of $150 a month in 1888. Before spring training, he remitted a telegram to his club, writing that "he is in fine condition and expects to do great work for us." He was ready for his first season in Organized Baseball. In an exhibition game on April 18 in Bloomington, he lost to the St. Louis Whites, a Chris von der Ahe owned club, 8-4. Von der Ahe also owned the major league St. Louis Browns. Bloomington committed seven errors. Playing first base that day for the Reds was the great pitcher Hoss Radbourn.[31] Griff was given the nod on Opening Day on May 1 at Bloomington. In his official Organized Baseball debut Griffith allowed just six hits en route to a 5-4-victory. From the *Chicago Tribune* on May 2, 1888:

"Bloomington, 5; Rockford, 4.

The season of the Central Inter-State League opened here today with a game by the Rockfords and Bloomingtons. The day was damp and chilly, but the attendance was quite large. The grounds were in poor condition. The game was a fine one. Score:

      Bloomington   3 0 0 0 1 1 0 0 0 - 5

---

[31] "Anson's Men Ahead," *Daily Inter Ocean*, Chicago, April 19, 1888, p. 3

Rockford   1 0 2 0 0 1 0 0 0 - 4

Batteries - Bloomington, Griffith and Newman; Rockford, Bates and Bowman. Base Hits - Bloomington, 6: Rockford, 6. Errors - Bloomington, 6; Rockford; 10. Umpire - Shoaf."³²

In his next start on May 5, Griffith shut down Peoria, 5-2, giving up only five hits and striking out eight. The game ended on a nice double play by shortstop Jack Reinagle. Clark started again on May 14 but lost to Decatur, 5-3. He gave up a mere five hits and struck out eight but Bloomington committed ten errors, half of which were made by their new righthander; he also threw four wild pitches. The sloppy play drew raised eyebrows throughout the league. Apparently, league officials had seen their share of gambling and game-fixing scandals in the past. The Reds players were called in front of league officials to account for their careless play. The investigation discovered nothing other than an off day in the field; nevertheless, five players were penalized for loose play and general disobedience. Griffith with five errors and the wild pitches was levied the stiffest fine, $15.

Griff defeated Dubuque on the 20th, 13-4, striking out eight men but showing a little wildness with a wild pitch and three hit batsmen. On May 23, he lost to Rockford 4-2 at home in Bloomington. From May 26 to June 13, Griffith won five games against only one loss, striking out sixty men in the six games. The latter game, against Dubuque, was a one-hitter that Bloomington won 13-4. The game on June 7 was a 9-0 shutout over Danville. He allowed only one run in a 4-1 victory over Decatur on the 11th. Griff proved to be a reliable starter and indeed a nice find. He was also hitting well, occasionally subbing at left or right field on off days.

His next time out on June 16 Griffith struck out ten but lost 8-4 to Rockford as the team committed an eye-popping fourteen errors. With rudimentary gloves high error figures were common in the nineteenth century, especially in the minors where the fields were typically shoddy. Unlike today, ground balls were not considered automatic outs. It's not uncommon to read a box score for a game where say fifteen runs scored but only five earned runs were charged to the pitcher. Two days later, he

---

³² Griffith's Hall of Fame file is littered with a box score claiming to be his first professional game. The date is indeed May 1, 1888 but it is from a game against Danville. This is not the case; Bloomington and Griffith opened the season against Rockford on May 1. Perhaps the Danville box score is from an exhibition game – not sure. There is also a box score of another league game versus Danville on June 22. Yet another claim is made that this was his last game with Bloomington. It was not; he pitched at least as late as June 28 with the club.

was beaten again, 6-3 by Davenport, despite striking out another ten men. On June 24, he defeated Lafayette 8-5 with seven Ks.[33] Danville defeated Griffith on the 28th 7-2.

Pitching every three to four days, Clark hurled 142 innings over sixteen games for Bloomington. His won-loss record stood at 10 and 6.[34] More impressive, he stuck out an average of over twelve men a game.[35] One of Griffith's battery mates that year was two-sport star Thomas H. McMahon.[36] He was also a top wrestler of the nineteenth century.[37] McMahon, a Detroit native born circa 1863, was wrestling professionally by age nineteen. He later served as a trainer for the Detroit Tigers during their pennant-winning 1907 season.

Charles N. "Pacer" Smith also played on Bloomington. Smith played for numerous minor league clubs from 1878-1894. Around 1886, he started to show signs of mental struggles that manifested into heavy drinking and run-ins with the law. At various times, he was indicted or suspected of larceny, burglary, assault and gambling. His baseball career soon ended as his drinking ran out of control in 1894.

In 1888, Smith married Maggie Buchert, despite the young lady's family's objections. The couple had a daughter, Louise, two years later. Smith soon began neglecting his wife and young daughter and the couple separated as his drinking increased. Mother and daughter moved in with Maggie's family in Decatur, Illinois. Smith occasionally visited his wife and daughter; however, as the married couple became estranged, Smith became habitually drunk. At times he was even known to threaten his family.

On September 28, 1895, Smith showed up drunk at the Buchert home at about 3 pm. with a gun. Maggie's 17-year-old sister, Edna, retrieved Louise from a neighbor's house. Upon her arrival, Smith pulled out his gun and shot his daughter in the neck. The girl fell down the

---

[33] From the best I could determine by reading *The Sporting News* via Paperofrecord.com, the score was 8-5; however, because of blurriness, it may have been slightly different. Unfortunately this may be true for the same reason on a few other games.

[34] His minor league season stats are taken from *The Encyclopedia of Minor League Baseball, Second Edition*, 1997.

[35] Brian Podoll. *The Minor League Milwaukee Brewers 1859-1952*, 2003, p. 47

[36] Griffith and McMahon played together with the 1887 Reds as well. McMahon may have caught Griff's first pro/semi-pro game. "Detroit Doings," *Sporting Life*, April 13, 1907, p. 11

[37] McMahon was an all-around athlete; he was also a sprinter and boxer.

basement steps and later died. Maggie took off running and Smith fired two shots that missed. He then killed Edna in the kitchen. He was arrested in a nearby alley, convicted of first-degree murder and sentenced to death. Smith was hung on November 29, 1895.

More important for his career, Clark met a Bloomington resident who would forever influence his pitching style, Hoss Radbourn. Radbourn played himself into shape with the Reds during spring training. At the end of 1887, he left his Boston National League club in a huff after team officials deducted money from his final paycheck. He openly declared, "They have driven me out of the business. You will never see me in another game of ball." His statement seemed all the more final when word leaked that he purchased a half-stake in the largest hotel in Bloomington.[38] Actually, he bought the saloon that resided under the Windsor Hotel.[39] As the season approached, Radbourn still hadn't come to terms with Boston, so he worked out with the local Reds, even playing in a few games as previously noted. He also found time to advise the young Griffith on pitching technique, teaching him to throw a sinkerball and helping refine his curve. On April 21, Radbourn left for the east coast after Boston management caved into all his financial demands.[40]

Radbourn was born in Rochester, New York and grew up in Bloomington, moving to Illinois before he was one year old.[41] He strengthened his arm as a teenager by repeatedly throwing the ball against a barn on his family's farm. By the mid-1870s, he was playing semi-pro ball locally and also played some games as a ringer for Illinois Wesleyan University.

In Bloomington on August 31, 1876 Radbourn, always a heavy drinker, went out on the town and tied one on. His club lost to Springfield the next day 4-1. Suspicions were immediately cast on the legitimacy of the contest, with many alleging game-fixing. Radbourn admitted to being offered $75 by local gambler Edward Stahl at Schausten's saloon on the night of the 31st. According to the local newspaper *The Pantagraph*, Radbourn "does not deny that he may have said that he would take the money, but, being drunk, was not responsible

---

[38] "Rad buys a Hotel," *Boston Globe*, January 22, 1888, p. 14

[39] *The Sporting News*, January 28, 1888

[40] "Radbourn leaves for Boston," *Chicago Tribune*, April 22, 1888, p. 13

[41] Some sources mistakenly list Radbourn as a resident of Bloomington, *Indiana*.

for his words."[42] Two other gamblers were also suspected of offering bribes to players. Game-fixing charges were levied against Bloomington players Gleason, Roach and John Flynn. On September 3, the stockholders met and expelled Gleason and Roach from the club. Flynn was apparently exonerated. Radbourn continued with the club through 1877.

Radbourn entered the minors in 1878, joining the Peoria Reds, an independent club. In 1879, he joined Ted Sullivan's Dubuque Rabbits. He played second base and the outfield and also pitched in six games, copping three victories. He then signed with Buffalo of the National League at the end of the year for $750.

The submariner was a hard drinker with a personality to match. His 309 victories rank among the all-time leaders. Having originally entered the majors as a right fielder, Radbourn suffered arm trouble while with Buffalo and quit the game in 1880 to enter the family business. Over the winter of 1880-1881, repeated telegrams from the Providence Grays seeking his services as a right fielder and part-time pitcher went unanswered. Finally, a friend replied with an acceptance of the offer in Radbourn's name and, then, pushed him on a train to join the club. Radbourn reluctantly embarked on his pitching career. On July 25, 1883, he pitched a no-hitter against Cleveland. He's also credited with seven one-hitters. Resilient, he pitched an amazing, by today's standards, 489 complete games.

Radbourn's 1884 season with the National League Providence Grays is particularly noteworthy. Providence's other pitcher Charlie Sweeney jumped the club at midseason. Radbourn offered to pitch the rest of the games if management forgave the suspension he was currently serving, gave him a bonus and released him at the end of the year to pursue his own deal. Providence had little choice but to acquiesce.

Radbourn pitched nearly every remaining inning. In the process he amassed many impressive statistics while leading the league in games, starts, complete games, wins, innings pitched and strikeouts. His 59 victories that year are an all-time major league high. At one point the righthander won eighteen straight. Staggering by today's standard, Radbourn pitched 678 innings. Equally impressive are his earned run average of 1.38 and 441 strikeouts. He also pitched eleven shutouts.

---

[42] Bill Kemp, Archivist/Librarian at McLean County Museum of History, "Famed 19th century ballplayer 'Old Hoss' came from Bloomington," April 6, 2008

However, the toll on his arm required a teammate to help him dress everyday.

Providence won the pennant. At season's end, the National League and American Association staged a series to determine the championship of baseball. Some recognize these contests as the first World Series matches. Radbourn won all three games: 6-0, 3-1 and 12-2. Instead of forcing his release at season's end, the pitcher accepted a $2,000 raise for 1885.

Radbourn retired at age 36 in 1891 to tend to his saloon business. At that time he was said to be worth $25,000. He attempted a return to the game in 1883 and again in the spring of 1884. The latter potential comeback was halted on April 13 when he was accidentally shot in the face by a friend while on a hunting trip. Unfortunately, Radbourn stepped from behind a tree at the precise moment that his friend fired a shotgun. He lost sight in his left eye and received considerable damage to his face, including partial paralysis and some speech loss.

The ex-pitcher's waning years were unpleasant. Because of his face, he became a recluse at his apartment. He also suffered from the effects of the paresis of the eye and other ailments and drank heavily. During at least his last year, Radbourn had severe cognitive troubles, perhaps brain damage from syphilis. He was also subject to convulsions, abnormalities with his nervous system and had trouble with "speech, feeling and locomotion." As the *Boston Globe* described in December 1896, "Charley Radbourn…is now at his old home in Bloomington, Ill., a wreck of his former self, owing to sickness."[43] On February 3, 1897 he suffered another convulsion which left him in a comatose state. He never woke up, dying at age 42 at his home two days later.[44]

The Reds ultimately land in fourth place with a 26-28-record in 1888. However, Clark was traded in early July.[45] He hitched a ride on a lumber wagon to catch up with his new club in Sioux City. Manager Jim Hart of the Milwaukee Brewers of the Western Association purchased Clark for $1,000 and pitcher John Struck, a recent amateur out of Louisville, on the

---

[43] "Baseball Notes," *Boston Globe*, December 21, 1896, p. 7

[44] See my Radbourn biography at the Society for American Baseball Research's Biography Project – easily located via Google.com - for further details on his career

[45] An article in *The Sporting News* of July 7, 1888 dated July 4 stated that Griffith was recently sold.

spot after Griffith defeated them in an exhibition contest.[46] Griffith was delighted with the pay raise to $225 a month from $150. Plus, he was now going to perform with and against better talent and in front of much larger crowds in such big cities as Chicago, St. Louis, Kansas City and Minneapolis.

Milwaukee, a town with long baseball roots, fielded minor league teams in the Northwestern League, Western League and Western Association during the 1880s. Back in 1877, Milwaukee was represented in the League Alliance, one of the first minor league organizations. They did well enough at the gate to land a National League franchise the following season; however, it was a dismal summer for the club in the standings and at the gate. The club dissolved in December still owing back pay to some of its players. In 1884 Milwaukee was a September call up in the soon-to-be defunct major Union Association, replacing a beleaguered Wilmington franchise. Griff later described the ethnic breakdown of Milwaukee as, "The Irish sat on the right field side, the Germans on the left field side. It was a standing rule that the manager had to have an Irish third baseman and a German third baseman."

Griffith won in his first game for the Brewers on July 8 in Sioux City 16-4. He struck out eleven men and scored three times himself. He split with Chicago in the middle of the month: losing on the 13th 5-1 and winning 5-4 two days later. Clark defeated Minneapolis on July 18 8-7. On July 22, at St. Paul he won again 8-1 in dramatic fashion by placing a hit and scoring three times. The *Chicago Tribune* raved, "Griffith pitched a magnificent game for the visitors," in front of 2,000 fans. Clark was just as efficient the next time out on July 26 as again he allowed only one run in a 6-1-victory over Sioux City. It was hit or miss after that. At the end of the season, his won loss record with Milwaukee stood at 17 and 12. The diminutive Griffith, comically, attributed his early success in Milwaukee due to the fact that he was hidden from the batters. He was initially issued a uniform that by his estimation would fit someone who was 6'4" tall.

Griffith was playing his third game in left field on August 6 when he let the winning run score on an error in the ninth. That was enough for manager Hart; Griff didn't appear in the outfield again in 1888. He did however win his first home appearance on August 8, 5-2 over Minneapolis; though, only 400 fans showed up to see the club's new righthander fan six Millers. Griff lost 5-4 to Sioux City on the 16th,

---

[46] The trade did happen as stated but I could find no verification of the exhibition game outside the recollection of Clark Griffith to Shirley Povich.

walking five batters and tossing four wild pitches. His catcher also had five passed balls.

On the 11th, Griffith defeated Des Moines 4-1 at Milwaukee on a cold August afternoon. It was so frigid that the boys who typically watched the game in a tree just outside Athletic Park couldn't stand the wind chill. They built a fire on the ground and rotated among themselves between the tree and fire. Griffith was delighted with the victory; it avenged the previous encounter with Des Moines in which he conceded seventeen hits. It was also against the highly-touted Yale pitcher Bill Hutchison. The *Milwaukee Sentinel* called it Griffith's finest performance to date; they were thoroughly impressed with his placement of the curveball.[47]

The Brewers returned to Bloomington on August 25 for an exhibition game and Griffith defeated his old teammates, 6-5 in front of 1,500 locals. He struck out nine Reds.[48] In Kansas City on the 29th he lost 8-3, ceding nine hits. Clark and team pulled out a win against Omaha on September 9 after a shaky Griffith allowed eight men to score in the first three innings. On the 13th, Clark dueled to a 4-4-tie when the game against St. Paul was called for darkness after eleven innings. Clark tossed his first professional shutout on September 19 against St. Paul for a 3-0-victory. He then shut down the Chicago Maroons on the 23rd 9-0, adding a double and two runs. He also won the first game of a doubleheader on the final Sunday of the season at Athletic Park on October 7, 6-5, notching four strikeouts versus Omaha. Milwaukee won despite collecting only three hits.

At times in 1888, Griffith looked brilliant for Milwaukee. In 228 innings, he gave up only 2.45 earned runs per game. His winning percentage, .500 at 12-12, surely could have been better; however, the Brewers, as a whole, fared worse, percentage-wise. They posted a losing 53-54-record, good enough for a fifth-place finish. Griff appeared on his first baseball card in the *Old Judge* cigar set in 1888. In October, Griffith was for the first time listed on the reserved roster of a club in Organized Baseball.[49] He was also listed on Milwaukee's reserved roster at the end of 1889 and '90.[50]

---

[47] "By Good Playing," *Milwaukee Sentinel*, August 12, 1888, p. 2

[48] *The Sporting News*, September 1, 1888

[49] "The Western Reserve List," *Daily Inter Ocean*, October 5, 1888, p. 2

[50] "Local News," *St. Paul Daily News*, October 4, 1889, p. 2, and "Western Players Reserved," *Daily Inter Ocean*, October 9 1890, p. 6

Clark played with two men that first year in Milwaukee that had recurring roles in his career. The first was speedy and graceful center fielder Jimmy McAleer who Griffith later succeeded as manager in Washington. McAleer, five years older than Griff, began his pro career in the early 1880s with a team from his hometown Youngstown, Ohio. More important was manager James A. "Jim" Hart. Hart pulled Clark from languishing on the west coast back to the majors near the end of 1893. Hart, Milwaukee's manager since 1887, managed in the majors with Louisville of the American Association from 1885-1886. He essentially secured his future in the game as a by-product of a plan to establish an international tour of ballplayers after the 1888 season. Al Spalding had the same idea. In order to eliminate a potential rival Spalding hired Hart to manage the American swing of his world tour. Hart then guided Boston of the National League to a second place finish in 1889. In 1890 he was brought in to help oversee Spalding's club in Chicago.

Also on the roster was Bobby Lowe, who became the first major leaguer to hit four home runs in a game in 1894 off Elton Chamberlain, and local hero Cal Broughton. In August the team traded for pitcher George Winkleman. He was a former sandlot teammate of John Philip Sousa, "The March King," on the Washington Bashfuls in 1883. Winkleman, Griffith's roommate in Milwaukee, appeared in one major league game for Washington in August 1886. In 1932, Clark hired his old teammate to help out around Griffith Stadium.

Clark signed for the 1889 season at the beginning of February[51] and joined the club for spring training in Louisville during the first week of April.[52] Milwaukee's new manager Ezra Sutton was looking forward to a full season out of the club's new righthander. Sutton was a top early third baseman; some claim that he was the best of the 1800s. His career started in the late 1860s as an amateur during the time of the famed traveling Cincinnati Red Stockings. Sutton was an initial member of the National Association, playing all five years of the professional organization's existence and continuing in the National League through 1888. He was one of the original men, along with Cap Anson and twenty-eight others, reserved via the new reserve clause system for 1880. Sutton was the first to hit a home run in National Association history; actually, he hit the first two on May 8, 1871.

---

[51] "General Sporting News," *Milwaukee Daily Journal*, February 2, 1889, page unknown

[52] "Bloomington," *Daily Inter Ocean*, Chicago, April 7, 1889, p. 11

Things went downhill for Sutton in his later years after his Hartford club disbanded in 1890. He left baseball to oversee the operations of his ice plant that eventually failed. He then became paralyzed for life due to a spinal disease. Later, flames overtook his wife when a lamp was dropped, igniting her dress at the dinner table. Due to his condition, Sutton could do nothing but watch. She died in the hospital six weeks later. He died destitute in a Massachusetts care facility a year later.[53]

Griffith didn't disappoint in 1889, winning his first three games. He defeated St. Joseph on April 23, 6-5, with ten strikeouts and knocked off Denver on the 27th, 13-6, and Sioux City on May 5, 13-9. In between, he was clobbered in Omaha 15-2 on April 30; but, he only gave up six earned runs, five walks, four passed balls and two wild pitches highlight the sloppy play. Griff struck out ten more on May 12, winning 12-9 and placing a double. He then played left field and batted fifth on the 17th, knocking a hit but making three errors in a 14-2-loss to Minneapolis. Clark took the mound the next day, losing 8-3 to Minneapolis again. Vindicated, Griffith defeated them, 8-2, six days later, posting six strikeouts and a double. On Decoration Day, May 30, he started both games of a doubleheader, losing the first, 13-12, but redeeming himself in the second, 11-7.

On June 13, Griffith led off and played right field versus St. Joseph. He walked twice and smacked two singles in a 9-6-victory. Two days layer, he relieved and won 10-3 while striking out six. St. Joseph responded by clobbering Griffith for thirteen hits in a 10-3-victory on the 19th. Despite seven strikeouts, Clark lost 10-8 against Sioux City on June 29. Similarly, he lost again on July 5, 7-6, but fanned eight Des Moines batters.

In a game shortened to five innings by rain on July 17, Griffith won 6-1 giving up a mere two St. Paul hits. He defeated Sioux City 8-3 on seven strikeouts on August 1. In a close one Griffith allowed only five hits in a 3-1-victory on the 21st. On September 10, Clark batted third and played left field in a 14-7-loss to St. Paul. He went 3 for 4 with a double. He played left field again in a 9-2-victory over St. Joe on the 19th. Next, he played both games of a September 22-doubleheader against Denver. In the first contest he struck out twelve men in a 7-4-victory. He also added a double and triple in four at bats. In the late game Griffith played center field and batted ninth, going 1 for 2 with a walk and a steal.

---

[53] For more about Sutton, look up my biography at the SABR Biography Project.

Milwaukee, now nicknamed the Creams, again finished in fifth place with a slightly worse record, 56-63. Clark was a shining light for the organization, posting 23 victories and eating up 328 innings over 43 games. Kid Nichols with 39 wins stood as the best pitcher in the league, as he would in the majors during much of the 1890s. The Western Association itself underwent its most successful season to date, thanks in no small part to favorable weather. Throughout his time in Milwaukee, Griffith often pitched for semi-pro clubs in and around the city to make extra cash. The men played for "hat money," donations from the fans that placed the cash in a hat passed around the grandstands.

Noticing Griffith's fine year in Milwaukee, John Montgomery Ward tried to sign the pitcher at the end of the year for the new Players League, which operated in 1890.[54] Ward was set to play shortstop and manage the Brooklyn franchise. The Players League grew out of Ward's unionizing efforts by Ward. Off the field, Ward gained a law degree from Columbia University. On October 22, 1885, with eight New York Giant teammates he formed and organized the Brotherhood of National League Players, baseball's first players union. Their main gripe was the reserve clause, and money of course which was always at the root of many problems. Ward then recruited and established Brotherhood chapters in every National League city.

While Ward was abroad with Al Spalding's world tour in early 1889, National League owners unilaterally adopted a salary classification plan that froze players' salaries in five tiers between $1,500 and $2,500. The magnates then tightened their control by blanketing the reserve clause over all players. A ballplayer was now fully bound to an owner that enjoyed exclusive rights to his contract, set territorial rights, a standardized pay scale and an unquestioned authority to fine and blacklist any player for virtually any reason. Such was the power of a monopoly.

Upon Ward's return to the States, the owners flatly refused to negotiate with him. In response, Ward called for the players to develop their own league at a meeting in July 1889. The Players League of 1890 was the result. It lured the biggest stars of both the National League and the American Association and, consequently, outdrew the two established leagues. In fact, 80% of the National League's players jumped their contracts for attractive offers. The new league had no reserve clause, salary classification or the dreaded blacklist.

---

[54] "After Griffith," September 20, 1890, un-cited article found in Griffith's Hall of Fame file

Griffith wasn't interested in joining the new league; he preferred to remain out west closer to home. Ward approached him several more times throughout the 1890 season but Griff held firm. Towards the end of the season in September, he had a change of heart and appeared to be leaning towards accepting Ward's offer for the upcoming season. It was soon too late; the league folded after only one campaign.

Under new manager Charles Cushman, the now re-renamed Brewers jumped to third place in 1890 finishing only five games behind Kansas City with a 76-47-record. Cushman, a forty-year-old from New York, umpired in the National League in 1885 and again in 1898. In 1887, he led Toronto to the International League championship. His star that year Ed "Cannonball" Crane pulled off the rare feat of leading the league in batting average, .428, and victories, 33. The International League was one of the last openly integrated top leagues. That year, African-American pitcher George Stovey shared the league lead in victories with Crane.[55] With Fleet Walker as his catcher, Stovey formed the minor league's first African-American battery. The lefthander is considered to be the first great African-American pitcher and the last to pitch in Organized Baseball prior to the late 1940s. Stovey was the object of Cap Anson's discontent in a July 1887 incident that is often overstated as the cause of total segregation in Organized Baseball.

The International League also boasted the great Frank Grant. An agile fielder and powerful hitter, Grant is the most acclaimed African-American player of the 19th century. The second baseman joined Buffalo in the International League in 1886. One of the better fielders of his day, Grant hit over .340 each season with Buffalo. His slugging average refused to dip below .520, an impressive number for the era. He led the league in home runs in 1887. In 2006, Grant and fifteen other Negro league players and executives were elected to the National Baseball Hall of Fame in Cooperstown, New York.[56]

Griff used the idea of Ward's offer to finagle more money out of Milwaukee. He still wasn't signed in late March, holding out for $2,000.[57]

---

[55] Lloyd Johnson and Miles Wolff, *The Encyclopedia of Minor League Baseball, Second Edition*, 1997

[56] Also at the SABR Biography Project are pieces on Ed Crane, George Stovey and Frank Grant.

[57] "Near Neighbors," *Daily Inter Ocean*, Chicago, March 23, 1890, p. 21, copy of article was blurry, the figure looks like $2,000 but may be slightly different

He finally signed at the beginning of April for $1,900 then left Bloomington on the 10th to join his club.[58]

Griffith won 8-4 on May 18, 1890 whiffing four. On the 25th, he shut down Sioux City 11-1 and fanned seven. Clark defeated Sioux City again on June 14, 14-2, with three strikeouts. Despite fanning seven on the 17th, Griffith lost 7-5 to Des Moines. Des Moines then ran into some trouble. The whole squad went on strike on June 20 because they hadn't seen a paycheck in awhile. Also on the 22nd, the entire team and umpires were arrested after the first inning for charging an admission fee on a Sunday, a violation of the law; they quickly posted bail and finished the contest. It was common for ballplayers to be arrested throughout the country during the nineteenth century for playing on Sundays.

On June 22, Griffith tossed a 2-0-shutout with four strikeouts versus Minneapolis in front of the largest crowd to ever attend a baseball game in Milwaukee. Many of the 7,000 were forced to stand in a roped off section in the outfield. Griffith won 4-2 over Des Moines on July 1, giving up only five hits. Griffith defeated Omaha 4-1 on July 20, fanning seven. He placed a double and beat Omaha again on August 3, 8-3, but was hit hard in a 16-10-loss to Sioux City on the 10th. Fanning five on August 23, Griffith defeated Lincoln 16-1. He also won 14-6 over Omaha on September 11.

Former major league star Abner Dalrymple manned left field for Milwaukee in 1890. He began his pro career in Milwaukee back in 1876. Clark and teammate John Thornton accounted for 56 of the team's wins, 27 and 29 respectively. Thornton led the league in the category. Griffith led the league in winning percentage, .794, with a 27-7-record in 44 games. On August 12 in Lincoln, Nebraska Clark umpired his first pro game. Anson brought his Colts to Milwaukee for an exhibition game at Athletic Park on October 1 and lost. Griffith didn't pitch as he was suffering from a fever, reportedly malaria;[59] amazingly, he posted those 27 victories while being sick off and on during the latter part of the season.

The league, as a whole, had another decent season financially in 1890 and even petitioned the National Association to be considered on par with the majors, the National League and American Association. The Milwaukee club itself posted a decent $6,000 profit. In August 1891, after Clark left, the club's owners bought out the Cincinnati Porkers of the American Association, merged the best talent and competed in the major leagues for the rest of the season. It was Cushman's only shot at the

---

[58] "Griffith starts for Milwaukee," *Milwaukee Sentinel*, April 10, 1890, p. 4

[59] More likely an extended cold

majors. It was also Dalrymple's last games in the big leagues and his first in three years.

Clark just finished two and a half successful seasons with Milwaukee in which he racked up 67 victories. The higher leagues were taking notice. Over the winter, Boston was interested in acquiring the righthander.[60] Also, two of the biggest names in the game came courting. Cap Anson stopped by Milwaukee on January 2, 1891 to propose a trade for Griffith.[61]

Anson was the nation's first sports hero. Only heavyweight bare knuckles champion John L. Sullivan eclipsed his popularity and legend during the 19th century. Anson had cigarettes and was the first to have a candy bar named after him. Discovered by Al Spalding in 1870 at Notre Dame, Anson spent 27 years in the majors, counting the National Association.[62] First, he joined Rockford in the National Association and hit .352 over the circuit's five-year existence. When the National League was formed in 1876, the first baseman joined Spalding in Chicago. Over the next twenty-two seasons, he won two batting titles, hit over .300 nineteen times and batted a solid .329. During two consecutive games in 1884, he hit five home runs, a feat that wouldn't be duplicated for 41 years. Anson managed and played for Chicago until he was 45 years old.

The lure of a personal invitation from Anson was surely compelling and very flattering. After all, the Colts had only once dropped below third place since 1879 when Anson took over as field manager. Either Anson didn't push hard enough or didn't present an enticing offer because Charlie Comiskey's pitch to join the American Association proved more enticing. Griffith was a Comiskey-type ballplayer, aggressive and intelligent on the field but controlled and thoughtful off, meaning that he was a focused athlete and wasn't one of the troublemakers or a lushes which seemed to define the era.

---

[60] "Base Ball Gossip," *Yenowine's Illustrated News*, Milwaukee, Wisconsin, February 1, 1891, p. 6, the exact quote reads, "The Boston club is after our pitcher, Griffith," unfortunately it doesn't note which Boston club, from the National League or the American Association

[61] "Ball Game at Auditorium," *Chicago Tribune*, January 3, 1891, p. 7, some reports suggest Anson was there to talk with Griffith; in others Anson denies any such interest at the time.

[62] It is a traditional belief that the National Association, which ran from 1871-75, is not a major league. This however is debatable.

The American Association was the 'other' major league. It was born in 1881 in part because Cincinnati, Philadelphia and St. Louis weren't represented in the established National League. The National League expelled Philadelphia after the 1876 season for failing to complete its schedule[63] and St. Louis dropped after 1877 in part because of the prohibition against Sunday games. Cincinnati was later ejected for a similar reason.

There was a lot of money to be made by selling beer at ballgames and by playing exhibition contests on Sundays, at least Cincinnati management thought so. The National League charter and propriety, however, forbade both at the time. The league put up with Cincinnati breaking the rules for a while but things came to a head in October 1880 when Cincinnati management refused to sign a resolution decrying beer sales and Sunday competition. Consequently, National League club presidents voted to expel the Reds. Understandably, the city's fans and backers were outraged. The National League made a tactical error. They tossed aside some of the largest, most rabid baseball fans in the union. Interests from these cities met to rectify the situation.

Cincinnati, St. Louis and Philadelphia became charter members of the new American Association, which began play in 1882. Many of the association clubs were owned by saloon keepers or brewers. The teams played baseball on Sundays where permitted, sold alcohol on the grounds and charged only a quarter per seat (for the most part). In contrast, a National League ticket cost fifty cents at the time. The Beer and Whiskey League, as the American Association became popularly known, was poised to outdraw the National League and pose a significant threat to its stability. First matter of business, they raided the established league for many of its top names and other disgruntled employees.

Like many, Comiskey hopped to the Players League for the 1890 season but had recently returned to St. Louis of the American Association - where he starred for many years - with the mass of ballplayers whose rights reverted to their 1889 team in either the National League or American Association. Those clubs retained exclusive rights, at least via their perception, to all players who were on their rosters prior to the Players League uprising.

The Players League, which operated for only one year, was formed as a result of considerable disgruntlement and perceived

---

[63] The National League ousted New York as well.

oppression on part of the ballplayers; thus, it had little trouble attracting talent. Nevertheless, it folded after one season due to the usual difficulty with financial backers; there weren't enough. Unable to recover financially due to the 1890 battle, the American Association followed a year later; it formally merged with the National League.

In 1874 at age 15, Comiskey, the son of a Chicago political boss, was sent to join his older brother at the Catholic St. Mary's Academy and College in St. Mary's, Kansas. By sending him far from home, the senior Comiskey was trying to defeat Charles' overwhelming thirst for baseball and make him into something useful, a plumber. Instead, Comiskey met an older student named Ted Sullivan who helped lead him from his father's path. Little known today, Sullivan was one of the most significant figures in baseball during the 19th century. He was the game's first significant scout and formed more leagues than any other man in the business. He also boasts perhaps the most diverse resume of any baseball man. The cursory headlines include: player, captain, coach, manager, league president, league founder, team owner, journalist, writer, promoter, agent, scout, cross-checker, business manager and international promoter.

In 1876, Comiskey joined Sullivan's Milwaukee-based semi-pro club, the Alerts, as a third baseman. The following summer he played for a club in Elgin, Illinois before finally breaking from his father and leaving home in 1878 to rejoin Sullivan with the newly formed Dubuque, Iowa Rabbits, an independent club. By 1879, Dubuque was one of the top clubs in the country not associated with the National League. The team displayed future notables, such as, Tom Loftus, the Gleason brothers, Bill and Jack, Hoss Radbourn, Bill Taylor, Laurie Reis and, of course, Comiskey.

Needing a league for his Rabbits, Sullivan formed and administered the Northwest League in 1879, which consisted of three other clubs representing Davenport, Omaha and Rockford. It was the first so-called minor league formed outside the east coast. Sullivan took steps to set a salary structure for the Northwest League and subordinated the league to the National League, which to some establishes it as the first legitimate minor league.

Dubuque won the pennant in 1879 and even scored a victory over Cap Anson's Chicago White Stockings in early August in an exhibition contest. Due in part to Dubuque running away with the pennant, the Northwest League folded after only one season. Comiskey stayed with the club through the 1881 season. With Dubuque Comiskey eventually settled at first base. He redefined the position as one of the first to increase his range by playing wide of the bag. An aggressive, hard-nosed ballplayer, he was described as a terror on the base paths and was also one of the first practitioners of the headfirst slide.

In 1882, Comiskey signed on with Chris von der Ahe's St. Louis Browns of the upstart major American Association. The 1882 Browns included several Sullivan graduates including Comiskey and the Gleason brothers. As a consequence, when von der Ahe replaced manager Ned Cuthbert at the end of the season, Sullivan was chosen as his replacement. At the end of 1883, the 23-year-old Comiskey himself replaced Sullivan as manager for the final nineteen games. Under Comiskey, the Browns won four straight pennants from 1885-1888 and placed second in 1889 before he departed for the Players League.

Entering the spring of 1891, Griffith was still among the reserved on the Milwaukee roster, though he was holding out for more money. On February 28, the club directors met and decided to drop all negotiations with Clark; he was asking for too much money.[64] On March 24, the *St. Louis Sporting Times* announced that Griff signed with the St. Louis Browns. Cushman thought the rumor was a hoax until he received a letter from Clark on March 28 informing him that he was jumping the club for a better offer from Comiskey. Griffith would happily be making $2,250, $750 more a year than Milwaukee offered.[65]

Milwaukee was distressed over losing Griffith.[66] The Western Association, as a whole was also upset. St. Louis, an American Association club, essentially raided Milwaukee's reserve roster, enticing Griffith to jump his contract. The two leagues were on good terms before this transgression. In response Western Association clubs went after some American Association reserved players returning from the Players League. Milwaukee, for one, offered a good deal of cash to St. Louis' Silver King. On April 10 Clark left Milwaukee. He was a major leaguer now.

The Browns were owned by Chris von der Ahe. He was perhaps the premier character of nineteenth century baseball, a combination of Gussie Busch, George Steinbrenner and Bill Veeck. A local tavern owner, von der Ahe entered baseball as early as 1876 to sell more beer. He knew little about the game but was smart businessman and turned much of the decision making over to Comiskey. Often overstated, Von der Ahe was

---

[64] "Smith the Secretary," *Milwaukee Sentinel*, February 28, 1891, p. 2

[65] "Prospects very good," *Milwaukee Sentinel*, March 29, 1891, p. 7, if Griffith had pushed the matter with Milwaukee, the club would have surely paid him more money.

[66] They also lost John Thornton.

kind of a joke around the league with his flashy clothes, ever-present dogs, thick German accent and complete ignorance of even the rudimentary aspects of the game.[67] Clark forever told stories of von der Ahe jumping out of his field box to argue contested plays with umpires. Adding to his flamboyance, the newspapers were full of stories of his mistresses, family battles and legal difficulties. However he was characterized in the press, von der Ahe was an astute businessman. He was also a grand showman who provided pregame carousel and carnivals rides, boxing matches and horse races.

Clark made his major league debut on April 11 at the original Sportsman's Park in St. Louis. The first Sportsman's Park housed the Browns, the current Cardinals, through their days in the American Association, 1882-1891, and for their first year, 1892, when the team en masse joined the National League.[68] The field, as most early ones, was huge by today's standards with the center field fence sitting at an unreachable 460 feet from home plate. The 350 feet to left field and 330 feet to right center seem comparable to today but in reality isn't. The ball wasn't wound as tight and rarely, if ever, traveled that far on the fly. It was only 285 feet down the right field line and under the right conditions a home run was attainable over the wall. Von der Ahe doubled the park's capacity to 12,000 in 1886 but for Griffith's debut only 3,500 showed to root on the club's newest find.

Clark didn't disappoint. The 21-year-old held Cincinnati batters to five hits and finished with a 13-5 victory after two hours and fifteen minutes. After three long seasons in Milwaukee, Clark finally reached the majors with its prestige and, more important, bigger paydays. In fact, Griffith looked like the next coming of Hoss Radbourn after rolling off five wins in his first five starts to begin his major league career. The victories, on April 11, 15, 19, 23 and 26, fueled interest around the league on St. Louis' little righthander.

It was the curve they all worried about. It baffled and, at times, appeared unhittable. He interwove it up with a fastball, if you could call it that, a changeup and an occasional sinkerball. But the newspapers cited, "Griffith's curves," as the focal point. Part of Griff's early success may have also been his willingness to pitch inside, perhaps a little too close. As

---

[67] Von der Ahe had a running feud with the Spinks, publishers of *The Sporting News*, a St. Louis-based paper and George Munson of the *St. Louis Dispatch*. A good deal of the anti–von der Ahe characterizations can be attributed to unjust criticism by harsh sportswriters.

[68] As part of the merger of the American Association and National League, St. Louis, Louisville, Washington and Baltimore joined the revamped 12-team National League.

the *Atchison Champion* noted, "They say pitcher Griffiths (sic) of St. Louis throws his fastball right at the batter's head."[69]

Clark had not yet developed the scuffball, spitball or the trademark screwball that he later claimed to invent (though Charlie Sweeney was throwing one in the 1880s). Those pitches, when added to the curve and Griffith's legendary control, mystified National League hitters during the 1890s. It might seem contradictory that he sits among the all-time leaders in hit batsmen, but that is just the byproduct of pitching inside – a sign of a tough and able competitor. The combination placed Griffith among the top pitchers of the decade. Bill James in his excellent review *The New Bill James Historical Baseball Abstract* ranks Griffith as the 70th best pitcher all-time.

It appeared in early 1891 that the curve was enough. That is until Griffith hit a wall and lost his next six starts. By the middle of July, his record stood at 11 and 8, not all that bad but he proved inconsistent after the initial string of victories including giving up an embarrassing four home runs on May 2 in a rain-shortened eight-inning contest. Comiskey wanted a fifth pennant and had an impressive lineup with himself at first and fellow Hall of Famer Tommy McCarthy in right field. The outfield was also filled with solid players and borderline Hall of Famers Dummy Hoy in center and Tip O'Neill in left. Jack Stivetts, a career 200-game winner, was the key on the mound with 33 victories and a league-leading 259 strikeouts.

The center fielder was perhaps the most interesting of the bunch. William Hoy developed meningitis as a boy causing him to lose his hearing and the capability to speak. The speedy center fielder had tremendous range despite never hearing the crack of the bat. On June 19, 1888, the rookie threw out three would-be scorers at the plate. The diminutive Hoy, only 5'4" tall, also swiped 594 bases, however statistics are skewed during the era because taking an extra base on a hit was credited as a stolen base until 1898. Hoy spent fourteen seasons with seven different clubs. In all, he scored 1,426 times in only 1,796 games, finishing with a .287 batting average and 726 RBI, while poking over 2,000 hits. When he passed away in 1961 at age 99, Hoy was the last surviving member of the American Association.

Some say that the basic umpiring signs, for safe or out, ball or strike and fair or foul were developed to inform Hoy of individual calls.

---

[69] "Diamond Chips," *Atchison Champion*, Atchison, Kansas, May 22, 1891, p. 7

Others also claim that signaling for a popup with one's arms dates back to Hoy's adventures in the outfield. It is true that Hoy is the best-known deaf player in major league history; however, there were others that preceded him in professional baseball.[70] Griffith played against John Ryn who is considered to be the first deaf player in professional ball while the latter was with Seattle in 1892. The presence of the deaf players encouraged their teammates, coaches and umpires to communicate with them through sign language, whether formal American Sign Language or impromptu gestures adapted to the situations that arose on the field.[71] Griffith, only Hoy's teammate for a short while in 1891, learned to communicate with his center fielder. They teamed up again a decade later.

Tip O'Neill, originally a pitcher, gained contractual freedom when John Day, owner of the New York franchises in both the American

---

[70] Deaf Major Leaguers:

Ed Dundon	pitcher	1883-84
Tom Lynch	pitcher	1884
William Hoy	outfielder	1888-1902
Reuben Stephenson	outfielder	1892
Luther Taylor	pitcher	1900-08
George Leitner	pitcher	1901-02
William Deegan	pitcher	1901
Dick Sipek	outfielder	1945
Curtis Pride	outfielder	1993-

Being that times and attitudes changed, Sipek was the first deaf-mute not to be nicknamed "Dummy." John Ryn is thought to be the first deaf ballplayer. His career may have started as early as the 1870s. In the minors deaf-mute George Kihm played first base from 1895-1911, racking up 2,245 hits and a .293 batting average. Lefthander Ryan Ketchner joined the Mariners' organization in 2000. There is a Dummy Murphy listed in the encyclopedias but that nickname seems to stem from his four errors on April 24, 1914 and subsequent misplays. I wrote biographies on several of these men for the SABR Biography Project.

[71] Nice article titled "The Deaf and the Origin of Hand Signals in Baseball" on this issue is contained in the 2008 issue of the Society of American Baseball Research's *The National Pastime*, p. 35, by Randy Fisher and Jami N. Fisher. It is interesting to note that the American Sign Language words for "out" and "free" remarkably resemble baseball's gestures for "out" and "safe," respectively.

Association and the National League, tried to move him between franchises. Day fail to wait the ten days required for such a transfer and O'Neill ended up with the Browns in 1884. Then, a sore arm forced him from the mound. No worries, O'Neill converted to the outfield, hit .350 in 1885 and helped the Browns clip four straight pennants. His 1887 season, in which he led the league in virtually every significant offensive category, is nearly indescribable and one of the truly stellar purely statistical performances in baseball history.

On June 27, Griffith knocked his first major league home run, a grand slam off Columbus' John Dolan in the bottom of the seventh. Comiskey released Griffith outright at the end of July, supposedly for ineffectiveness.[72] Rumors abound that he had a sore arm. Nonetheless, Clark, the salesman, peddled himself to other association clubs and nearly landed with Baltimore but in the end signed with Boston for the pennant run. He was not traded for pitcher Jack Easton nor did he jump the Browns as some have noted. Easton was released by Columbus on July 23 and agreed to a contract with Boston but backed out over a hitch with the bonus and signed with Comiskey in St. Louis.

While with St. Louis, Griffith showed signs of his system bucking potential. Yes, he was creating waves with management from his first season in the bigs. Catcher Bill Moran was signed off a Joliet, Illinois roster by Ted Sullivan for the Browns. The problem was Moran was owed a $200 bonus but von der Ahe wasn't forthcoming with the cash. After talking the situation over with Griff, Moran quit the club and left town in protest. Von der Ahe then threatened to "thrash" Clark for his interference and the loss of his catcher. In the end, Moran ended up with the Browns as they switched to the National League in 1892.[73]

The Boston Reds were managed by Art Irwin. Irwin, a local boy, first joined the majors in 1880 when his minor Worcester club en masse joined the National League. A bit unusual for the time, he threw righthanded but batted from the left side. Coaching for years at the University of Pennsylvania and Harvard, he became one of the premier college coaches of the time. In April 1894, his college team defeated the National League Phillies. In 1893, Irwin unveiled an invention which became the first football scoreboard when it was used on November 30, 1893 in a game at

---

[72] "Summer Sports," *Yenowine's Illustrated News*, Milwaukee, August 2, 1891, p. 7

[73] *The Sporting News*, July 30, 1952

Harvard. Similar scoreboards were used throughout the northeast at stadiums, theaters and such for decades to come. At the time of his death in 1921 he was still collecting royalties on the invention.

Irwin played and managed in majors through 1899. Save a long stretch as a New York Highlander scout and official from 1908-1915, he managed in the minors from 1903-1921. In June 1921 while managing Hartford in the Eastern League, he was taken to the hospital, suffering from abdominal trouble. The doctors found cancer and gave him a bleak outlook, expecting him to expire within a short time, perhaps weeks. Irwin relinquished his manager position and left the hospital to go home to his wife May at their New York apartment.

On July 14, Irwin left New York on the steam ship *Calvin Austin* bound for Boston. He was headed for his hometown and his other wife Elizabeth, whom he married in 1883. During the trip, friends said that Irwin was depressed and talking about ending his life, stating that he was, "Going home to die." He also discussed his medical issues and the fact that doctors gave him a bleak outlook. The ship arrived in Boston on July 16 but Irwin was nowhere to be found. His clothes and luggage were in his stateroom; it was assumed that he jumped overboard at some point, committing suicide and dying in the Atlantic Ocean.

While in Philadelphia as manager from 1894-1895, Irwin met a local lady named May, thirteen years his younger. They were later married. The 1900 and 1910 U.S. Censuses list Irwin as living separate lives with both families. Neither family knew about the other family. Neither wife knew about the other wife. None of Irwin's friends or business associates seemed to know about the two wives either. He had children with both women. At some point he virtually abandoned his Boston family, living with May in Manhattan. He made infrequent trips to Boston to be with Elizabeth and their children; though, he ceased supporting them. By 1920, Elizabeth was near destitute. The families learned about each other for the first time while visiting Irwin in the hospital. It became a public scandal immediately after Irwin's death.

The Boston club boasted two Hall of Famers at first base and right field, Dan Brouthers and Hugh Duffy, respectively. On the mound, righthanders George Haddock and Charlie Buffington carried the load, winning 63 games between them. Around the same time Griff signed with the Reds so did the legendary King Kelly, the most flamboyant of the 19th century stars.

The Reds were in first place, 2.5 games up on the Browns when Clark joined the club. Griffith made his first start on August 3 against

Comiskey's boys but lost. He won his next three starts on August 10 and 18 and September 4. Boston won the pennant by 8.5 games over St. Louis. Griffith could feel proud that he spent a month and a half with the association's best team but there was work to be done on his game. Pitching for the two best teams in the league, Griffith finished with a respectable 14-9-record, which was the sixth best winning percentage in the American Association. He also exhibited the genesis of the fine control which became his trademark, finishing fifth in fewest walks per game and seventh in strikeout to walk ratio. Another Griffith trademark and portend of his pioneering of relief pitching is highlighted by his league-leading totals of relief wins and games finished.

If it wasn't evident then, it is in hindsight. Griffith needed to tweak his pitching style to measure up to major league competition. The curves would only fool them for so long. Griffith was only 5'6" and 155 lbs. at the time; he couldn't wow them with a speedball. Plus, the pitching distance would soon be stretched to the current 60'6". Two other factors came into play. The American Association was about to disband, the first of three leagues to collapse under Griffith.[74] There were significantly fewer major league slots available in 1892. Unfortunately, Boston was not one of the four American Association teams absorbed by the National League.

There was another upside to his first experience in the majors. During the era, utility players often doubled as ticket takers before games.[75] Griffith did this for von der Ahe in St. Louis. He later said that the experience opened his eyes to the business end of the sport and made him focus on plans beyond merely playing ball. Griffith, though low-key, became a bit of a showman himself. The experience also made him well rounded in his view of the game and more focused in how he approached his opportunities in the future.

Clark was given his unconditional release by Boston on September 21. The previous day he played left field in Milwaukee, scoring a crucial run in the 5-4 victory. Rumors still abound concerning his sore arm, but Cleveland offered him a contract to join their rotation in tandem with their new ace Cy Young for 1892. First, Clark petitioned president Nick Young to see if he was eligible to play in the National League. He needed

---

[74] American Association in 1891, Northern Pacific League in 1892 and California League in 1893

[75] Besides collecting tickets, von der Ahe's men also performed numerous jobs around the ballpark including grounds keeping chores.

to find out if the National League still considered him property of Milwaukee, the club he jumped. The issue ironed itself out as Milwaukee withdrew from the Western Association and consequently the National Agreement; Griff never did join Cleveland or any National League club in 1892.[76]

After being released, Griff hung around Milwaukee for a few weeks to gauge his opportunities for the following season. He played in a few exhibition games and was pressed into service as an umpire on October 12. It was the last day before the Milwaukee players headed home for the winter. They were playing the St. Louis Browns, when excessive kicking by Milwaukee caused the umpire to walk out in the fourth inning. Clark was quickly recruited to finish the game.[77] The next day he left for Helena, Montana to spend the winter with his brother punching cattle and working on a ranch. He left with an offer from Cushman to rejoin the Milwaukee club, which was joining the Western League.[78] He also played a little ball in Montana to get his arm in shape.

It was clear in early 1892 that Griffith wasn't going to catch on with a National League club. There were just too many arms to be had with the folding of the American Association. No need to add a pitcher with a potentially bum wing and little experience in the show. Clark decided to move on from Milwaukee; in early April he signed with Tacoma, Washington of the independent Pacific Northwest League.[79] Professional baseball was in its infancy in Tacoma; in fact, the first professional game in the area didn't take place until 1890. The league itself had a history of financial struggles and, true to form, wasn't in operation come September.

The Tacoma club itself recently underwent reorganization. Club president W.B. Bushnell, a local ice entrepreneur,[80] recently refurbished the club's ballpark but the sheriff sold the club and grounds in November 1891 to satisfy the mortgage.[81] Bushnell branched out his ice business to the larger Seattle.[82] The manager of his Seattle plant was Elmer Rockwell.

---

[76] "League after Players," *Milwaukee Sentinel*, September 26, 1891, p. 5

[77] "Last of the Season," *Milwaukee Sentinel*, October 13, 1891, p. 5

[78] "Where the Ballplayers Go," *Milwaukee Sentinel*, October 14, 1891, p. 2

[79] "In the World of Sport," *Milwaukee Sentinel*, April 10, 1892, p. 8, though the paper incorrectly identified the team as Seattle

[80] Owner of the Tacoma Ice and Refrigeration Company

[81] *The Sporting News*, December 5, 1891

[82] 1890 Census: Seattle population, 42,000; Tacoma, 36,000.

Many sources cite Bushnell as the president of the Pacific Northwest League in 1892; however, Rockwell handled the league's administration and was continually identified in the press as the league's president.

Griffith's arm troubles weren't structural as much as just a general soreness; his arm tired easily his first couple of years in pro ball. He tried to pitch through it over the winter and into the spring but the tenderness remained. Clark worked through the problem, posting a fine season in Tacoma. The league consisted of four clubs, representing Seattle, Portland, Spokane and Tacoma. Rosters around the league included Bill Lange, Gil Hatfield, Howard Earl, Charlie Irwin, Tom Parrott[83] and Gil McGinnis for Seattle, Abner Dalrymple with Spokane and Jake Stenzel, Edgar McNabb and George Tebeau for Portland. At the time Lange was a young catcher. *The Sporting News* noted, "The pitching department of the various clubs are very evenly matched. Tacoma seems to have slightly the best of it now. The signing of Griffith was a good move and the young twirler will make friends for himself if he does well. He is a good batter for a pitcher."[84]

The Tacoma Daisies, under manager Farmer Bill Works, opened with a victory on April 13 and continued to do well. Works won the Triple Crown in the Texas League in 1890 as outfielder, first baseman and manager for Galveston. Ed Cartwright, Bill Goodenough and Works himself, who led the league in hits, supported Tacoma's young pitchers at the plate. Phil Routcliffe and Chuck Lauer also played for the club. They ended up with the league's best record, 41-32, but won neither the first nor second half, much like the modern Cincinnati Reds in 1981.

Hugh Fullerton of the *Chicago Tribune* delighted in telling and retelling the story of Griffith pitching in Seattle one day in 1892.[85] The pitcher was getting rocked. Every pitch seemed to end up banging off the outfield wall. About to make another delivery to the plate, Clark heard a huge commotion coming from the bleachers. He turned to see the local clothier ripping his sign off the center field fence that offered a free suit to any batter that could hit his billboard. "That's the toughest roast I ever got in baseball," declared Griffith years later.[86]

---

[83] Parrott also played for Tacoma in 1892.

[84] *The Sporting News*, April 16, 1892

[85] Clark Griffith was a favorite of sportswriters Shirley Povich in Washington D.C. and Hugh Fullerton in Chicago.

[86] Hugh S. Fullerton, "Pitchers I have Known," *Chicago Tribune*, January 14, 1906, p. A2

On April 17 at Tacoma, Griff was clobbered by Seattle for eleven runs on six hits in the fourth inning and pulled from the game. The final score was 14-4. He didn't start another game until May 8, as *The Sporting News* noted, "Griffith has had the grip and is not yet in shape."[87] On the 8th he lost to Seattle 5-1. Clark won a wild one on May 13 11-10 over Spokane. Seattle defeated Griffith on the 18th at Tacoma 5-4, despite Griff striking out six and placing a double. He lost again on May 25 and was knocked out of the box in a 10-9 contest versus Spokane.

He won the first game of a doubleheader on June 5 Griff 4-3 versus Seattle, despite four walks and three wild pitches. He also placed a double. Three days later, he lost 3-0 to Portland, giving up six hits and two walks but striking out six. Clark beat Portland 6-3 on the 12th. The following day he played right field and batted second because Goodenough was ill.[88] Clark split with Spokane in the middle of June, beating them on the 17th 7-1 and losing on the 19th 10-9 in ten innings. Tacoma and Griffith were hit hard on the 23rd, losing 21-17. Clark entered in relief and gave up 15 hits and six earned runs. Between both teams, 39 hits were placed. During June, Spokane made a bid for Clark, but Tacoma wasn't interested.[89]

Griff was in right field again on June 26 and July 2. Tacoma won 4-1, but lost the shutout on an error by Clark on the latter date. On the 7th in Seattle Griff lost in eleven innings 8-7; he also knocked a double. On July 10, Griff entered in relief in the sixth inning; Seattle scored 13 times that inning for a 14-10 victory. He had an off day on July 13, walking four and losing to Portland 9-5. He had a hard time finding the plate, blaming his problems on the umpire. The next day he played first base in a 9-7 win over Portland. Griff played first base again on the 16th during a 3-2 loss to Portland. On the mound again, Clark defeated Seattle 4-1, ceding only four hits and striking out seven. Erratically, he walked two and hit four batters.

He defeated Seattle on the 23rd 4-1 and shutout Portland on the 28th 9-0. Griff triumphed over Portland on July 30 8-4, striking out ten against only one base on balls. He also smacked a three-run double. On August 4, he shutout Spokane 11-0, ceding only four hits and striking out nine. The next time out, two days later, he only allowed one run in an 8-1 triumph over Spokane again. On the 10th, Clark pitched well against

---

[87] *The Sporting News*, May 7, 1892

[88] The Tacoma club fielded the same eleven, including the three pitchers, men all season. Of the box scores I found, no other names appeared.

[89] "Gossip of Sports," *Morning Oregonian*, Portland, June 26, 1892, p. 20

Seattle, shutting them out until the sixth inning when two runs scored on a wild pitch. He was then tossed from the game for excessive arguing. He pitched and won versus Portland 10-9 on October 16. The game was played in Salem, Oregon. Clark lost 10-4 to Portland two days later.

In total, Clark put up solid numbers once again in 1892. Over 28 games and 221 innings, he won 13, lost 8 and posted a 1.59 ERA. He also batted .241, his best mark to date. Tacoma's season ended more with a thud than a pennant celebration. Throughout the league, players hadn't received paychecks in a while. The league called it quits on August 21. Griff pitched and won 8-6 over Portland that day. He also knocked a double and scored three times. Luckily Griffith and boys were playing at home in Tacoma. Some on other clubs were stranded away from home without any cash.

Money, in fact, was tight all year. On August 5, the Tacoma club met to decide whether to call off the season or not; apparently, the men must have received some sort of payment that day as they decided to continue on. They were still owed back pay. As *The Sporting News* noted, "The Tacomas could not make good the last guarantee."[90] Plus, the players couldn't locate management. The *News* continued, "The worst state of affairs however seems to be in Tacoma where a regular game of hide and seek is going on between the players and the directors."[91] Manager Bill Works was especially disgruntled concerning his time in Tacoma. He explained, "I gave them a good team that played first class ball from start to finish, and a lot of gentlemen as well. This is the way they treated us: They refused to pay our salaries. I have placed our accounts in the hands of Wirstling & Wirstling, attorneys in Seattle."[92] They filed suit in Superior Court in King County, Washington. The men were owed $657.31, $75.10 to Griffith personally. On September 22 a judgment was rendered in their favor; league assets were attached to pay the debt.[93] Seeing this successful recovery, the Spokane players also filed a suit. After the lawsuits, some of the players drifted into California or other parts of the country to find a payday.

Works received a telegram from club owner Frank Higgins in Missoula offering to maintain the salary of any interested players in traveling to Montana to play ball. The Montana State League operated outside Organized Baseball in 1892, which meant they refused or weren't

---

[90] *The Sporting News*, September 3, 1892, article dated August 27

[91] *The Sporting News*, September 3, 1892

[92] *The Sporting News*, November 19, 1892

[93] "Hal Pointer's Time," *Morning Oregonian*, Portland, September 23, 1892, p. 8

permitted to sign the National Agreement binding them to the National League and lower classifications.[94] The league was organized earlier in the year and showcased franchises in Helena, Butte, Missoula, Philipsburg, and some cities which didn't finish the season, all western towns. The season got a late start, beginning on May 30 and running until October 5.

As such, the outlaw league signed whomever it wanted and paid no attention to existing player contracts or the despised reserve clause. At times in baseball history men were blacklisted from Organized Baseball for merely playing with or against outlaw clubs. The National League in 1892 made threats about the jumping of pitcher Tony Mullane to Butte. Works, perhaps considering this, threw the telegram away but Griffith fished it out of the trash. He talked the entire squad, including Works, into following him to Missoula to finish out the season. Clark later recalled this period as the first time he was able to organize and lead men.

Griff was familiar with the area; his brother lived there and he spent the previous winter working and playing ball in Montana. In fact, one of the Montana State League's early organizers in 1892, umpire Charles Kilpatrick, was a friend. To promote the upcoming season, Kilpatrick sent word back to *The Sporting News* in February 1892 boasting about the quality of play in the area and the beauty of the area's mountainous scenery. His biggest selling point was Griffith. He boasted, "Clark Griffith, the pitcher, is winning here at Helena and is in the best of condition. Mountain air seems to agree with him and next season will see him pitch the game of his life. Griffith and myself walked up Mount Helena yesterday a distance of 12,000 feet."[95]

Former teammate Tom Parrott headed to Montana as well. Others of interest in the league that year were Elmer Foster, Tommy Hernon, Art Twineham[96] and pitching star Tony Mullane. Mullane jumped his Cincinnati National League club at midseason due to a salary dispute and then joined the Butte club.[97] The entire Tacoma squad actually relocated

---

[94] The 1892 Montana State League is listed outside Organized Baseball by all sources I could find. However, the "The Second Series," *Morning Oregonian*, July 16, 1892, p. 6, states that the league was admitted as a Class-B league under the National Agreement.

[95] *The Sporting News*, February 27, 1892

[96] Twineham also played with Griffith in Bloomington in 1887. He was a noted polo player as well.

[97] Mullane was at times an ambidextrous pitcher. Occurrences of ambidextrous pitching in major league history:

    Tony Mullane   July 18, 1882   4th-9th innings

to Missoula. The Montana everyday roster of O.J. Patten, Goodenough, Works, Cartwright, Arthur Sippi, Routecliffe, Mike Cody and Kid Speer matched the Tacoma starting eight. *The Sporting News* remarked, "The entire Tacoma ball club has been transferred to Missoula to play the balance of the season in the Montana State League. All seemed well pleased with the prospect, as they have been virtually advanced two month's pay by the Missoula management."[98]

The men arrived in Missoula at the turn of the month.[99] There was a wild celebration when the players stepped off the train. Missoula was a booming mining town straight out of Hollywood westerns, at least the section where the players congregated. There were gambling joints and saloons and a huge drunken Sunday night party after Griffith won the first game 6-5 with five strikeouts. *The Sporting News* commented, "A hard game was won by Missoula at Helena September 4 in the tenth inning."[100] The hat was passed and $700 landed in the pitcher's pocket, lesser amounts for the other men. Yes, the players could be happy here for a while! They played into November, well after the official season ended.

The town looked forward to a fine showing against archrival Helena in the upcoming weeks. Higgins, the state's future Lieutenant Governor, promised Griffith $200 if he won the next contest and local newspapers estimated that $100,000 in bets were placed on the game. Griffith squeaked out the victory, 5-4, to the delight of a raucous, gun-toting throng. The new Missoula crew proved especially strong; they won the second half of the season.[101] Griff defeated Butte 20-6 on September 17. He struck out five and smashed two triples. He topped Butte again the following day 24-5, placing another triple and a double. On the 24th, he

Larry Corcoran	June 16, 1884	four innings
Elton Chamberlain	May 9, 1888	8th & 9th inning
Tony Mullane	July 14, 1893	ninth inning
Greg A. Harris	September 28, 1995	ninth inning

Mullane is said to have pitched with both hands periodically. The first and last known dates are listed above.

[98] *The Sporting News*, September 3, 1892

[99] *The Sporting News*, September 3, 1892

[100] *The Sporting News*, September 17, 1892

[101] Modern researchers for *The Encyclopedia of Minor League Baseball, Third Edition* state that Missoula won the second half. Contemporary *Sporting News* issues claim that Helena won the second half.

tripled yet again and defeated Helena 10-6. On the mound the following day, he was knocked out of the box, then moved to first base and hit a double, during a 16-4 loss to Helena.

The men enjoyed there time in Missoula, especially after being jilted on their paychecks in Tacoma. As Bill Works exclaimed, "I never was fronted nicer that I was during the time I was a member of the Missoula club."[102]

Griff again spent the winter in Helena working on a ranch with his brother and playing a little ball around Missoula. In a few years Clark and Earl bought a ranch in Montana that Earl oversaw during the baseball season. In 1911, Griff took a second mortgage on that ranch to fulfill his dream of buying into a major league franchise. By the end of the 1910s, he sold it and all the livestock to gain controlling interest in the Washington Senators.

Griffith joined another financially shaky circuit in 1893, the California League, which operated outside Organized Baseball the previous year. California fielded its first baseball clubs, organized by cricket players, back in 1859, first in Sacramento and then in San Francisco. The first organized games in the state took place the following year. The first enclosed park was built in 1868 in San Francisco. The hunger for the game grew exponentially after the famed Red Stockings of Cincinnati toured the state the following year. The first professional league, the Pacific Base Ball League, was formed in 1878 and centered in the state's economic base, San Francisco.

San Francisco was the hub of the west coast well into the 20th century. Tens of thousands of Americans and immigrants settled there after gold was discovered near Sacramento in 1848. In 1879, the rival California League was first organized, lasting through Griffith's time there in 1893. Unfortunately, organizers were unable to secure grounds to play at in San Francisco so the league based itself in Oakland, a serious detriment since the city only had about 14% of the population that San Francisco did. Oakland's population base didn't begin to catch up until after 1906 when an earthquake and related fires nearly destroyed San Francisco. The National League Cincinnati Reds and Chicago White Stockings toured the west coast in October 1879, further promoting the sport. It finally secured grounds in San Francisco in 1880. Exhibition tours by major league clubs dramatically increased throughout the 1880s.

---

[102] *Sporting News*, November 19, 1892

Al Spalding made a heralded stop in California during his world tour of 1888-1889.

In 1886, the California League finally branched outside the San Francisco area to include Sacramento, approximately sixty miles away. That same year the league applied and was granted admission to the National Agreement, formally linking it with Organized Baseball, and asked to be placed in charge of baseball decisions on the west coast. In 1892, Los Angeles joined the California League for the first time, spending a lot of money to capture the flag. That year saw a great deal of upheaval within the league both on the administration end and with player relations. The root of the problem derived from financial pressures, due to an economic downturn, the Panic of 1893.

At the end of January 1893, the California League, often misidentified as the Pacific Coast League in relation to Griffith, was still unsure which cities would be represented during the upcoming season. Only one club, Oakland, was set to field a team. The trouble centered on the shaky Los Angeles franchise that represented the fastest growing city in the state and the financial key to the league's success or failure. An additional dilemma arose as many of the ballplayers didn't like traveling a far south as Los Angeles, nearly 400 miles, just to play a few games.

Griffith was set to pitch for Col. Tom Robinson's Oakland Colonels. Robinson was an aggressive, well-liked baseball promoter who was held in high esteem throughout the area for his many years of service as a local sportsman; however, recent financial troubles found him sliding hard in the standings and continually battling the fans and the press. The hurler must have come at a high price because the *Los Angeles Times* continually referred to him as "the costly Griffith" or "the expense Griffith" or the "high-priced hurler." He mailed in his contract in February and arrived from Montana on March 14. The Oakland squad played a few games with University of California and Stanford College nines to work themselves into shape.

After backers were enlisted and all the details ironed out, Opening Day was set for March 25. Since Griff entered professional ball he was pitching from 55'6". The rules established in 1887 set a pitcher's box that was 4 feet wide and extended from 50' to 55.6" from home plate, or home base as it was called. It should also be noted that there were no mounds during the 19th century; they were delivering from flat ground. The pitchers kept one foot on the back of the pitcher's box and could take one step forward as they delivered; thus, they were pitching from 55'6". For 1893 the pitcher's box was eliminated for a fixed pitcher's plate, which was placed at 60'6" from home, an extension of five feet.

The plate was initially 12" x 4" but was changed two years later to the current 24" x 6".

Griff brought his catcher from Tacoma Mike Cody with him. Bill Works was also in the league, playing for San Francisco. The league opened with clubs in Los Angeles, Oakland, San Francisco and Stockton.[103] The moderate weather on the coast allowed play to continue through November and possibly later, with major leaguers joining the fold at the end of their season. Oakland was set to play a 159-game schedule, every Wednesday through Sunday until November 5. In reality, the California League only completed 99 official league contests that year. Oakland opened up with a 4-2-victory and rarely slowed down. Griffith lost the following day in the ninth inning in San Francisco 6-5 before nearly 10,000 fans; he allowed only five hits while striking out four. Griff won on the 30th 7-3 over Los Angeles. He also placed two hits and scored. He won again on April 1 8-3, ceding only six hits. He doubled to left field with the bases loaded for three RBI and scored.

Clark won Oakland's home opener 5-3 on April 8, holding Stockton scoreless until the eighth inning. He defeated Stockton again on the 16th 12-7 but was manhandled by Los Angeles 14-4 on the 20th and 11-4 on the 23rd. Griff topped San Francisco on April 27 9-7 and again two days later 5-4, winning the latter game in the ninth. San Francisco got its revenge on the 30th, defeating Griffith 7-4 in the second game of a doubleheader. He lost again, to Los Angeles on May 7 10-9, before defeating San Francisco 7-3 on the 11th. While still in town, he lost two days later in the final inning 7-5. The following day, Griffith pitched the second game of a doubleheader, being knocked out in the third inning before Oakland won in the ninth 10-9. Griff split with Stockton, losing 9-8 on the 19th and winning 6-3 on the 21st also placing a double. He took two of three games from San Francisco at the end of the month, losing 15-6 on the 25th but winning 16-5 on the 27th and 7-6 the following day.

Clark defeated Stockton on June 3 and Los Angeles three days later, each by a run. On June 11, he relieved in the later innings during a loss to LA in the first game of a doubleheader and lost himself in the second game 10-9. Still in Los Angeles on June 15 he won a sloppy game 10-9, ceding 15 hits. He lost two days later in a high scoring game 16-11. On the 21st and 23rd Griff defeated Stockton 7-4 and 11-8 respectively. On June 25, he defeated Stockton again 2-1 and moved to right field and in the second game that day. He defeated San Francisco on June 30 9-2 and July 2 14-6. On July 4, San Francisco topped Oakland 16-8. Clark

---

[103] Sacramento later replaced Stockton.

entered in relief, but was hit just as hard as the starter. He split with Sacramento, Stockton's replacement in the league, losing 12-8 on the 7th and winning 16-5 two days later. He hit well in each game, tripling in the first and scoring three times on three hits including a double in the second. Every Oakland player scored in the latter game. On July 13, he won over Los Angeles 7-6 but lost on the 15th 6-2 and split with San Francisco on the 19th and 21st, winning the latter game. On July 23, Griff was tapped for nine hits and seven runs in the first two innings versus San Francisco. Oakland lost 8-3. On the 27th, Griff won over Los Angeles 8-5. He received an ovation in the second inning after striking out the side. Los Angeles defeated Clark two days later 7-4.

At the beginning of August, Oakland had a series with Sacramento; Griff won three games, on the 2nd, 4th and 6th. On August 7, he was called into action as an umpire, same clubs. On the 10th, he defeated San Francisco 5-1, the only run scoring on an error, and shut them out two days later 8-0. The following day, August 13, the league disbanded.

The league's attendance faltered from the beginning. Robinson quickly moved some of his home games to the heavier populated San Francisco. By early May, he couldn't pay his men. On May 2 the players revolted, demanding payment before boarding a train headed to Los Angeles. The train, in fact, left without the ballplayers. Robinson quickly came up with some cash and the men departed the following day and played a doubleheader. Again on May 18, the Oakland players refused to play, Stockton this time, unless paid. The following day, Oakland businessmen Louis Gieschen and Edward Noblett took over the club from Robinson for $750, a little more than he owed in back payroll.

As the Stockton owner Mike Finn noted of Robinson, "The league has not been making money, but the rest of us pay our men regularly…He buys himself diamonds and then comes around and tells me the ladies gave them to him." Allegations that Robinson was skimming the profits drew the ire of players and fans. It was also discovered that he was providing over one hundred and fifty free tickets to friends and associates for each contest. *The Sporting News* added its two cents about the Oakland owner, exclaiming, "Robinson is too talkative, and it is almost impossible to tell when he is really telling the truth."[104]

The club did have an expensive payroll, $1,300 a month, of which Griffith demanded a large share. The new owners immediately replaced team captain O'Neill with Cantillon and cancelled the free passes. By the

---

[104] *The Sporting News*, April 1, 1893

end of May, the California League was falling apart because of low attendance and bickering between franchises. The Stockton team dropped out with Sacramento taking its place. League president John J. Mone, who had led the league since 1882, was ousted on June 5.

The league ended its first half after a July 4-doubleheader, with Los Angeles a couple games up on Oakland. The second half began the next day. The league hit another financial wall in mid-August and suspended play. Arguments among league owners, particularly between Sacramento and Los Angeles, sparked by meager turnouts at the gate and other squabbles proved disastrous.

The league, on paper, rose again but fell apart within a couple days. It was pronounced officially dead again on August 18. Plans were made to revive half the league, San Francisco and Oakland, the following week but things again hit a snag in Oakland on the 25th. Geischen wasn't paying the players regularly either. Griffith saw this before in Tacoma and wasn't going to stand pat. The players hadn't seen much money for the ten weeks since Geischen's initial payment. He was doling out only $5 or $10 at a time to the men. They all owed room and board and couldn't pay. Many hotels didn't much care for ballplayers anyway because of their nasty habit of chewing tobacco and their general rowdy behavior. Geischen was pushed for the cash but he claimed poverty and couldn't come up with the $2,000 to $2,500 he owed the players. The men demanded promissory notes but Geischen honestly declared that they'd be worthless.

Griffith took up the cause for all the players. Every other team paid their men. What had Geischen done with all the gate receipts since June? In San Francisco Griffith and company refused to come out of the dressing room and play the day's game. They sent a representative to plead their case to the crowd, a local politician. Surprisingly, the players received an ovation as they departed the park without playing.

In the end, Griffith, in his first experience pitching from 60'6", put up impressive numbers, 30 victories against only 17 defeats. He surpassed one the toughest hurdles of the era; many other hurlers would never successfully make the transition. Griffith and Jack Horner accounted for all of Oakland's sixty victories. Each led the league in the category and Clark also copped the strikeout crown with 151 over fifty games and a career-high 427 innings pitched. Obviously, the club didn't need much relief help. In fact, the two pitchers had little trouble with the new pitching distance, asserting "that they experienced no mound difficulty in controlling the ball."[105] They were supported offensively by shortstop Charley Irwin who led the league in runs and first baseman Howard Earl who did the same in hits. Griffith showed a glimpse of things to come by batting .265. The figure was close to the league average. Due to the increased pitching distance, batting averages in the California League jumped from .241 in 1892 to .268. Runs per game also jumped from 10.4 to 14.0. On the mound Griffith, Horner and Los Angeles' George Borchers were the clear standouts in the California League.

The star of the Oakland team was captain, second baseman and local favorite Joe Cantillon who became a close friend of Clark's. Joe was born in Janesville, Wisconsin in August 1861 to Ireland-born parents Patrick and Catherine Cantillon. The Cantillons came to the United States at a young age to work for the railroad. All eight of their children were born in Wisconsin.[106] Most of the male Cantillons went to work for the railroad as well. Joe, the fourth child, did so by his mid-teens; however, he caught the baseball bug and began his career as a second baseman in 1879.[107] He played in and around his home state with Green Bay, Eau Claire and Winona, Minnesota, among other stops. In 1888 as manager of Eau Claire, Cantillon met Ted Sullivan who became a life-long friend and great influence on his baseball career. Cantillon first played on the west coast in 1889 with San Francisco.

He became a huge favorite in California after a fabricated story by San Francisco sportswriter Charley Dryden, the man famous for later coining the phrase "Washington – first in war, first in peace, and last in the American League." Dryden received numerous inquiries regarding the nationality of Cantillon. In an article, the writer fictitiously stated that Joe's real name was Pongo Pelipe Cantillon, the son of an Italian nobleman who moved to the United States seeking fame and fortune. After that, Italian-Americans flocked to the ballpark to catch sight of their countryman.

Following stints in the Interstate Association and the Western Association, Cantillon returned to the west coast with Oakland in 1892. After playing with Griffith, Cantillon found jobs as manager and second baseman for Rock Island, Illinois and Dubuque, Iowa. He then began working as an umpire in Ban Johnson's Western League in 1895. During

---

[105] *The Sporting News*, April 1, 1893

[106] Per the 1870 and 1880 U.S. Census

[107] Joe was still listed as a railroad employee in the 1880 U.S. Census.

the rest of the decade, Cantillon hopped between field management and umpiring positions.

When the American League became a major in 1901, he umpired during the first season. In 1902, Cantillon worked in blue for Nick Young in the National League. Starting in 1903, he managed the Milwaukee Brewers of the American Association through 1906 when he was named manager of the Washington Senators. In D.C., Cantillon sealed his name in baseball lore when he signed a young righthander named Walter Johnson.

Also on that Oakland squad was captain and third baseman Norris L. "Tip" O'Neill, not to be confused with the two major leaguers with the same nickname. This O'Neill was born on February 1, 1867 in Rouseville, Pennsylvania to Irish-born parents. O'Neill first made a name for himself as catcher for Allentown in the early 1880s. There, he was the battery mate of John "Phenomenal" Smith. O'Neill first played out west in 1889, joining Tom Robinson in Oakland. He continued to play in the area through 1898. From there, he umpired in the American Association and developed a strong friendship with White Sox owner Charles Comiskey, eventually moving to Chicago.

He served as president of the Western League from 1905 through 1915. Strangely, O'Neill did not live nor hold an office in a Western League city. He worked out of Comiskey Park. The fact that he lived in Chicago eventually wore on the league owners. In 1914, they gave him an ultimatum to move to a league city or find another job. He promptly drove to Des Moines and established a mailbox but refused to relocate. The glib manner in which he did do, protesting that, "I shall live any place I damn please," led in part to his ouster in December 1915.

O'Neill maintained an office at Comiskey Park for many years, working as a representative for Comiskey and the White Sox. He handled many of the administrative and financial dealings for both of Comiskey's international tours, in 1913 and 1924. He also acted as a scout for the club and often oversaw spring training. In September 1917 he sold an oil well on family land for $200,000.

O'Neill was a minor figure in the Black Sox scandal. National League president John Heydler stated that, "Tip O'Neill, former Western League president, came to me after the first World Series game...and told me Comiskey and Gleason felt that something was wrong, but that they did not want to go to Ban Johnson because of the bad feeling between him and Comiskey…"[108] O'Neill was also the one who physically handed the eight players their suspensions in October 1920.

White Sox manager Kid Gleason, O'Neill and film producer Clyde Elliott went to St. Louis shortly after the series to question gambler Harry Redmon, at the time the hottest lead Comiskey's investigators had, about his knowledge of the fix. Elliott was a friend of Redmon's. Comiskey also sent O'Neill to question Chicago gambler Mont Tennes at 6 am the day after Game One of the World Series.[109] His report of the conversation led to Gleason issuing a warning to all the players. O'Neill was also among the first men to testify in the Black Sox case, doing so before the grand jury on October 5, 1920.[110]

Griffith hung around the San Francisco area through August. He had an offer to join the Chicago Colts but he didn't immediately jump at it.[111] The Colts were languishing in tenth place in the National League; consequently, manager Cap Anson was looking to revamp his squad. He brought up quite a few minor leaguers in August and September, including second basemen Bon Glenalvin from Los Angeles and John O'Brien from Augusta, third baseman Lew Camp, outfielder Henry Lynch from Springfield and pitchers Frank Donnelley from Macon and Jim Hughey. Griff joined the club as well in September as did Oakland shortstop and Chicago native Charlie Irwin.

The California League attempted to reorganize in September but not until the Oakland boys received some financial relief after threatening legal action. In the end, Oakland posted the best record, 60-39, seven games ahead of Los Angeles. Griffith took particular pride in standing up for the men and later surmised that his actions probably hastened the death of the league. There may be some merit to that since the California League, or any other area league for that matter, failed to operate for five years.

California organizers initiated another series of exhibition games between the two surviving teams, Oakland and San Francisco. Play began

---

[108] "Former Bengal, Jean Dubuc, named in Baseball Scandal," *Washington Post*, September 27, 1920, p. 8

[109] Information about O'Neill and Tennes came from Charles Comiskey's testimony at the 1924 Milwaukee trial.

[110] A biography of Norris O'Neill can be found at the SABR Biography Project

[111] Initial word of his signing came on August 20; though, Griff remained in California into September.

on August 30 with Griff in center field.[112] One noteworthy game on September 1 saw Clark catching for Horner. The backstop tripled that day. Clark was departed; the National League was calling. He received telegrams from his old manager, Jim Hart. Hart was now the secretary and business manager for Al Spalding's Chicago Colts managed by Cap Anson and heard of the fine season Clark was putting forth in California.

Hart originally impressed Spalding as the business manager for his world tour of 1888-1889. After managing Boston to a second-place finish in the National League in 1889, Hart joined Chicago as club secretary. Spalding, disillusioned and stressed after the recent Brotherhood battle that brought about the Players League, soon resigned the club presidency to concentrate on his other business ventures. In April 1892, Hart was elected president and remained with the club until 1905. Spalding ultimately sold the franchise to a venture group led by Hart in 1902.

Spalding himself was one of the pioneers of the National League. Joining the Chicago White Stockings in 1876, he pitched the league's first shutout on April 25. Spalding already led the National Association the previous four years in victories. His Boston team won the pennant each of those years. In the National League's first year Spalding also led in victories with a 47-12 record and eight shutouts. Arm strain relegated him to playing first base the following season. Spalding was the first professional to win 200 games. In the National Association, he put together a 207-56 record over five years that included twenty straight victories to begin the 1875 season. Spalding quit playing baseball at age 28 to devote himself to the sporting goods company that still bears his name. The business eventually made him a multi-millionaire. Back in 1882 Spalding assumed the presidency of the Chicago National League club upon the death of William Hulbert, founder of the National League.

Griffith initially balked at the Colts' offer, preferring to stay on the west coast.[113] He eventually thought otherwise and wired Chicago admitting that he couldn't afford the train fare. Hart wired the money and the deal was done. The Colts released John O'Brien to make room on their roster.[114] Clark arrived in Chicago in early September. The Colts, today known as the Cubs, were in tenth place, 31.5 games behind the Boston

---

[112] *The Sporting News*, September 9, 1893

[113] "Baseball Again," *Los Angeles Times*, August 25, 1893, p. 4

[114] "Sunday Baseball," *North American*, Philadelphia, August 21, 1893, p. 5

Beaneaters, when Griff joined the club. There would be no pennant chase for the newcomer but Anson was auditioning for his pitching staff in 1894. Clark had some friends on the club, as fellow west coast teammates and competitors Bill Lange, Charlie Irwin, Bob Glenalvin and Tom Parrott also held roster spots.

Clark made his debut for Chicago at South Side Park II on September 7 versus the Philadelphia Quakers with 2,443 in attendance. South Side Park II was originally the built for the Players League back in 1890. The first Comiskey Park was later built on the same plot of land with the field at spots overlapping. Griffith pitched a complete game, giving up eight hits but striking out six. The Colts lost however, 7-3, leaving sixteen men on base. Though he gave up a home run to longtime catcher Jack Clements, the *Chicago Tribune* praised Griffith for his "fine speed and excellent control."

It was also the first meeting between Clark and Big Ed Delahanty. As an omen of things to come, Delahanty went 2 for 4 with two singles, a stolen base and two runs scored. Griffith didn't fare much better against the big slugger over the years. In 87 at bats against Clark, Delahanty placed 36 hits for a .412 batting average.

Delahanty was one of the finest hitters in baseball history and the premier power hitter of the 1890s, averaging an impressive 186 hits, 8 home runs, 107 RBI and a .354 batting average during the decade. The eight home runs are more extraordinary than they may appear. His career .505-slugging average is impressive by any era's standard. On July 13, 1896, Delahanty became the second man to hit four home runs in a game, all inside the park; however, it wasn't enough for his Phillies to defeat the Chicago Colts that day. Philadelphia's outfield of the era boasted Cooperstown-bound Delahanty, Billy Hamilton and Sam Thompson, one of the finest groups ever assembled. In 1894, they each hit over .400. In fact, the entire team batted a collective .350, still a record. His legendary career is overshadowed only by the events surrounding his death.

In June 1903 with his Washington Nationals team on a western trip, Delahanty failed to show up for a game in Detroit, probably due to drunkenness. As the *Washington Post* stated, Delahanty missed the June 29 game "nursing a very bad headache." Manager Tom Lofton suspended the outfielder but allow him to travel with the club. On July 2, Delahanty jumped the club, nowhere to be found. He hopped a train headed for home. Aboard, he became uncontrollable even threatening the conductor with a razor. The conductor escorted the drunken slugger off the train at Niagara Falls, Ontario, Canada, as the train was about to cross an international bridge. The train pulled away and the drunken Delahanty reportedly tussled with and pushed past a night watchman and followed. That was the last time anyone saw him alive. News of his disappearance didn't even hit Washington papers until July 5. Delahanty's body was discovered a week later twenty miles down the falls. He had apparently fallen off the bridge and been swept away. He was 35 years old.

Griffith relieved rookie Frank Donnelly in the second game of a doubleheader against Boston on September 13 in what the *Chicago Tribune* described as the "most remarkable scene of the year." With the game tied in the sixth inning and Boston at bat with darkness quickly approaching, the Colts started delaying the proceedings after Tommy McCarthy reached second base. The infield began tossing the ball around in no particular hurry to return it to the pitcher. After that ran its course, Anson, one of the great all-time umpire baiters, initiated an altercation with umpire Tim Hurst. Eventually, the entire Chicago squad chimed in. Once Hurst restored order, Anson changed pitchers to prolong the delay. Griffith came in, taking his time warming up. Finally loosened up, Clark threw wide to batter Billy Nash several times to buy more time. Nash entered the fray, demanding that the umpire forfeit the game to Boston. Griffith finally pitched to Nash who connected but when McCarthy broke for third he tripped, breaking two toes. This caused another delay and ultimately the game was called for lack of sunlight. Over 6,100 were on hand to witness the 8-8-tie.

Griffith made his second start and collected his first National League win the following day, September 14, in front of a sparse crowd of 1,153. Uncharacteristically, Philadelphia's Gus Weyhing gave up 17 hits on the way to losing 12-5. Though he gave up nine hits himself, Griffith was only in trouble in the ninth inning at which time the game was virtually wrapped up. The *Chicago Tribune* commented, "Griffith is a good man and hard hitter. His style is much like that of [Bill] Hutchison and his control of the ball is excellent." Clark went 2 for 4 that day with a sacrifice and a run scored.[115]

Griffith made his final appearance of the season on September 19 against Washington in relief of Fritz Clausen. He picked up the loss, 7-6, after allowing a run in the ninth. Interestingly, all of the Colts games that September were in Chicago. The season ended eleven days later. Griffith finished with a 1-2-record over four games, striking out 9 and walking five.

---

[115] "Weyhing's Pitching was easy," *Chicago Tribune*, September 15, 1893, p. 6

Griffith headed back to California with some fellow National Leaguers, arriving in Los Angeles on October 23. Local organizer George Vanderbeck put together a series of midwinter exhibition contests to take place into November, pitting an Oakland club against his Los Angeles squad. Each team displayed an impressive lineup of young and experienced professional talent. Oakland included George Van Haltren, Jerry Denny, Lou Hardie, Joe Cantillon, Norris "Tip" O'Neill and pitcher Jack Horner. Los Angeles boasted Bill Lange, Howard Earl, Charlie Irwin, Tom Parrott, Sam Dungan, George Treadway, Bob Glenalvin, captain, Heinie Reitz and Griffith and Edgar McNabb pitching. Jim McDonald umpired the contests. McDonald, a former major leaguer and San Francisco native, was hoping to catch on with the National League.[116] He was well-known throughout the sporting world as one of the few men to defeat local boxing hero James Corbett.

Griff pitched on October 25 but gave up 11 hits and lost 5-3. He pitched every other game, playing first base on the days he wasn't on the mound.[117] On the 27th, he won 6-3, giving up only four hits. He also knocked a single and double and scored a run. The following day he played first and scored twice with one hit. On October 29, Griff started the game but was knocked out of the box after the second inning with the score 6-6. He moved to first base; Los Angeles ended up winning 10-9. The *Los Angeles Times*, looking back on a fine year, referred to Clark as "the most scientific twirler on the coast."

Griff also joined the Petaluma squad in a loose six-team Central California League that emerged in September.[118] Lange and Irwin also played for Petaluma.[119] One game of note on November 9 at San Francisco took only 47 minutes to complete. On November 19, Clark played in the field against Santa Rosa, hitting a double in the 10-8 loss. That winter, he also hooked up with some fellow "amateurs" in a so-called amateur battle for the championship of California. Two rival towns were competing for bragging rights. Griff was enlisted and asked to bring

---

[116] He would in 1895.

[117] Howard Earl was to play first base; the reason he failed to join the club will be explained shortly.

[118] Per minor league researcher Carlos Bauer at his blog minorleagueresearcher.blogspot.com, the Central California League included two San Francisco squads, Petaluma, Santa Rosa. It was later revamped to include Oakland and San Jose.

[119] *The Sporting News*, November 25, 1893

some "ringers" with him. As he explained, "So I secured Charlie Irwin, Mike Cody and several other well-known players and…when we had put on some old uniforms we sneaked out on the field to limber up. The other team had not put in an appearance, but there was a big crowd on hand…Suddenly there was a cheer and the other team showed up. Before betting any money of my own I thought I would take a peek at this rival outfit and when they came into view the first man I saw was Jerry Denny, behind him was Big Bill Brown, the New York catcher, and also Fred Carroll, together with other professionals. Then I concluded not to bet. We did not recognize on another, however, for we wanted to get our money. All of the amateurs sat on the bench and we went at it. The game was a heart breaker, but we won it, and also won other games, which landed the 'amateur championship' of the coast."

Griffith also joined a Sacramento club in December 1893. The club was part of a midwinter league created by local businessman John H. Batcher. Joe Cantillon captained the club, which also included Bob McHale, a local catcher who finally made the big leagues in 1898, Heinie Reitz, Irwin and George Borchers.[120]

Once again, Griff was part of a lawsuit filed for back pay from Oakland management at the end of 1893. For simplicity sake, the Oakland players consolidated their suits under one teammate's name, signing their claims over to team captain and first baseman Howard Earl. The suit was settled on December 15 with $40 being deducted from each player's claim. Earl allegedly swindled his teammates, telling them the settlement was for 50 cents on the dollar instead of the actual 82.5 cents. In total, he absconded with a $500 profit, of which $175 belonged to Clark. To boot, the men were too poor to even sue Earl.

Los Angeles' owner Vanderbeck recently purchased the Detroit club and was in the process of placing it in Ban Johnson's revamped Western League for 1894. He recruited west coast players, including Griffith and several teammates. However, he signed Earl first which alienated the others.[121] Regardless, Clark accepted terms with Chicago;[122] he was in the majors to stay.

---

[120] *The Sporting News*, December 30, 1893

[121] "Earle's Alleged Crookedness," *Milwaukee Sentinel*, December 16, 1893, p. 6

[122] National League president Nick Young announced Griffith's contract with Chicago on February 23, 1894. "Baseball Contracts," *Weekly Herald Dispatch*, Decatur, Illinois, March 3, 1894, p. 10

Another group of National Leaguers made California their home during the winter of 1893-1894. The squad, mainly made up of Boston players, was led by Billie Barnie and Billy Nash. The roster was filled out by Kid Nichols, Mal Kittridge, Tommy McCarthy, Herman Long, Dummy Hoy, Hugh Duffy, Jake Beckley, George Davis and Kid Carsey. They arrived in San Francisco on October 26 and played into February. Griffith played at least one game against the squad, manning second base as part of an Oakland squad in San Francisco on January 2.

The Boston club suffered a couple of tragedies that off season. First was an accident involving catcher Charlie Bennett. During a hunting trip in Kansas in January 1894 with his buddy and future Hall of Famer John Clarkson, Bennett attempted to re-board a moving train, slipped and was run over. He lost both legs, one at the ankle and the other at the knee. Confined to a wheelchair, Bennett ran a newsstand in Detroit for the next thirty years. Later, the city named their American League ball field Bennett Park in his honor. Second, Hugh Duffy brought his ill wife with him to California, hoping the warm weather would do her well. She was suffering from tuberculosis. Unfortunately, she took a turn for the worse and died within hours of returning home to Massachusetts on March 31.

Edgar McNabb, Griffith's mound mate with Los Angeles and Sacramento would be dead before Opening Day. McNabb, known as Pete on the west coast, also played against Griffith in the Pacific Northwest League in 1892. In the same league in 1891 McNabb met and began seeing a pretty blonde named Louise Rockwell, wife of PNL president William Elmer Rockwell. The Rockwells lived in Seattle. As the *Los Angeles Times* so condescendingly put it, "Like many other American women, Mrs. Rockwell had little else to do except dress well and amuse herself, and she was a constant at the baseball games, where she met the pitcher."[123]

W.E. Rockwell, called Elmer, began pitching in his late teens for a Keithsburg, Illinois, a small town on the Mississippi River, club called the Ictorias. His catcher was 16-year-old future Hall of Famer Bid McPhee. Both were then signed by Davenport of the Northwest League for the 1877 season. During one of their games together, McPhee took a foul tip to the nose, breaking it in the days before catcher's gear. After that, he became a second baseman.

When the PNL collapsed in August 1892, McNabb took off for Los Angeles with his catcher Kid Baldwin. Mrs. Rockwell left her

---

[123] "The Wages of Sin," *Los Angeles Times*, March 5, 1894, p. 7

husband and child to follow. The couple continued their relationship through McNabb's rookie season in the National League in 1893. During which he fell ill and returned to California. With money tight she began performing with vaudeville troupes as a "skirt dancer" under the stage name of Louise Kellogg. Meanwhile, McNabb signed on with Grand Rapids for 1894, accepting a $250 advance.

Money became tight, as Kellogg may have lost her job perhaps because she was "a poor performer."[124] On the afternoon or early evening of February 28, 1894 Kellogg arrived in Pittsburgh, her parents lived in Braddock not far from the city, from New York City. She asked McNabb to meet her on Fifth Avenue. He secured a room earlier in the day at the Hotel Eiffel, registering as Mr. and Mrs. E.J. McNabb. They had plans to meet up with Louis Gillen, a friend, to attend the theater that evening. Sometime after the couple met that day, Kellogg announced her intention to break up with McNabb. She told him that she cared for someone else, possibly considering reconciling with her husband. The couple then made their way to the Eiffel Hotel. Shortly after entering the room, McNabb pulled out a gun.

The shots were not heard by anyone in the hotel, as a nearby fire drew the attention of the guests and staff. No one met Gillen so he went to the hotel looking for the couple. Arriving at the room at about 8:30 pm, he heard Kellogg groaning. He retrieved the police as City Hall was just across the street, who busted in the room. They found a bloody mess. Kellogg was lying on the floor with three shots to her head and neck. McNabb was next to her dead from two shots to the head. She was taken to the Homeopathic Hospital. Kellogg though was growing weaker by the hour. Doctors could not operate due to the fact that one of the bullets was lodged against her spine. At about midnight the next evening she slipped into unconsciousness and died at 4:40 am on March 2.

Awaiting the startup of the 1894 season, Cantillon and Griffith, both nearly broke, drifted along the coast looking for a payday. They ended up at the seedy Barbary Coast, a San Francisco neighborhood, of all places. The Barbary Coast first become a popular hangout during the California Gold Rush in the late-1840s. The area was well known for its vices: gambling, prostitution and viscous criminal activity. Nowhere in the United States, perhaps all of North America, were more heinous atrocities committed with such regularity.

---

[124] Letters found indicate that Kellogg was financially supporting McNabb over the winter of 1893-94.

The two found employment oddly enough in a honky-tonk music hall. Griffith played bass fiddle and the pair acted in a skit each night. Cantillon starred as a cowboy who, twice a night, killed a wandering Indian, Griffith. Clark called on his childhood memories to conjure "authentic" Native whoops and hollers. Like Doc Holliday and Wyatt Earp, Cantillon and Griffith worked as faro dealers, a card game popular in the American West during the 19th century. Griffith described many years later how drunks would be lured into a backroom of the saloon and knocked out. By the time they awoke, they were at sea headed for some unknown calamity, perhaps slavery - hence, the origin of the term shanghai.

CHAPTER THREE

OLD FOX

The previous year was a long one. The season begins early in California and ends late. Plus, Griffith joined an exhibition tour after his three-week stint with the Colts. He threw over 500 innings in 1893, from 60'6" for the first time. His arm was tired. During spring training in 1894 in Hot Springs, Arkansas, Clark experimented with several different deliveries to offset the soreness. The righthander found that by releasing his curve on the other side of his middle finger, off the ring finger, the ball broke away from lefthanded batters and in on righties. Griffith stumbled upon an effective out pitch, the screwball or popularly called the fadeaway. He later claimed to have invented the delivery that Christy Mathewson made famous a decade later. In truth, he probably learned the pitch from Johnny Horner at Oakland the year before. His main weapon, though, was still the curve. In fact, Griffith's answer to the rule lengthening the pitching distance was to gain greater control over the bender.

The Colts had seven pitchers in training camp in 1894, a lot for the era. A *Chicago Tribune* report from camp noted, "Griffith is regarded by his fellow players as being the coolest and shrewdest of the seven." The club also was hoping Bill Hutchison, a graduate of Yale University, would bounce back from a mediocre 1893 and perform to the standard of the three previous years when he averaged over 40 victories; however, he only won 14 games. Hutchison's career nose-dived after the mound was pushed back. Of the others, only Griffith and Willie McGill made any significant contributions. The *Tribune* proved prophetic; the Colts found their new ace.

Griffith started his first game on May 11, the fifteenth game of the season, with a 4-2-victory over Louisville. His next start was another victory over Pittsburgh at the new ballpark, located outside the city two miles west of downtown Chicago. West Side Grounds with a capacity of 16,000 housed the club through 1915. It was 340' down the left field line and 316' to right. From there, the grass extended to an astounding 560' to dead center, too far to reach but ample room for the prized overflow crowd.

The hitting stars of the club were the ever-present and aging Cap Anson, shortstop Bill Dahlen and Bill Lange. Griffith roomed with Lange and always claimed that he was one of the top center fielders of all-time. Lange was a San Francisco native who ran away from home as a teenager to live with his older brother in Port Townsend, Washington. He played amateur ball in both San Francisco and Port Townsend. After high school, he joined the Seattle club in the Pacific Northwest League, his first professional assignment, until it folded in 1892 and then hopped to Oakland with some teammates. In 1893 he joined the Chicago Colts a few months ahead of Griffith.

Even though his batting average resides among the career leaders and few matched his stolen base totals, Lange, nicknamed Little Eva, will never make the Hall of Fame; he left the game too soon. Lange quit baseball at the height of his career at age 29 to wed the daughter of a San Francisco real estate magnate. Her father had forbidden the marriage to a lowly baseball player, an attitude that many in American society shared at the time. Lange was quoted as saying, "Plant flowers on my baseball grave out in center field, for I am in love and will never play there again." Despite the offer of a substantial pay raise from Griffith at the upstart of the American League and even though his marriage ended in divorce, Lange never returned to play in the majors.

On the evening of June 13, Griffith stepped off the train in the city in which he would forever be linked, Washington D.C., for the first time. He won there three days later. Griffith pitched a fine game on July 11, defeating perhaps the finest pitcher of the 1890s, Kid Nichols, 13-1. On August 5, a discarded cigar sparked a fire in the bleachers at the West Side Grounds during the seventh inning. The large Sunday crowd of 9,500 panicked, particularly the 5,000 in the bleachers. Hundreds were injured as they jumped and clawed their way out of the park. The Colts' George Decker, Jimmy Ryan and Walt Wilmot used their bats to detach barbed wire so fans could escape. Luckily, few were seriously injured. The game was called with Griffith getting the victory, 8-1. Cincinnati's only run scored on an error by third baseman Charlie Irwin. Fires also caused extensive damage in Baltimore, Philadelphia and Boston in 1894. Two days later, Dahlen's 42-game hitting streak, which started on June 20, came to an end. He quickly started another that extended to another 28 games. In all, Dahlen clubbed a hit in seventy of 71 consecutive games. Dahlen, perhaps overlooked by Hall of Fame voters, spent twenty years as a National League shortstop amassing numbers that still reside on the all-time leader board, despite his era's primitive gloves. He was known as "Bad Bill" which aptly described his personality – temperamental, volatile, stubborn and argumentative.

Cap Anson had been insisting for years that a baseball could be caught from the Washington Monument; in fact, he had a running bet with the management of the Arlington, Virginia club. Work began on the Egyptian-inspired monument back in 1848, but was halted in 1854 due to political controversies and funding issues. Construction didn't start up again until 1880, which led to its completion four years later. In 1888 it was opened to the public. Paul Hines tried the stunt back in 1885 but refused at the last moment to attempt the catch, probably because he was barehanded.

  Egged on by Anson, Griffith, Bill Hutchison, Jiggs Parrott, George Decker, Scott Stratton, catcher Pop Schriver and two officials from the Arlington club headed out to the Washington Monument with bucket of baseballs on August 25. They wanted to be the first to successfully "pitch" and "catch" a ball from the monument. Griffith and Hutchison took the elevator to the highest point allowed, a window about 500 feet off the ground. Clark tossed the first ball out the window but Schriver just let it bounce to judge the velocity and the impact. He caught the next one to a rounding applause just as the police arrived to chase them off.[125]

On September 30 Griffith played his first of four career major league games at shortstop. He batted second but was pulled after making three errors and being hooted by the crowd. Clark finished the season strong, winning his last six starts. Unfortunately, the Colts weren't as efficient. They finished in eighth place with a 57-75-record. Griffith did considerably better, leading the team with 21 victories against 14 losses

---

[125] "Schriver's Great Feat," *Washington Post*, August 26, 1894, p. 3

over 36 games and 261 innings.[126] Griffith could do this! He stuck in the majors this time. Jim Hart quickly inked the righthander to a contract for 1895 on September 24.

The team met in Galveston, Texas for spring workouts in 1895. Griffith got the nod on Opening Day on April 18 and won, 10-7. He was already being called The Old Fox for his pitching cunning and prowess and, perhaps also, for his hunting and trapping skills. On May 20, Clark became one of the few pitchers to place five hits in a game. He went 5 for 5, all singles, plus a walk but only scored once. He also copped the win, 24-6. Over the years, Griffith proved to be an able batsman. In 1895, he hit .319 in 142 at bats and hit over .300 again in 1901. At retirement, Griffith's batting average was .233 over 1,380 at bats with 321 hits, 8 home runs, 49 doubles and 17 triples. He also scored over 200 times. Modern fans of the *Moneyball* era would be glad to hear that he walked 166 times, among the all-time leaders for pitchers.

A team picture that year shows Griffith with the typical big, thick mustache of the era, looking every bit the seasoned veteran. The mustache appeared as early as 1890 photos and as late as 1898. Much later in life, Clark was recognized for his full head of striking gray hair and thick, white eyebrows.

In a strange occurrence by today's standards, the umpire announced loudly to the crowd of 10,000 prior to the game on June 23 that the proceedings would be held up for five minutes after the third inning. Cordially, the entire Chicago squad was going to be arrested and president Hart posted bail and then the game continued. The specific charge was "aiding and abetting the forming of a noisy crowd on a Sunday." The incident was orchestrated by a local reverend. In the end Griffith won 13-4. The men stood trial on July 9 with the judge ruling against the Sunday noisemakers and assessing a $3 fine to each man. Presumably, the club picked up the tab.

The whole affair was a run around the controversial Blue Laws. The cities of Chicago, Cincinnati and St. Louis permitted Sunday baseball as far back as the 1880s. The National League lifted its own ban against playing on Sunday in 1892 when the influx of four American Association teams demanded it. Until 1934 when Pennsylvania repealed its Blue Laws, there were many one-day jaunts on Sundays to fit in a profitable game to

---

[126] In 1994, Griffith won 20+ games with one of the highest ERAs for a 20-game winner; however, the year was filled with 20+-game winners with high ERA. Pitchers were still getting accustomed to the greater pitching distance.

avoid strict cities. For example, it was not uncommon for the Philadelphia A's to travel to Cleveland or Washington after their Saturday game and then slide to another city on Monday. Also, some clubs played away from their normal venue on Sundays. At times, New York teams hopped to New Jersey for a profitable contest.

Clark lost a heartbreaker to Amos Rusie on July 9, 1-0, on an error by center fielder Bill Lange. It was his first home loss of the season, before 6,000 locals. Griffith did notch two impressive victories against stellar pitchers Kid Nichols on July 18, 2-1, and Jack Stivetts on September 5, 7-1. On July 31, the club erupted in a mini-revolt, questioning one of the domineering Anson's decisions. In Pittsburgh in the sixth inning with the score tied 6-6, Anson was injured trying to steal second base. At the change of innings he put rookie pitcher Walter Thornton in to play first base. Griffith and a few others decided that it would be better to have the team's other catcher Tim Donohue take over first. Donohue arrived at first at about the same time as Thornton. Play was delayed as Anson asserted his authority and removed Donohue from the field. Griff was clearly irked, throwing a fit on the mound and slamming his glove to the ground. He then proceeded to lob the ball to batters in defiance. For their part, the fielders also tried to throw the ball wide of Thornton at first. Eventually, tempers subsided. Luckily so, Thornton ended up contributing an important hit and the Colts won 11-6.

The *Washington Post* published a rare glimpse into nineteenth century pitch counts on August 27, 1895. The article tabulated the pitches of Griffith and Win Mercer during the game the previous day in D.C., which just happened to be a 9-9 eight-inning tie shortened due to darkness. The two pitchers virtually matched each other pitch for pitch with Mercer throwing 160 offers to the plate and Griffith with 162. Griffith threw 28, 23, 27, 13, 12, 33, 20 and 6 pitches, in order by inning.[127]

The Colts improved to 72-58 in 1895, good for fourth place. They drew nearly 400,000 in paid attendance, second best in the league. Griffith won over twenty games again, 26 to be exact against only 14 losses. He was the workhorse of the staff, amassing 353 innings over 42 games. Against the league, Griffith finished fourth in wins, fifth in complete games and sixth in winning percentage, fewest walks per game and innings pitched. By now, he was well known around the league for his control.

---

[127] Mercer by inning: 17, 8, 26, 27, 14, 24, 12, 32

Griffith was offered the position of baseball coach at the University of Wisconsin for the 1896 season. Fred Pfeffer, who coached the team in 1895, recommended him. Griff turned it down in order to head south in March for preseason workouts.[128] He held out in early 1896 for the first time with the Chicago club.[129]

Griff started the 1896 season with a loss to St. Louis on April 21, 7-3, the fifth game of the season. On May 8, he was winning 5-3 in the top of the ninth with one out and men on first and second. Philadelphia's Billy Nash came to the plate and worked the count full. As soon as he received the ball from the catcher, Griffith fired it back. The quick pitch, delivering the ball before the batter is set in the box, was legal at the time. Nash, startled, half swung at the ball. The little dribbler started a game-ending double play. The Old Fox pulled another fast one. Clark always made sure the game was played at his pace. He'd quick-pitch or slow the proceedings to a near-halt, whatever proved to be successful.

On June 6 he defeated Nichols again, 4-1. The results were the same on July 22 and August 28. However, he lost to another skilled hurler, Cy Young, on June 9, 9-6. The Colts finished the season in fifth place with a 71-57-record. Griffith won 23 contests against 11 losses over 36 games and 318 innings. Against the league, he placed third in strikeout to walk ratio. Throughout the season, Griffith maintained a sometimes heated feud with one of his catchers, Mal Kittridge. Kittridge supported Republican Presidential candidate William McKinley while Clark preferred the Democrat, William Jennings Bryan. Griffith was said at times to cross up Kittridge, sneaking in a fastball when he was expecting an off-speed pitch during the feud.[130]

To blow off steam, the Colts played a game they called "Living Pictures." They created a mock stage wherever they were at the time and put on a performance. At the Worth Hotel in Chicago in August, the men decided that that evening's performance would be based on William Shakespeare's play *Romeo and Juliet*. Griff and Dahlen argued over who would play Romeo; the pitcher won out. While spewing his lines, Griff's ladder gave out beneath him. Luckily, he wasn't seriously injured.

By 1896, Cap Anson was losing control over his men. Near the end of the season, he ordered morning workouts but only three players posted for duty; the men were growing tired of his totalitarian methods.

---

[128] "Pitcher Griffith's Offer," *Milwaukee Sentinel*, February 1, 1896, page unknown
[129] "Some Baseball Gossip," *Morning Oregonian*, February 11, 1896, p. 2
[130] Rich Eldred, "Malachi Kittridge" biography in *Baseball's First Stars*, 1996

Griffith pitched what is listed as the final game of the season on September 20, as continued rain in Chicago and Cincinnati washed out the scheduled remaining games. Amid the rainouts, Griffith took off for home without a word to team management. Clearly, Anson was losing grip of the club.

Clark and teammates Dahlen, Jimmy Ryan, Fred Pfeffer and Anson lived in Chicago year round. They spent the winter together, often hanging out at Mussey's Billiards Parlor. Griffith, Dahlen and Herman Long also played a little indoor baseball, a sport that originated in Chicago and is the precursor of softball. Griffith, the serious one, enrolled at Northwestern University to study law over the winter.[131] His newfound interest didn't last very long once the thoughts of the ball field crept back into his mind. To counteract the effects of the lethargic off season, the group hopped a train early to spring training to get a few extra days of workouts before the others arrived.

The news out of Hot Springs in early 1897 focused on Bill Lange. He was holding out for a reported $500 raise. Chicago eventually ponied up the extra cash but he still didn't report to camp. What he really wanted was to attend the heavyweight championship fight between his hometown hero, James J. Corbett, and Bob Fitzsimmons on March 17. Feigning injury, Lange refused to report until after the bout. That night, Fitzsimmons began a two-year title reign. Incidentally, the bout sparked the age of video sports coverage, earning an estimated $750,000 for the Veriscope Company.[132]

Anson continued having difficulties with his charges. He grandly proclaimed, "My men are a bunch of anarchists. Clark Griffith is the ringleader."[133] At the time, Griff was negotiating with Jim Hart for a $500 raise to $2,500; however, this would have violated the $2,400 salary cap that the National League established after the Brotherhood war. Hart therefore decided not to entertain the pitcher's demands. Consequently, Clark began speaking out against the salary cap and recruiting ballplayers from the Colts and other clubs to join his cause. Herein lays the genesis of the labor movement that would come to a head at the turn of the century.

Anson wasn't pleased. He wanted the men to know they were being watched. He warned, "Clark Griffith is at the head of the mutineers

---

[131] "Sporting Matters at Home and Abroad," *Denver Evening Post*, December 9, 1896, p. 8

[132] Charles Hirshberg, *ESPN25*

[133] "Discontent is becoming Serious," *Chicago Tribune*, April 27, 1897, p. 8

on the Chicago team and he has some willing lieutenants. They have been doing missionary work in Cincinnati and I understand they intend to try it here, but let me say this – The ringleaders are known. The league has spotters everywhere and no steps can be taken without the club owners being posted as to every detail."[134] The league had little to worry about in 1897. As the *Steubenville Herald* noted, "A diligent inquiry among National League teams shows very little inclination to fall in with Griffith's plan."[135] Undaunted, Griffith continued his rants against the system. At the end of 1900 they helped change the game forever.

The National League, like the other two major leagues, lost money during the Brotherhood struggle in 1890 that spawned the Players League. On top of that it went into hock to buy out some American Association owners at the end of 1891, perhaps as much as $140,000. This was also right around the time that the economy was becoming pinched due to the oncoming Panic of 1893. Naturally, league officials blamed their financial woes on the players. Consequently, they initiated the salary cap and a few other belt-tightening measures. Furthermore, the league instituted a 10% assessment against each team's profits through 1895 to pay for the American Association expenditures. Under this scenario, the magnates cared little about the salary gripes from the players. This was especially true in Chicago, where Spalding turned over day-to-day operation of the club to James Hart because he was particularly disgusted over the events.

To make matters worse in 1897, the owners unilaterally decided to push payroll dates back. Traditionally, the men received their first check on April 1. This was especially helpful since most were broke by the time spring training rolled around and many actually were borrowing cash to get them through to April. Also, as a policy, players were never paid for spring training. Out of the blue, the owners unilaterally decided to issue the first checks that year on April 15, causing some undue hardships on the men. Griff was livid and he wasn't the only one. At the time, he had little choice but to sign his new contract for the league maximum and accept the owner's terms. The players had no recourse, a legal one perhaps but that would create more problems than solutions. However, those two weeks without pay created a lot of ill will.

---

[134] "Ball Players' Union," *Milwaukee Journal*, April 26, 1897, page unknown, other union backers include Ed Doheny and Jim Donnelly of the Giants, *Steubenville Herald*, June 28, 1897

[135] "Advantages at Home," *Steubenville Herald*, June 28, 1897, p. 7

Clark started on Opening Day April 22 but lost to Cincinnati. He tossed a masterful game on May 22, allowing only one Washington run on six hits. A forever-disputed milestone occurred on June 18 when Cap Anson notched his 3,000th hit.[136] Chicago set the still-standing record for runs scored in a game in support of pitcher Jimmy Callahan, nicknamed Nixey, on June 29. On thirty hits, the Colts tallied 36 runs against only seven for Louisville. Callahan first drew interest as a pitcher on a Massachusetts textile team and, later, in semi-pro ball. In 1895, he led the Eastern League with a 30-9 record for Springfield. The Colts plucked him from Ban Johnson's Western League where he won 24 games in 1896.

Griffith notched another impressive victory over Kid Nichols on July 8, 2-1; though, he lost to Nichols on two other occasions in 1897. After over 170 major league starts, Griffith finally tossed his first shutout on August 13, a 2-0-victory over Cincinnati. Rare, it was Chicago's second and last shutout of the season. Griffith had a superstition about shutouts; he feared they were a harbinger of future losses. Strangely, he later went to great lengths to avoid them.

Other starters of the era such as Amos Rusie, Kid Nichols, Bill Hutchison, Gus Weyhing and Cy Young posted significantly more shutouts than Griffith. Unlike these men, Clark was not a fastball pitcher. Fewer strikeouts meant he put more balls in play, which in turn led to a greater potential for errors during this era of the primitive glove. The best pitcher of the era, Nichols, had only 48 shutouts in an astounding 532 complete games, a 9% ratio. Match that to a present-day starter like Randy Johnson at 37%, 37 shutouts in 100 complete games.

Griffith ran into some trouble on August 26 in a game versus Amos Rusie of the Giants in New York. Giving up eight runs in the first inning, he turned to Anson and asked to be relieved. Anson denied the request. Griff was ultimately tagged for 23 hits and 19 runs. In the *Brooklyn Eagle's* estimation, "Griffith showed a spirit of insubordination and simply lobbed the ball over the plate. He did not want to pitch, but Captain Anson kept him in…His work was so poor that the spectators hissed him. New York men fattened their batting average and overwhelmed their opponents with base hits and runs."[137]

Another interesting chapter in baseball history took place with Griffith on the mound on August 30 in New York. With darkness

---

[136] Anson's hit total has been roundly debated since the publication of the first MacMillan *Baseball Encyclopedia*. A brief description of this can be found at Anson's bio at Wikipedia.com.

[137] "Other Games," *Brooklyn Eagle*, August 26, 1897, p. 4

approaching, Anson, in the batter's box, argued with the umpire Bob Emslie in an effort to delay the game. He was ejected. Unfortunately, there was no one on the bench to take his place. Emslie declared an out since no replacement batter readily appeared. To make matters worse, Bill Lange left first base during the argument and was tagged out, although time had actually been called. The Colts then took the field but only had eight players dressed. Emslie was prepared to forfeit the game. Just then, pitcher Danny Friend jogged out of the clubhouse and manned left field. However, he was wearing an overcoat, one of the team's insignia ulsters and not an often-reported bathrobe, to conceal his street clothes. Of course, Giants manager Bill Joyce caused a stir over this but Emslie let the game proceed anyway. After two outs with Joyce still complaining loudly, Emslie forfeited the game to Chicago. Newspapermen were unsure of the final score. Was it 7-5, the score through eight innings, or 10-5, the score in the ninth, or the forfeited-score of 9-0? In the end they settled on 7-5.[138]

The season ended on October 3 with a doubleheader that ultimately became Anson's final game as a player and as the Colts manager. The 45-year-old had played ball professionally since 1871. He went out with a bang, blasting two homers in the first contest. In February 1893, Anson signed a five-year contract with Chicago. His last few years with the Colts were marred by increased tensions with his players and club president Jim Hart. Anson and Hart developed a dislike for each other in 1888 during Spalding's world tour. The players resented Anson for his strictness against drinking and smoking, readiness to fine any player and his foul temper. After Anson publicly blasted the team in 1897, Spalding withdrew his support of the manager. Hart, tired of second-division[139] finishes and of Anson himself, decided not to renew his contract and chose Tom Burns to manage the club. Anson managed New York briefly in 1898 and continued to play ball, semi-professionally, until he was 59 years old.

After the departure of "Uncle" Anson, the Colts became known as the Orphans. The Colts dropped all the way to ninth place in 1897, a distant 34 games behind Boston. Chicago, being a ravenous baseball town, still placed fourth in league attendance with 327,000. Griffith performed nicely with his fourth of six consecutive 20-win seasons. In 41 games and

---

[138] The 7-5 score stands at Retrosheet.org.

[139] The use of the term division in early baseball has a different meaning than today. There were no formal divisions at the time. Being in the first division meant being one of the top-4 clubs in an eight-team league. Similarly, being in the second division in 1897 meant being one of the lower six clubs of the 12.

344 innings pitched, he won 21 and lost 18. League-wise, Clark placed seventh in wins despite his club's poor showing, third in innings and led all in complete games with 38. On October 20 new Pittsburgh manager Bill Watkins visited Jim Hart seeking a trade for perhaps Griffith and others. He was matter-of-factly told that Griffith, Bill Lange, Bill Dahlen and Jimmy Callahan were untouchable.

Throughout 1897, Griffith continued to espouse change in the treatment of ballplayers. He railed against the reserve clause, salary scale and the fining system – all measures unilaterally imposed by the owners which provided the players little recourse. This was also right after a heated feud between Giants' star Amos Rusie and their despised owner Andrew Freedman, which resulted in Rusie sitting out all of 1896.[140] Ballplayers were starting once again to display the displeasure with the system that marked the end of the previous decade.

Over the winter, Griffith again attended law classes at Northwestern University. He contemplated leaving baseball altogether in 1898 after being offered a chance to study and practice law with a "prominent" Chicago lawyer. He also played indoor baseball again for a few extra bucks and was looking for other ways to keep in shape and make a little money. He cast an eye at football, wanting to recruit fellow Colts into forming a team. He somehow believed, "that it isn't brutal as compared to facing a runner who is coming on spikes first…" In his mind he had the squad picked out: Thornton and Connor as guards; Decker and Donahue as tackles; Everett and Ryan as ends, Griffith at quarterback; Lange at halfback; Friend, McCormick, Briggs and Kittridge as subs. He boasted that such a team would outweigh and outrun all but the top college elevens. It would be a pure moneymaker.[141] In early February, Griff went on a rabbit-hunting trip with Joe Cantillon, Adonis Terry and Kid Speer.[142]

Eighteen Ninety-Eight was Griffith's best year against the league save perhaps for 1901 which was in a different circuit. The truly dominant pitchers of the 1890s were Kid Nichols, Cy Young and Amos Rusie. Each boasted a blazing fastball that continually kept the batters uneasy. Clearly, these were the three most effective pitchers of the decade. Young is a household name today particularly because of the award named in his

---

[140] The issues between Rusie and Freedman would ignite again after 1898.

[141] *Sporting Life*, December 4, 1897, p. 5

[142] "Hart scores Johnson," *Milwaukee Sentinel*, February 3, 1898, p. 6, Speer was a minor league catcher, not the major league pitcher who would only be 11 years old in early 1898

honor. Most know that he won more and lost more games than any other twirler. An interesting fact about Young is he didn't play his first professional game until the age of 23. After 31 games in the minors and a no-hitter for Canton, he was sold to nearby Cleveland of the National League. It wasn't until 1899 that Young played for a team based outside his birth state.

Nichols moved to Kansas City with his family at age 11, signing his first pro contract with that city's Western League franchise six years later in 1887. He won 39 games with 368 strikeouts for Omaha in 1889 for a total of 83 minor league victories. Manager Frank Selee took his superstar with him to Boston of the National League the following summer. Nichols hit the majors running at age 20 and didn't slow down until he had 350 wins through 1904.

Rusie was born in Indiana, hence the "Hoosier Thunderbolt" nickname. He quit school while still young to work in a factory and play semi-pro ball. He was signed by the Indianapolis club of the National League after shutting out both Boston and Washington of the National League in exhibition contests. Indianapolis folded after the 1889, transferring control of its players to the league, which sent Rusie and several teammates to New York. He became the first big New York sports star, winning 233 games for the Giants from 1890-1898. Rusie also had an effective hard curve that he'd throw on any count.

John Clarkson, another Hall of Famer, also dominated in the 19th century with a rising fastball and a drop curve but he pitched nearly his entire career from a 55'-mound. So did speedball pitchers Hoss Radbourn, Charlie Buffington, Bill Hutchison and the Cooperstown-enshrined Tim Keefe. Buffington won 233 games over an eleven-year major league career. His specialty was the fastball and an overhand, hard-sinking curveball that he placed with amazing accuracy. In 1884 while pitching for the National League Boston Beaneaters, Buffington amassed 48 victories and 417 strikeouts. The previous year he led the team to the pennant. Buffington once fanned seventeen Cleveland players in a game, eight of them in a row. The American Association failed in 1891 and, in turn, the National League ordered across-the-board pay cuts. Buffington, one of the league's highest paid players at $2,800, refused to accept Baltimore's offer and simply quit. At thirty, he never played professional baseball again.

From 1890-1892, Chicago Colts pitcher Bill Hutchison won 120 games, struck out 862 batters and compiled a 2.73 earned run average. The righthander led the National League each year in starts, innings pitched and victories. In 1892 alone he fanned 312 men. Hutchison crumbled when the mound was pushed back in 1893; he simply waited too long to develop a curve. His earned run average ballooned to 4.75 then 6.06 in 1894. Over the next four seasons, Hutchison lost 62 games against only 44 wins. The rule change affected "Wild Bill" more than most.

A list of top fastball pitchers of the era also includes Jack Stivetts, Pink Hawley and lefties Frank Killen and Ted Breitenstein. Stivetts won 203 games and played a little outfield on the side, hitting .298 with 35 homers. The slugger hit two home runs in three separate games. Hawley centered himself after three losing seasons and posted 31 victories in 1895 under Pittsburgh manager Connie Mack. In all, he won 167 games in ten seasons with the club. Killen another hard thrower won over thirty games twice on his way to 164 career victories. Breitenstein, a St. Louis native, pitched a no-hitter in his first major league start for the hometown Browns of the American Association on October 4, 1891. He is the only man to throw no-hitters from 55'6" and 60'6" mounds.

Curveball pitchers Kid Gleason, future manager of the infamous Black Sox, Gus Weyhing and Vic Willis also rank among the best of the era. Gleason was virtually done by 1895 and Weyhing stumbled with the mound change. He won 177 games from 1887-1892 but only 87 more in a major league career that lasted until 1901. Weyhing is the only ballplayer to win thirty games in a season in three different major leagues: American Association, Players League and National League. Willis had the best curve of the decade but didn't join the league until 1898. He was finally enshrined in Cooperstown in 1995, perhaps other deserving 19th century players continue to be ignored.

In certain ways Clark Griffith can be compared today to Greg Maddux in pitching technique. Neither had an elite fastball but each utilized their superior intellect and outstanding control and changed speeds and moved the ball in and out, up and down to keep hitters off balance. Both had command over a wide array of pitches and would throw any of them on any count. The times were quite different but they both pitched through the two most hitter-dominant eras in major league history. However, it should be noted that Maddux has a legitimate claim as one of the top five pitchers in major league history, if not the top spot.

Griffith tossed the ball from six different delivery angles and did a few other things that are either prohibited today or impractical. Several nineteenth century rules differ from today. Throughout Clark's term in the National League, foul balls were not counted as strikes. Specifically, foul tips and bunts were counted as strikes by 1895 but players like Willie Keeler made a living off chopping balls foul, without penalty, awaiting something they could lay into. The National League adopted the modern rules in 1901, the American League two years later.[143] This gave nineteenth batters an advantage that they don't enjoy today.

Again, Griffith was small in stature, listed as 5'6.5" tall, shorter than the others mentioned. Rusie, Stivetts, Young, Buffington, Killen and Willis were all over six feet. Clark was at least three inches shorter than all except Gleason. He needed an edge. Righthanded pitchers under six feet aren't common today unless they can throw with exceptional heat. Like Maddux, who throws at least seven different pitches, Griffith threw an assortment of slow-breaking and sharp-breaking curves, a screwball, sinker, changeup, fastball, emery ball,[144] spitball and a scuff ball, which he also claimed to invent. Some historians even speculate that he also threw some form of a slider, a delivery that wasn't popular until after his death.[145] He also quick pitched and, at times, delayed his offering until the batter was frothing; anything to keep them uneasy. He was a master of shadowing, which is hiding the ball from the batter until the last possible second and otherwise trying to limit the batter's vision of the ball. Noted Chicago sportswriter Hugh Fullerton, a longtime admirer of Griffith, claimed that, "No brainier pitcher ever lived."

Griffith was the last to routinely use shadowing. That is, after he released the ball he maneuvered or contorted his body in such a fashion that his uniform became the backdrop of the ball from the batter's perspective. If done successfully, the batter wouldn't pick up the ball as quickly as usual since the uniform backdrop was gray.[146] One of his favorite deliveries was to hide the ball behind his front leg as he kicked and pushed toward the plate. If done right, this would make it seem that the ball was shooting from his leg.

He scuffed or otherwise marred the ball in any manner possible. He did it even during his delivery, dragging the ball across his spikes after kicking his leg up to pitch. At times, he was known to kneel on the mound and remove the dirt from his spikes by blatantly beating the ball

---

[143] There is a persistent and engaging story involving a showdown between Griffith and John McGraw. It goes that McGraw fouled off pitch after pitch of Griffith's one day in an attempt to find an offering he could hit. Griffith became particularly irate about the incident, complaining to major league officials. Supposedly out of this argument, the modern foul-strike rule developed. The problem is I can't nail down the date of any such incident and I can't find reference of another who could. Hopefully, if there is merit to this story, another will be able to mine this nugget.

[144] Peter Morris, *A Game of Inches: The Game on the Field*, 2006, p. 168

[145] Peter Morris, *A Game of Inches: The Game on the Field*, 2006, p. 175

[146] Peter Morris, *A Game of Inches: The Game on the Field*, 2006, p. 113

against them. He also beat the ball against his belt, little pebbles or any other object lying about. This created little slits in the ball, perfect for him to dig his fingernails and fingers into to hopefully enhance his curveball.[147] Amusingly, he once received a bill for $11 from an opposing team for damaged baseballs. A thrown ball that is scuffed is more likely to be affected by opposing forces, such as, wind and still-air.

Fullerton claimed that Griffith was the modern founder of the delivery. "One of the big features of the pitching of the old days was nicking and scuffing the ball. Not one in five pitchers really understood how to handle a ball. One of them was Hoss Radbourn, who seldom pitched a ball unless it was nicked, sanded or greased. He taught his art to Clark Griffith, who became one of the great pitchers of the world, chiefly through using the tricks that he had been taught by Rad. Griff taught some of that stuff to other pitchers, and he was the father of the trick pitching, really, in modern baseball."[148]

Griffith later claimed that he never threw a spitball but that was a time when he was politicking for its ban. The overall key to his game though was control. Clark earned his nickname, The Old Fox, by his crafty manner on the hill. It had nothing to do with his age, as he received the nickname by age 25. Cy Young described Griffith as a "dinky-dinky pitcher. He didn't have anything, but he had a lot of nothing, if you know what I mean."[149]

By 1898, Griffith became what could be politely called an umpire baiter and rabble-rouser, anything to gain an edge. He never backed down from an argument and, in fact, started many of them if he thought it would help his club. Cap Anson expected as much from his players. Griffith wasn't above jawing at the batter and opposing bench or otherwise abusing the umpire about his strike zone; these skills, by the way, were not limited to John McGraw and the old Orioles. A celebrated confrontation with Kip Selbach in 1900 illustrates this point.

Selbach was a nervous type in the batter's box, easily riled by delays and other nuisances. Like Mike Hargrove many decades later, Selbach constantly adjusted his belt, cap and trousers and cleaned the dirt from his spikes before each pitch. With runners on second and third and Chicago up a run, Griffith pitched Selbach wide to entice a strikeout, but Selbach worked the count full. Griffith then reputedly yelled, "Here, hit

---

[147] Peter Morris, *A Game of Inches: The Game on the Field*, 2006, p. 170

[148] *New York Evening Telegram*, September 12, 1921

[149] John Thorn, *The Relief Pitcher*, 1979

this you big stiff," and lobbed the ball underhand. Selbach swung wildly, came up with air and stumbled to his hands and knees.

Selbach though held a great respect for Griffith. He enjoyed watching him work. As he described, "When a pair of foxes like Clark Griffith and Al Maul are brought together, you never fail to witness a duel of baseball diplomacy in the center of the diamond. The rivalry that has existed between them for years becomes hotter as the seasons come and go, and when these two twirling members of the seasoned class meet they combine their brawn and brain for action. Some of the best games pitched this season have had the veteran contemporaries doing battle on the rubber."[150]

Addie Joss, in speaking of Griffith said, "Besides being a successful twirler, Griffith was one of the wisest men that ever stepped in a box. He was not blessed with the natural qualifications of the successful twirler, that is, speed and strong physique and had to resort to strategy to get results.

"Always on the lookout for a chance to slip one over on the opposition, on anything that might make his task lighter, Griffith immediately took advantage of the rule which was passed some years ago allowing the pitcher but the small rubber to stand on when getting ready to deliver the ball.

"The rule is that the twirler must stand with both feet on the rubber, or with one foot on it and the other ahead, when in the act of delivering the ball. Most box artists interpreted the rule to read that they must stand so that they ball of the foot is on the rubber; but not so Griffith.

"He used to stand with his heel against the front end of the pitcher's plate, and then, just as he was ready to pitch, would slide a foot or so, and, in this manner, be able to steal that much of the distance to the plate on the batter.

"Where a pitcher is throwing on an average of 150 balls in a game, it can be seen that this was something of an advantage. If the opposition was not watching him every minute Griffith was liable to be anywhere from 1 foot to 3 or 4 feet closer to the plate."[151]

Hall of Famer Joe Kelley was quoted as saying, "Clark Griffith is one of the finest judges of the weak points in a batsman, and as he stands

---

[150] "Sporting Miscellany," *Sandusky Star*, Ohio, September 12, 1898, p. 2

[151] "Don't want Elberfeld," *Washington Post*, January 18, 1909, p. 8

on the runner, sizing up the foe in front of him, there is a light of confidence, mixed with disdain and indifference, written all over his face, and he almost makes the batting enemy feel like a farm hand from far back. But aside from Clark's mental ability, there is plenty of mechanical skill in his good right arm and he has almost perfect control of the ball."[152]

Opposing manager Art Irwin also noted that, "Griffith is the nearest approach to Radbourn of any pitcher in the league. His control of the ball is almost perfect. His change of pace reminds me of Radbourn, and he has a large stock of reserve force. Griffith never takes his eyes from the ball. He watches the batsmen closely, and after pitching in two games against a strange batsman he has his man sized up. When Griffith goes up against a batter of the heroic type, such as, [Ed] Delahanty, [Larry] Lajoie or [Buck] Freeman, he depends on pace mixture. He will deliberately waste the first ball by tossing it outside the plate. The next one may also waste, and the third one will be slow, but over the base, and the next a fast, sharp-breaking curve. But as a rule he tosses up a slow curve, one of those of the Tim Keefe vintage, when the heavy sluggers are at the bat and no one on base…"[153]

Fullerton of the *Chicago Tribune* was a great admirer of Griffith and his one-time mentor Hoss Radbourn. Here, Fullerton describes the science of countering base running. "They [Radbourn and Griffith] had a balk motion guaranteed to draw runners away from first, and each had a deceptive motion in pitching that kept a batter in doubt as to whether the ball was slow or fast until it was upon him…He [Griffith] would work a nervous base runner into hysterics by his tantalizing throws, and eventually he would snap the ball suddenly to the baseman, catch the runner off balance and nip him off base." Fullerton described this method as being especially successful against nervous runners like Joe Kelley but that it wouldn't work against a skilled base runner like Willie Keeler.

Clark attributed his success to taking care of himself physically. He ate well and rarely over indulged at the saloon. In his words Griffith "never drank or smoked or kept late hours." As he noted, "When I was working regularly, I prepared myself for games under a perfect system. The day after I had been in the box I made it a point not to do any pitching whatsoever. I would go out to the outfield and develop my wind by chasing the ball out there. The next day I would assume pitching practice until limbered up; then stop and do no more until I went in the

---

[152] "Baseball Notes," *Washington Post*, June 27, 1898, p. 8

[153] "Baseball Notes," *Washington Post*, August 7, 1899, p. 8

box the next day. I was always careful what I ate; especially at lunch on the day I was going to pitch...I always found it a good plan to take a nap after lunch on the day I was going to pitch. That brings a man's faculties all back."[154]

Furthermore, Griff was a master at reading batters and recognizing their flaws. He explained, "There is a great deal in understanding a batter's feet. It is by studying them that I am able to tell what kind of a ball the man is expecting, and consequently give him something he doesn't want. Every batter has a different position of the feet when he expects a fast one or a floater, a high or a low ball. They try to fool the pitcher when they are going to bunt, and can, too, on a way they hold the bat, but their feet give it away almost invariably. A batter's feet are better to watch than his head in this respect."[155]

Griff preferred to work in heavier atmospheres, believing it aided the effectiveness of his curveball. Thus, he was cognizant of the various changes in the barometer and in the humidity. He also felt that his curveball reacted better at lower altitudes.[156] Along these lines, he'd fit in with modern major league pitchers who prefer to avoid pitching in Denver.

Griffith won at least twenty games each season from 1894 to 1901, save 1900. His seven 20-win seasons sit among the all-time leaders. After leaving the National League, Griffith pitched the Chicago White Sox to the American League's first pennant as a major league. He also pioneered the use of relief pitching as a pitcher, manager and club executive. Clark pitched sporadically after 1906 but, in the end, toed it up in twenty major league seasons.

He won 237 ball games against 146 defeats for an impressive .619 winning percentage. His 3.31 earned run average is bloated due to the early 1894-1897 campaigns and the fact that those years fit directly within perhaps the most prevalent hitter's era in major league history. He also tossed 22 shutouts but at times went out of his way to avoid them. Clark started 372 games and finished 337 of them, 26th on the all-time list. He relieved in another 81 contests.

---

[154] "Eating and Pitching," *Washington Post*, February 26, 1905, p. A9

[155] *Sporting Life*, May 31, 1902, p. 6

[156] "Some Queer Baseball Curves," *Cincinnati Enquirer*, page and date unknown, article in Griffith's Hall of Fame file

For the era 1893-1919, *Total Baseball* ranks Griffith ninth in Total Pitcher Index and 24th in Total baseball Rank. The 2001 edition of *Total Baseball* places Griffith 45th all-time in Total Pitcher Index and 160th in Total Baseball Rank. The old-timers committee elected him to the Hall of Fame in 1946, by which time the Baseball Writers Association of America was virtually ignoring 19th century players.

Griffith faced the top clubs of the day, a charge to the contrary that at times has been lodged against others, such as, Lefty Grove. While with the Cubs, he tossed his most innings against New York and Boston, two of the top clubs of the era. Over 22% of his time on the mound was spent facing those two clubs. He faced the other premier club of the era, the Baltimore Orioles, roughly 8.3% of the time; hence, Griffith sent 30.5% of his time facing the three top clubs, well above the normal percentage split of 27.27.[157]

The sample size is too small for a meaningful evaluation in the American Association; however, he did pitch 964.2 innings in the American League. Considering that Griffith only pitched full-time from 1901-1905,[158] the top opponents were Philadelphia, Boston, Cleveland and Detroit. Those are incidentally three of the top four clubs he faced.[159]

Griffith signed his contract for 1898 in spring training at Hot Springs for the same figure as the previous year, the league-maximum $2,400. The pitcher claimed that he never felt better and welcomed the upcoming season. He started Opening Day again on April 15 and won a well-pitched game, 2-1, in St. Louis. There was another fire the following day in the second inning at Robison Field in St. Louis with 7,000 in attendance. This one was more serious. Within three minutes the flames engulfed the wooden planking and some present were badly burned and otherwise seriously injured. Patrons were leaping from the stands with their clothing

---

[157] There were twelve clubs in the National League during Griffith's tenure, meaning eleven opponents. Purely on statistical average, he would be expected to face each club 9.09% of the time. The percentage of innings pitched per opponent varies for each pitcher. Here is Griffith's breakdown against NL opponents: New York 11.2%, Boston 11.0%, Pittsburgh 9.4%, Brooklyn 9.2%, Cincinnati 9.0%, Philadelphia 8.6%, St. Louis 8.6%, Cleveland 8.5%, Baltimore 8.3%, Washington 8.1% and Louisville 8.0%.

[158] Though, he was a reliever for much of 1905.

[159] There were eight clubs in the American League during Griffith's pitching tenure. Obviously, his innings pitched will be way down against both Chicago and New York, as he played for and managed both clubs. Here is the breakdown per team: Philadelphia 22.8%, Washington 15.4%, Detroit 14.4%, Milwaukee/St. Louis 12.5%, Cleveland 12.3%, Boston 9.8%, Chicago 7.6% and Baltimore/New York 5.3%.

afire. Browns' catcher John Clements was burned on the face. Brown and Orphan players helped the throng escape and all made it out within an amazing seven minutes. The game was replayed the following day after temporary circus seating was installed overnight. Luckily, the right field bleachers were still intact.

The wooden ballparks only had a life span of about five years during the nineteenth century due to flames and general decay. Problems persisted until concrete and steel structures were erected soon after the turn of the century. Teams employed spotters whose sole job was to police the stands looking for potential blazes. Honus Wagner's father did this in Pittsburgh. Incidentally, the use of concrete and steel allowed multiple tiers to be built, thus, expanding seating capacity – and potential profits.

Clark was known to have a superstition about tossing a shutout;[160] he'd avoid it if possible. On April 29, he had one going against Louisville in the eighth inning. True to form with a huge lead, he took measures to stop it. He yelled for first baseman Bill Everitt to intentionally drop a ball that was hit by Honus Wagner to shortstop Bill Dahlen. The first baseman did, allowing General Stafford to score from third. The Orphans were up by sixteen runs at the time. The story has been retold using Frank Chance's name instead of Everitt's. It was in fact Chance's first major league game; however, he caught the eighth and ninth innings and did actually muff a fly ball but it wasn't at Griffith's behest.

In April, the National League pushed through a resolution, a 21-point "purification plan," initiated by Cincinnati owner John Brush. He sought to cut down on foul and abusive language by the players and general rowdy behavior, a defining character of late nineteenth century baseball. Brush's impetus originated from an incident in Boston in late 1897 in which a Baltimore player shouted obscenities at spectators. The dirty-trick reputation of ballplayers, especially the Orioles, and their crass behavior on the field defined the basic stereotype decent people had of professional athletes at the time. In order to widen the game's appeal, especially among female clientele, baseball officials needed to tone down the profane behavior. Naturally, the men that defined the era, many rough and tough ballplayers, saw few benefits to altering their approach. John McGraw, perhaps the embodiment of this scrappy type, led the charge against those who wanted to clean up the game. He openly insisted that

---

[160] For his part, Griffith always denied having any issue with shutouts.

he would rather quit the game he loved than see it bow to levels of decency of polite society.[161]

Brush, a Civil War veteran, opened a department store in Indianapolis in 1875. Entering baseball in 1887, he purchased that city's American Association franchise. He soon bought into the New York Giants for the cost a couple player transfers and purchased the Cincinnati Reds for a mere $23,000. He became a force in baseball politics through his position as head of the Board of Arbitration and, later, as leader of the three-man National Board before the leagues merged in 1903.

Griffith was the first to be held accountable for his actions in front of the Board of Discipline. It stemmed from an argument with umpire Tom Lynch on May 24 that resulted in his ejection. Tim Hurst, a former umpire and currently the Browns' manager, even chimed in and attested to Griffith's fine record and gentlemanly demeanor. Clark could have found a better character witness. Hurst, in his one season out of blue, turned on his fellow arbiters and carried on worse than most.

Hurst received his start officiating pedestrian and bicycle races, boxing and wrestling matches and roller polo contests. A Pennsylvania native he found a slot umpiring in the Pennsylvania State League in 1888 and moved up from there. Griffith first met the umpire in mid-1889 when Hurst joined the Western Association as an arbiter after the collapse of the Southern League. The following year Hurst managed the Minneapolis franchise to within a game of the championship. After a dispute with the front office, he landed a job in blue for the National League in 1891.

Griffith was *forced* to throw four shutouts in 1898 since the Orphans were up by a relatively small margin in each game, thus, preventing any shenanigans. On June 7, he blanked New York 3-0. Two starts later, St. Louis fell 4-0. He also blanked Cleveland on July 25, 7-0, and New York again 1-0 on August 30. Griffith participated in a tie game on August 15. The game was called because of darkness in the tenth inning after each side scored twice. Griffith was on the mound and ahead, 2-1, in the fifth inning on September 16 when the umpires forfeited the game to Philadelphia because shortstop Sam Mertes wouldn't stop arguing.

Griffith and some teammates skipped the game against Brooklyn on June 25 to catch Chicago's popular *American Derby* horse race event at Washington Park. Griffith, sore back, Bill Dahlen, sore finger, and Jimmy

---

[161] Frank Deford, *The Old Ball Game*, 2005, p. 29

Callahan, pitched the day before, had their manager's permission. Bill Lange, on the other hand, made up a story about being in a wedding.

On August 13 at New York, Griffith was tossed out of the game before he even entered it. In the top of the first inning Bill Everitt was called out on a close play at third. Clark jumped off the bench and cussed umpire John Hunt, resulting in the ejection. Walt Woods was rushed into service in the bottom of the inning to pitch.

The Orphans finished in fourth place with an 85-65-record under Anson's replacement Tom Burns in 1898. They drew more than 424,000 customers, tops in the league and an all-time Chicago high. In 38 games and 326 innings, Griffith posted a 24-10-record. He led the league in earned run average with a 1.88-mark and finished third in WHIP, walks and hits per inning pitched. He was also in the top-10 in wins, winning percentage, walks per game, strikeouts, complete games, shutouts, strikeout to walk ratio and opponent on-base percentage. *Total Baseball* ranks him number one in their Clutch Pitching Index and second to Kid Nichols in Total Pitcher Index and Total Baseball Rank, which includes position players. The crafty Griffith was in his prime at age 28. His 1.88 ERA set the season record for the 60'6" pitching length; it was broken by Cy Young in 1901 and in the National League by Jack Taylor the following year.

Griffith spent the winter in Chicago but traveled to Minnesota and Montana to hunt and see his brother, Earl. He also went bear hunting in Wyoming.[162] Clark spied a ranch in Montana that he soon purchased. The property served in the future to help finance his initial stock purchase in the Nationals in 1911 and later when he gained controlling interest of the club in 1920.

When he wasn't at the ballpark, Griffith could often be found at a nearby racetrack. In fact, the *Chicago Tribune* joked upon his return from a hunting trip in early November that Griffith was jittery from being away from the ponies for so long. He was said to be "a knowledgeable track man that could recite the breeding, record, condition of the track, distance, weight carried, owner, jockey and trainer for every horse that won a race in the last decade." A running joke claimed that Griffith was on his horse hunting one day when two fawns jumped out of the brush beneath him. He jumped from the saddle but didn't bother to shoot.

---

[162] "National League Notes," *Daily Review*, Decatur, Illinois, October 7, 1898, p. 6

Instead, he merely bet his companion which one would reach the clearing first.

Teammates and fellow enthusiasts Bill Dahlen, Bill Everitt, George Decker and Bill Lange often accompanied Griffith to the track. The hotheaded, argumentative Dahlen picked fights with arbiters to purposely get ejected from games to gain an early jump on the betting. At the winter meetings in December, a trade rumor was batted around involving the Cubs and Giants. Famed righthander Amos Rusie and club owner Andrew Freedman were at odds. The Giants owner was possibly looking to unload his star. The proposal involved Griffith and shortstop Dahlen for Rusie and second baseman Kid Gleason. The deal was never consummated.

The Orphans conducted spring training in New Mexico in 1899. Griff traveled to the training site in an unique way per the *Lincoln Evening News*, "Clark Griffith of the Chicago club rode all day through Texas and a portion of New Mexico sitting in a [train] car window with a rifle across his knees looking for a chance shot at a buffalo, an antelope or some big game...It was a tired boy he was when he reached Albuquerque without having had to blow the smoke out of his rifle barrel."[163] That same day, the *Milwaukee Journal* described a close call, "William Phyle, pitcher for Chicago, had a narrow escape from death at Hudson Hot Springs, New Mexico yesterday. A ball from a *Winchester* rifle fired by Clark Griffith while hunting barely missed his head."[164]

Griffith started and won Opening Day on April 14, 1899 at Louisville, 15-1. He was ejected five days later. After a close call in the second inning, he started hounding umpire Oyster Burns about his strike zone. In the fourth, Burns had enough and tossed the pitcher. Griffith was particularly irked about being called for a balk earlier in the game. The National League instituted a new balk rule for 1899 and Griffith had been telling reporters since spring that there was going to be trouble over the matter. The umpires knew it wouldn't be long before Griffith hit the roof; he warned such. He was ejected again on the 27th. Tommy Connolly chased him for making a threatening gesture and abusive remarks. The largest crowd, 27,489, ever to see a baseball game in Chicago showed up at West Side Grounds to see the Orphans take on the Browns. The stands were jammed tight with bodies encircling the field.

---

[163] "Sports of the Week," *Lincoln Evening News*, March 25, 1899, p. 6
[164] "Finish Western League Business," *Milwaukee Journal*, March 25, 1899, p. 12

Griffith was tossed yet again on June 5 after dropping to his knees on the mound and screaming, "Murder!" after umpire Ed Swartwood called a ball. The crowd became incensed and police were called in to protect the umpire and restore order. Baltimore's John McGraw was also ejected from the same game. Murder was not a good term to use with Swartwood. After leaving the game, he became the official hangman for Allegheny County, Pennsylvania. A diligent and respected worker, his services were highly sought by surrounding counties as well.

Griffith pitched some nice games in June. He threw five-hitters on the 11th, 17th and 24th. On the 20th, Griffith faced his old foe Kid Nichols again and was victorious, 5-1. Clark, true to form, refused to complete another shutout against Cincinnati on June 17. Leading 12-0, Griffith, ignoring the clamor from the stands seeking a shutout, started the ninth by lobbing the ball to Dusty Miller who *unfortunately* flied to left for the first out. Griffith lobbed pitches to Jake Beckley and Tommy Corcoran who both drove singles. Harry Steinfeldt flied to right fielder Danny Green. Clark yelled for Green to let it drop but was ignored. Charlie Irwin grounded to third but this time Jim Connor heeded Griffith's screams and threw the ball wide of second, allowing Beckley to score. Relieved, Griffith promptly closed out the game for a 12-1 victory.

August 27 saw Griffith ejected once again. The to-do started when he hit Willie Keeler but Clark claimed the batter didn't try to avoid the pitch. Following another disputed play in the fourth inning, umpire Tommy Connelly ejected Griffith for making a threatening motion towards him and arguing excessively. The Orphans ended up losing 6-2. Griffith pitched all eight innings of another tie game, 10-10, on September 18 that was called for darkness. He pitched another fine game versus Louisville's Rube Waddell on October 2, winning 6-1. He faced Waddell again six days later on the backend of a unique doubleheader. In Chicago three teams faced off. The Orphans' Jack Taylor shut out the Cleveland Spiders 13-0 in Game 1. Griffith won a shortened second game against Louisville, 7-3, when darkness descended on the field in the fifth inning.

Chicago dropped to eighth place in 1899 but Griffith put up his usual solid season on the mound. He won 22 and lost 14 over 38 games and a stout 320 innings. Again, he placed in the top-ten in a number of major pitching categories and ranked fifth in Total Pitcher Index.

Tom Loftus was named manager for the 1900 season. Griffith probably felt that he deserved a shot at running the club, but that wouldn't have happened as Jim Hart found him to be somewhat of an instigator and troublemaker - the whole union sympathizer argument. As a player, Loftus had two brief stints in the majors as an outfielder in 1877 and '83. He started managing minor league clubs in 1878 but left baseball two years later. Friends Ted Sullivan and Charles Comiskey lured him back to the game in 1883. The following year, Loftus became one of the top recruiters for the major Union Association. He is the only man to manage clubs in four different major leagues.

Griffith made his final Opening Day start for the Orphans on April 19, winning 13-10. On June 19, he out-dueled Pittsburgh's Rube Waddell 1-0 in the game of the year and the longest shutout in Cubs history, 14 innings. Griffith himself knocked in the winning run. For his part, Waddell struck out twelve. It was Griffith's first of a league-leading four shutouts. The others occurred on June 29, 1-0 against Brooklyn, August 16 2-0 versus New York, and a 0-0-tie against St. Louis on September 29. The latter was called for darkness after seven innings.

On an off day, August 17, Griffith went to the track. He was supposedly minding his own business when a stranger walked past him twice, stepping on his toes each time. When Griffith protested, the man attacked Griffith and knocked him down with his binoculars. Clark bounced up and started slugging away. No arrests were made. The Orphans wrapped up the season in sixth place. Griffith had an off year, posting a 14-13-record over 30 games and 248 innings. His won-loss record may have been better considering that he received terrible run support, about 21% less than the league average. In truth, he was distracted; there was too much going on off the field. His unionizing activities encompassed much of his thoughts away from the diamond, as did his impending marriage to a Chicago, by way of Scotland, lady that was set for early December 1900.

In December, Pittsburgh manager Fred Clarke and Chicago president Jim Hart bantered about trade possibilities. Clarke was having a hard time controlling his young lefthander Rube Waddell, as would every one of the pitcher's managers. Orphans' manager Tom Loftus handled Waddell successfully in the minors so Clarke thought a straight-up trade for Griffith might help both teams. Griffith was known to be unhappy in Chicago and club management was getting tired of his "anarchistic tendency." The trade never came off partially because of the encroachment of the American League. Griffith stayed in Chicago in 1901 but he was pitching for an entirely different squad. In total he won 152 games for the Cubs, third on the team's all-time list behind Bill Hutchison and Larry Corcoran.

Waddell was one of the most effective lefthanded pitchers in major league history. However, four different teams were only too happy to be rid of his disruptions. He possessed a fastball that has been compared to Walter Johnson's and a sharp-breaking, overhand curve. He routinely struck out batters in an era when most choked up and merely slapped at the ball. His strikeout per game ratio is the best in baseball prior to World War II. Moreover, his strikeout total nearly triples his walks, signifying great control on the mound, a trait he didn't possess off it. From 1902-1907, he led the American League every year in strikeouts. His 349 in 1904 strikeouts weren't eclipsed in the majors until Sandy Koufax's 382 in 1965 and in the American League by Nolan Ryan's 383 in 1973.

Rube, a Pennsylvania semi-pro ballplayer, was originally signed by Louisville of the National League in 1897, transferring with owner Barney Dreyfuss to the Pirates in a syndicate deal. Within a week, Waddell jumped the team to escape the club's disciplinarian manager Fred Clarke. After returning, he was shipped to Connie Mack in the Western League, back to Pittsburgh and then finally on to the Cubs in May 1901. Even Tom Loftus was forced to suspend Waddell for the final month of the season.

What irked his managers and teammates the most was his penchant for skipping out on the team whenever it suited him to drink, wrestle alligators, join minstrel shows, hang around firehouses, chase fires, tend bar or go fishing and hunting. No one could control his wanderlust. Undiagnosed in a less than sensitive era, Waddell was probably mentally ill. Baseball history is littered with colorful stories about men with eccentric lifestyles or habits. Today, we'd probably encourage those individuals to seek counseling.

Waddell joined Mack again, this time with the Philadelphia Athletics in the American League in 1902. Apparently, Mack discovered a method to limit his carousing. He paid the pitcher in installments, $5 and $10 at a time. Once, he distributed his star's salary in $1 bills to try to make it last longer and to try to keep him under control, coming back for more. Waddell shined in Philadelphia, going 24-7 his first season. On July 2, he became the first recorded major league pitcher to strike out the side on nine pitches. From 1902-1905, he won at least twenty games a season, notching 97 in all. The southpaw also fanned 1,148 batters and posted a meager 1.88 ERA. Hall of Famers Waddell, Eddie Plank and Chief Bender formed the best rotation in the American League.

In 1905, he won the pitching Triple Crown by leading the league with 26 wins, 287 strikeouts and a 1.48 ERA. In a 20-inning classic that year he out dueled Cy Young. Waddell was sorely missed in the postseason after sustaining an injury to his left arm in a row with teammate Andy Coakley. Unsubstantiated rumors abound that gamblers paid him off to skip the series. Two years later, his teammates had enough and forced the pitcher's sale to the St. Louis Browns. In his first game against his old teammates Waddell struck out sixteen on July 29, 1908 to set the American League record. By 1910, the Browns released him to the minors.

While in Kentucky in 1912, Waddell helped build a levee to fend off a flooded river. To do so, he stood for hours in freezing water. Rube became sick and never fully recovered. The following year he collapsed while playing in the Northern League and ended up in a Texas tuberculosis sanitarium. He died there on April 1, 1914.

CHAPTER FOUR

BUCKING THE SYSTEM

Arthur Soden, the Boston Beaneaters owner and father of the reserve clause, summed up the general attitude of the owners during the 19th century, "When a player ceases to be useful to me, I will release him." As the statement suggests the players had little say in their plight and, in fact, had a lot to fear from the magnates. The blacklist, for one, was a favorite weapon of employers in the late 19th century. It helped to hold down wages and to keep workers from branching out to seek competitive offers from other employers. It was especially effective in industries where monopolies existed. Major League Baseball has always been a monopoly, even more so after the concept of "Organized Baseball" was instituted. Here, a major league could exert its influence over not only its own members but lower classifications, as well.

Blackballing was a constant threat held over the players' heads. It was such a powerful weapon that the mere mention of it was often enough to keep would-be rebels in line. Most ballplayers of the time did not have the education or the means to pursue professional careers. Baseball often was the only vehicle keeping them out of the mines or from similarly arduous labor. They knew they had a good job and were afraid to have it taken away. Club owners understood this and acted accordingly, forcing their terms on the labor force.

The blacklist was exponentially threatening in combination with the reserve clause that was introduced by Soden in 1879 in response to losing the service of George Wright and Jim O'Rourke. At first, each team was permitted to protect only five players on its roster, meaning that the club had exclusive rights to their services. In truth, a gentleman's agreement established exclusive rights to all players. Eventually, all became the formal reserved property of their owners.

Legitimately, league officials were concerned that ballplayers might jump their contracts and sign with a competitor, or be enticed by outside leagues or perhaps engage in fraudulent conduct, such as, game fixing. In truth, the blacklist was a highly regarded method of controlling the workers, players. Once a man was placed on it, he could not play for another club within Organized Baseball and his salary was terminated. It must be noted that during this period it was not uncommon for a player to be owed weeks or even months of back pay. What a powerful threat indeed.

Reserve clauses were written into contracts to bind players to a specific club. There were no free agents. A player had to renew his contract with his team or be ineligible to play for another league club. After a détente was adopted between the National League and American Association, they honored each other's reserve clauses with the signing of the National Agreement in 1883. Basically, a club decided where one would or would not play. Many have described this as 'slave labor.' Organized baseball is and was a monopoly. Where could a man find a job at a comparable salary?

The National League was especially fervent in applying and threatening the blacklist in response to player desertions to the American Association, Union Association and Players League. The American Association, because it last for ten years, also utilized blacklisting. Executives even threatened players with blacklisting if they didn't sign their offered contract as-is within thirty days, a strong negotiation ploy and one that a single ballplayer had little remedy against. Basically, sign it or get out. Major League Baseball's control became even greater as minor league teams began signing the National Agreement and adhering to its provisions. Hence, club owners from every part of the country banded together to control the labor force.

Of course, these events threatened the ballplayers who now had fewer and fewer options. National League magnates could sell or transfer a player's contract at whim. They could also unilaterally decide not to negotiate or to just sit on a contract, forcing a ballplayer to remain idle without pay. Recent cases involving Amos Rusie and Bill Joyce particularly irked the players. The one-sidedness of contracts in the owners' favor signaled the helplessness of the individual player, whether star or journeyman and especially the newcomers.

The players were not totally without power. Blacklisted players received a reprieve and were welcomed into the American Association, Union Association, Players League and later the American and Federal Leagues at their onsets. In fact, the list was in part responsible for the formation of these leagues. The new leagues could count on qualified, talented, disgruntled players to fill their rosters. This is exactly what Ban Johnson counted on during his attempt to attain major league status for the American League.[165] He needed a man on the inside, a man who could help fill those rosters with major league-quality talent. Enter Clark Griffith, a man who just happened to have been pushing the players' cause for quite some time. As luck would have it, both Johnson and Griffith lived in Chicago and both were good friends with Charles Comiskey. The American League was beginning to take shape; it now had a legitimate shot at rivaling the National League.

As early as spring training 1897, Griffith was pushing for the players to unionize. As always, the main gripe centered on money. Salaries were frozen in a tiered system between $1,500 and $2,400. Clark was at the top with nowhere to go and had been negotiating with Jim Hart for a raise and an increase of the salary ceiling. Griffith had a history of organizing the boys back in Tacoma and Oakland, learning the art of persuasion. Soon, some of the Colts were close to revolting; it was easy to identify the ringleader. During one game shortly after Opening Day 1897, manager Cap Anson censured Griffith for conspiring with the other players in the clubhouse.

The owners argued that the players brought the problems upon themselves during the Brotherhood war that resulted in the formation of the Players League in 1890 and which, in part, led to an expensive merger with the American Association. The National League, they argued, was still paying the debt and so would the players. But by the end of the decade, that seemed like a long time ago. The players were no longer buying this argument; the merger expenses had actually been paid off by 1895. The grumblings were voiced in 1897 thanks to Griff. In response, the owners threatened the rabble-rousers with blacklisting in April. This was just an initial tremor; the players weren't organized at this point. A lull ensued.

Griffith won 137 games from 1894-1899 with the same salary the last three years. Since 1897, he continued to be outspoken about the pay

---

[165] Johnson's hope for a successful American League was also greatly boosted when the National League contracted from twelve clubs to eight after the 1899 season.

structure and other perceived injustices, to the frustration of club president Jim Hart who at times entertained offers for his best pitcher, the troublemaker. By 1899, Clark was joined by stars Bill Lange, Jimmy Ryan, Tim Donahue, Joe Kelley, Hugh Duffy, Wilbert Robinson, John McGraw, Willie Keeler, Ed Delahanty, Billy Hamilton and others in his unionizing effort. However, at this point they were still unable to rally the league as a whole.

The men first contacted Samuel Gompers, a rabid baseball fan and head of the American Federation of Labor, in the summer of 1899. Gompers recalled, "…I was approached by labor leaders in Chicago who had been in consultation with several players of the Chicago team, with a view to bringing about a players' union. A conference was arranged…here in Washington at Federation headquarters, but as we could not secure delegates from all the league clubs, the matter was delayed…The agitation of a players' protective association…was inspired by the noted pitcher Clark Griffith."[166]

Cap Anson, who retired in 1898, was looking to get back into the game. In September 1899, rumors surfaced that he and others were interested in reviving the old American Association to challenge the National League for supremacy at the top of Organized Baseball. In this effort H. D. Quinn from Milwaukee, Chris von der Ahe and Alfred H. Spink, the St. Louis sportswriter who with his brother founded *The Sporting News,* joined Anson. Griffith turned his eye to the possibility.

The *Chicago Tribune* caught up with Anson in October in Chicago where he was said to be recruiting players. Anson was advising players not to sign their 1900 National League contracts and was boasting of already securing commitments from pitchers, Griffith, Amos Rusie, Jack Dunn, Jimmy Callahan; catchers, Mal Kittridge, Donahue, Mike Heydon; infielders, Dick Cooley, Heine Reitz, Bill Dahlen, Jimmy Williams; outfielders, Jesse Burkett, Delahanty, Lange, Sam Mertes. Griffith was antsy by this point. He was good friends with Anson and had no great love for Chicago management. A Baltimore contingent including McGraw, Kelley, Robinson, Boileryard Clarke and Hughie Jennings were also threatening to join the association if the Orioles were dropped from the National League, as seemed likely.

Ban Johnson of the Western League, now re-named the American League, began to make waves about encroaching on the National League. It would seem that the National League was daring someone to try; they dropped their presence in Baltimore, Washington,

---

[166] "Union of Ball Tossers," *Washington Post,* April 3, 1900, p. 8

Louisville and Cleveland in January 1900. To counter the upstart American Association, the National League entered into smokescreen discussions with the American and Eastern Leagues about potentially creating a 24-team major league. Grandiosely, the western-based American League would post clubs in Chicago, Louisville, Kansas City, Cleveland, Milwaukee, Buffalo, Detroit and either Indianapolis or Minneapolis and the Eastern League would represent Baltimore, Washington, Philadelphia, Providence and four cities from the New England and the New York areas.

Over the winter, Griffith began to push hard for the wage ceiling to be raised to $3,000. He also wanted owners to pick up the tab for the players' uniform costs. When the new leagues failed to materialize and the salary issue wasn't addressed, Griffith declared in spring training 1900 that he was done with baseball. He was headed to Cape Nome, Alaska to mine for gold with Charlie Dexter, the Orphans' new catcher. Griffith talked about Alaska all spring. He had friends there willing to pay the ballplayers $20 a day to help mine. Griffith declared that he was tired of the game and its politics and wanted to seek his fortune elsewhere. For his part, manager Tom Loftus paid little attention to Griffith's ramblings. Gold mining in Alaska wasn't going to lure Clark from the diamond but the thought of it was clearly a symptom of the pitcher's dissatisfaction with the baseball business.

In April, Samuel Gompers publicly backed the baseball players and suggested the formation of a union. As he declared, "Although I cannot divulge the plans at the present time, I will readily admit that the sentiment of our body is strongly in favor of organizing professional ballplayers. The movement has been one long delayed, not so much through lack of interest on our part as by timidity on the players' side. Events of the past few seasons, together with the prospects of a war among baseball men next year, have given the players more determination and confidence. It looks as if the coming year will present exceptional opportunities to bring about the long-sought-for organization."[167]

Twenty-three player representatives met with Daniel Harris, Gompers' representative, on Sunday June 10 at the Sturtevant House in New York City. Harris led the discussion. By the day's end, the Protective Association of Professional Baseball Players was officially formed. Officers were elected but their names were not disclosed. The new organization decided to include minor leaguers and seek a legal representative. But timidly, they planned to avoid antagonizing National

---

[167] "Union of Ball Tossers," *Washington Post*, April 3, 1900, p. 8

League owners, thus they politely declined affiliation with the AFL. Hughie Jennings gave the press briefing. Informally, Griffith was the most vocal member of the contingent. He was adamant that no player signs a National League contract for the upcoming season.

The officers were later identified as Chief Zimmer, president; Clark Griffith, vice president; Boileryard Clarke, treasurer; Hughie Jennings, secretary. Lawyer, and former ballplayer, Harry Taylor was selected as the union's counsel and handled most of the formal communication with the league. Nearly one hundred ballplayers met on July 29 to formally adopt a constitution and organize the union. The following list highlights their demands:

- Increase in wage ceiling

- No selling, trading or farming of players without their consent

- 3-year limitation on the reserve clause

- Limits on suspensions and fines

- Payment of medical bills and uniforms by the club[168]

- Provision for a board of arbitration

- Seek a player's right to void his contract within ten days if owners defaulted, similar to the current right held by the employer.

The players also set about penning their own universal contract and pledged not to sign any contracts for 1901 until authorized to do so by the union. Griffith elected himself the "official bomb thrower." His first target was Arthur Soden who had refused giving him two passes during a recent series in Boston. Typical in baseball history, the National League's formal response was no response. They refused to formally recognize the union, as they ignored the charge of the American League, as well.

The story of the American League begins with the hiring of Ban Johnson as president of the dormant Western League in November 1893.[169]

---

[168] Major leaguers purchased their own uniforms until 1912. At that time they cost about $30, not an insignificant amount.

[169] Leagues don't really lie dormant; they simply collapse, for the most part, due to financial strains. A new league with the same name may eventually rise with some of the previous backers, but in reality it is a completely different league. For simplicity sake many simply group the leagues together by their name and draw some sort of a common history. For example, there were several Western Leagues in organized baseball. By date, they are: 1885-88, 1892, 1894-99 that was renamed the American League in 1900, 1900-37, 1939-41 and 1947-58.

Johnson, much disparaged at the end of his career, brought considerable talent and ambition to the floundering minor league. The league, in fact, didn't even schedule any games in '93 and may have faded into obscurity without the influx of this new blood. The area thirsted for a professional baseball league.

Johnson, a Cincinnati sportswriter and editor, secured the job with the help of friend and then-Reds' manager Charles Comiskey. Comiskey soon joined the new president in the endeavor, purchasing the Sioux City franchise. Johnson empowered his umpires to clean up rowdy play and backed them when necessary. The best available talent was also courted. As a result, attendance grew steadily. The increased profits delighted the club owners and drew admiration throughout all of baseball. Building a minor league from scratch and making it profitable was no simple feat during the depression of the 1890s.

Like all minor leagues, the Western League felt the sting of the majors as it lured their talent, leaving little or no compensation behind. Of particular contention was the draft system whereby major league clubs could pluck talent from a lower classification for a mere $500. Creating a de facto farm system, Cincinnati Reds' owner John Brush a longtime Johnson foe shuffled players without regard from the majors to his Western League franchise in Indianapolis. To irk Johnson and the other Western League owners, Brush drafted players from other rosters and transferred them to the Reds. Eventually, some players would funnel back to Indianapolis to compete against their former Western League clubs.

Johnson and his good friend Comiskey soon felt that it was time to buck the system. With the expiration of the formal Western League charter in 1900 the renamed American League was no longer bound to the National League via the National Agreement. The plan was coming into focus. But first a few upgrades in financing, locality and player talent were needed before their product warranted major league status and national recognition.

Economically, Johnson met a godsend while visiting Cleveland to find a backer for a local team. His name was Charles Somers, a coal and shipping fortune heir. Eventually, Somers put millions at Johnson's disposal to help the league through its initial rough spots. It could be said that Johnson was the brain behind the new American League but certainly Somers was the might. Besides supporting the Cleveland franchise, he staked the A's and Browns and carried the Red Sox for years. Somers also provided the capital for the building of Comiskey Park.

As if on cue, the National League pared to eight teams after the 1899 season, dropping Washington, Cleveland, Baltimore and Louisville.

Johnson saw his opportunity. It was obvious that he couldn't compete on a national level with clubs representing such cities as Grand Rapids, Columbus, St. Joseph and Toledo. In order to excel Johnson needed to court eastern fans and their money. Eventually, franchises were added in Philadelphia, Baltimore and Washington. Comiskey, a Chicago native, relocated to his hometown, the Grand Rapids club shifted to Cleveland and Buffalo officials set up stakes in Boston. From the Western League's traditional base only Detroit and Milwaukee were retained.

The American League offices were located in Chicago in 1900. Johnson and Comiskey were stationed there and so was Griffith. The three met in the fall at the Polk Street Café on Chicago's West Side to discuss matters. Griffith couldn't promise anything but it was obvious to the magnates that he could draw talent to help fill the American League rosters. The three spent a lot of time together over the next few months talking baseball and perhaps plotting the future of the game. Johnson followed the meeting with an announcement on October 13. Heeding Griffith's concerns, the American League promised to limit suspensions, provide medical care for on-the-field injuries, disavow player transactions without their approval, limit the reserve clause and agree to binding arbitration. Not coincidentally, these were the main union gripes.

National League officials continued to put the players on hold until at least their annual meetings in December. At some point Griffith, hedging his bets, also tried to convince Jim Hart of the Orphans to breakaway from the National League and establish an entirely new circuit. Griffith did think on a grand scale.

Although the American League formally withdrew from the National Agreement in January 1900, thus becoming an independent league, it had not encroached on any existing National League contracts. Johnson didn't stand pat. In October and November, he decided to find backers and playing sites in Baltimore, Washington and Philadelphia. In response to antagonistic interviews by National League president Nick Young, Johnson announced on November 19 that the American League was set to operate in the east in 1901. Moreover, he declared that the league would not sign the National Agreement unless its bylaws were changed. The American League had drawn its sword, the fight was about to begin.

Few ballplayers from the National, American and Eastern Leagues signed contracts entering December. The National League magnates met at the Fifth Avenue Hotel in New York beginning on the 10th. Initially, the owners refused to hear the players' demands. Griffith publicly threatened trouble and reiterated that the players were united and resolved to gain concessions.

Union officials - Griffith, Zimmer and Jennings - finally met with a contingent of owners on December 12 and presented their case. The league even heard union lawyer Harry Taylor. Conceding nothing, the owners stated flatly that they were not there to negotiate. They just listened. That evening, Boston manager Frank Selee of the National League fired the first shot in the player war. He telegraphed second baseman Dick Padden of Comiskey's White Sox to offer him a contract. Furthermore, Selee vowed that his actions were only the beginning.

Within the first hour of their meeting on December 13, the National League owners universally rejected all demands made by the players. It then set out to destroy the union. Over the next three days, to squeeze the players further, the owners shrank rosters to sixteen and cut the salary ceiling from $2,400 to $2,000. The union kept its cool. It drew up a petition requesting another hearing and handed it to National League president Nick Young to give to committee chairman Arthur Soden. The union received no reply to their petition. Griffith and Zimmer decided to attend the December 15 meeting anyway.

Waiting to be heard, they were forewarned by Nick Young that, "They [the owners] aren't going to give you a thing." As warned, the meeting was adjourned with Griffith and Zimmer still sitting there waiting to present their case. After the meeting, sportswriter Tim Murnane approached Soden at the hotel bar about the players' request for a hearing with Griffith and other ballplayers present. Soden innocently replied that he hadn't received such a petition. Then tauntingly, he casually pulled it from his breast pocket and snidely claimed, "Can this be it?"[170] Some reports suggest that Soden and Griffith nearly came to blows.

Griffith was livid. It was probably at this time that he unequivocally decided to leave the National League; although, negotiations, led by Zimmer and Taylor, dragged on until March. Griffith supposedly wired Ban Johnson, "Go Ahead: You can get all the players you want." For his part, Johnson agreed to recognize the union. Clark, on his way home to his new bride, declared "that he was out for business and would not stand to be turned down. He said he would give the league a lot of bother after the season opened, if not sooner."[171]

---

[170] Harry Casey, "The Story of Baseball (Part III)," *Baseball Magazine*, April 1912, page 28

[171] "Will Protest," *Boston Globe*, December 16, 1900, p. 7

On December 16 the union issued formal orders for all to refuse to sign National League contracts. Zimmer took off to meet Ban Johnson. The two later had a falling out. Zimmer claimed that Johnson asked him to en masse bring all the National League players into the American League. Zimmer refused this notion on the premise that it would be stabbing the existing American League players in the back. Nearly all of them would be out of a job. Johnson denied this charge.

Talk of a strike was in the air. Charlie Ebbets of Brooklyn, speaking for many of the owners, declared that the players were bluffing and dared them to test the owners further. This seemed to be the National League's approach all along. They felt that they were in charge and thus weren't about to cede anything.

In 1901, Griffith the entrepreneur formed the Clark Griffith Co., located at 153 LaSalle Street in Chicago, and made plans to develop and manufacture a baseball, hoping to break Spalding's stronghold in the marketplace and sell baseballs for use in the American League and in the minors. He was making plans for 1901 and the National League clearly wasn't among them. The union formally endorsed the Griffith ball. The Southern Association adopted it in 1902, as did some semi-pro and amateur clubs in baseball-ravenous Chicago. Unfortunately for the Griffith Co., the American League adopted the Reach ball.

The Clark Griffith ball was marketed for years. Advertisements appear in the *Sporting Life* for it in 1902. The ad pictures Griffith in a bow tie declaring, "I inspect every ball." The balls were manufacture at the American League's standards.[172] Further ads appear in the *Sporting Life* in 1907. At that time a ball cost $1.25 a piece and was manufactured by the Monarch Sporting Goods Mfg. Co. of Chicago. Griffith attempted to sell the ball for official use in the major leagues several times. One time of note he made a bid for the 1911 National League season. Controversy erupted that year over which manufacturer would supply the official ball. Garry Herrmann and Stanley Robison withdrew from the rules committee over the issue.[173]

To counter the American League, the American Association was revived on paper in early January; this time with the backing of the National League. National League executives talked Louisville into withdrawing

---

[172] *Sporting Life*, February 8, 1902, p. 8

[173] "Halt Tenney's Deals," *Washington Post*, January 24, 1911, p.8

from the American League and entering the American Association with old friend Harry Pulliam as team president. Though the American Association was a league on paper only and was puttering around for over a year, the National League was in a unique position to help. They still owned leases on ballparks in the abandoned cities and had any number of potential backers at hand. Picking sides, several Pittsburgh Pirates, including Rube Waddell, broke with the union and signed with their generous owner Barney Dreyfuss. The National League was gearing up for the fight as well.

Boston became an American League city on January 23. Six days later, the American League officially declared itself a major league. Schedules were handed out, most union conditions were formally accepted and contract provisions were set. The new league offered contracts between three and five years in length; there was no salary cap. At the end of each contract a player would become a free agent. No player could be traded, sold or farmed without his consent.

Hugh Duffy signed to manage the Milwaukee franchise. American League field managers Connie Mack, Jimmy Manning, George Stallings and Jimmy McAleer were held over. Soon Griffith, McGraw and Jimmy Collins were announced among the contingent. These men became the main recruiters for the encroachers. Covertly, they were already at work signing National League talent.

By the middle of February, the National League magnates backed down and declared their willingness to compromise. By this time, Griffith was already rumored to have signed with Comiskey. On the 26th and 27th, union president Zimmer addressed the National League owners and came to an understanding. He announced that many of the players' demands were met and then authorized the men to sign with National League clubs, and only National League clubs. Thus, Zimmer was now fully allied with the National League. The disbanding of the American Association was also announced.

On the February 28, Griffith, in St. Louis, declared that he was still unsigned and was available for the best offer. More likely, this was a ploy to distract from his recruitment tour for the American League. Zimmer's agreement essentially disregarded all the American and Eastern League players, a huge percentage of union members. He also failed to win over many National Leaguers. In response, Clark pressed the union for a statement allowing the men to sign with the American League. Harry Taylor formally gave this okay. Zimmer, feeling undermined, threatened to resign from the union and suspend any player that doesn't uphold his commitment to the National League. It's was too late, though. Most players abandoned the union; it had served its purpose. The signings begin in earnest with spring training rapidly approaching. The American League set Opening Day for April 24.

Of the first thirty-nine cherry-picked players the American League sought, only one failed to sign, Honus Wagner. Clearly, National League players were disgruntled with their current situation. Many former major leaguers who were dismissed when the National League pared to eight teams also signed. In all, 111 of the 182 men on American League rosters that first year were former National Leaguers. In fact, Chicago won the pennant in 1901 with a roster stocked of former major leaguers. These men immediately raised the caliber of play in the American League to the point of competing on par with the National League, or perhaps above as many have argued.

For his part, Griffith spent much of February and March recruiting. He traveled into New England, along the east coast, through the south and as far as Kansas City. It wasn't really that hard of a sell. He was offering higher salaries and greater benefits to men who were already disgruntled with their employer. Clark tread three miles through heavy snow to get to Fielder Jones to sign in Shinglehouse, Pennsylvania. Griff also hit the National League hard for Jimmy Callahan, Sam Mertes, Fielder Jones and Billy Sullivan.

Griffith claimed to have helped sign the American League's biggest coup, Napoleon Lajoie. Clark had a lot to do with enticing many players to jump to the upstart league. The most amusing story involves his attempted signing of Honus Wagner. Upon hearing Griffith was headed to his hometown, Carnegie, Pennsylvania, Wagner hid from the Old Fox at a local hotel and refused to meet with him. He was afraid of Griffith's persuasiveness. Wagner called March 2, "Wouldn't that make a brass statue laugh, to see big Hans running to little Barney with tears on his cheeks begging him to keep a 110-pounder like Griffith from kidnapping him?"[174]

Court battles, ticket pricing wars and roster raiding continued throughout 1901 and '02. Going head-to-head for fan support in Boston, Philadelphia, Chicago and later St. Louis, the American League outdrew the established teams, alarmingly so. Finally, Reds' president Garry Herrmann, Jim Hart and Cardinals' owner Frank Robison approached Johnson about a truce in December 1902.

---

[174] "Star Players for Comiskey," *Chicago Tribune*, March 2, 1901, p. 6

The peace agreement was penned the following year, readapting the ruling body. The National League established the National Board after the 1901 season to oversee league operations. It included Hart, Soden and John Brush as chairman. The new three-man board, called the National Commission, was comprised of the American and National League presidents and an elected owner who were now empowered to oversee both major leagues and to resolve disputes. The elected official was Herrmann, president and minority owner of the Reds, who, despite being a National Leaguer, tended to side with Ban Johnson. This established Johnson as the most powerful major league executive until Kenesaw Mountain Landis, a Chicago jurist appointed by Teddy Roosevelt, replaced the commission in 1920.

CHAPTER FIVE

THE AMERICAN LEAGUE

Charles Comiskey's Chicago White Stockings won the American League flag in 1900 with an 82-53-record, four games in front Connie Mack's Milwaukee club. At the gate, the minor American League was incredibly strong, drawing about 927,000 in paid admissions with Buffalo as its only east coast city, and a weak one at that. The National League attracted about 1.75 million fans. The White Sox led the American League with 175,000, which was on par with New York and more than Brooklyn and Cincinnati in the National League.

Comiskey was hoping for a repeat of the same in 1901, but with the massive influx of former National League talent it would be a crapshoot. The race was officially on in March as countless players switched leagues or renegotiated their previous contracts, vying for the sweetest deal. Many, in fact, committed themselves before March but that was in secret; we'll never know the whole story there.

During the tussle between the two rival major leagues, clubs, in relation to their wealth, expanded their rosters to grab as much talent as possible. Everyone wanted to secure as many qualified men as possible. The core of the 1901 White Sox was returnees. First baseman Frank Isbell, shortstop Frank Shugart, third baseman Fred Hartman, center fielder Dummy Hoy, left fielder Herm McFarland, as well as, pitchers Roy Patterson and Jack Katoll worked for Comiskey in 1900. Patterson led the league in winning percentage with a 17-6-record. Katoll won 16 games.

The 1900 White Sox, the original Hitless Wonders, won the traditional way, with pitching and defense. They were dead last in batting; their leading hitter was backup catcher Joe Sugden. Griffith courted National Leaguers Sam Mertes, second base, Fielder Jones, right field, and Billy Sullivan, catcher, to remedy that. He also brought the Orphan's other ace Jimmy Callahan with him.

After nearly twenty years as a field manager, Comiskey turned the reigns over to trusted friend and advisor Griffith. Clark was the obvious choice to take over the White Sox. For one, he was intelligent, quick-thinking and possessed a solid baseball mind. Many in the industry knew that it was only time before he took over a club, despite the fact that few pitchers followed this path. Secondly, he was revered in Chicago for his pitching battles over the past seven seasons; he was a shining light on a second-division club. He proved to be a natural leader. This was evident to both Ban Johnson and Comiskey as they pulled him into their confidence over the past year. Griffith proved instrumental to the upstart league, as he would for another fifty-plus years. Comiskey even offered Griffith and his good friend Callahan 40% of the club for $11,000 but they couldn't come up with the cash.

On January 31, 1901, St. Louis sports promoter C.W. Daniels went to Chicago to make a proposal to Comiskey and Griffith. He was interested in starting an association football, which is soccer, league to be played by professional baseball players. On the surface it was not a bad idea. The games were to be played during baseball's off-season, bringing the players additional income and helping them stay in shape. Plus, there would be instant name recognition for the league, which would obviously spark interest at the gate. The first professional soccer league in the United States was actually started by several major league baseball owners back in 1894 but Chicago wasn't involved at the time.

A game actually took place in St. Louis during spring training. On St. Patrick's Day, Griffith and John McGraw played and led soccer teams comprised of Jimmy Callahan and others. Comiskey ran with the idea at the end of the baseball season. On September 27, the Associate Football Clubs of Chicago was formed to play in the fall at the White Sox' ballpark and other local venues; smartly, it was comprised of experienced and talented soccer players. The above referenced date, January 31, makes one pause at just how early Griffith was formally allied with the American League. Union issues weren't even settled until the end of February or the beginning of March. Griffith was in all likelihood the first National Leaguer to jump to the upstart league even though the official announcement was weeks, perhaps months away.

For his part, Orphans' president Jim Hart repeatedly stated to the press throughout 1901 that he was more than glad to be rid of the troublemaker Griffith. He was obviously sore about the whole American League affair and Griffith's involvement. Naturally, he felt betrayed, and perhaps rightfully so. Hart was in part responsible for Griffith's advancements in the game, first in Milwaukee and then in Chicago. However, a few hundred dollars might have gone a long way to appeasing his star pitcher. Reading between the lines, it's obvious that Hart didn't want to part with Griffith, an extremely popular personality in Chicago. He passed at least twice on proposed trades for Clark. Perhaps what particularly irked Hart was that Griffith also absconded with Jimmy Callahan.

Before heading to Excelsior Springs, Missouri to meet up with his entire squad for spring training, Griffith headed to Hot Springs, Arkansas in early March to work himself into shape. During the era, Hot Springs was a typical stop for baseball men looking to purge the excesses of the winter and tighten their muscles and gain their wind for the grueling upcoming summer battles. Griffith was quite familiar with the area after spending previous springs there with the Colts. At Hot Springs, he met up with John McGraw, manager of the new Baltimore Orioles franchise, and more than a few other like-minded individuals.

On March 8 or the 9th, McGraw and Griffith worked out a 25-year-old Cherokee Indian second baseman named Tokahama. He supposedly approached the managers at the Eastman Hotel where he worked as a bellhop[175] and requested a tryout.[176] Griffith hit grounders and pitched to the recruit. McGraw, impressed, told newspapermen that he was bringing the second baseman with him to Baltimore, where the Orioles were conducting spring training.[177]

---

[175] It was not uncommon for black ballplayers to work at hotels in the South during the off-season, occasionally picking up some cash when an exhibition match could be arranged.

[176] How exactly Griffith and McGraw met up with Grant is left to conjecture. There are several ways this could have happened. McGraw and Griffith, one or both of them, may have known Grant on sight or by reputation. McGraw and Griffith may have spotted Grant playing ball and approached him. Grant may well have approached the managers. A go-between, such as another player or reporter, may have introduced Grant to the major leaguers.

[177] "Frangible's Bush Cup," *Chicago Tribune*, March 10, 1901, p. 18

Tokahama was almost immediately identified in the *Baltimore Sun* as "the Cherokee Indian Grant"[178], suggesting that the baseball men knew Tokahama's true identity, Charlie Grant, an African-American with the Chicago-based Columbia Giants.[179] At age eighteen in 1896 Grant joined the famed Adrian, Michigan-based Page Fence Giants that was founded by all-time greats Bud Fowler and Home Run Johnson. Grant took over second base and stayed with the club until it folded after the 1898 season. With many of the Page Fence Giants, he shifted to the Chicago-based Columbia Giants the following year.

In 1901, black ballplayers were shunned by Organized Baseball, a light-skinned Native American just might pass though. Grant's parents were mulatto; he was light-skinned with high cheekbones and straight hair. The ruse continued as few probably noticed the tiny snippet about Grant in the Baltimore newspaper. A longer, more detailed, piece appeared in the *Baltimore Sun* five days later but for some reason the Grant name was never mentioned at that point. McGraw played his hand well. When some first sought to call him on the discrepancy, he played on further confusion that misidentified Tokohama as the popular Frank Grant rather than his true identity, Charlie Grant. Grant himself then gave interviews, declaring himself as the product of an Indian mother and white father.

It wasn't long before the cat was out of the bag. By March 31, the story linking Tokohama and Grant began to hit the major newspapers. He never did make the trip to Baltimore, rerouting instead to Chicago to rejoin the Columbia Giants.[180]

In mid-April, Callahan broke his arm and consequently didn't make his first regular season start for two months. The White Sox opened at South Side Park III on April 24. Due to three rain postponements, it was officially the first contest of the revamped American League. Patterson won 8-2 over Cleveland. That weekend, the White Sox also hosted the league's first Sunday contest. A standing room only Chicago crowd of 15,000 showed to see their old hero Griffith surrender just one run on seven hits for a 13-1-victory. The mob surrounded the field necessitating that all batted balls into the throng be registered as ground rule *singles*.

---

[178] *Baltimore Sun*, March 12, 1901

[179] Actually, some reporters confused him with Frank Grant, one of the top 19th century black ballplayers.

[180] A biography of Charlie Grant with more specific details of the Tokohama story can be found at the SABR Biography Project.

Griffith, realizing this, induced ground ball after ground ball. Comiskey, smiling from ear to ear about the huge turnout, promised to erect more seating before the next Sunday contest.

Griffith was up to his old tricks on May 2, his second start. After a throwing error by third baseman Hartman, Detroit took the lead in the ninth. The Sox began stalling, hoping for rain and darkness to force a premature ending to the contest which would then revert the score to a tie. Refusing to register the third out, Hoy let a fly ball drop and the infield refused to tag Ducky Holmes who just stood between second and third surrendering. Umpire Tommy Connolly was forced to forfeit the game to the Tigers and was rushed by the throng for his decision. It was the first American League forfeit.

On May 23, the A's scored twice in the ninth to close to 11-7 with the bases loaded and no outs. Griffith relieved Zaza Harvey and, in an extremely rare occurrence before World War II, intentionally walked Philadelphia's Napoleon Lajoie, forcing in a run. Clark then induced three groundouts to complete the victory, 11-9. This is further noteworthy because Clark despised the intentional walk throughout his career as a pitcher, manager and front office executive. It was the only time in American League history that such a free pass was issued.

On Sunday May 26, Griffith pitched his first of a league-leading five shutouts in 1901 at home before 12,500 spectators. He won 5-0 with four strikeouts in a clean game that tallied no errors. Griffith also knocked two safeties. Griffith pitched the first game of a morning-afternoon doubleheader on Thursday, Memorial Day, May 30, winning 8-3 over Boston. The much-maligned separate-admission, day-night doubleheaders of today have a historical predecessor. Seventeen hundred fans showed for the first game and an incredible 13,000+ lined up to see the afternoon contest.

On June 10, Griffith claimed a victory after pitching the final two innings. The White Sox score three times in the tenth for their field leader to edge Washington 13-10. Griffith blanked Philadelphia 4-0 on six hits and five strikeouts on June 21. Before the club left town, Clark shut them down again four days later, 5-0. This time he allowed only four hits and struck out three with his old cohort Joe Cantillon umpiring. Clark also placed two doubles and a sacrifice and scored twice. The *Washington Post* headlined, "Griffith the Whole Thing: His Pitching and Batting the Only Feature Worthy of Mention."

The players' union was still puttering along on June 23. Griffith and the other American League jumpers were finally accepted back into the fold after being suspended by Zimmer. Zimmer was reelected but immediately resigned, feeling vindicated. However, many still felt that the union president had shifted his loyalty from the players to the National League owners. Griffith tossed shutouts again on July 14 and the 31st. The latter was a 2-0-gem that sparked three consecutive team shutouts of the Tigers. Clark allowed just five hits. Hoy and Griffith were the only two to score, as Clark notched a hit and a steal. Detroit limped out of town with an 8-6-victory in the final game of the series.

By midseason, it was obvious that the revamped American League was proving to be a success. However, Johnson still had a few problems. He built his reputation on cleaning up the rowdy image of the game during the 1890s. He had done a fair job with it in the Western League but in 1901 he brought many of the toughest kickers, so called for kicking up a fuss, from the National League into his fold. The three main culprits were managers Hugh Duffy, John McGraw and Griffith. The managers played the game as they always did, with intensity and a strong desire to win; however, there was a new sheriff in town and new rules to follow. Someone had to bend. For a while both sides did; eventually, Johnson's vision prevailed, more or less.

The American League began the season with quite a few inexperienced umpires. The players and, of course, the managers saw an opportunity in this. Shortly after the season began, McGraw found himself suspended for five days. At the same time Griffith was barred from the coach's box for the same duration. Johnson issued his first warning. Clark was ejected again in the 8th inning on June 12 for arguing balls and strikes in Baltimore. The incident sparked a rash of disputes between Griffith and umpire Jack Sheridan.

On August 3, Sheridan again ejected Clark after he wandered into the field of play during a triple by Jack Katoll. On the 7th, Sheridan tossed Griffith in the seventh inning for excessive kicking. Amusing, he had been chased from the coach's box earlier in the game, meaning in essence he was tossed twice in one game, first as a coach/manager and then as a player. Two days later, Sheridan ejected Clark again for arguing. By this time, some were questioning the hiring of Griffith as a field manager. He seemed to be out of control at times and rather than reigning in his players was, himself, leading the fight. Many admired this competitive quality in a field leader; however, times were changing. *The Sporting News* in particular was a harsh critic of the offenders. It should be noted that the *TSN* consistently supported virtually every endeavor of Ban Johnson, often to the detriment of all differing opinions or actions.

The American League pennant race was tight all summer. Comiskey was chomping at the bit. After managing and being in control on the field for nearly twenty years, he had a hard time ceding the reins.

The tight race only intensified his stress. Griffith had to at times take the owner's heat, sometimes justified, sometimes not. On July 20, the White Sox lost 8-6 to the A's. The team committed eight errors, four by shortstop Frank Shugart, and made a miscue or two on the bases. Comiskey blew up after the game, giving Griff an earful. The *Chicago Tribune* nearly blushed as it noted the pervasive foul language used by the White Sox owner in the exchange.[181] Despite the fact that the club was 47-27 at the time, only 1.5 games in first, Commy expected better results. He continued to ride the club and especially his manager for the next month and a half.

Comiskey clearly overreacted on August 12. He sat in the stands continually making critical comments about his club to reporters. He especially regaled them with stories about how his old St. Louis teams would be doing better. Funny thing, the team was up five games on Boston in first place and had just beaten Cleveland 17-2 on nineteen hits. The events of August 21 proved that Comiskey was right to keep pressing his team. The club virtually imploded that day in Washington. In a fit pitcher Katoll threw the ball at umpire John Haskell, striking him in the leg. Later in the game, Frank Shugart, in the batter's box, began arguing with Haskell. The umpire pulled out his watch, a common ploy, and gave the batter a few seconds to take his position in the box. Shugart lunged at the watch and then began punching the umpire. Both Chicago players were arrested. Two days later, Johnson suspended Katoll and permanently expelled Shugart, all with Comiskey's blessing. Haskell was hobbled for weeks and eventually required surgery on his leg. That same day, Mike Donlin smacked a liner up the middle that broke Griffith's middle finger on his pitching hand. To make matters worse, Griffith, in a fit of anger, spouted off some silly threats about initiating a strike over Shugart's expulsion.

The White Sox were poised for a pennant run but had just lost their starting shortstop and best pitcher. Callahan was also suffering from malaria.[182] Plus, they were up only a half game on Boston. Whispers around the league questioned Griffith's ability to lead and control his players. There was cause here. The entire incident was an embarrassment to Ban Johnson and his efforts to present a more family-friendly atmosphere at American League parks. The *Chicago Tribune* also saw it as an embarrassment to Comiskey and the city. They pushed for Comiskey to take back the club from Griffith, roasting the manager in the paper.

---

[181] "Remnants win All Four," *Chicago Tribune*, July 21, 1901, p. 19

[182] "League in Dire Straits," *Chicago Tribune*, August 25, 1901, p. 19

"The infusion of more National League blood into the teams of the new league than could be readily assimilated resulted not in elevating the new players to the American League's standard of diamond deportment, but in lowering the American League's standard pretty close to that of the National League."[183] This was a clear shot at Griffith, by a hometown paper nonetheless.

The *Tribune* backed Johnson down the line, blasting Katoll, Shugart, Griffith and two others who attacked umpires, Baltimore's Burt Hart, also expelled from the league, and Milwaukee manager Hugh Duffy, who was soon looking for another job. The newspaper was particularly harsh on Griffith, noting "the failure of Griffith to make good as a manager. Comiskey believed there was the making of a great manager in the veteran pitcher and has given him every chance to demonstrate that belief. Instead, Griffith has shown his inability to control players and, though a wise, plucky field general, thoroughly experienced in the game and its finest points himself, he has not been able to inspire the players with the same spirit they had so much of last season and because unable to control his own disposition to berate the umpire, has lost the respect of the better classes of American League patrons…"[184] *The Sporting News* was also critical of Griffith's penchant for airing his gripes in public.

The *Tribune* noted on August 30 that, "Comiskey will take the reins today for the rest of the season…" This never happened but it is a clear indication that Griffith's job was in jeopardy. The White Sox were too strong a club to warrant a change. Griffith rejoined the rotation on September 9. That day, they swept a doubleheader, placing them in first by a comfortable seven games. They captured the pennant on September 21. Many casual fans today cite Boston as the first top American League club, perhaps the confusion stems from the first World Series dating only to 1903. It was Clark Griffith's Chicago White Sox that led the drive that first year.

Whatever problems Johnson had with some of Griffith's impulsive actions, they were tenfold with the treachery of John McGraw. McGraw was a hard-nosed kid who was forced to grow up in a hurry as a child on New York streets. At age twelve he ran away from home, escaping an abusive father soon after his mother and four siblings passed away during a diphtheria epidemic. Fortunately, he found a positive outlet in baseball, playing professionally by age 17.

---

[183] "League in Dire Straits," *Chicago Tribune*, August 25, 1901, p. 19

[184] "League in Dire Straits," *Chicago Tribune*, August 25, 1901, p. 19

Nearly from the beginning of Johnson and McGraw's association the independent McGraw was conspiring against the American League, even as he was assuming the reigns of one of its clubs. He was allegedly involved, and probably initiated, a drive by the National League to place franchises in Baltimore, Detroit and Washington for 1902. He was even rumored to have approached Nationals' manager Jimmy Manning about taking over the proposed National League Washington club. By mid-1901, McGraw was openly and dramatically talking of jumping to the National League and dragging his buddies with him.[185] On the field, no one kicked more often and louder than McGraw, which clearly put him at odds with Ban Johnson.

Things came to a head in July 1902; McGraw nearly single-handedly destroyed major league baseball in Baltimore, the town with which he was supposedly strongly linked. Actually, he succeeded. On June 29, 1902, Johnson suspended McGraw yet again for excessive kicking and abusive and foul language. McGraw then set his plan in motion. He covertly saw that the majority of the club's stock was transferred to the control of New York Giants' owner Andrew Freedman. McGraw and Freedman then took over the Baltimore franchise and set about to destroy it and, hopefully, the American League in the process. McGraw jumped to the Giants, released Joe McGinnity, Dan McGann, Roger Bresnahan, Jack Cronin, Joe Kelley and Cy Seymour from their Baltimore contracts and transferred them to the National League. The men bolted the club while Wilbert Robinson was at his mother's funeral. Since the club only carried fourteen players, it couldn't field a team. Robinson was left to pick up the pieces. Decimated, the club soon relocated and Baltimore would be without a major league franchise for over fifty years.

In the end it was evident that McGraw couldn't handle being under the thumb of disciplinarian Ban Johnson. The American League was just getting started and trying to portray a family image. In the minors, Johnson increased his fan base by prohibiting profanity and rowdiness from players and managers on the field. This was in direct contrast to how the National League operated in the 1890s. Umpires were given total authority, which Johnson backed up with fines and suspensions. The strategy was particularly effective at increasing female turnout and promoting a more fan-friendly environment. It eventually sparked an attendance explosion and general acceptance of the sport by the public, especially after Harry Pulliam and the National League followed suit. Major league gates topped three million in 1901, four

---

[185] "Calls M'Graw a Traitor," *Chicago Tribune*, July 27, 1901, p. 7 and "Baltimore may Bolt," *Washington Post*, July 27, 1901, p. 8

million in 1903, five million in 1904, six million in 1907 and seven million in 1908, all previously unmatched heights.

It also didn't help McGraw's mood as he realized that Johnson was probably going to turn over the proposed New York franchise to Griffith, a trusted friend and advisor. In fact, this may go to the very root of McGraw's unhappiness. Clark, over time, adapted to the new requirements of decorum. The game itself was sorely in need of leaders that did.

The White Sox finished 1901 with an 83-53 record, four games ahead of second place Boston. Skilled on offense and defense, the team finished first in runs scored and earned run average. Griffith's boys also ran well, stealing 280 bases, over seventy more than the second-place club. Clark posted a stellar 24-7-record to lead the league in winning percentage. He also finished in the top-four in earned run average, wins, WHIP, walks per game and opponent on-base percentage. It should also be noted that Griffith received terrific run support in 1901, 42% above league average.[186] Cy Young was clearly the best pitcher in all of baseball in 1901 but the Sox could boast two of the finest in Griffith and Callahan, who came on strong after his arm healed. Clark one-upped Young; he became the only man in modern major league history to post twenty victories and manage a club to the pennant. At the plate Napoleon Lajoie copped the Triple Crown, putting up the finest single performance of the year. Griffith was at his best that year holding Lajoie hitless in three games.

The White Sox outdrew their cross-town rivals, the Cubs, 354,000 to 205,000 and continued to do so in 1902, by 74,000. The American League, as a whole, came on strong at the gate, attracting 1.7 million fans, about 200,000 less than the National League. Surprisingly, the American League outdrew the National League by about a half million in 1902, 2.2 million to 1.7 million. The upstart league was particularly successful in Boston, nearly doubling the attendance of the Braves that first season and tripling it in 1902. After 1901, the Phillies' support collapsed, falling over 300,000 behind the Athletics in 1902. Upon the transfer of the Milwaukee franchise to St. Louis in 1902, the Browns outdrew there as well.

---

[186] According to *The 2006 ESPN Baseball Encyclopedia* Griffith received about average run support throughout his career, actually 1% above normal. Some years were better than others though (a score of 100 is average with a higher number meaning better run support): 1891, 115; 1893, 113; 1894, 107; 1895, 93; 1896, 86; 1897, 90; 1898, 106; 1899, 113; 1900, 79; 1901, 142; 1902, 105; 1903, 76; 1904; 1905, 112; 1906, 76; 1907, 146.

Unlike today, there were few, if any, general managers during the Deadball Era. Comiskey and Griffith worked year round administering the club. As soon as the season ended, Griffith headed to New York as an emissary for the American League to scout locations for a possible franchise to operate in that city. There, he further rocked the National League by coaxing Giants' manager George Davis to sign a White Sox contract for 1902 to replace Shugart at shortstop. Davis had played for New York since 1893 and had even taken over the managerial reigns in 1900. Davis came easily after the much-despised Giants' owner Andrew Freedman refused to enter a bidding war for his manager's services. Griffith later filed an affidavit in 1911 attesting to Freedman's indifference in the Davis matter. The hated owner was still being sued by his players nearly a decade after leaving the game. Griffith also clipped Brooklyn for longtime Dodger and twenty-year pro veteran Tito Daly to man second base. The additions allowed Mertes to move back to his traditional spot in the outfield.

Also in October, Griffith put up Ed McFarland in a Philadelphia hotel to discuss the upcoming season with the catcher. McFarland demanded $500 cash to become a White Sox. Clark didn't have the money so he went to Phillies' owner Tom Shibe under false pretenses and borrowed it. Amusingly, he stole Shibe's player with Shibe's money. Back home in Chicago, Griffith enticed outfielder Danny Green to jump the Orphans. Moving quickly, Comiskey signed nearly his entire squad by December except for Hartman who jumped to the Cardinals. Griffith then signed ex-teammate Sammy Strang in January to replace Hartman at third base. He landed Strang after the New York Giants took a little too long in re-signing him.

Clark sponsored a semi-pro club in Chicago in 1901 called the Griffiths. In early 1901, Griffith and the club's management led a drive to form a separate league. The new league, donned the Amateur Managers' Baseball League, was formed in early April.[187] It also adopted the Griffith baseball for use in league games. By the end of 1902, about 150 clubs comprised the league. There were hundreds such clubs around the city vying for fans and grounds. Many joined associations that handled their booking, setting their schedule and guaranteeing a venue on the busy weekends. The Griffiths played many teams in and around the area, including college nines, the White Sox and strong black clubs like the Chicago Unions with

---

[187] "Pfeffer losses his Case," *Chicago Tribune*, April 7, 1901, p. 17

Rube Foster and the Columbia Giants with Charlie Grant. Having an in, the club was able to line up profitable matches at American League Park when the White Sox were out of town. Career baseball men like Tony Mullane and Cap Anson could often be found umpiring the contests.

The Griffith club was renamed Clark Griffith's Chicago Maroons in 1902. It was one of the stronger clubs that year in the Amateur Managers League,[188] as noted by the *Chicago Tribune*, "Clark Griffith's Chicago Maroons…have a long string of uninterrupted victories with strong out of town teams to their credit…"[189] Contests between the Maroons and the Columbia Giants both started and ended the local baseball season in 1902, April 6 and November 8 respectively.

In early January, Griffith, Comiskey and Johnson returned from Clark's 5,000-acre Craig, Montana ranch where they spent the New Years' holiday hunting. The three joked at length with reporters about each's shooting prowess. As he had in previous winters and would in the future, Griffith spent a good part of his off-season at the ranch, which was run by his brother Earl during the baseball season.

The White Sox trained in Excelsior Springs again in 1902; however, the players spent nearly as much time shoveling the diamond as playing on it. The men battled the snow and Chicago cold into June. Griffith made his debut on April 30 with a 4-0 shutout of the Cleveland Broncos against rookie Addie Joss. Joss made his major league debut four days earlier, a one-hit shutout of St. Louis. He is probably the least known of the great Hall of Fame pitchers of the 20th century. His 1.88 earned run average is second all-time and no one in baseball history allowed fewer base runners per game, 8.73. That is less than a man per inning. In fact, Joss, with such great control, walked an average of only 1.43 batters per game.

On October 2, 1908, during the final week of the season in the heat of a pennant battle between Cleveland, Detroit and Chicago, all within 1.5 games of first place, Joss pitched a perfect game. The clutch performance came against Big Ed Walsh of the White Sox in a year in which Walsh won forty games. Joss notched another no-hitter on April 20, 1910 against Chicago again. In April 1911, Joss passed out on the bench during a preseason game. He died one week later of tubercular meningitis at age 31. The Hall of Fame waived its ten-year rule to include Joss in 1978. The move to include him in Cooperstown began soon after

---

[188] The Amateur Managers League comprised about 150 clubs in 1902.

[189] "Many Amateur Games Today," *Chicago Tribune*, June 22, 1902, p. 11

the momentous publication of the MacMillan *Baseball Encyclopedia* in 1969. Utilizing this work, historians and fans could now statistically compare the greats, and not so greats of the game. Joss' stats shined.

On May 13 in Detroit, Griffith was at it again, earning an ejection from umpire Jim Johnstone for kicking and abusive language; he was subsequently suspended for five days by Ban Johnson for the outburst. After being handed the suspension letter on May 15, Griffith was still irate, exclaiming that the umpires needed protection from Johnson because "…they're so rotten, some of 'em."[190] On May 19, the White Sox took a one-day jaunt to Detroit. Clark shut out the Tigers 1-0 on three hits. Sam Strang scored the only run of the game in the first inning due to two infield errors. The Detroit club was so dismayed by the loss that they deducted $11 from Chicago's purse for scuffed balls by Griffith. Six dollars was assessed for a like number of balls from the May 19 game and another $5 deducted for damaged balls from Griff's last visit to Detroit's mound on May 12. According to the *Sporting Life*, Griffith's reaction to the slight "cannot be found in Sunday school books."[191]

Clark took a beating in the third inning on June 2, giving up homers to Ed Delahanty, Bill Coughlin and George Carey of the Washington Senators. He pulled himself from the game. After many years of competition, Griffith finally posted a victory over Cy Young on June 11, 3-2. Then, Griffith came down with a gall stone ailment and only pitched once between June 23 and July 25. Fearing a possible operation and in pain, Griff at times turned over the club to Frank Isbell. For a time, it was feared that he would be forced into retirement. Incorrect rumors abound that he had a catarrh of the stomach.[192] Clark never did feel right throughout the rest of the season and was still severely weakened well into August.

Shortly after Johnson praised Griffith for his recent self-control, the manager was tossed by umpire Jack Sheridan on July 7 in Cleveland. Still riled, he was ejected again by Sheridan the following day. Clark relieved Wiley Piatt in the fifth inning on August 4 and collected the victory in the eleventh, 8-7. On the 12th, Chicago found itself in first place, ready to make another pennant run. But, by the time they returned from a two-week road trip, the White Sox resided in third place, five games back of Philadelphia. They never climbed any higher. Griffith lost a

---

[190] "Manager Griffith Disappointed," *Sporting Life*, May 24, 1902, p. 1

[191] "Detroit Dotlets," *Sporting Life*, May 31, 1902, p. 4

[192] "Baseball Notes," *Washington Post*, June 29, 1902, p. 9

heartbreaker to Rube Waddell on August 16, 2-1, but beat the lefty three days later, 5-2.

On August 28, the White Sox split a doubleheader at home with league-leading Philadelphia. Griff was in New York doing some recon for a potential American League franchise in the city. With his manager away and not scheduled to pitch that Thursday, Ned Garvin[193] skipped the games to get loaded. By 6:00 pm, he succeeded. Out of cash by then, he asked a saloonkeeper for a loan. After being refused, Garvin brandished a gun and demanded the cash. Bar patrons fled the establishment and hailed a policeman. The policeman entered the bar and demanded that Garvin turnover the firearm. The pitcher then hit the policeman with the gun and fired two shots at the fallen man's head but missed. The bartender jumped in the melee, saving the policeman's life. As they wrestled, Garvin fired into the bartender's left shoulder. As he went down, Garvin fled the scene.[194]

Garvin, a self-professed proud Texan, had previously shot at a man several times in Milwaukee in August 1901 because he didn't like his shoe-shining technique. He had also stabbed a man before in another bar fight. The following day, August 29, Garvin appeared at the ballpark to grab his things. Charles Comiskey intercepted him and fired the pitcher on the spot, giving him his outright release. He was arrested the next day. Other than losing his job little punishment befell the pitcher. He was fined a mere $100 and costs for disorderly conduct. He quickly caught on with a local semi-pro club, the Spaldings, and then signed with a National League team, the Brooklyn Dodgers by mid September.

On September 7, the second game of a doubleheader in Chicago was tied in the fourteenth inning. Up to their old tricks, the White Sox started delaying the game by hiding the game ball, so the umpire tossed Washington pitcher Bill Carrick a new, cleaner ball. Carrick just chucked it in the stands. Griffith started arguing and calling for a forfeit. Instead, the umpire ejected Clark from the game. An overflow crowd descended upon the field, causing the game to be called for darkness. The next day, the White Sox played an exhibition game in Muncie, Indiana against a local nine. The men played out of position with Griffith in left field; he told the home club that he would play anywhere they chose. The White Sox players clowned around on the field to amuse the five hundred in

---

[193] Garvin was a better pitcher than his overall win-loss record shows. Over his career, he received about 11% less run support than the league average. Moreover, he continually put up decent ERA+ figures during losing seasons.

[194] "Garvin Wild with Gun," *Chicago Tribune*, August 29, 1902, p. 1

attendance, a future trademark of Griffith's clubs. On September 20, Callahan threw the only no-hitter of the first three seasons of the American League, a 3-0 defeat of Detroit.

The defending champions dropped to fourth place in 1902. They still outdrew the Cubs, 338,000 to 264,000. Griffith started twenty-four games and racked up a 15-9-record. He finished within the top-seven in winning percentage, walks per game and shutouts. Clark also had the distinction of being ejected from the most games in 1902. He wouldn't be with the club in 1903, he was off to New York. Following a brief respite in Montana from mid-November to early December, he had a franchise to build. After 98 career victories, Jimmy Callahan left mound and took over the managerial duties and manned third base for the White Sox.

CHAPTER SIX

BIG APPLE

Ban Johnson knew from the beginning that he had to get into the New York market to secure his league's survival. The American League was successfully challenging the established league at the gate and on the field. Johnson and company lured significant talent from the National League to the point that many historians consider it a stronger league during its first few seasons. All that was needed was a little structural tweaking. The transfer of the Milwaukee franchise to St. Louis was a plus but Manhattan Island had 2.2 million residents. That was the place to be.

Two major impediments stood in Johnson's way. First, the notoriously corrupt nature of New York politics was a jolt to the executive's senses. He hadn't come across such problems in his other ventures. Tammany Hall cronies had their fingers in all aspects of city life, especially real estate and construction. There were palms to grease, egos to stroke and channels to weed through. It seemed everyone wanted a cut of the business. At first, Johnson was befuddled, then angered. Indignant, he wasn't going to pay their price and he wasn't about to bring such men into his league. More than anything Johnson needed a site to put a ballpark but how was he going to circumvent these men? The second problem was the vindictive Giants' owner Andrew Freedman who would not stand for the American League invading his territory.

Tammany influence in New York baseball dates back to a least the era of Boss Tweed who held power within the Mutuals baseball club during the amateur National Association of Base Ball Players from 1860 until his incarceration in 1871. Though they were not the first or only ones for that matter, Tweed's administration highlights a classic example of how men were compensated to play the game during the supposed amateur era. Many of his players were listed on the payrolls of city administrations, such as, the coroner's office or the street cleaning department, though they never actually showed up to perform their duties.

History books show that William Marcy Tweed sat at the helm of New York's Tammany Hall, a Democratic Party organization known for its strong influence over New York politics and ceaseless corruption. Tweed's looters are thought to have absconded with between $100 and $200 million of taxpayers' money. Many future generations of New York baseball owners owed allegiance at one time or another to Tammany Hall. The relationship continued well into the 20th century.

Andrew Freedman was one of these men. He purchased control of the debt-ridden New York Giants in 1895 for $50,000 and accrued a long list of offenses against the game before finally being ousted in 1903. For example, if a sportswriter offended him, Freedman barred him from the grounds even if he presented a ticket. He went as far as to punch a young *New York Times* reporter. Freedman attorneys could often be found filing lawsuits against journalists and others or answering any numbers of claims against the club owner himself. Like a New York magnate a century later, Freedman employed a ridiculous twelve managers in eight years. *The Sporting News* exclaimed, "He had an arbitrary disposition, a violent temper, and an ungovernable tongue in anger which was easily provoked and he disposed to be arbitrary to the point of tyranny with subordinates." Freedman often did as he pleased as weak-kneed National League president Nick Young and other league owners stayed out of his way. Freedman was vindictive if nothing else as highlighted by his strong-handed approach with players, such as, Amos Rusie.

Hall of Famer Amos "The Hoosier Thunderbolt" Rusie was an outstanding pitcher of the late 1800s. Some say his speed was the primary reason for the pitcher's mound being pushed back to 60'6" in 1893 because the fireballer struck out 982 batters the previous three seasons. In his ten-year career Rusie won 248 games, 164 of them from 1890-1894, and amassed 1,950 strikeouts and thirty shutouts, a significant amount for the era. However, in 1895 he ran contrary to one of the most oppressive and loathed moguls in baseball history, Freedman. After winning 24 games, Rusie found $200 in fines deducted from his last paycheck for a reason he couldn't readily determine.

Rusie insisted that the money be restored to him in his 1896 contract. Freedman refused and the pitcher sat out the entire season. New York fans were going nuts losing the services of one of the best pitchers in baseball. Freedman's name became a four-letter word throughout the industry. Rusie hired Monte Ward to defend him but lost his case in front of league officials. Ward decided to seek remedy from the courts and take the opportunity to challenge the reserve clause as well. The last thing National League officials wanted was a challenge to the reserve clause to be overseen by the judicial system. The case was still in the courts in the spring of 1897. Freedman stood firm even after the other league owners begged him to capitulate. Shortly after, Rusie signed; the others paid all his lost salary. In turn, Rusie agreed to drop the lawsuit. Even after Rusie reported, Freedman refused to use the pitcher until a fan uprising demanded it.

Politically, Freedman was connected. He joined Tammany Hall right out of college and was a longtime friend of the current Tammany boss Richard Crocker. Just as important, Freedman gained his wealth through real estate and construction and, as such, was among the city's leaders in each. He sat on Tammany's policy board and on their finance committee, directly involved in all decision making. He was also on the board of directors of the Interborough Rapid Transit Company, the firm constructing the city's subway system for $35 million. There seemed to be no way to circumvent Freedman's influence to erect a ballpark for a potential American League franchise.

Johnson was determined. Near the end of 1901, rumors suggested that the Baltimore franchise was destined for New York. John McGraw, as manager of the Orioles, appeared to be the man to lead the American League into New York. But, it was Griffith who had Johnson's ear, confidence and loyalty. A *New York Times* reporter caught Clark at the Fifth Avenue Hotel in New York City soon after the season ended on October 10. The Chicago manager had just clipped the New York Giants of their manager George Davis and was courting Tito Daly from Brooklyn. From there, Griffith was headed to Boston and Philadelphia, pursuing other National League players. Clark admitted to the reporter that he and McGraw were sent to New York to line up some Wall Street men for financial backing and to scout potential sites for a ballpark. Johnson wasn't pleased that Griffith's boasts landed in the newspapers, so much for a clandestine operation. Moreover, Orioles' president Sidney Frank was downright irate about the relocation talk, perhaps he was unaware of Johnson's intent. Griffith and McGraw made several of these secretive trips over the winter; however, the American League president would be making all the press announcements in the future.

Rumors placed the Orioles in New York by Opening Day 1902. Symbolically, Johnson temporarily moved his American League office from Chicago to the Big Apple before the season started. Freedman wasn't going to let the American League in. He either purchased outright or gained options on all parcels of land appropriate for Johnson's needs or had friends do likewise. He also threatened, through his political influence, to route all subway or streetcar line construction away from any proposed ballpark. Beaten, the American League didn't make it into New York in 1902.

On June 29, McGraw was placed on indefinite suspension by the American League president. It was clear to McGraw that he no longer fit into Johnson's New York plans. McGraw fled to Freedman's office of all places and concocted a hostile takeover of the Orioles with a shift of the manager and his key men to the Giants. The American League's biggest foe now controlled of an American League franchise. The insurrection took place during a series with St. Louis, resulting in the forfeiture of the July 17 game. McGraw and his men joined the Giants, in the process relieving second baseman Heinie Smith of his managerial responsibilities.

Johnson hurried to Baltimore and called Griffith and other advisors to the city for consultation. It was too late; the men were gone. Johnson invoked the American League's right to acquire 51% of the franchise and regained control of the club. Nonetheless, the damage was done. The baseball community was stunned with many predicting doom for the upstart league. Johnson wouldn't be caught unawares again. Instead, he was determined more than ever to bring the National League to its knees.

Though nothing was announced, it became clear to many that Griffith was slated to be the New York manager; indeed, he was the league's point man. It was an obvious choice and he was an ideal candidate to oppose McGraw in New York. Comiskey was not pleased to lose his manager but he realized that it was best for the league. On the offensive, Johnson and Griffith eyed the best team in the game, the Pirates. By mid-August, they made substantial offers to many Pittsburgh regulars despite Pirates' manager Fred Clarke's complaints. On August 26, Griffith announced that the Orioles were relocating to New York for 1903; to instill confidence in the Baltimore players, he signed several of them to 1903 contracts.

Questions arose about why Griffith was acting on behalf of the American League and signing players for the upcoming year. Apparently,

Johnson hadn't consulted the other American League owners. Consequently, Clark was called to Philadelphia to meet with Johnson, A's owner Ben Shibe and Connie Mack. There, Johnson laid his plans before all, informing the press on the 28th. It was now official; the existing Baltimore stockholders would be bought out by the league and the club transferred to New York. Griffith was named that club's manager and, in fact, had long ago been slotted as such.

Johnson was jumping the gun. He still didn't have a site to play ball on. Circumstances were working in his favor. A reform movement in New York City ousted Crocker from his Tammany office and ushered in progressive mayor Seth Low in 1902. Low's term is noted for its rarity: honesty and competency. Freedman's power was waning as Tammany Hall fractionalized. Griffith told New York reporters on October 7, "There are no ifs and ands about it. We are coming in here without doubt, and with a strong team. We have the grounds and everything is all ready."[195] It was merely a boast; they actually had neither and Johnson was later forced to back away from the statement.

On October 25, Johnson officially dropped his bomb. The American League had supposedly signed nineteen National Leaguers. The Pittsburgh franchise was particularly assaulted. After the details were ironed out, Griffith secured pitchers Jack Chesbro and Jesse Tannehill, catcher Jack O'Connor, third baseman Wid Conroy and outfielder Lefty Davis from the Pirates. It was a huge coup. Chesbro was 28 years old and coming off two excellent seasons. Tannehill, also 28, was a four-time 20-game winner.

Griffith also took a go at Christy Mathewson and Tommy Leach and, in fact, they were both listed as jumpers to the American League. In the end Mathewson and Leach stayed in the National League. Clark was also pursuing Brooklyn captain Willie Keeler since at least the fall of 1901. Near the end of 1902, Clark enlisted Boston manager Jimmy Collins in the effort. After several discussions, Griffith was pessimistic that Keeler could be signed. Collins believed Keeler would come around and bet Griffith and Johnson $100 that he would. Finally, while Keeler was headed west after the season he stopped in Chicago to meet with Clark. Griffith took him directly to Johnson's office where Keeler signed for $10,000 with a $2,000 bonus. As Johnson was mailing Collin's money, he joked with Griffith, "If we lose a few more bets like that, there won't be any National League."

---

[195] "New Baseball Players for New York," *New York Times*, October 7, 1902, p. 6

Griffith landed longtime Boston Braves captain Herman Long to play shortstop. Long had been playing since 1889, amassing over 1,000 runs batted in. Many consider him one the finest shortstops of all-time. He then purchased first baseman John Ganzel from Louisville of the independent American Association where he led the league with a .366 batting average and 194 hits. Griff also secured Dave Fultz who McGraw was also eying. In all, Griffith's recruiting drive during the winter of 1902-1903 was just as impressive as the previous year's, perhaps more so.

From Baltimore Griffith kept second baseman Jimmy Williams, outfielder Herm McFarland and righthanded pitcher Harry Howell as regulars in 1903. On paper Griffith had a stellar cast.

The combination of O'Connor and Howell proved disastrous in 1910. That year, the race for the American League batting title came down to the last day of the season between two of the game's greats, Cleveland's Napoleon Lajoie and Ty Cobb of the Tigers. Lajoie was well liked and admired throughout the league and already won three batting titles and the Triple Crown in 1901. His 1901 batting average was .075 better than his nearest competitor, a still-standing record. His team was even nicknamed the Naps in his honor. Cobb, only 23 years old, copped the last three batting titles and would go on to win every one through 1919 save 1916. He was as despised as Lajoie was adored.

The problem occurred on October 9 as the St. Louis Browns attempted to deprive Cobb of the batting title and the automobile that the Chalmers Motor Company promised the winner. In a doubleheader versus the Browns Lajoie in nine plate appearances compiled a triple, six bunt singles, a sacrifice bunt and a shot to shortstop Bobby Wallace that was ruled a hit on an errant throw. Thus, he went 8 for 8 and apparently won the title.

Uproar ensued in Detroit that prompted an investigation by Ban Johnson. Young Browns' third baseman Red Corriden admitted that team manager Jack O'Connor ordered him to play deep whenever Lajoie came to the plate, thus allowing potential bunts to roll for hits. "Rowdy Jack" O'Connor was a hard-living, hard-drinking 21-year major league catcher and long-time battery mate of Cy Young. The American Association expelled him back in 1892 for habitual drunkenness, disorderly conduct and insubordination. The heart of his career was spent with the aggressive National League Cleveland Spiders of the 1890s, a team that rivaled the Baltimore Orioles of the era for hard-nosed tactics. O'Connor once broke the jaw of umpire Jack McNulty.

Johnson further learned that Browns pitcher-coach-scout Harry Howell wrote a note promising the official scorer a suit of clothes if he ruled close plays in the favor of Lajoie. He was also seen popping in and out of the scorer's box throughout the game, presumably trying to influence his decisions. Howell was one of baseball's first spitballers, winning 134 games in thirteen major league seasons. Demonstrating the looseness of the era, he had been arrested back in 1906 for book making.

Johnson questioned O'Connor and Howell to no avail. They were officially cleared but Johnson forced their dismissal and sought to exclude them from Organized Baseball. No action was taken against the young Corriden, who spent over fifty years in baseball. When the official statistics were issued, Cobb was declared the winner anyway. Seeking to capitalize on the publicity, Chalmers gave both players an automobile. A *Sporting News* researcher in 1981 found an error in the official calculations that mathematically gives Lajoie a higher batting average for the 1910 season. A Bowie Kuhn ruling chose to ignore the discrepancy; consequently and probably rightfully, Major League Baseball still recognizes Cobb as the winner.

O'Connor never again appeared in Organized Baseball; but, he did find a job with the Federal League. The manager was in the middle of a two-year contract when dismissed from the Browns. He sued and recovered $5,000. In his only season as a major league manager he lost 107 games. Despite Johnson's efforts to exclude him, Howell found employment as an umpire in the minors and, later, in the Federal League.

Dave Fultz is an interesting figure. He was born in Staunton, Virginia in 1875. His maternal great-great grandfather John Morton was a signer of the Declaration of Independence. Fultz's father was a captain of an artillery unit during the Civil War, seeing action at the Battle of Chancellorsville. He also practiced law in Staunton and was a multi-term mayor of the city. The family moved to Pennsylvania in the mid 1890s. Fultz followed in his father's footsteps relating to vocation, religion, education, military and politics.

In 1894, Fultz enrolled at Brown University in Providence, where he ran track and captained the baseball and football squads. He was an All-American in both sports in 1896 and '97, becoming the first Brown football All-American.[196] Both sports teams were among the tops in the country during his tenure, also featuring future major leaguers Daff

---

[196] Fultz's career marks of 174 points and 31 touchdowns wouldn't be topped by a Brown player for a century.

Gammons and William Lauder. Fultz played halfback and second base. He graduated from Brown in 1898. Though he entered professional baseball and coached various college squads, he continued to study law, earning a degree from Columbia University in 1904.[197]

Fultz remained active in professional and college football well into his 50s as a player, coach, official and administrator. He played professionally from 1899-1901 for the Pittsburgh based clubs representing Duquesne and Homestead. Gammons also played for each of those clubs. Former major league pitcher Mark Baldwin coached the Duquesne squad.

Within a month of graduating from Brown, Fultz signed with the Philadelphia Phillies. He was extremely fast and proficient at bunting and stealing bases. Some sportswriters claimed he was the best bunter in the game. He also had excellent range in center field until his legs began to give out after years of taking abuse on the gridiron. He was quickly released by the Phillies but landed with the Orioles as a free agent. Just before spring training in 1900 he was transferred to Brooklyn then sold to Connie Mack, manager of the Milwaukee franchise in the minor American League.

He was actually drafted off the Milwaukee roster by Brooklyn in September, but the American League had other plans for its men as it declared major league status. Fultz remained with Mack, playing center field for the A's in 1901 and '02. In 1902, he helped drive the club to the pennant with a .302 batting average, 44 steals and a league-leading 109 runs.

Fultz perennially insisted on a clause in his contract that stipulated that he didn't play on Sundays. He also never cussed, drank or smoked and was well-known for counseling other ballplayers against the vices. Mack was particularly fond of Fultz and his work ethic. He used Fultz as an example of the value of good college athletes, stating, "It was Dave Fultz, a graduate of Brown University, who got me started going to the colleges for pitchers. Dave was one of the greatest outfielders that ever lived. In 1902, the first year the Athletics won the flag, his work was marvelous. Not even Jimmy Fogarty, whose memory is still revered in Philadelphia, ever did better playing. Fultz played inside ball. His arms and legs were mere factors in the game. His brain dominated his work. He impressed me so that I have since looked to the colleges for players, and have seven of them on this team – [Chief] Bender of Carlisle; [Eddie] Plank of Gettysburg; [Jack] Coombs of Colby; [Harry] Krause of St.

---

[197] He passed the New York bar in February 1905.

Mary's; [Jack] Barry of Holy Cross; Eddie Collins of Columbia and [Harry] Davis of Girard."[198]

Fultz's legs started to give out in 1903 after years of taking hits out of the backfield. He appeared in 79 games for the Highlanders and another 97 in 1904 despite perpetual knee pain. In late 1904, he obtained his law degree and set about to study for the bar exam. Passing the bar, Fultz decided that 1905 would be his last season in professional ball. It was in his 129th game of the season that that decision became all the more firm. On September 30, 1905, Fultz, playing center field, chased a fly ball hit by the Cleveland Indians' Bill Bradley. He collided with shortstop Kid Elberfeld. Both were knocked unconscious. Elberfeld was eventually helped from the field disoriented and bleeding above the eye and across the nose. Fultz however didn't regain consciousness for two hours. He awoke in the hospital with a broken jaw and multiple lacerations. He subsisted on a liquid diet for nearly a month. Tough, he was soon on the football field officiating games with his face bandaged and a cast still in his mouth.

With that he left the ball field as an active player; he did however remain close to the game. He coached college baseball at the U.S. Naval Academy in Annapolis and Columbia University from 1908-1911. He also did legal work and advised professional ballplayers as a practicing attorney in New York. About 1910, some players took their gripes to Fultz about their plight in trying to negotiate and work within the framework of the contract designed by and for Major League Baseball. Basically, the men were reiterating the problems which had plagued professional ballplayers since at least the advent of the reserve clause and other collusion-based treatment from club owners.

Fultz soon started touring minor and major league cities trying to drum up supported for his new creation, the Fraternity of Baseball Players. When Ty Cobb was suspended in May 1912 for fighting with a fan, his teammates rebelled and sat out a game. Fultz quickly inserted himself in the dispute and unilaterally crowned himself as president of the new players' union. The new players' union was formally chartered on September 6, 1912 and was administered from Fultz' law office. By 1914, the union had a membership of about 1,100 men, mostly minor leaguers.

The union gained significant leverage with the emergence of the outlaw Federal League. Throughout the Federal League era, major league executives were constantly threatening ballplayers with banishment for jumping to the new league. Fultz stood his ground, returning the threats

---

[198] *Sporting Life*, June 5, 1909, p. 5

and soothing the players during the contentious times. With these assurances, union membership rose to over 1,200 by the end of 1916. However, with the decline of the Federal League by the end of 1915 Fultz and the union lost much of their negotiation power. Major League Baseball officials soon reneged on virtually all the promises they made with Fultz and the players over the last couple of years.

Irate, Fultz issued a set of demands to baseball executives near the end of 1916. In January 1917, the National Commission rejected most of them. National League president John Tener then announced that the National Commission would no longer hear appeals from the Fraternity. Fultz called for a general strike on February 20, 1917; however, the players were losing steam and failed to back him. In short major league officials were aggressive in their reaction and the players backed down. Fultz then released them from their strike pledge and the union eventually disintegrated. He later served as an aviator during World War I and, back in baseball, as president of the International League.

Griffith spent a good portion of the winter on the road, mostly in New York, ironing out details for his new club; however, Clark did find time to go bowling with Johnson, Comiskey and Nationals manager Tom Loftus before leaving Chicago.

He also needed to find a new apartment in New York. Addie Griffith lived in Chicago since emigrating from Scotland in the early 1890s. She was living with her mother, brother and sister when she married in December 1900[199]. The Griffiths took Addie's mother, Jane, with them to New York. She resided with Clark and Addie for the rest of her life. Throughout their tenure in New York, the Griffiths resided at a hotel on the southeast corner of West 155th Street and Amsterdam Avenue.

"ALL DISPUTES AT END," read the headline on January 11, 1903. The two leagues came to an agreement the night before. The baseball war was over. Each league now respected the other's player contracts, adopted the reserve clause, played under uniform rules and signed the National Agreement. Naturally, the sticking point was the assigning of disputed player rights. McGraw was incensed when Ed Delahanty was sent to the Washington Nationals and not his club.

---

[199] Living arrangements as listed in the 1900 U.S. Census

Another consequence of the armistice was the eventual slashing of salaries and a reneging of promises made to the players union in early 1901 by both the American and National Leagues. Griffith adopted management's stance on this account and took a lot of heat for doing so. He was the most visible rebel and pusher for reform. But, he was now heavily involved in league management and was expected to help ease the transition. In this effort, Griffith held numerous one-on-one conferences trying to rationalize his new stance to his colleagues and quell their concerns. Yes, he revised his outlook but it was inevitable; he was now a part of management and was eventually looking to join the ranks of the club owners. Peace between leagues had and would always work in management's favor. The players would have another chance during the rise of the Federal League.

As part of the agreement, Johnson was given the okay to move into New York. As a bargaining chip, he threatened to set a franchise in Pittsburgh. It was only a threat but it provided leverage when dealing with the National League. The American League was heading into New York anyway so the compromise was set. Johnson still needed to secure a site to play ball. He hated to do so but a deal with Tammany Hall had to be made.

A faction opposed to Freedman offered a track of land in Washington Heights at 168th and Broadway, beautifully overlooking the Hudson River and New Jersey Palisades. It was owned by the New York Institute for the Blind and was once a Revolutionary War battleground that George Washington supposedly crossed. It's the current site of New York-Presbyterian Hospital. One catch, the Orioles were sold to a group headed by coal magnate Joseph Gordon for the ridiculously meager sum of $18,000 on March 11. It quickly came to light that Gordon was fronting for two notorious Tammany figures Frank Farrell and Bill Devery. Farrell was among a contingent that operated hundreds of gambling outlets of all varieties throughout the city. Devery was a former New York City police chief who amassed a fortune soliciting cash from any and all in the vice industry. Not the type of individuals Johnson particularly wanted in the game but all in all just two in a long list of questionable characters in the game prior to the hiring of a commissioner.

Griffith now had greater responsibilities in New York with the team being sold to non-baseball men. In Chicago Comiskey and Clark bounced ideas around, two experienced baseball men. In the days before a general manager many chores fell on the manager. In New York, Clark had but himself to run day-to-day operations. Even during the off-season, he tended to club business from his ranch. He'd typically take off for Montana by late October after the World Series. There, he'd relax and tend to his business interests, both in Montana and New York, until close to or shortly after Christmas or the turn of the year. Occasionally, he'd hop a train to sign a player or attend a league meeting. Returning to New York, Griffith set out to sign his players for the upcoming season, usually mailing out contracts in early January.

There wasn't a great deal of rush to dole out contacts since all men were bound by the reserve clause and couldn't offer their services elsewhere without Clark's approval. Griffith almost exclusively handled all player transactions throughout his tenure in New York and many of the other administrative duties. For the most part during their early relationship, Farrell just rubberstamped his manager's decisions. To illustrate, Clark later revealed the he never actually signed a written contract while with the Highlanders throughout his tenure. Why would the boss, the man running the company, need to sign himself? Griff's initial compensation with the club was $6,000 a year.

Clark and Frank Farrell, the active partner, actually became quite tight. Farrell also ran a stable of horses. Griffith, an experienced frontiersman and a member of the Dillon horse-breeding family, housed some of the magnate's horses on his ranch and bred them. By 1905, he had about fifty horses in all on his ranch. Farrell kindly sent some of his stallions and high-class mares to Montana to help improve Griff's breed of horses. Farrell named one of his prized Kinley Mack racing colts "Clark Griffith." Amusingly, the name just seemed natural after the two-year-old horse kicked a stable hand, nearly tearing his arm off. In Farrell's mind, Clark, the baseball kicker, and the kicking horse were a match.[200] Clark Griffith, the horse, proved quite successful, winning purse after purse from 1905-1906. It wasn't until later when Farrell became more active in on-the-field matters that problems developed between the two. Devery was actually the controlling owner, but was a silent partner. Griff didn't even know that fact until his fourth year with the club.

The new club, initially called the Americans, departed for spring training in mid-March. Opening Day was set for April 22. They spent most of their time in Atlanta and New Orleans playing the Crackers and Pelicans, respectively, of the Southern Association. The New York newspapers were initially hostile to the new ball club. Freedman still had some connections after all. Griffith hired reporter Jim Bagley to travel with the

---

[200] "Baseball Notes," *Washington Post*, April 27, 1905, p. 8

team and remit stories back to several Gotham dailies. Clark also paid sports editor Jim Price of the *New York Press* to cover the southern trip. Bagley's stories proved sufficiently entertaining that the city's main papers were forced to pick up coverage of the Americans. The American League was now legitimate in New York.

Meanwhile, Farrell tapped his Tammany connections to have a ballpark built. Demolition and construction cost $200,000 and another $75,000 for the park itself. Blasting didn't even begin until March 18. It took five hundred men working day and night to complete the job before Opening Day, well nearly complete at least. The grounds were a mess, leveling proved a nightmare. The ballpark sat atop a hill, requiring a lot of dynamite to make headway. Overseeing matters, Griffith amassed a collection of arrowheads and 1776 vintage grapeshot and canisters during the digging. The field became known as Hilltop Park after an initial christening as American League Park. Along the same lines, the team itself eventually adopted the moniker Highlanders.

The season opened with the construction incomplete. There was no roof and 5,000 folding chairs were needed to make up for an unfinished grandstand and bleachers; but, seating was available for about 16,000. The field was the biggest problem. The infield was nicely rolled but the *New York Times* described the outfield as, "rough and ragged." Ropes circled the field marking ground-rule double territory. There would be no triples or homers unless the ball left the entire grounds. Keeler had little room to cover in right since most of it was cordoned off. The ground there proved particularly troublesome to level. It was a sinkhole and never really settled until 1904. Keeler was used to uneven grounds as his groundskeeper in Baltimore deliberately left a hill in right field. Keeler could deftly manage the protrusion but it wreaked havoc with visiting outfielders.[201]

Griffith made his first start on the mound on April 27. However, the day belonged to Connie Mack's newest find out of Dickinson College via the Carlisle Indian School, Chief Bender. The Chippewa Indian shutout Griffith's men 6-0 in his first major league start. Opening Day in New York took place on April 30. Ban Johnson tossed the ceremonial first pitch before a crowd of 16,243. Jack Chesbro won the first game at American League Park 6-2.

---

[201] *Level Playing Fields*, Peter Morris, 2007

The Highlanders became the victims of unmerciful heckling through the first weeks of the season. Griffith suspected that new Giants' owner John Brush and McGraw were behind the outbursts. Farrell dealt with the problem the way he knew how. He had some Tammany cronies knock the hecklers around a little. They confessed to working for Brush and were permanently chased from the field.[202]

Griffith defeated the A's Eddie Plank on May 6, 6-1. After giving up a couple hits in the ninth, he was ejected for kicking and abusive language by umpire Tommy Connolly, his first of the year, after Connolly gave an Athletic a ground rule triple. Once again, Johnson issued warnings to all his managers and players about rowdy behavior. Both Griffith and Boston manager Jimmy Collins were suspended for three days to kick the season off. Keeler oversaw the club in Griff's absence. The National League also started tightening the belt in relation to excessive behavior. Honus Wagner was suspended for three days for "threatening to strike Umpire [Bug Holliday]."[203]

On Sunday May 17, the Indians and Highlanders played in Columbus, Ohio to skirt Cleveland blue laws. Addie Joss topped Griffith 9-2. Dave Fultz declined to play on God's day, as he would his entire career. In St. Louis on the 23rd, Griffith defeated the Browns 3-1 on two hits. He also placed a double and scored. With the team in seventh place in June, Highlanders' president Gordon threatened Griffith's job if he didn't right the ship. So to add some punch, Griffith first sought a trade for Delahanty from Washington but that was a no go. He then set his sights on 28-year-old shortstop Kid Elberfeld who was unhappy with his employers in Detroit. He first contacted manager Tigers manager Ed Barrow but he was asking too much. Instead, Clark went directly to Tigers' owner Sam Angus who accepted shortstops Ernie Courtney and Herman Long for Elberfeld who then joined the Highlanders on the 13th.

Griffith tossed the first shutout in Yankees' history on June 16, a 1-0 victory over Comiskey's boys in front of a hometown crowd of 2,130. Chicago's Doc White was just as impressive giving up an identical six hits but losing on a sacrifice fly by Jimmy Williams in the fifth inning, which scored the pesky Keeler. The Highlanders were shutout by Joss eight days later. Griffith won 2-1 on a six-hitter in St. Louis on the 30th. He also placed a couple of singles.

---

[202] Shirley Povich, 33-part series on Griffith, "Clark Griffith; 50 Years in Baseball" for the *Washington Post* in January and February 1938

[203] "Pittsburg, 9; Cincinnati, 4," *New York Times*, May 9, 1903, p. 7

In July, the Giants threatened the peace agreement by contesting the transfer of Elberfeld to their American League rival in New York. Legal injunctions were sought and tensions heightened yet again. The problem lie in the assignment of players after the peace agreement was penned in January. The Giants were miffed at losing out on George Davis, Ed Delahanty, Elberfeld, Dave Fultz and Napoleon Lajoie, all men they believed would be joining the club in 1903. The Giants viewed the Elberfeld trade as a personal affront. They saw it as a direct American League action to siphon fans from the Giants to the cross-town Highlanders. The team's new owner John Brush approached National League president Harry Pulliam about derailing the peace agreement.

To appease Brush, Pulliam sent a letter in late June to Ban Johnson charging the American League with violating the "spirit" of the peace agreement. The actual letter of the pact wasn't violated since Elberfeld was assigned to the Tigers who could dispose of him in any way they pleased. Brush also asked and received permission from Pulliam to field shortstop George Davis, a disgruntled player assigned to the White Sox. Davis, property of an American League club, actually played for the Giants on June 26. National Commission chairman Garry Herrmann, himself a National Leaguer, was livid, writing a letter and publicly questioning Pulliam's motives and actions in violating the peace agreement. It was surely a lapse of judgment on Pulliam's part and perhaps an identifying characteristic when it came to dealing with the New York owner.

Comiskey quickly obtained two injunctions in the Davis case. In all, Davis appeared in only four games for the Giants before sitting out the rest of the season and then joining the White Sox in 1904. Brush kept harping on the losses of Elberfeld, Davis and Delahanty. On July 10, he obtained a temporary injunction preventing Elberfeld from playing with the Highlanders. It was five days before the New York Supreme Court dissolved the baseless injunction, allowing Elberfeld to rejoin his club.

The vindictive saga of 1903 repeated itself the following season as Brush and McGraw once again stood in defiance of the best interests of Major League Baseball. With the Highlanders driving for the pennant in 1904, they refused to enter into post-season play. Their hatred of the American League far outweighed any sensibilities to the contrary, even a considerable financial windfall.

It obviously took Brush and McGraw longer to accept the peace between the leagues than all others involved. That is clearly evident by their refusal to participate in the 1904 World Series and an intercity series in 1903. Similar contests had already been set, and were profitable, in Chicago, Philadelphia and St. Louis. And, of course, the Pittsburgh Pirates and Boston Americans were destined to make history in October. Sarcastically, Brush declared to the *New York Times*, "I do not care to recognize the American League in New York. I do not know who these people are."[204]

On July 20, Griffith topped Joss 7-3 and did the same to Bender eleven days later, 3-1. On August 9, Griff sent a challenge to John McGraw of the Giants to play a postseason seven-game series, but was rebuffed.[205] Sticking to their guns, the Giants didn't officially recognize the American League. Griffith then shut down St. Louis, 6-1, on August 20 and Chicago, 6-5, three days later. On September 1, he topped Plank again 5-1. On the 9th, Clark tossed his second and last shutout of the year, a 4-0 gem over Philadelphia and Bender. Griff had been hounding Browns' manager Jimmy McAleer for muscular outfielder John Anderson since early in the season but was continually denied in trade discussions. That changed when Anderson booted a ball in late September and McAleer finally agreed to the trade.[206] It was consummated at the end of the season on October 6.

On "Shoot Straw Hats" day, September 1, the club was traveling by ferry to Philadelphia. Griffith and boys ran amuck attacking all the passengers and tossing their hats overboard. The Highlanders never threatened for the league lead the entire season; but, they did come on in the second half to land in fourth place with a 72-62-record. Clark secured his job with Gordon. The club drew 212,000 to Hilltop Park, less than half of the Giants' 580,000 patrons. On the mound, Griffith won fourteen games and placed on the leader board in his customary control categories of fewest hits per game and WHIP. It was a bit of a struggle on the mound considering that he received about 24% less run support than the average league pitcher. Griff still put in the innings, 213 for the second straight year. The next two seasons, his final major contributions on the mound, he contributed about 100 innings each year.

Clark umpired the final two games of the season against Detroit, making him the only Hall of Famer to umpire in three different major leagues. In 1891, he worked behind home plate on August 13 in an American Association game between Boston and Cincinnati. He umpired at first on July 27, 1894 in a National League contest pitting Chicago and

---

[204] "Sends Challenge to Brush," *Chicago Tribune*, September 5, 1903, p. 6

[205] "McGraw Challenged by Griffith," *Washington Post*, August 10, 1903, p. 8

[206] Shirley Povich, 33-part series on Griffith, "Clark Griffith; 50 Years in Baseball" for the *Washington Post* in January and February 1938

Cincinnati. He did the same the following year on May 31 with his Colts taking on New York. In the American League on September 28, 1903, Griffith umpired at first but was behind the plate the following day. Obviously, all his work in blue was as a substitute, filling in for absent arbiters.

Detroit Tigers' owner Sam Angus put the team up for sale at the end of 1903. The story broke on November 8 that Griffith was in Detroit offering the owner $40,000 for the franchise. However, Angus was said to be holding out for $45,000. Ban Johnson confirmed the existence of the offer but he disputed the dollar figures. Clark didn't have a solid financing plan at the time; he just wanted into the ownership ranks. He was quickly eliminated from the bidding. As Johnson said, "Griffith will have to be with New York next season, and besides that, I understand that the persons he was depending on to help him out with the financial part of the transaction have dropped out."[207]

Griff's first taste of ownership actually came in the Eastern League. With Ed Barrow and Frank Farrell, Clark purchased the Montreal franchise on February 27, 1906.[208] He put up $6,000 of the $20,000 purchase price with Farrell as the main stockholder. The men held onto the club through 1907. The club served as an unofficial farm club. Men like Louis Leroy were first stationed there before joining the Highlanders.

Before departing south for spring training in 1904, Griffith made two acquisitions. On February 21, he purchased longtime backstop Deacon McGuire from the Tigers. Of particular note, McGuire began his career sharing the catching duties with Fleet Walker, the first acknowledged African-American player in major league history, in 1884 with the Toledo Blue Stockings of the American Association. Out hitting McGuire by 78 points, Walker's major league career was over at season's end while McGuire's would see another twenty-five springs. To round out his rotation, Griffith acquired fellow Bloomington native Jack Powell from the Browns for Harry Howell.

Clark arrived in Atlanta on March 9 to kick off the spring. The club also traveled to New Orleans before returning to New York on April 8. One of the hot issues of the spring stemmed from the Giants and Dodgers insistence on opening in New York City on the same date as the Highlanders. Griffith threatened to rewrite his entire schedule to oppose

---

[207] "Detroit Baseball Team for Sale," *New York Times*, November 10, 1903, p. 10

[208] *Sporting Life*, March 3, 1906, p. 4, Farrell was the majority owner

the Giants head-to-head all season if they didn't reschedule Opening Day at the Polo Grounds. The National League acquiesced, opening in Brooklyn instead.

The Highlanders opened the season on April 14 with Jack Chesbro out dueling Cy Young of Boston 8-2. The year belonged to Chesbro; he carried the club almost single-handedly all summer. He started 51 games and completed 48 of them, amassing 454 innings and four relief appearances along the way. He posted 41 victories for New York against only 12 losses and notched a 1.82 earned run average. Chesbro's start, win and complete game totals are all twentieth century highs.

The key to Chesbro's 1904 season was his newfound spitball. Chesbro saw Elmer Stricklett use the pitch in a spring training game. Stricklett wouldn't share his secret but Chesbro began tinkering with it anyway. Problem was, Griffith wouldn't allow the pitch to be used in a game.[209] However, after Chesbro alternated wins and loss for a slow start and a 4-3 record, the manager cut him loose on May 14. Chesbro won his next fourteen starts.

The newly acquired Powell also added 23 victories for the Highlanders. After watching the pair all summer, *Boston Globe* reporter Tim Murnane wrote an article declaring that the spitball was revolutionizing the game. The Old Fox helped usher in a new era. Griffith, himself, was backing off the mound at age 34. He only started eleven games in 1904 and five of those were designed to give his staff a breather, being the day after a doubleheader or the second game of one. He only tossed 100 innings in 16 games for a 7-5-record. For his career, Griff was the most active pitcher-manager in baseball history. He toed the rubber in 146 games that he also managed, by far the most. The other top four in order are Monte Ward, 117, Al Spalding, 61, and Kid Nichols, 36.

On Opening Day in Philadelphia, April 21, Griffith had a run-in with a photographer. The photographer asked if he could get a team photo but a ceremonial parade was about to start. When Griffith refused to line his men up, the man became belligerent, shouting several "offensive epithets" at the manager. Griffith clocked the man, giving him a "badly bruised face." A warrant was issued for the manager but he settled the matter for $4.50, though the photographer wanted a full $5.

Despite assurances to the contrary, several Brooklyn Dodgers and Phillies were arrested on April 24 for playing a game on a Sunday in New

---

[209] At the time Griffith believed the pitch was inherently dangerous to his catchers. It's unpredictably would surely lead to hand injuries for his backstops.

York City. The 13,000 in attendance paid 25, 50 or 75 cents for a program that supposedly denoted their seating assignments and, thus, was not an admission fee. City officials were not fooled. Blue laws were repealed in New York in 1919.[210]

Griffith made his first start on May 27 and the rust was evident. He surrendered 13 hits, a wild pitch and hit two batters in a 7-5-loss to the A's. He straightened himself out on June 12 before a huge Sunday crowd in Chicago; allowing six hits and striking out five, Griffith shutout Comiskey's men 2-0. He also placed a double and a sacrifice. The *New York Times* raved, "Griffith used every trick known to the game, never putting the ball across the middle of the plate. He worked every corner and edge with a wonderful control, supplemented with knowledge of every batter's weakness."[211]

On the 17th, Clark shipped Bob Unglaub to Boston for left fielder Patsy Donovan. On June 22 Griffith defeated Washington 11-6 and again topped Rube Waddell, 5-2, in the second game of a July 4-doubleheader. However, Cleveland crushed Clark 16-3 on the 13th. He righted himself with a 3-1 three-hit victory over George Mullin and Detroit on Sunday July 17[212] before losing his next two starts. Pitcher Al Orth was acquired from Washington on July 20 and won eleven games for the Highlanders over the second half of the season. By the end of the season, Orth was tossing the spitball as well; he particularly admired its sharp break. He used it extensively in 1905 as well, posting eighteen victories. The following season he won a stunning 27 games.

Griffith frequently battled Farrell throughout his tenure in New York over administrative issues. With the team bouncing between second and third place in late July, Farrell approached Cubs manager Frank Selee,

---

[210] Chicago, Cincinnati and St. Louis permitted Sunday baseball as far back as the 1880s. The others:

Boston	1929	Brooklyn	1919
Cleveland	1911	Detroit	1910
New York	1919	Philadelphia	1934
Pittsburgh	1934	Washington	1918

[211] "American League; New Yorks shut Chicago team out without a Run," *New York Times*, June 13, 1904, p. 8

[212] The game was played at Wiedenmayer's Park in Newark, New Jersey with 6,700 in attendance.

offering him a substantial boost in income to manage the Highlanders. Selee declined, using the offer to coax a raise out of his boss, Chicago president Jim Hart. When the story broke on July 25, Clark said he knew Farrell was in consultation with Selee but was misled to believe that the owner was working as an agent for Ban Johnson trying to lure Selee for another American League club.

Griffith and the American League were battling a war of words with the Giants. On July 27 John McGraw announced, "The Giants will not play a postseason series with the American League champions. Ban Johnson has not been on the level with me personally, and the American League management has been crooked more than once."[213] McGraw and Giants' owner Brush were reigniting their feud with the new league. It was their feud; nearly all other participants came to terms with the new structure of Organized Baseball. Of particular concern to the Giants was that the Highlanders were in the race for the American League flag until the last day of the season. History shows that indeed no World Series was played in 1904 because of the Giants' animosity. Brush soon became conciliatory after incurring the ire of the entire baseball community for canceling the marquee series. To exact some measure of revenge, Griff sat on Philadelphia's bench during the opening game of the 1905 World Series.

Griffith was at it again on August 8 in Cleveland. In the fourth inning of a 9-1-loss umpire Silk O'Loughlin called John Ganzel and Dave Fultz out on disputed plays. Clark jumped into the middle of the fray and, with Fultz, was ejected. The pair refused to leave the field. A police officer was summoned to escort the men from the grounds. Ban Johnson once again suspended the manager. Soon after, *The Sporting News* blasted Griffith for his continued beefs with umpires and his wild statements to the press. "The heaviest handicap of the Highlanders is the senseless kicking that its manager does and encourages his players to engage in…Griffith discusses his 'complaints' against the officials of the American League with the newspapers, pronounces the umpire, who has disciplined him incompetent and with amazing effrontery declares that he will never again be permitted to enter 'my' park…Griffith's services to the American League are held in high appreciation, but his conduct on and off the field has given rise to scandals, which has affected its prestige with patrons. It is high time for him to be taught that umpire-baiting is a handicap and not a help to an American League team." Clearly, Griffith took his time

---

[213] "John McGraw Chronology," July 27, 1904, baseballlibrary.com

adopting Johnson's full vision for the American League. Of course, Johnson, an administrator, wasn't on the field battling for a pennant everyday either.

Griffith ran into some more trouble with the law on August 13. Jack Powell ran a $46 tab at a Chicago bar but jumped a train to St. Louis before paying the debt. When Griffith refused to accept a garnishment writ, the police threatened to execute a warrant on the Highlanders and the manager himself.

Griffith pitched a superb game on the backend of a doubleheader on September 6 against Philadelphia. He won 2-1 and surrendered a mere three hits, only one left the infield. Rube Waddell struck out 14 men in the opener that day. Clark lost to Waddell three days later, 5-1.

Nineteen Hundred Four was the first pennant showdown between the Red Sox and Yankees; but, the clubs went by different nicknames at the time.[214] They were within a game of each other through much of September, trading the top spot back and forth. On September 29, the two clubs sat tied atop the leader board. Griffith relieved Orth in the sixth inning in St. Louis on October 3 after the starter suffered arm troubles. The two combined on a four-hit shutout. Clark yielded two of those hits and struck out three batters.

After the October 5 contests, Boston was up a half game heading into a four-game series against the Highlanders to end the season and determine the championship. New York took the first contest on October 7 at home to reverse the standings. In one of the biggest blunders by team executives in history, Highlander owners Farrell and Devery scheduled a football game between Columbia University and Williams College on the 8th at Hilltop Park. Consequently, the baseball clubs hopped a train and head to Boston. The relocation to Boston allowed the insertion of another game into the schedule, a makeup for a previous rainout between the clubs. Contemporary rules only permitted rainouts to be made-up in the city they occurred; hence, October 8 was rescheduled as a doubleheader. Now, four games remained that would determine the pennant, a doubleheader in Boston on the 8th and another in New York on the 10th.

With the home field advantage Boston swept on the 8th to go up by 1.5 games with only two to play. Both towns were in frenzy. New York Governor Benjamin Odell and his staff trekked to Boston to see the

---

[214] Actually, the origin of the Yankees name can be traced at least to 1904; however, it was just an informal nickname at that time used by a few sportswriters and fans.

contests. On the way home Griffith chartered another train to avoid Odell's planned celebration. The governor still sent his best wishes for the upcoming contests but slipped in a few zingers for Clark's avoidance. With their backs up against the wall the Highlanders needed to take both games on the 10th. Over 28,500 ravenous New Yorkers showed up to root the boys on. Unfortunately, they lost 3-2 on a wild pitch by Chesbro in the ninth inning of the first game. Boston won their second consecutive American League pennant.

The Highlanders finished with a 92-59 record. Clark took the club to within a game of winning his second American League flag in four seasons. His men drew 439,000 fans to what was really an inferior ballpark. The Giants attracted 610,000 followers. Ban Johnson's vision proved a success. With over a 100% increase in patronage, the Highlanders still only ranked fourth in the league in the category. The American League seemingly conquered the world in four short seasons. They became the first baseball league to draw over three million paid admissions.

Griffith made another important acquisition at the end of 1904. On October 4, he drafted pitcher Doc Newton and a seemingly benign first baseman named Hal Chase from Los Angeles of the Pacific Coast League. Newton had just led the league with 39 wins; however, he copped only twenty victories in five seasons with New York. Chase was a find, the first homegrown Yankee superstar. Some still call him the best fielding first sacker of all-time. He was also the most corrupt player of the twentieth century outside the eight men who threw the 1919 World Series. Chase was openly accused of game fixing by three major league managers and suspected by countless others. He was considered the master of the "indifferent play" for his ability to swing the score while making it look like another's error or misplay.

Ironically, he is often credited as being perhaps the finest fielding first baseman of his era. This is despite the fact that he led the league in errors seven times and committed an incredible 402 errors in a fifteen-year career, an average of 27 errors a year, at first base yet - quite a testament to his fielding skills or perhaps more appropriately a testament to his fraud. *The Sporting News* in 1913 wrote, "That he can play first base as it never was and perhaps never will be played is a well-known truth. That he will is a different matter."

In the minors Chase gained a reputation for great defensive play. He quickly became a fan favorite after joining New York in the American League. The Highlanders were ecstatic about the future after Chase finished third in the batting race in only his sophomore season in 1906 with a mark of .323. The first baseman quickly dashed those hopes after he began jumping the team to seek extra cash and once after he was spurned the manager's job.

In 1910, New York manager George Stallings accused Chase of throwing games. Ban Johnson investigated and issued a statement praising the "sterling" character of Chase. Later, Stallings was fired and replaced by Chase of all people. Chase was himself replaced as manager after the 1911 season. In '13 another New York manager, Frank Chance, accused Chase of throwing games and shuffled him to the White Sox in May. In 1914 Chase jumped the White Sox for the Federal League. The Federal League was an independent third major league that challenged Organized Baseball from 1914-1915. After the Federal League folded, Chase caught on with the Cincinnati Reds, as he had worn out his welcome in the American League. Cincinnati manager Christy Mathewson suspended Chase for "indifferent play" in August 1918.

The National League initiated an investigation into Chase's conduct; nevertheless, in 1919 National League president John Heydler cleared him citing lack of evidence. It was an obvious whitewash and a portent to that year's World Series difficulties. Ridiculously, John McGraw stated prior to the hearing that if Chase was cleared he wanted to sign him and consequently he did. The inability, or indifference, of the National Commission to stymie Chase reminded many of similar circumstances surrounding pitcher Jack Taylor the previous decade. Taylor was repeatedly charged with and even openly admitted to fixing games and just as repeatedly he escaped sanction. Not only was this a forewarning to some in the game, especially an outspoken Barney Dreyfuss, but it was also fodder for subsequent indiscretions.

Disclosed later, Cincinnati Reds second baseman Lee Magee charged Chase with bribing him to lose games in 1918. Chase, Magee and Heinie Zimmerman were all forced out of the major leagues at the end of 1919 for suspected crooked play. They were never officially expelled but were persona non grata nonetheless. In August 1920, Chase was banned from Pacific Coast League ballparks for trying to bribe Salt Lake City players and umpires. He was also expelled from the Mission League and the outlaw San Joaquin Valley League. Later, Chase joined the outlaw Copper League in Arizona and Northern San Joaquin Valley League and played with fellow disgraced players Buck Weaver, Chick Gandil, Lefty Williams, Jimmy O'Connell, Harl Maggert and Tom Seaton. In 1931, Chase penned a letter to Judge Landis inquiring about his status in Organized Baseball and apologizing for his past indiscretions. Landis replied that the first baseman was in good standing with Organized

Baseball for all he knew but, coyly, asked Chase to describe these indiscretions. Chase's lawyers advised him against replying.

Chase's name naturally popped up early in the grand jury investigation of the throwing of the 1919 World Series. He had heard early on about a possible scam and contacted various parties to confirm the rumors. Nothing delighted him more, a predetermined outcome. What his exact role was in the affair is still unclear due to the fact that he wasn't compelled to testify; it was reported however that he won money betting on the Reds, possibly $40,000.

The mere fact that Chase was able to work the system and profit from it for so long surely led, in part, to the 1919 Black Sox scandal. The entire industry had some idea of Chase's misdeeds and, more important, major league officials seeming indifference to them. Certainly, unnamed others prospered in undisclosed fixes. Major League Baseball refused to confront its flaws and, as such, fed the greatest scandal in American sporting history. The National Commission soon ceded its power to a stern disciplinarian judge from Chicago.

Willie Keeler was the first Highlander to sign for 1905. Out of the blue, he walked into Frank Farrell's offices in the Fuller Building at 23rd and Broadway on November 22 and penned his name to a contract. The club didn't expect any others to sign until Griffith returned from his Montana ranch sometime around Christmas. Walter Clarkson, recently signed out of Harvard University and brother of Hall of Famer John Clarkson, spent November and December at the Griffith ranch hunting and trying to put on weight for the upcoming season.

Griffith's time at the Montana ranch wasn't always a relaxing vacation. There was work to be done and business interests to oversee. More than a few times, he drove cattle and other livestock to the local railroad depot for transport and sale. He accompanied his investment to Chicago or another major city where they were sold. He saw to all the minor details along the way. In essence, the ranch was a business and all that that entails. Like any business, there were market and economic concerns. As he described in a 1907 interview, "I had a long talk with Secretary [William] Loeb when I was in Washington this week. The Standard Oil Company practically owns the State [Montana]. The Beef Trust has all the cattle raisers broke and between the Standard Oil, the Beef Trust and the railroads, the people of that country are simply slaves...I saw the finest kind of cattle starving last winter while waiting for promised cars to take stock to the markets. I made some money, as I was in a position to put in plenty of fodder and hold my stock over. In fact, I fed for other people, but the conditions are something awful for the ranchers in Montana, and it is all due to the trusts."[215]

A *Washington Post* article on December 11 examined, "Players who are rich." After discussing Al Spalding, Al Reach and George Wright who all made a killing in sporting goods, the article declared, "Griffith is a well-to-do ranch owner with Montana land enough, if it was in New York City, to out rich the Astor estate." Of course this is misleading; there was quite a difference in value between a 5,000-acre spread in Montana and one in New York City.

Chesbro and Powell combined for 845 innings in 1904. Their arms didn't rebound so quickly in 1905, especially, with the cold weather encountered in the spring. Orth was also experiencing arm troubles. Griff added Bill Hogg to the roster to pick up some of the slack but it is his own relief pitching and management of his entire pitching staff that year that eventually changed the game. Griffith became one of the game's first effective relief pitchers in 1905 and '06. He started only seven games in 1905 and two the following year; however, Clark led the league both years in games finished seventeen and fifteen, respectively. In 25 games and 102 innings in 1905 Griffith posted a 9-6-record with a 1.68 earned run average. He led the league in relief games, wins and earned run average. In 1906, his last significant year on the mound, he recorded a 3.02 earned run average over sixty innings.

On the management end, Griffith made far more pitching changes than any other manager in history to date. Historian John Thorn described Griffith as, "the first manager to make full use of his bullpen."[216] In fact, Griffith contemplated extensive relief pitching as far back as 1902. Before the season commenced he was planning on pulling the plug on White Sox pitcher Ned Garvin, "relieving him the moment that he begins to show his weakness." Garvin had a poor showing in 1901 with Milwaukee, posting a 7-20 record.[217] The concept of relief pitching, especially on a grand scale, upset baseball purists such as Henry Chadwick, the dean of sportswriters.

The Highlanders tossed only 88 complete games in 1905; no other team had less than 117. There were only 258 games in the American League that were not completed by their starters and New York accounted for 25% of them, 64. Griff seemed to make the right choice

---

[215] *Sporting Life*, June 15, 1907, p. 9

[216] John Thorn, *The Relief Pitcher*, 1979

[217] Garvin himself had actually relieved ten times in 1901 to lead the league.

when it came to pulling the starter, considering the club still led the league in shutouts. Though it was not a new idea to pull a pitcher for a pinch hitter, Griffith took the practice further than anyone had before. The late inning strategic replacement came from the wily mind of the Old Fox.

The new methods, as they always do, produced some backlash. Jack Taylor expressed the feeling of some on Griffith's staff, "As a manager, I think Griffith is prone to expect too much from his pitchers. He forgets that other pitchers hadn't the head and control he possessed. He knows what he used to do in a pinch, how he liked to have three balls and two strikes on a batter when the game was a tie and a runner at third, and still curve one over when the batter thought sure he would trust to nothing but a straight fastball. Because Griffith could do this kind of thing is what made him a great pitcher, but there are mighty few who can duplicate him. I've heard kicks that he yanks a man out too quickly. He expects them to do what he used to do and they can't do it."

Again, Griffith had fewer complete games than any other manager in 1906. With his strategic shuffling Griff was able to coax a second-place finish out of a club that was fifth in team earned run average. Extensive relief pitching wasn't the only innovation Clark contributed during his time in New York. On August 2, 1906, he started the eighth inning in relief of Jack Chesbro and switched catcher Red Kleinow with Ira Thomas. Rotating the batting order, Griffith inserted himself in the #8-slot where the catcher was batting and Thomas in the #9-slot where the pitcher was batting. A common ploy now especially in the National League, it is the first-known double-switch in major league history.[218]

Clark also popularized the squeeze play in 1905, making the Highlanders the first club to consistently capitalize on the strategy.[219] Some say he even named it. The *Washington Post* exclaimed, "Manager Griffith says he has a new one called the 'squeeze play,' which is working wonders."[220] He claimed the idea came to him during a 1904 contest when Jack Chesbro misread a sign. On third base at the time Chesbro thought he saw the steal sign, so he took off for home. Startled to see Chesbro barreling home, batter Willie Keeler virtually threw his bat at the ball, in essence bunting the pitch. Both men landed safely.[221]

---

[218] "Detroit easy for New York," *New York Times*, August 3, 1906, p. 8

[219] The squeeze play was first utilized on June 16, 1894 in a game between Yale and Princeton. "The Most Perfect Thing in America," *Everybody's Magazine*, 1911, p. 445

[220] "Baseball Notes," *Washington Post*, April 9, 1905, p. S1

[221] "How Squeeze Play Began," *Washington Post*, January 12, 1908, p. S4

Spring training 1905 started with a squabble. Los Angeles Angels' owner Jim Morley didn't want to give up Hal Chase. He claimed Chase was drafted illegally and signed the first baseman to a contract with the Angels for the upcoming season. In the middle of the argument was Los Angeles' manager Pop Dillon, Griffith's cousin. After trading barbs in the press Clark sent a representative to California to drag Chase away. The newest Highlander arrived in camp on March 28.

The club opened with a 4-2 victory by Jack Chesbro on April 14. Griffith started his first game on the 27th and tossed a four-hit, 1-0 shutout over Philadelphia's Eddie Plank. Clark's second start on May 22 was also a shutout over Detroit but he was ejected in the second inning. After warming up, Griffith tossed his first offering of the inning. Umpire Tom Kelly called it a ball and Griffith hit the roof. The pitcher was removed in favor of Hogg who completed the 2-0-contest with eight strikeouts. Clark, still fresh, started the next day, losing 5-4. He didn't make another start until September.

With the club in last place on May 31, Farrell and Griffith sat the team down at the hotel and blasted them for sloppy play. John Anderson was shipped to Washington. Griffith vowed to find replacements for any slackers. Patsy Dougherty was suspended for poor performance. When Dougherty retorted that he'd rather retire to his farm, Griffith stood firm, "Well Pat, old boy, retire as soon as you like and it will save me the trouble of releasing you."[222]

During an argument in the fifth inning on June 9, Griffith charged to the plate to enter the fray. Cleveland catcher Fritz Buelow threw his glove at the Highlanders' manager. The benches emptied, requiring police to intercede and escort Griffith, Buelow and Indians pitcher Addie Joss from the park. On Sunday August 6, Clark fell ill of food poisoning after spending the day at Coney Island.[223] Future great Ty Cobb made his major league debut against Chesbro on August 30. Griff tossed his second shutout on September 6, a seven-hitter won with two runs in the ninth. He tossed a 10-1, complete game victory over Detroit on October 3. The Highlanders sank to sixth place in 1905 with a 71-78-record; yet, they drew a strong 310,000 fans.

Clark joined the American League's rules committee over the winter in January 1906, remaining a member even through his tenure with

---

[222] "Pat Dougherty Suspended," *Washington Post*, June 1, 1905, p. 8

[223] *Sporting Life*, August 12, 1905, p. 5

the National League and for many years to come. He would now be changing the game's rules from the inside.

The Highlanders performed well in 1906, finishing second with ninety wins. They also outdrew the Giants for the first time, 435,000 to 403,000. This was made possible by the extension of the subway, which finally reached Hilltop Park by summer. Farrell boasted of a $90,000-profit. Griffith worked his pitching staff much the same way as in 1905 but he only toed the rubber in seventeen games. After this season, Clark's pitching career was virtually over. Never a big strikeout threat after reaching the majors, he finished among the all-time leaders in fewest whiffs per nine innings, 2.54, behind Eddie Rommel and Ted Lyons.

A few years later, Griff described why he quit pitching, "Baseball is constantly changing. Why I had almost as much speed when I quit pitching as ever in my career. I had more curves, far better control, and I think more generalship…Take a great pitcher of today, for example. He may have wonderful speed and marvelous curves, but the batters get wise to him after a while. Then his day is over. I remember in my own experience. I always had a jump on the ball, its life, in other words. But finally that left. It happens all the time."[224]

On May 4, Griffith and the Highlanders' bench rode opposing starter Chief Bender particularly hard, calling out ethnic slurs to get the pitcher's goat. It proved effective as Bender was tossed from the game after slamming his glove to the ground and arguing a play in the fifth inning. It's worth noting that New York's starter that day Louis Leroy was a Native American as well. Philadelphia sent an impressive stable to the mound that day, Bender, Rube Waddell and Eddie Plank, in the 6-2 loss. Bender exacted his revenge the following day, pitching a complete game 9-3 victory against the Highlanders and also smacking a three-run home run to the right field wall.

On May 7, Griffith got into a row with umpire Tim Hurst. Managing on the base paths, Clark tossed his hat in the air in protest to a Hurst call and charged the umpire. During the argument, Griffith accidentally stepped on the umpire's foot. Hurst reared back but stopped short of punching the manager. He then took Clark by the lapel and arm, ushering him to the dugout. Griffith pulled away but ended up with a fat lip anyway. Washington third baseman Lave Cross interceded, calming Griff and walking him to the bench. It didn't take long for Clark to find

---

[224] "Sees Game changing," *Washington Post*, January 2, 1910, p. S4

another fault with the umpire and the two were at it again. Police entered the fray and escorted Griffith from the field.[225] Ban Johnson thought about it for a week and finally suspended both men for five days.

Clark made his first start on May 31, a complete game victory over Philadelphia. In St. Louis in early August Griffith was teaching his men a lesson with a cue stick when they decided to play a trick on him. They conned the manager into a pickup game with an "elderly gentleman." Griffith sat down while the stranger broke but he never got the table back. Amazed, Clark asked the man his name and he was revealed to be former world billiards champion Alfredo de Oro.

De Oro once come to the rescue of a raw seventeen-year-old ballplayer lost in Cuba. In early 1891, Al Lawson organized a barnstorming tour of the country. John McGraw was a part of the contingent. After one of the games, McGraw became separated from his fellow Americans, ending up lost four miles from his hotel and amid a mob of Cubans whom he couldn't communicate with. Luckily, he ran into de Oro who hailed the youngster a cab back to the hotel.

At the onset of August Clark saw a specialist in Detroit for a supposed "nervous condition." A doctor recommended that he quit his job. Obviously, that was out of the question.[226] His recovery was slow, as he felt ill much of the latter part of the season.

Griffith was suspended indefinitely after being ejected again on August 27. He refused to leave the park, managing from the grandstand. Ban Johnson witnessed the spectacle, banning the manager until September 5. Clark's boys set a record while he was away, by sweeping five doubleheaders in six days. Griffith started his second and last game on the 20th. He left after the fourth inning of what ended up being a 2-2-tie caused by a rain washout in the eighth. Griffith caused quite a stir among the newsmen with a claim that Detroit pitcher Bill Armour somehow slipped a rubber ball into the September 24 contest. Umpire Tim Hurst just ignored the manager's ravings.

Clark used some old National League delaying tactics on September 27 after the Highlanders tied the score in the fifth inning in the backend of a doubleheader in Cleveland. The game was called for darkness, causing 12,000 patrons to chase the New Yorkers from the field.

---

[225] "Umpire and Player Clash," *New York Times*, May 8, 1906, p. 6

[226] *Sporting Life*, August 11, 1906, p. 3

Like other winters, Ban Johnson spent a week in November at Griffith's ranch hunting and amassing new stories for the newspapermen. Also in November, Clark led a hunting party into Canada.

The Highlanders slipped to fifth place in 1907. Griffith, the pitcher, only entered four games all in relief. Before the season even started, it was evident that Clark was getting restless. He entered into a partnership with his old California buddies Joe Cantillon and Norris L. "Tip" O'Neill to buy a sheep ranch in Montana. The plan was to each put up about $7,000 as an initial stake. O'Neill, president of the Western League, would oversee the operation during the summer while the other two attended to their ball clubs. Clark was already successfully raising cattle but saw a bigger windfall in sheep. The idea never left the planning stages. In the fall, Griffith contemplated leaving baseball to breed horses full-time. He already had over a hundred on his ranch, and figured the enterprise would be much more lucrative than baseball. Perhaps the graying manager was looking to settle down at age 37 after twenty years in the game. Clark made even bigger plans in 1908; he wanted a ball club.

An interesting game took place in Chicago on May 26. Big Ed Walsh had a 4-1 lead in the fifth inning as rain began to fall. Griffith pulled starter Al Orth to delay the game, hoping for a rainout before the contest became official. Inserting himself on the mound, Clark took forever to warm up. It was pouring by then and umpire Jack Sheridan called for a delay. The ploy backfired on the Highlanders, as play resumed after only ten minutes. Griffith did his best to delay further, even allowing a ball to roll through his legs so the last out wouldn't register. Sheridan threatened to forfeit the game to the White Sox but it actually lasted into the sixth inning. Walsh was immortalized with a rain shortened, five-inning no-hitter.[227]

Griffith was ejected for excessive arguing by umpire Jack Sheridan on June 4. The Highlanders were crushed on June 12, 16-4, making eleven errors in the process, enough to make any manager irate. Griffith became absolutely livid when his hometown crowd began cheering for the Tigers and booing his men. While he was leaving the field after the game, Griffith encountered a local dry goods merchant, Mr. Frank, who was complementing the Tigers' budding star Ty Cobb. Griffith clocked the man in the jaw and was chased to the clubhouse by

---

[227] The Highlanders' only run occurred in the first inning after Walsh walked Kid Elberfeld and Hal Chase. Two wild pitches later, Elberfeld scored.

the businessman's friends. Frank threatened to swear out a warrant. In court Griffith declared self-defense and paid a fine.

The Highlanders lost 16-5 on June 28 in a game noted for sore-armed catcher Branch Rickey allowing thirteen Washington stolen bases.[228] Washington manager Cantillon was sitting around a New York hotel on June 29 between games with Griffith's club, when he received a phone call from Cliff Blankenship. Blankenship, the Nats' backup catcher, was injured so Cantillon sent him on a scouting expedition to Weiser, Idaho. Cantillon learned of his newest acquisition, Walter Johnson, the man who brought Griffith his greatest riches and happiest moments in the game. Blankenship also signed Clyde Milan during the same trip. Griffith remained sore about the acquisition, until he became the Senators manager of course. His pitcher Bill Hogg received a telegram from a friend in Weiser about Johnson three weeks before Blankenship signed the pitcher. Hogg simply tossed it aside without any further thought.

The story illustrates just how time sensitive spotting budding talent was prior to the institution of the amateur free agent draft. Teams were often overwhelmed with tips on prospects. Senators' executive Ben Minor received a favorable report on Johnson much earlier. It was just one of hundreds of casual tips he'd received over the years. He discarded the initial one. After several more communiqués on Johnson, he finally mentioned it to Cantillon.[229] If Blankenship hadn't been injured, there is no telling when the Senators might have gotten around to looking over the young ballplayer. This just goes to show how a little luck, a quick-response and having an experienced scouting staff can change a team's fortunes. In this instance that club could very well have not been Washington.

Clark started having some personnel trouble in 1907; the men were grumbling, especially Kid Elberfeld. In part, they were disgruntled with the manager's new policy against smoking cigarettes. Elberfeld was feuding all season with Wid Conroy, Jimmy Williams, Ira Thomas and Hal Chase. In July, Frank Farrell had enough and suspended Elberfeld for "indifferent play in the field and at bat." The shortstop was pulling the same malaise routine he did with George Stallings in 1903 to force a trade. It didn't work this time. Finally, Elberfeld apologized to Griffith and the team and was reinstated on August 15. The Highlanders sputtered all

---

[228] After that, Griffith started talking about making an outfielder out of Rickey. *Sporting Life*, July 27, 1907

[229] Frank H. Young, "The Ivory Hunters of Baseball," *Washington Post*, June 2, 1929, p. SM3

season, dropping to the second division with a 70-78 record. Off season rumors suggested that Griff's days in New York were numbered, potentially being placed by Stallings or George Davis as manager of the franchise by Opening Day.

In December, Griff traipsed to Grand Island, Nebraska to talk Fred Glade into joining the Highlanders after acquiring the pitcher in a trade. Glade didn't want to play for an east coast club, having grown up in rural Nebraska. Over the previous four years with the St. Louis Browns, he posted a 52-63 record, which may have been significantly better with a little more run support. Glade loved baseball but wasn't financially dependent on it; his family owned a decades-old, profitable milling business. He first entered pro ball in 1898 with Fort Worth. From there, he was purchased by Des Moines in 1900 and signed by the Chicago Cubs at the end of 1901.

The pitcher took part in spring training with the Cubs in 1902 but mysteriously disappeared before the season opened and was promptly suspended. He finally contacted manager Frank Selee in mid May and rejoined the club. His major league debut took place on May 27, being tagged with the loss while giving up eight runs in eight innings. That was the end of Glade's career in Chicago. He finished the year with St. Joseph in the Western League. However, he did make an impression on at least one baseball man. In a post season interview, umpire Hank O'Day mentioned that the fastest pitcher he'd seen all year was Glade and he had high hopes for the righthander when he learned to control his wildness.

He continued to pitch for St. Joseph until being picked up by the Browns for the 1904 season. He turned in a solid rookie season with an 18-15 record in 35 games. On July 14, he struck out 15 Senators. At the end of 1907, Glade, disgruntled in St. Louis, was making noise about quitting baseball to run the family business. Browns manager Jimmy McAleer was only too happy to unload the pitcher to Griffith. With New York he pitched five games, losing four, for the Highlanders. By June 1908, Glade had a sore arm, a touch of malaria and really didn't want to be in New York. In St. Louis on June 21, he was pulled from the game by Griffith and fined $25 for failing to cover first base. In a huff Glade told Griff he was leaving the club and going home. The manager shot back, "Go on home and stay there until you are ready to pay the fine. You can't pitch another game until the fine is paid."[230]

---

[230] *Sporting Life*, June 27, 1908 and June 6, 1908

The trade acquiring Glade and his ineffectiveness for the club was one of the final nails in Griffith's New York coffin. He tried to trade for Glade as early as 1906. On November 5, 1907, he gave up Jimmy Williams, Hobe Ferris and Danny Hoffman for Glade, Charlie Hemphill and Harry Niles. Hemphill proved to be the only plus from the trade, while Williams and Hoffman did well for the Browns.

After Griff resigned, Glade promised new manager Kid Elberfeld that he'd rejoin the club, but it never happened. The pitcher signed a contract with the Highlanders in February 1909 but later sent then-manager George Stallings a letter stating that he would be unable to join the club at the start of spring training. He had business obligations to attend to in Nebraska. Despite rumors and communications to the contrary, Glade never rejoined the team.

After his father passed away, Fred became president of the Henry Glade Milling Company in August 1911. Within two years the mill was operating 18 hours a day and producing nearly 400 barrels a day with annual revenue that topped $650,000. Business hit a snag during World War I, necessitating a merger with three other milling enterprises to form Nebraska Consolidated Mills. In 1922, NCM doubled its capacity with the purchase of the Updike Mill in Omaha. NCM now produced enough in one week to feed the entire state for a year. In 1971, the operation was renamed ConAgra. Through a complicated evolution and extensive diversification the company thrives today. Their brands are readily recognized today: Banquet, Chef Boyardee, Healthy Choice, Hunt's and Libby's, to name just a few.

Griff headed back to New York from his ranch in late January. Along the way he stopped in Chicago to make a trade and see his tailor. During spring workouts in Atlanta, Clark was rocked when he took the mound and never did enter a game during the regular season. On May 5, President Teddy Roosevelt received Griffith and his men at the White House. Roosevelt was never much of a baseball fan but the President talked of his youngest son, Quentin, who loved the game and played on a team with Secretary of War William Howard Taft's son, Charlie. Clark grandly threw his support behind Roosevelt for a third term. Ten-year-old Quentin pitched a fit when he discovered that he missed meeting some of his baseball idols.

That same day, Griffith was suspended indefinitely for arguing with umpire Tommy Connolly on the 4th and failing to leave the park as told. Clark simply parked himself in the pavilion behind third base. On June 9, the Highlanders stood in fourth place a mere half game out of first. It fell apart and the team tanked, losing twelve of the next 13 games to end up in sixth place with a 24-32-record. After a 6-6-tie called for darkness on June 24 against the A's, Griffith summoned team owner Frank Farrell to the Majestic Hotel in Philadelphia. The manager resigned feeling discouraged over the losses and believing that a replacement might bring better luck to the boys. At least that's what he told the press. To highlight his frustration, Griffith was ejected from his last game as the Yankees manager by umpire Rip Egan.

A host of problems were later unearthed between Farrell and Griffith. In truth, it is unclear whether the manager was actually fired or resigned or was forced to resign, possibly after a huge blowup. For one, Clark was unhappy with Farrell's interference, particularly concerning the owner's attempt to suspend pitcher Bill Hogg after a poor outing. Griffith was also being told which pitchers to start. Further frustrating the manager, Farrell and Devery were refusing to fund any new acquisitions. On the other hand, Farrell was irate over the recent losing skid and had been complaining about unsuccessful trades that Griffith made sending Jimmy Williams, Joe Yeager, Danny Hoffman and Hobe Ferris to St. Louis for Harry Niles, Fred Glade, Charlie Hemphill and Branch Rickey. Rumors also suggested that Kid Elberfeld was undermining the manager, which is wholly believable considering his disposition.

In reality the losing streak doomed the manager. Farrell and Devery decided that a change needed to be made. The above-mentioned trade also sorely stuck in the craw of the Highlander owners, especially since the Browns were riding atop the league at the time. St. Louis also had former Highlanders Jack Powell and Harry Howell, obtained in trades with Griffith, who were consistently winning for the club. The Highlander executives felt that Browns' manager Jimmy McAleer was consistently getting the best of Griffith.

The owners wanted Willie Keeler to take over the club, but Keeler got wind of this idea. Not wanting the job and especially with the circumstances of replacing his friend Griffith, Keeler went to Philadelphia to hide out for a couple of days to avoid the situation. Farrell then contacted Ned Hanlon about taking over the club but after being turned down gave the job to Kid Elberfeld. Elberfeld proved a disaster; he didn't have the temperament to run a club. He later admitted to consulting his wife on his starting rotation throughout the season.[231] The club was demoralized under his leadership. First baseman Hal Chase, upset at not

---

[231] Terry Simpkins, "Kid Elberfeld" entry in *Deadball Stars of the American League*, 2006

being chosen manager, jumped the club in September and returned home to California.

Clark made some off-the-cuff remarks about being done with baseball. He was exhausted. The *Washington Post* claimed that he was "a nervous wreck as a result of the Highlanders poor showing."[232] The *Sporting Life* summed up the situation, "Up to the time Clark Griffith became a manager he was a jovial fellow of good health. Today he is a nervous wreck."[233] He considered a trip out west to a resort in Wisconsin to fish and recuperate. Instead, he stayed close to the game, joining Joe Cantillon in Philadelphia to watch a Nationals-Athletics contest and rest for a few days.[234] He didn't stand pat for long. Within a week he was negotiating to purchase the Birmingham Barons of the Southern Association for $30,000. That didn't pan out but Griffith kept looking. August rumors had him managing the St. Louis Cardinals[235] or perhaps the Washington Nationals. He even talked about forming a whole new baseball league, one in his estimation that would rock the baseball world. His plan called for a group of midwestern clubs with the possibility of an eastern presence like Pittsburgh. This didn't come to fruition either.

Clark hooked up with Reds' president Garry Herrmann at the World Series and spent much of October in Cincinnati. Rumors naturally circulated that he would soon take over the team, irking John Ganzel who was recently given the job. The idea of Griffith returning to the National League was a shocker. Seemingly just a few years ago, he was the man leading the charge away from the established league. Griffith initially turned down the Cincinnati job. At the time the minors were in a dispute with the majors and there looked like a possible secession was in the making. He wanted to see how things would play out, possibly easing his way into club ownership, either in the minors or in the show.

At the end of October, Griff headed to his ranch to prepare some cattle for transport for sale in Chicago. The cattle reached Chicago on November 13. Clark and his brother Earl handled the business transactions over the next week. At the time, Herrmann was relentlessly trying to ink Griff to a deal to manage his club. On November 18,

---

[232] "Griffith Resigns Job," *Washington Post*, June 25, 1908, p. 8

[233] *Sporting Life*, July 4, 1908, p. 11

[234] "Team is Home Again," *Washington Post*, July 2, 1908, p. 8

[235] "Current Notes picked up from Sporting Arena," *Washington Post*, August 23, 1908, p. S3

Griffith tersely wired Herrmann from Buffalo that, "You better cut me out as am not ready to talk business."[236] Clark rethought the wording of the telegram and immediately fired off another stating, "I just wired you that you better cut me out of the Cincinnati proposition. I did not do this because I have signed with anyone else but because I am undecided what to do and I think it is up to me to tell you where I stand."[237]

Undeterred, Herrmann contacted Ban Johnson and requested that he intercede on his behalf in the negotiations with Griffith. Johnson immediately wired Griffith in Buffalo, advising him to take the Reds' offer. Johnson claimed that he was mystified why Griffith hadn't accepted the offer, but expected him to eventually sign.[238] The reason for Clark's hesitation was soon evident; he was negotiating to take over a minor league franchise.

Clark hooked up with minor league owner George Tebeau and Joseph O'Brien, president of the American Association, in November. Rumors suggested that Tebeau was planning to sell Griffith his Kansas City franchise for $25,000 and perhaps his Louisville one as well for $35,000. Tebeau, in turn, was also looking to purchase the Buffalo franchise in the Eastern League. The fact that O'Brien was in the mix suggested a deeper plan in the works. Baseball men wonder if the trio was perhaps plotting the introduction of a third major league.[239] Clark wanted his own club since the formation of the American League. It wasn't to be; the National Association settled its dispute on December 10.

After months of haggling, Clark was finally cornered by Cincinnati official Max Fleischman. As a result, he signed with Herrmann on December 11 to manage the Reds. The Old Fox was headed back to the National League. John McGraw and others happily welcomed him back into the league.

---

[236] *Western Union* telegram dated November 18, 1908 found in Griffith's Hall of Fame file

[237] *Western Union* telegram dated November 18, 1908 found in Griffith's Hall of Fame file

[238] Letter from Ban Johnson to Garry Herrmann dated November 18, 1908 found in Griffith's Hall of Fame file

[239] "Talk of New League," *Washington Post*, November 25, 1908, p. 8

CHAPTER SEVEN

BACK IN THE NATIONAL LEAGUE

Griffith took over a lackluster Cincinnati club in 1909 that hadn't placed in the first division since 1904. In fact, the club had never really challenged for the pennant since moving into the National League in 1890.[240] He popped them to fourth place that first year but they still resided a distant 33.5 games out of first place. For getting them into the first division, the manager earned a $1,000 bonus, a clause written into his contract.[241] The Reds didn't fare much better Griffith's other two years 1910-1911, fifth and sixth place, respectively, 29 games out each year. There were no pennant chases in Cincinnati for Clark. The congenial Griffith got along with club president Garry Herrmann well, as he did with everyone, save perhaps umpires. He was also well paid, $7,500 a year, but Clark never felt truly at ease being back in the National League. He was also getting very antsy about joining the ranks of the club owners.

Herrmann, a Cincinnati native and typesetter by trade, entered local politics at age 23 in 1882, becoming a member of the Cincinnati Board of Education. He later found a job as a printer working for a local newspaper publisher. In 1887, he was hired as an assistant clerk in the Police Court. In his spare time Herrmann studied the laws governing municipalities,

---

[240] The Reds were originally an American Association club.

[241] *Sporting Life*, October 16, 1909, p. 11

becoming the local expert on such. Cincinnati's Republican Party boss George B. Cox noticed this and soon promoted him to the position of Water Works commissioner. He proved to be quite competent introducing modern management principles to the municipal government. It was under Herrmann that Cincinnati's modern water works system was built.

Herrmann became one of Cox's lieutenants, Rudolph Hynicka the other, administering the affairs of government and his commercial endeavors. Hynicka oversaw Hamilton County and Herrmann administered city affairs. It was said that Herrmann carried Cincinnati's financial stats in his head. As the *New York Times* stated, "For years the word of these two men in their separate fields was final." The graft system fed Cox, his two lieutenants, and others hundreds of thousands of dollars for years. Harold Seymour in his work *Baseball* painted a more comical picture of Herrmann. "Herrmann was a political tool of George B. Cox, boss of Hamilton County, Ohio. Lincoln Steffens reported how Herrmann and Cox's other lieutenant, Rudolph Hynicka (sic), once were talking to some outsiders when Cox broke in, "...when I whistle you dogs come out of your holes, don't you? They were still. "Don't you, Garry," he repeated. "That's right," said Garry.[242]

In July 1902, Herrmann opened discussions with John Brush about purchasing the Cincinnati Reds. Later in the month after the Baltimore Orioles debacle, Ban Johnson visited Cincinnati intent on adding an American League franchise in that city for the 1903 season. Herrmann was seen holding a private discussion with Johnson, which naturally fueling speculation. Further pressure was placed on Brush as Cox threatened to run a streetcar line through the center of his ballpark, the newly restructured Palace of the Fans. On August 9, the announcement came that Brush sold the club to Cox, Herrmann, Cincinnati mayor Julius Fleischmann and his brother Colonel Max Fleischmann of the famous Fleischmann Yeast Company family. The new coalition paid $150,000 for all but 1/20 of the club.

Though Herrmann at all times owned an insignificant portion of the club, he was elected president and retained that position until his retirement due to poor health in 1927. The genial Herrmann was also elected to head the new National Commission after the signing of the renewed National Agreement in 1903 that brought relative peace between the National and American Leagues. The position offered no salary but perhaps more importantly provided Herrmann with a significant expense

---

[242] Harold Seymour, *Baseball: The Early Years*, 1960, page 9

account, $12,000, which financed his love of high living: travel, food and drink.

The commission also comprised the two league presidents. The nominal head of the commission, Herrmann tended to let Ban Johnson, an old friend from his days as a Cincinnati sportswriter, lead the commission. That point is usually overstated as the Cincinnati boss was at the center of most controversies during his time on the commission. Back home, Herrmann continued to oversee political affairs in Cincinnati until the Cox organization was defeated in the mayoral race that elected a Democrat in 1912.

The first major controversy of the 1909 season was sparked on April 23. In the sixth inning, Honus Wagner jumped from one batter's box to the other trying to disrupt the pitcher after amassing a 3-0 count. Reds' pitcher Harry Gasper was in the middle of his windup at the time. Griffith protested to umpire Bill Klem to no avail. After the game, a 2-1 Reds loss, he filed a formal protest with the league. National League president upheld the Reds, declaring the contest a no decision.[243]

New league, old habits - Griffith was ejected for arguing with umpire Stephen Cusack on May 13. The next day acting National League president John Heydler suspended the manager and his outfielder Bob Bescher and catcher Frank Roth for three days.[244] The National League jumped from 94 ejections in 1908 to 119 the following year. Helping to up the numbers, Griffith was ejected three times in 1909,[245] topped only by Cardinals' manager Roger Bresnahan with four. For his career, Clark was ejected 68 times, 62 of them as a manager. His totals for career ejections and ejections as a manager ranked second only to John McGraw at the time.[246]

During Clark's tenure in Cincinnati there were quite a few disputes centering on trades. Most of them involved Herrmann's penchant for loosely playing with the rules but Griffith had his troubles as well. The Highlanders and American League filed charges on August 20 against their former manager for allegedly tampering with pitcher Hippo Vaughn. Vaughn was property of the Highlanders, playing a couple of games for the club in 1908. In August 1909, he was ordered to report to

---

[243] "East hears of 'Dr. Creamer,'" *Chicago Tribune*, April 25, 1909, p. C1

[244] "Clark Griffith Suspended," *Washington Post*, May 15, 1909, p. 8

[245] He was also ejected on September 1.

[246] Lyle Spatz, *The SABR Baseball List and Record Book*, 2007

Rochester, but en route he ran into the Reds' manager. Griffith enticed him to skip his train and join the Reds, claiming that the Highlanders violated the rules by farming the pitcher two years in a row. As such, Griffith believed that on appeal the National Commission would award Vaughn to his friend George Tebeau in Louisville who would in turn transfer his contract to Cincinnati. Vaughn worked out with the Reds in uniform for a week. The Highlanders protested and ultimately regained their pitcher. Griffith may have had his hand slapped over the incident but he proved a wise judge of talent. Vaughn went on to post 178 major league victories, mostly with the Cubs. Griffith actually did obtain Vaughn, claiming him off waivers from New York in June 1912 while with the Senators; however, he traded him two months later.

Griffith took the mound for the only time in 1909 on the next to last day of the season, October 3. On the backend of a doubleheader at home he went all nine innings, giving up eleven hits and losing 8-1. By 1909, other managers were adopting Griffith's method of pulling their starters, including his old friend Joe Cantillon in Washington. Complete games were significantly reduced in Pittsburgh, Cincinnati, Philadelphia, St. Louis and Boston in the National League. Boston, New York and Washington followed suit in the American League. Griffith still changed pitchers more frequently than any other manager but the gap was closing.

Griffith took off for Montana shortly after the World Series. Joe Tinker, among others, stopped by the ranch to spend time with the Griffiths and take in some hunting and discuss the possibility of joining the Reds for 1910. Tinker was also rehearsing for an upcoming vaudeville act. Clark an old frontiersman loved to deer hunt. His experiences, advice and strategies filled a column for the *Washington Post* on December 12.

Griffith was always trying something new to help his men improve their skills. In January 1910 he mailed a self-made apparatus to Bob Bescher's house designed to help him develop into a switch hitter. Thick rubber cords reaching from the floor to the ceiling suspended a baseball about waist high. The regulation-sized ball was fitted with an extra cover to promote longevity. The point was for the batter to hit the ball and to keep hacking away while it was in motion, a forerunner of the modern baseball trainers. Bescher was a natural lefthander who was forced by coaches when he was young to bat strictly from the right side. With Clark's help he switch-hit in the majors for eleven seasons. Bescher and Griffith were like-minded men. They spent a good amount of time together during the off-seasons at the Griffith ranch hunting and tending to the cattle. Bescher worked punching cattle on a Nebraska ranch after high school.

At spring training in Hot Springs in February Clark unveiled his newly invented pitching machine. Obviously, he spent the off-season tinkering with gadgets. The device was similar to a shooting gallery. Wires were strung which suspended discs; a pitcher standing 60'6" away would try to hit the discs and in theory improve his control on the mound. The machine also included a ball return. Clark had scorers keeping count of hits and misses, thus tabulating strikes and balls, to gauge how his recruits were doing.

Clark continued to gain a reputation as an early Captain Hook, if you will. It was not uncommon for him to use fourteen or sixteen players in a game, virtually unheard of before. Nearly his entire squad could be called on any given day.

One of Clark's challenges in Cincinnati was starting catcher Larry McLean. In 1909, Griffith named McLean team captain and even had him run the club for a few days while he was sick. Problem was, McLean was a heavy drinker and couldn't always be counted on. Eventually, the title was stripped at the end of 1910 after a drinking binge that resulted in a week's suspension.

It's always interesting when coming upon salary distributions. On June 14, 1910, Griffith penned his salary list on stationary from the Copley Square Hotel in Boston.[247] It reads: Griffith $10,000; Frank Bancroft, club secretary, $2,700; Mike Martin, team trainer, $1,050; Bid McPhee, scout, $1,500; Fred Beebe $3,300; Bob Bescher $2,500; Bill Burns, of World Series fix fame, $4,000; Tommy Clarke $2,000; Tom Downey $2,400; Joe Doyle $2,700; Dick Egan $3,200; Art Fromme $3,100; Harry Gasper $2,400; Dick Hoblitzell $3,200; Hans Lobert $3,200; Larry McLean $4,200; Tommy McMillan $1,800; Ward Miller $1,800; Mike Mitchell $3,800; Dode Paskert $2,400; Art Phelan $1,500; Frank Roth $2,200; Jack Rowan $2,000; George Suggs $2,400; Sam Woodruff $2,100. The total payroll was $71,450 or $56,200 just for the players.

Late in the year, Griffith drafted former White Sox Daredevil Dave Altizer off the Minneapolis roster of the American Association, where he led the league with 111 runs scored. Clark told the ballplayer he didn't need him in 1910 but to be ready for spring training. With the minor league season over, Altizer returned home to Chicago. In early October Griffith decided he did indeed need Altizer but he couldn't locate the player. Apparently, he was busy planning his wedding and was nowhere to be found. Not to be denied, Clark placed the following classified ad in the *Chicago Tribune* on October 3:

---

[247] A copy resides in his Hall of Fame file.

PERSONAL - WILL DAVE ALTIZER, BASE-
ball player, please report to the Cincinnati Baseball Club at once?

CLARK GRIFFITH

manager

A reader who knew the whereabouts of Altizer woke Griffith's good friend in Chicago Jimmy Callahan at 7:30 a.m. Callahan promptly rounded up the ballplayer and shipped him to Cincinnati.

Like previous winters, major leaguers traveled to Cuba to play some exhibition games after the 1910 season, in November and December. The group included many Detroit Tigers and Philadelphia Athletics and was headlined by Ty Cobb. The two major league clubs played some tough Cuban teams and even each other. The Havana club was fortified with several black players from the Chicago Leland Giants, Pete Hill, Sam Lloyd, Grant Johnson and Bruce Petway.[248] The Almendares club boasted three men who also played in Organized Baseball with the New Britain of the Class-B Connecticut League, Luis Cabrera, Rafael Almeida and Armando Marsans.

Ban Johnson and Charles Comiskey took a vacation together in Cuba in January, while there they studied up on the baseball scene.[249] Cincinnati Reds' secretary Frank Bancroft, business manager Frank Van Croft and scout Louis Heilbroner joined the barnstorming trip, even sending back scouting reports. It wasn't Bancroft's first trip to the islands. He first traveled to Havana in December 1879 as manager of the barnstorming minor National Association Worcester, Massachusetts club. At the time, Cuban baseball was in its infancy; the first Cuban baseball league was just formed the previous year. In November 1908, Bancroft returned to Cuba with the Reds for a thirteen-game barnstorming trip.

Bancroft, born in 1846, joined the union army during the Civil War while still in his mid-teens. He became a drummer boy and eventually joined the cavalry. He never actually played professional ball, but nonetheless was signed to manage New Bedford of the International Association from his home state of Massachusetts in 1878. He proved to be a skilled organizer both on and off the field. Away from the game, Bancroft owned a hotel, a theatre, a roller rink and opera companies and

---

[248] "Joy in Cuba when Cobb Strikes Out," *New York Times*, December 18, 1910, p. C6
[249] "Johnson to study Baseball in Cuba," *New York Times*, January 19, 1911, p. 12

managed several hockey clubs. He managed major and minor league clubs until assuming the duties of business manager of the Reds, a post he held from 1892-1920. Bancroft managed more major league clubs, seven, than any other man. His only pennant came in 1884 with Louisville when Hoss Radbourn almost singlehandedly carried the club into the postseason.

Heilbroner sent Herrmann reports on Almeida. The scout recommended signing the player, stating that he is "worth some money...good fielder with good arm..." He cautioned however that, "He is a mulatto, speaks fair English."[250] "If he were a white man, he might be good for the big show."[251] After hearing the reports and learning that Cabrera, Almeida and Marsans were all property of New Britain, Herrmann contacted team owner Dan O'Neil trying to purchase all three. He also contacted several New England sportswriters to gain their opinions of the men. Their responses were mixed, positive on their playing ability, yet sprinkled with a few racially negative responses.

Griffith later enjoyed telling the story that he contacted Almeida about a tryout only to be conned into springing for a second train ticket for his interpreter. Unfazed, Clark bought the two tickets. He then recalled walking onto the field and seeing Almeida and his "interpreter" both shagging flies in the outfield. The interpreter was in full baseball uniform. The more he watched, the more Griffith focused on the interpreter, Marsans. It's an amusing story but fiction nonetheless. The Reds from the get-go were after all of O'Neil's Cuban players. Perhaps the point of Griffith's story was that he received quite a few favorable reports on Almeida but in the end he was especially enamored with Marsans' potential.

On June 15, O'Neil and Herrmann negotiated a thirty-day option on the players, settling on the price of $3,500 for Almeida and $2,500 for Marsans.[252] Cabrera was out of the picture by then. Problem was Almeida and Marsans had yet to report to New Britain; they were still in Cuba. When they heard of the interest from a major league club, they hopped on the U.S.S. *Mexico* on June 22, arriving in New York three days later.[253]

---

[250] Memo dated December 30, 1910, Nick C. Wilson, *Early Latino Ballplayers in the U.S.*, 2005, p. 25

[251] Memo dated January 4, 1911, Nick C. Wilson, *Early Latino Ballplayers in the U.S.*, 2005, p. 25

[252] Pirates' owner Barney Dreyfuss was also interested in the Cubans but wasn't about to pay $6,000.

[253] Immigration and Emigration, New York Passenger Lists, June 25, 1911 at Ancestry.com

Then they boarded a train for Connecticut. O'Neil's son accompanied the pair to Cincinnati to receive payment. The *Cincinnati Enquirer* notified their readers on June 23 that two "very dark-skinned" men were about to join the Reds.[254] Nervous about seeing their dark complexion, Herrmann met the men at the train station on the 28th. One report suggested that Herrmann nearly had a heart attack after seeing two African-American porters disembark, confusing them with the ballplayers.

"The decision taken by Cincinnati Reds' owner, president August "Garry" Herrmann and field manager Clark Griffith to sign Almeida and Marsans changed the direction of baseball forever."[255] Griffith didn't initiate the signing of the Cuban players in 1911 but it never would have happened without his backing. He was the manager; men before him and after him had and would quash such a plan. Griffith wanted to improve his floundering club, any way possible within his allotted budget. There is no truer sign of a baseball man. Almeida and Marsans would have to earn their way onto the roster just like very other member of the club.

It's hard to realize today just how revolutionary their decision was. The plan would never get off the ground, if the Reds didn't sell the two men to the racially conscious baseball community and general public. The first course of action was to wage a public relations campaign to outdo any potentially negative press the men's dark appearance might garner. The Reds decided to take the offense on several fronts: the men's character, their heritage and, failing that, formal documentation. The club and the press so intricately wove truth and falsehoods that it's nearly impossible to separate fact from fiction today.

To boost their character, the press focused on the players' wealth, as if that defined them. Almeida, in particular, was from a wealthy family. He was among the few who attended the University of Havana and in early 1911 he reportedly inherited $200,000, further marking him as a man of class and dignity. The press pushed the fact that the men were from families of affluent landowners and commercialists. Marsans, so the claim went, was among the select few Cubans to attend a university in the United States.[256] After the wealth factor was portrayed, the men supposedly passed several tests that no white ballplayer ever had to. Herrmann specifically state, "Both are perfect gentlemen." The

---

[254] *Cincinnati Enquirer*, June 23, 1911, quote found in Nick C. Wilson, *Early Latino Ballplayers in the U.S.*, 2005, p. 29

[255] Nick C. Wilson, *Early Latino Ballplayers in the U.S.*, 2005, p. 23

[256] The institution was never named and, in fact, the timeline didn't fit either.

Philadelphia Inquirer also chimed in, "Neither one drinks, are quiet and inoffensive players."[257] Was a Caucasian ballplayer ever qualified as such?

Almeida and Marsans' heritage received the most press. Their families had to be scrutinized. The plan was to distance them from their Cuban heritage, in essence to counter many Americans' negative perception of such. It was essential that they appeared to be racially pure. Almeida was declared a product of Portuguese royalty, a descendent of a Marquis. His father was Portuguese, his mother, born in Cuba, was a product of two Spanish parents. An elaborate and swashbuckling story was concocted of Marsans defiance of Spanish occupation in Cuba at age eleven. One of the biggest boosts the pair received was from Cuban sportswriter Victor Munoz who declared, "Both of these men are pure Spaniards, without a trace of Colored blood." With these requirements met the Cincinnati Enquirer proudly introduced the pair as, "Two of the purest bars of Castilian soap."[258]

Times being what they were, the men first had to produce documentation stating that they were of "Castilian and not Negro heritage." Lucky for the Reds, then New Britain owner Billy Hanna already gathered the necessary papers in the winter of 1909. He went to Cuba in response to fellow Connecticut League owners who were challenging the racial purity of his recruits. Hanna brought back documents, whether authentic or not, which hopefully resolved the issue.[259]

All this evidence was meant to counter negative stereotypes. Truth is many knew they were being duped. The pair surely "had some Afro-Cuban blood."[260] Negro league pioneer Rube Foster even jested that, "There were more Negroes on the team than there were Cubans."[261] There is no denying that Almeida and Marsans endured racially motivated taunts and threats throughout their professional careers, as did many of Griffith's Cuban recruits through the years.

---

[257] Nick C. Wilson, *Early Latino Ballplayers in the U.S.*, 2005, p. 30, quote taken from the Philadelphia Enquirer

[258] Adrian Burgos Jr., *Playing America's Game*, 2007, p. 98, quote taken from the *Cincinnati Inquirer*

[259] He obtained favorable documentation on all his Cuban players except Luis Padron; as a consequence, Padron had to be released.

[260] Peter C. Bjarkman, reference from Nick C. Wilson, *Early Latino Ballplayers in the U.S.*, 2005, p. 25

[261] April 1914 interview, reference from Nick C. Wilson, *Early Latino Ballplayers in the U.S.*, 2005, p. 25

The Cubans were introduced to the majors on a road trip in Chicago on July 4. Each pinch-hit late in the game and then took the field. Marsans hit .261 in 58 games in 1911, Almeida .313 in 36. Marsans played in the majors with four clubs through 1918, working full-time in about four seasons. Almeida only played for Cincinnati; his major league career was over in 1913, never appearing in more than fifty games in any given season. Interestingly, Almeida and Marsans were two of seventeen men to play in the Negro leagues or pre-Negro leagues and the major leagues prior to Jackie Robinson in 1947.[262] Five of the 17 worked for Griffith.

Griffith came under fire shortly after the 1911 season began. The club was floundering, frustrating team ownership and fans. He didn't take kindly to the negative portrayals in the press. As a result, he spent nearly the entire year feuding with Cincinnati sportswriters Jack Ryder and Bill Phelon.[263] By June, he wasn't even speaking to the pair.[264] Griff managed to keep his job at an ownership meeting on June 5 but the directors were clearly divided. By July, the team was openly discussing a replacement for 1912. Unbeknown to Griffith, Herrmann held secret meetings trying to lure Mike Donlin to take over the club during the summer. Rumors even suggested Griff's cousin, Frank Dillon, as a possible successor.

Clark was suspended again on July 29 for arguing with umpire Jim Johnstone. After the season Herrmann announced on October 12 that Griffith would not be brought back in 1912. Then, Herrmann vacillated after being petitioned by his ballplayers to keep the manager. In Clark's mind he was done with Cincinnati nonetheless. The Reds' president didn't make a move one way or the other, claiming surprise and anger when Griffith finally took it upon himself to sign with another club.

Rumors quickly put Griffith with the Browns or Nationals. New Red Sox owner Jimmy McAleer was also talking about signing Clark. Looking towards ownership again, Griffith thought about into buying the

---

[262] The list includes (with major league debut noted): Fleet Walker 1884; Weldy Walker 1884; Rafael Almeida 1911; Armando Marsans 1911; Mike Gonzalez 1912; Jack Calvo 1913; Alfredo Cabrera 1913; Angel Aragon 1914; Dolf Luque 1914; Jose Rodriquez 1916; Ricardo Torres 1920; Jose Acosta 1920; Pedro Dibut 1924; Mike Herrera 1925; Oscar Estrada 1929; Chico Hernandez 1942; Izzy Leon 1945.

[263] Phelon, a longtime reporter for the *Chicago Daily News*, had known Griffith since his first days in the majors.

[264] *Sporting Life*, September 16, 1911, p. 3

Providence club in the Eastern League. He enlisted Frank Navin of Detroit and plans were made for both to invest in the club, Griffith to run it and Navin to season young ballplayers there.[265] Griff was also rumored to be interested in the Lincoln franchise of the Western League.[266]

Clark hopped between New York and Chicago near the end of the year, making plans and getting advice. One of his stops was to Ban Johnson's office. There, Griffith expressed his interest in returning to the American League. The pair decided that the Nationals were a perfect fit; they were in desperate need of some direction. Johnson asked Washington president Tom Noyes to meet in Philadelphia on October 23. Clark then headed to D.C. to meet with the club's directors. The announcement was made on October 30. Given a three-year contract, Clark was the new manager and part owner of the Nationals. In fact, he was the largest single shareholder.

In 1911, Griffith picked up an option on a track of land near Joe Tinker's apple orchard in Yamhill County, Oregon near Newberg. The plan was to enter the fruit business. They joined up with Fielder Jones who sought an orchard in Sheridan, near Portland, Oregon. Griffith, Billy Sullivan, Patsy Dougherty and Doc White purchased acreage on Jones' spread. Griffith chipped in for ten acres.

Griffith was a victim of a Montana ranchers joke in December. While at his ranch in November, Clark admired an Angora goat, even commenting that it would make a fine mascot for his new club. He forgot all about the animal upon moving to Washington. That is until December 10 when he received a call at his office from his wife. The goat was delivered to their apartment, with a $7.50 delivery charge. They housed it in the basement of the apartment building and took it to the ballpark to graze.

---

[265] "Griffith unlikely to direct Nationals," *Washington Post*, October 16, 1911, p. 8

[266] "Griffith after Lincoln Team," *Chicago Defender*, November 18, 1911, p. 6

CHAPTER EIGHT

THAT BASEBALL GRAVEYARD

Washington was an initial member of the American League in 1901. It was perhaps the weakest member. The phrase "Washington – first in war, first in peace, and last in the American League" was already being bandied about before Griffith took over. Seven managers preceded him in the nation's capital. Throughout that time, the club failed to climb higher than sixth place, never winning more than 67 games. It was a challenge just to break fifty in the win column. They perennially posted attendance figures among the lowest in the game, in part, because they had the smallest population base to draw from in the American League. By any definition, the American League version of baseball in Washington was a complete flop.

In 1911, Thomas C. Noyes, Benjamin S. Minor and Edward Walsh administered the club. Noyes was born in January 1868 in D.C. to well-to-do parents. After graduating from Princeton, he became a reporter on the city staff of his father's newspaper the *Washington Evening Star*. He ascended to assistant city editor, then city editor before becoming treasurer after the death of his father.[267] In 1911 he was named vice president of the company.[268] Noyes became interested in baseball management as early as 1901. At that time he was among the contingent

---

[267] Thomas' father Crosby S. Noyes was a longtime Editor-in-Chief of the *Washington Star*.
[268] He was also president of the D.C. Board of Trade.

looking to revive the old American Association. In March 1904 Noyes and William Dwyer purchased 75% of the club out of receivership. Noyes then assumed the presidency in February 1905.

Minor joined Noyes as a club director in 1905, assuming the titles of secretary and general manager. Minor was born in July 1865 in King George County, Virginia. He graduated from law school in 1887 from the University of Virginia, where he also played for two years on the baseball squad as an outfielder and backup catcher.[269] He then moved to D.C., a Mecca for budding attorneys.[270] By the turn of the century, Minor built a large practice representing numerous local businesses and was well known as the general counsel for the Washington Gas Light Company. In 1903, he began representing Ban Johnson and the American League and was assigned the task of reorganizing the Senators at the end of the year.[271]

Noyes and Minor brought stability to the club; it turned a profit for the first time in 1905. The men had other full-time jobs. Running the Senators was almost a sideline. Day-to-day administration was left to the club's field manager. In 1911, that manager was Jimmy McAleer; however he bailed on the team on September 15, having recently purchased shares in the Boston Red Sox with John I. Taylor and Robert McRoy, Johnson's assistant.[272]

The team was deeply in debt in 1911 and attendance revenue, among the lowest in the league, wasn't paying the bills. On March 17, 1911 a plumber's blowlamp torched nearly the entire grounds at American League Park, save a small section of bleachers. Noyes decided to completely rebuild and to refurbish the entire field as well; he estimated the initial outlay to be in the neighborhood of $100,000.[273] The park reopened eighteen days later but without box seats or a roof. It was completed anew on July 24. To offset the costs, the Senators were considering doubling their outstanding capital stock. This was Clark's in to the ownership ranks.

The fact that McAleer had just bought into a major league club was further incentive for Griffith. McAleer was one of the initial managers

---

[269] Minor also played ball for the Bethel Military Academy.

[270] His father was a merchant in D.C., which helped spark Ben's practice.

[271] Minor's law firm was called Minor, Gatley and Drury. The name would change over the years, eventually to Drury, Lynham and Powell. They served as the Nationals' legal representative for well over fifty years.

[272] Ban Johnson himself was also rumored to be a part-owner of the Boston club.

[273] "Senators' Ball Park Burns; Plumber's Blow Lamp Cause," *Chicago Tribune*, March 18, 1911, p. 17

and recruiters for the American League. They were also teammates with Milwaukee back in 1888. He was now a club owner, as was John McGraw, Connie Mack, who begun investing in clubs back in 1890, and George Stallings. Griffith wondered when his time would come. When Garry Herrmann gave Clark his release in Cincinnati, it was almost a blessing. Griffith was a baseball man. That was all he wanted from life since he was seven years old. Sure he talked about getting out of the business and he had investments that would help with any transition, but all roads led back to the game for him. He tried at times to purchase major league clubs and had a slew of minor league opportunities but all fell through or didn't last for long. He just didn't have the financing to enter the major leagues at the time; the minor leagues weren't really where he wanted to be. He was at a crossroads in 1911, as he clearly related, "If I couldn't become part owner of the stock of a major league club, I decided to acquire one in the minors. I was through with managing teams for a salary. I wanted to get my money invested in baseball. I ought to have had it years ago. I helped to organize the American League you know."[274]

Griffith began shopping himself at the World Series in 1911. He was 42 years old and believed the time had come to make the ownership leap at the major league level. Clark had a long talk with Edward Walsh, an insurance broker and vice president of the Nationals, concerning the managerial vacancy. Griffith amassed numerous friends in the game. He knew everyone in the business and they knew him. This goodwill paid off soon enough. Clark not only saw an opportunity to manage the Nationals, he wanted in the boardroom. The first step was to bring the idea to Ban Johnson. Everything was done with Johnson's consent in those days, or usually at his urging. Fortunately, Johnson wanted him back in the American League and went to bat for him with Washington's chief stockholder and president, Noyes.

Clark was on friendly terms with Noyes, since they were members of the rules committee in January 1906. Griff even expressed an interest in the Washington position before. As Griffith later relayed, "I have never before told it in public, but it is a fact, nevertheless, that as early as 1908 I tried to purchase a large block of stock in the ball club here. Conditions at that time were such that there was nothing doing, but when the fire came that swept the old park, I had my chance and I grabbed it."[275]

---

[274] Clark C. Griffith, "Building a Winning Team," *Outing Magazine*, May 1913, p. 131

[275] Excerpt from a speech given at the Gayety Theater in June 1913. "Boosters in Rally," *Washington Post*, June 17, 1913, p. 8

Noyes was also considering Billy Murray and George Stovall as the team's new manager. The Nationals' directors met at the Commercial Club near the White House in late October 1911. The first order of business was debt management. As planned they decided to double the club's outstanding capital stock to 20,000 shares, a total of $200,000 at a par value of $10. Clark offered to buy out whoever was willing. The smaller stockholders, sensing a large payday, jacked up their price. The deal initially fell through.

Noyes, Walsh and Minor stepped in and offered 1,200 shares to Griffith at $12.50 each and suggested that he purchase as much as he could afford from the others. Clark agreed to buy 800 more shares at $15, giving him 10% of the club. He emerged from the October 30 meeting, "Yes, I have purchased a large piece of the stock in the Washington club. I am the largest stockholder. This does not mean that I have the controlling interest...I have signed a three-year contract." He signed for a reported $7,500 a year, supposedly the same figure he was making with the Reds.[276] There was also the possibility that Griffith could soon become the team's president, as Noyes was considering retirement. The $7,500 figure proved to be low; by 1913 he was making $10,000 a year, which matched his earnings in Cincinnati.

Clark now had a new mission and there were things to do. Mrs. Griffith closed down the apartment in Cincinnati, found another in D.C. and set about fixing it up. Clark departed for Chicago; he had to come up with $27,000. Johnson promised a $10,000 loan but he quickly reneged. Comiskey also refused to sink any money into "that baseball graveyard," as he referred to Washington. That was certainly an understandable reaction considering the club's performance since its inception. Comiskey himself was especially lucky to settle in one of the two cites that could support two major league franchises throughout the 20th century. Griffith had to look elsewhere; he left Chicago empty handed.

He returned to Craig, Montana and his 5,000-acre ranch, which he owned with his brother since 1898. Clark had about $8,000 in cash and sold off most of his, sheep,[277] cattle and alfalfa, from a smaller 800-acre

---

[276] As cited in the previous chapter, Griffith was making $10,000 in 1910. This was from an internal memo though. The fact is newspapermen weren't always privy to exact payroll figures. Griffith's initial salary with the Senators may have been $10,000 or he may have taken a cut to $7,500 to attain his dream. He would soon be making more money, among the tops in the game.

[277] He had about 2,000 sheep at the time.

ranch, to help make up the difference. He then gained a second mortgage on the ranch from the First National Bank of Helena, Montana for the remaining amount. Clark returned to the nation's capital with the cash in hand in time to have Thanksgiving dinner with his family in their new apartment. The family later purchased a property at 2821 Ordway Street. In December, Clark opened an office in the Southern Building and set about revamping the club. The 1912 version of Senators would be a completely different commodity. The city's rooters were soon rattled as he purged one fan favorite after another.

As it turned out, Noyes passed away on August 21, 1912 at age 44 from pneumonia. Minor was elected club president by the stockholders at the end of the year in the same meeting Griff was elected to the Board of Directors. Griffith continued to operate as he had in the past; he was the manager and general manager, to borrow a modern term. However, major financial decisions had to be cleared through Minor. There was no great antagonism between Griffith and Minor but eventually Clark wanted a bigger say, especially after nearly losing Walter Johnson due to Minor's stubborn negotiation tactics.

CHAPTER NINE

SENATORS, NATIONALS OR NATS

Griffith sent shockwaves through D.C. in December 1911. He dismantled the existing Senators' squad, trading or releasing ten veterans. He rebuilt the team around pitchers Walter Johnson, and center fielder Clyde Milan and shortstop George McBride.[278] Milan was one of the best center fielders in Washington history. His speed allowed him to play nearly as shallow as the great Tris Speaker. In his career, Milan snatched 495 bases, topping at 88 in 1912. Milan roomed with the Johnson for fifteen years. Promoted to field manager in 1922, Milan was let go because of his easy-going nature, a trait that Walter Johnson needed to overcome as well. Milan retired as a player, finishing with 2,100 hits, 1,000 runs scored, a .388 on-base percentage and a .285 batting average. He embarked on a long career as a minor league manager and coach for the Senators. After hitting fungoes in the Florida heat during spring training in 1953, the 65-year-old suffered a fatal heart attack.

Washington fans were stunned when Griffith unloaded Johnson's main catcher Gabby Street, a local favorite, in favor of the younger Eddie Ainsmith and John Henry. The squad was completely revamped. By the season's end, only two men over thirty were on the roster. Griff also brought in his own pitching coach, Nick Altrock, who averaged over

---

[278] Check out an eleven-page article Griffith wrote in *Outing Magazine* in May 1913 if you'd like to get a full understanding of his motives and actions in revamping the club that first season. Clark C. Griffith, "Building a Winning Team," *Outing Magazine*, May 1913, p. 131

twenty wins a year with the White Sox from 1904-1906 until his arm went dead. Altrock was one of the main starters that carried the "Hitless Wonders" to the world title in 1906, also winning five games in relief that year. Altrock remained with the Senators well into the 1950s, performing a host of duties with the club. He was among the first to arrive every year at spring training, running camp and putting the men through their paces. Altrock's lasting fame is derived from his clowning in the coach's box during games and running amuck in pregame drills. He teamed with Germany Schaefer and later Carl Sawyer and Al Schacht as part of Griffith's traveling show, as they would perform on the road as well.

Team trainer Mike Martin also transferred to Washington. Martin was with Griff since 1904 with the Highlanders after the former yelled from the stands claiming to be able to heal sore arms and other aches. He also joined the Reds with Griffith. At age 19, Martin became one of the first full-time trainers in baseball. He worked at the New York Athletic Club and Columbia University, first honing his skills with the legendary trainer Mike Murphy at the University of Pennsylvania. Martin worked with basketball, baseball and football players and rowers, trackmen and other athletes, such as, world champion bike racer Marcus Hurley and boxing champ Terry McGovern. He also took a nursing course at Roosevelt Hospital in New York. Like Altrock, Martin was among the first at training camp every year working the men into shape. Both men were often sent on scouting missions for the boss. In fact, Martin switched to scouting full-time in 1946. He died in an auto accident in June 1952, heading to Griffith Stadium to meet with Clark to go over a few prospects.

Griffith completely took charge of the entire franchise, expanding his duties well past field management. He purchased more land surrounding the ballpark to add bleacher seating and install a new entrance and set out to extend the park's roof to protect the fans from the elements. He also needed to find a spring training site and eventually settled on Charlottesville, Virginia. The Nationals never actually had an official office. Griffith secured a lease in the Southern Building and hired a personal secretary. To kick off the year, contracts went out on January 3. To be sure, no baseball man was busier than Griffith from December to March that off-season.

Perhaps most important of all, Clark reached out to the community. He sponsored the YMCA and set up an "Amateur Baseball Day" in the District. For decades the winner of the amateur tournament was awarded the Clark Griffith Trophy. In fact, the Clark C. Griffith Collegiate Baseball League thrives today. Also, he joined the local

Masons[279] and tirelessly worked during the off-season developing community relations. No club in major league history offered their stadium pro bono as often as the Senators did during Griffith's reign. Free use of the park was given to civic, local and federal government and military groups and, especially, to functions hosted within the black community, wherein the stadium itself sat.

There's always been confusion over the club's nickname. Which was it, Senators or Nationals? Both nicknames were actually used during the 1890s in respected to the National League franchise. The Nationals nickname is easily understandable; it stemmed from the club's representation of the nation's capital and ethnocentric pride. Baseball clubs had similar names since at least the 1860s. Some say the nickname Senators has its roots in the influence of Arthur Pue Gorman, a noted Baltimore baseball figure during the amateur era and an influential U.S. Senator during the 1890s.[280]

Either way, the new Washington franchise was being called the Senators even before Opening Day 1901. In February 1905, club management asked the fans to write in potential new nicknames. On March 26, team president Thomas Noyes officially renamed the club "Nationals."[281] Fan Frank L. McKenna, described as an old-time fan, was the first to send in the suggestion and consequently won a season pass. Though newspapermen and fans haphazardly refer to the club as the Senators or Nationals or the abbreviated Nats, throughout Griffith's tenure the club was officially known as the Nationals; however, his heir Calvin Robertson Griffith officially reverted to the Senators moniker on October 30, 1956.[282] To add to the confusion, newspapermen routinely referred to the club as the Griffiths, Griffs or Griffmen well into the 1940s.

The Nats played at American League Park, which, like many old-time parks, was melded into the community and had distinctive characteristics as such. The center field wall snaked around five houses and a huge tree. The tree even jutted into the field of play. It had, and

---

[279] Local Harmony Lodge No. 17, raised on October 12, 1921, made a lifetime member on April 25, 1928, elected honorary member of the Grand Lodge of D.C. on May 8, 1940 as noted in Harmony Lodge No. 17 F.A.A.M. Bulletin from April 1945

[280] A baseball-based biography of Arthur Gorman can be found at the SABR Biography Project

[281] "Senators' New Name," *Washington Post*, March 26, 1905, p. S1

[282] Bob Addie, "Bob Addie's Column," *Washington Post*, October 31, 1956, p. D3

would have until Mr. Griffith's death, one of the largest field dimensions in the majors. Left field was 405 feet from home, spanning out to 420 to 457 feet in dead center. Right field was a cozy 320 feet from the plate but a thirty-one-foot footwall kept many hits in the park.

The season started on a somber note as President Taft declined an invitation to attend Opening Day in wake of the *Titanic* disaster, which included the death of his friend and military aide Archie Butts. Vice President James S. Sherman tossed out the ceremonial first ball instead. The club was hovering in sixth place at the end of May and Griffith was pushing the directors to spend some money to beef up the club's talent level. Noyes ponied up $12,000 with which Clark bought heavy-hitting first baseman Chick Gandil from the Montreal Royals of the International League. It proved to be a great move; Gandil batted .305 and knocked in 81 runs and finished tenth in the league in slugging. The club slid into a groove, winning seventeen in a row. The first sixteen were away games, a new record. The town was going nuts. Never had baseball caused such frenzy in D.C., at least not in the current century.

Seemingly the entire U.S. government showed up at American League Park on June 18, including the President, Vice President, Speaker of the House and Secretary of State, for the first home game since the streak began. In all, 15,516 paid their way into the park. After the 5-4 win, the Nationals stood in second place. They remained there. Taft appeared at the park one more time as President, on August 13 while on the campaign trail.

Griff's lust for team ownership continued even after he bought into the Senators. He pulled some associates together in Cleveland in July 1912 for the purpose of buying a minor league club. Aware of the rules against farming, they decided to purchase a club outright, perhaps one from the South.[283] The plan never developed beyond the initial stages.

The season ended with Griffith's boys finishing fourteen games behind the Red Sox, a huge success for Washington. Attendance jumped over 100,000 and the club's receipts were up 50%. On October 24, the manager's salary was bumped to $10,000 in appreciation of his efforts, and results of course.

Unfortunately, the biggest show of the season took place in Boston. The 1-0 showdown between Joe Wood and Walter Johnson on September 6 drew 30,000 fans. Clark gave the fans one final show on

---

[283] "Griffith to buy a Minor League Club," *Hartford Courant*, July 29, 1912, p. 10

October 5 with second place wrapped up. In the seventh inning the showman received word that Philadelphia lost, thus, securing runner up status for the Nationals. He sent in his clowning tandem, Altrock to pitch and Schaefer to second. Forty-three-year-old scout Jack Ryan was sent to third. After Altrock was banged around, Schaefer called for Griffith to replace him. In his only appearance of the year Clark tossed one pitch; Hal Chase hit it out of the park. Thus, he became the first man to face only one batter in a season and give up a homer, not to mention it happened on the first pitch. Schaefer and Griffith then switched positions. The 42-year-old Griffith even racked up a couple of assists at second but struck out in his only at bat. It was the last game at Griffith's old stomping grounds Hilltop Park in New York.

Clark seemed to mellow a little in 1912, not getting ejected or suspended as much. He also endeared himself to the players by signing to play lucrative exhibition games in September and October. One game on September 9 at the New York State Fair in Syracuse netted $1,000 for the men. As usual, Griffith took off for Montana after the World Series but returned after Thanksgiving to pursue trading possibilities.

An engaging story came out of Helena, Montana in November. Clark was out hunting one day when either he or one of his companions dropped a deer, well so they thought. It was only wounded. The deer then charged straight at the group. Griffith raised his rifle but it jammed. He then looked around and found a rock, flinging it at the wounded animal. He hit it between the eyes, knocking it senseless. He then walked up to the animal and killed it with the butt of his rifle. A tall tale many thought, but this one was confirmed by all present.

Third baseman Eddie Foster was one of Griff's prized pupils. Clark developed a play around Foster's acclaimed bat control. He didn't invent the "run and hit" play, similar to the "hit and run," but it was routinely utilized with Foster at the plate. Runners often took off, trusting Foster to connect with the ball.

Baseball Magazine weighed in to congratulate Griffith on his fine season resurrecting the perennially weak Washington franchise. They exclaimed, "Griffith is one of the shrewdest managers in the game. He has always been noted for his cautious planning and has a knowledge of the most intricate points of the game which is excelled by none."[284]

---

[284] "Washington Notes," *Baseball Magazine*, June 1912, page 92

Griffith met the eighteen-year-old son of a local saloonkeeper on December 29, 1911 and invited him to spring training. Joe Engel, later known as the "Barnum of the Bushes," embarked on a 36-year relationship with Griffith as a player, scout and farm system director. He also may have been the first to give Baltimore Orioles owner-manager Jack Dunn the heads up on a young kid named Ruth, George Herman. Engel's first connection with the Senators came as a batboy under manager Joe Cantillon.

Nineteen Thirteen brought another second place finish. In fact, only Boston and Chicago won more game than Washington during the rest of the decade after Griffith arrived. Hurting for pitchers and using all sources available, Clark placed an ad in the *Washington Post* for hurlers. Doc Ayres, Jack Bentley,[285] Harry Harper and Jim Shaw were signed this way. Griffith also brought the fourth and fifth Cubans, outfielders Merito Acosta and Jack Calvo, into the majors in 1913. He also tried to deal for Armando Marsans to no avail.[286] Griff was extremely popular in Cuba; in fact, Cuban officials were quite distraught when a planned postseason tour of the islands by the Nationals failed to pan out. Decades later when he finally made that trip, hundreds mobbed him upon arrival at Havana Airport.

Newly elected President Woodrow Wilson threw out the first ball on Opening Day. He attended five other games in 1913 as well. In early May, Griffith had another blow up with an umpire. Angry, he swore off talking to them altogether and even bet Walter Johnson and Ray Morgan that he wouldn't utter a word to one the rest of the year. Two weeks later on the 21st, Clark lost his wager when Silk O'Loughlin tossed him for foul language. The manager bought the pair a suit of clothes. After Ban Johnson suspended Altrock on May 26, the volatile Washington manager screamed to reporters that he was done forever with the American League president. In 1913, Griffith also began pushing for the system by which the top-four teams in each league received a cut of the World Series monies.

The big news of the summer hit on August 13 when the Nationals pulled into Detroit. Clark handed Tigers' owner Frank Navin a $100,000 check for Ty Cobb. Navin didn't quite know what to make of the offer but he promised Griffith he'd take it under advisement. Truthfully, Navin didn't believe Washington even had $100,000 but he

---

[285] After signing Bentley, Griffith decided to turn him into a pitcher.

[286] Griffith tried to purchase Marsans in the spring of 1912 for $5,000.

admired Griffith as the "check-writing champion of the world." In truth the Nationals didn't have the money. The offer nearly caused strokes throughout the boardroom. Clark had a plan. If Navin gave him two weeks, he'd sell 100,000 game tickets at $1 a piece to fund the deal. Navin knew he couldn't part with the great Cobb; he turned down the offer two days later.

The Nationals put on another show on the last day of the season, October 4. For one, the team used an unprecedented eight pitchers. Griffith pitched a scoreless eighth inning for his only appearance of the year. He then moved to right field and into center, knocking a double in his only at bat. Griffith, age 44, and catcher Jack Ryan, 45, formed the oldest battery in major league history. Walter Johnson played center field but the comical Schaefer once again stole the show. He pitched and played right field and center. But, he hung around between second and first instead of manning his proper position in the outfield. When he did venture onto the grass he either took a nap or sat atop the outfield fence while the action took place around him. At times the umpires were allowing four outs in an inning.

After the World Series, Cap Anson came to D.C., and with Griffith, was received by President Wilson at the White House on October 16. Clark was later asked to name his all-time team.[287] It follows:

Catcher	Buck Ewing
First Baseman	Charles Comiskey
Second Baseman	Eddie Collins
Shortstop	Herman Long
Third Baseman	Jimmy Collins
Left Fielder	Bill Lange
Center Fielder	Tris Speaker
Right Fielder	Ty Cobb
Pitchers	Amos Rusie
	Cy Young
	Christy Mathewson
	Walter Johnson.

---

[287] "Manager Griffith places Johnson on All-Time Baseball Combination," *Washington Post*, April 26, 1914, p. S2

John T. Powers formed the outlaw Columbian League in February 1912 based in the Midwest. In August 1913, the league owners ousted the conservative Powers in favor of Chicago businessman Jim Gilmore. The re-named Federal League merged with some interests from the defunct United States League. Gilmore immediately announced that the group would challenge the American and National Leagues for talent, attendance and monies in 1914. Essentially, they were claiming major league status as the American League had a decade and half ago. To compliment franchises in Chicago, St. Louis, Pittsburgh, Indianapolis and Kansas City, the Federal League added East Coast clubs in Baltimore, Brooklyn and Buffalo.

Gilmore's threat seemed attainable as he admiringly recruited wealthy businessmen into the fold: himself, a coal dealer and machinery manufacturer; Phil Ball, a St. Louis ice machine mogul; Harry Sinclair, an Oklahoma oilman and later of the infamous Teapot Dome scandal; Robert Ward, a Brooklyn banker; and Charles Weeghman, a Chicago restaurateur. To entice quality players, the Federal League offered signing bonuses, fewer contractual restrictions, a 5% annual raise and free agency after ten years. Browns' first baseman George Stovall was the first to breach the reserve clause and join the upstart league. He also became one of the Feds' top recruiters.

Joe Tinker was the first big name to jump. Eighty others followed. A furor arose when the league nearly lured the great Walter Johnson from Washington. Numerous lawsuits were initiated from both sides. One accused Major League Baseball of violating the nation's antitrust laws. It was argued before noted monopoly buster Chicago jurist Kenesaw Mountain Landis who merely delayed any ruling until Major League Baseball could work out a settlement, endearing him to baseball executives.[288]

Part of the Federal League's strategy was to put as much pressure on their local competition as possible. In Baltimore, for example, they built their park directly across the street from Jack Dunn's International League Baltimore Orioles. Dunn was forced to relocate to Virginia and sell Babe Ruth to the Red Sox to offset costs.[289] Also, Connie Mack claimed that one reason he had to sell off his first dynasty, one that took him to the World Series four times from 1910-1914, was that he could not

---

[288] The judge was known as a monopoly buster for his landmark ruling against John D. Rockefeller's Standard Oil for a record $29 million.

[289] "Has Plan to save Baltimore Club," *New York Times*, June 20, 1914, p. 7

compete with the salary inflation caused by the onslaught of the Federal League.

Alas, financial woes brought down the league. Much of the league's financial backing was lost with the death of Robert Ward at the end of 1915. After that, Ball and Weeghman were enticed into purchasing into the established major leagues; the league then fell by the wayside. Most Federal League owners settled out of court with major league officials. The Baltimore club however pursued the issue to the Supreme Court into the 1920s. Out of this came baseball's antitrust exemption.

Griffith's year started off rocky at home; on January 18, someone broke into his house at 2821 Ordway Street and stole a cold-storage box and jewelry valued at $42.[290] In May, the Federal League reared its head, as Tinker began courting Walter Johnson and other Washington players. Clark and executives around the league spent much of 1914 trying to appease their players and keep them in the fold. Gilmore cockily boasted that Johnson would be pitching for the Feds in 1915. The battle for the pitcher took place at the end of the year.

There was a major blowup in Philadelphia on June 26. In the third inning of the first game of a doubleheader, the A's began complaining that Joe Engel was pitching with both feet off the rubber. In the fourth, umpire Ollie Chill started calling Engel's pitches balls for the illegal delivery. Griffith ran onto the field to argue and refused to leave. Chill forfeited the game to Philadelphia. Connie Mack entered the fray with some silly comments about banning Clark from baseball for his hotheadedness. Griffith rebutted, "I admit I lost my nut but umpire Chill did more so. Anyhow, he is an incompetent umpire. I have appealed to Johnson." In the end, the Nationals were fined $300 and Griffith another $25 personally.

Clark closed out his active career on October 7. It was the third year in a row he organized a farcical game for the last day of the season; this one was much tamer. Continual lineup changes were made, including Tris Speaker's only mound appearance of his career. Clark pitched a perfect ninth inning, striking out one. He even placed a double off Speaker.

Griffith signed another three-year contract at the beginning of the 1915 season for $10,000 annually. The *Washington Post* reported that he was

---

[290] "Police News Notes," *Washington Post*, January 19, 1914, p. 9

among the highest paid men in the game behind only John McGraw, Tris Speaker, Ty Cobb, Eddie Collins and Walter Johnson. Connie Mack and Ban Johnson could surely be added to this list. President Wilson tossed the ceremonial first pitch on Opening Day in 1915 and 1916. He was prevented from doing so the rest of his term because of war concerns and health issues.

Clark added two men to the club in 1915 that anchored the team for years to come. He was looking for a first baseman to replace Chick Gandil who couldn't seem to limit his carousing or curtail his chain smoking.[291] Griffith was again railing against the effects of smoking on an athlete. He took off to Buffalo to scout outfielder Charlie Jamison. The club owner wanted $7,500 for him. Griffith countered with $8,000 if he threw in first baseman Joe Judge. The slick fielding first sacker remained a fixture in D.C. into the 1930s.

Clark earlier provided an $800 loan to the owner of the nearby Petersburg club of the Virginia League. In July, the league was on the verge of collapse so Petersburg sent pitcher Sam Rice to the Nationals in lieu of repayment of the loan. Rice impressed Griffith in batting practice and as a pinch hitter and was soon turned into a right fielder, remaining with the club until 1933. Rice had been through a lifetime of troubles the past few years. He married at age eighteen in 1908. Four years later, his wife, two children and parents were killed in a tornado. Distraught, he wandered the country and joined the Navy. It was there that he was discovered playing ball.

On February 3, 1915, the emery ball became the first pitch ever banned by a major league, the American League. The pitch at the time was popularized by Russ Ford who for years disguised its delivery as a personalized version of the spitball, going as far as to lick his fingers before pitches to throw off batters and officials. He first started throwing it in 1908. By 1913, his secret was out; he was slicing or scratching the ball in order to gain some unexpected movement on his pitches.[292] Griffith led the charge to ban the pitch. Sure he scuffed the ball back in his day, but this was 1915 and it didn't favor his club. He was the opposing manger on the losing end of the proposition now.

---

[291] Dan Ginsburg, "Chick Gandil" biography in *Deadball Stars of the American League*, 2006

[292] T. Kent Morgan and David Jones, "Russ Ford" biography in *Deadball Stars of the American League*, 2006

When the season started, Griff was the first to call out a potential violator. On April 17, the Nats lost to the Red Sox 7-5. Griff accused pitcher Ernie Shore of throwing an emery ball; he collected five allegedly scuffed balls and remitted them to Ban Johnson.

In July 1915 a slew of baseball men put up about $1,000 each to purchase a 2,436-acre hunting and fishing resort in Dover Hall, Georgia, a dozen miles from Brunswick. The original idea was to build the foremost baseball training facility on the planet. That never came about but they kept the property as a winter resort. After the construction of a $50,000-clubhouse and numerous cabins, it was christened the Dover Hall Club. Baseball men spent part of their off-season there vacationing with their families and otherwise enjoying themselves. Perhaps, even a little business was conducted between hunting and fishing parties and the evening entertainment. Griffith spent a weekend here or there enjoying the atmosphere and the thrill of the hunt with Cap Huston, George Stallings. Ty Cobb, Ban Johnson, Charles Comiskey, Damon Runyon, John McGraw, Ed Barrow, Jacob Ruppert, John Tener, sportswriters, wives and others. Wilbert Robinson and Huston enjoyed the area so much they retired there.

On June 30, 1916, a fight broke out in the third inning in a game against Boston after Red Sox pitcher Carl Mays hit George McBride with a pitch. McBride threw his bat at Mays and the benches cleared, even some fans joined in. Griffith was walking to the mound arguing with Mays when catcher Sam Agnew came up from behind and slugged him in the nose. Griffith staggered and then rushed Agnew. Players and police separated the two; the catcher was hauled off to jail. Clark refused to press charges and the matter was dropped.

After a respite spent at the track and partaking in other family activities after another long season, Clark and family set about closing the Montana ranch. Griffith was eyeing controlling interest in the Nationals. He sold most of his horses to English and French officials for the war effort in late 1916.[293] He needed to unload the property to gain the needed capital. He was looking for someone to buy it outright or perhaps temporarily lease the property. Clark made a self-described error the previous summer turning down a $30,000-offer for the ranch. He countered with $33,000 but never heard a reply.

---

[293] Stanley T. Milliken, "Says Control of Club is sought by Griffith," *Washington Post*, December 31, 1916, p. S1

Griffith was a little frustrated with his limitations within the Senators' organization. He was at the forefront of the community trying to instill the club into every fiber of the community. He spoke to church groups, provided loving cups for various local tournaments and spent countless hours at benefits and fundraisers. When the Masons asked for use of American League Park for a ballgame, they were charged $200. The group looked elsewhere for their activities. Clark was not only a Mason, with Almas Temple, but the organization had 12,000 members. Griffith couldn't understand why the club alienated that many people for a mere $200. In short, he wanted a greater say; he wanted things done his way.

The ranch finally sold in February 1917 for $35,000. By then, the property included 9,000 acres, 4,000 of which the Griffiths owned outright. The rest was held on lease by the state. The remaining seventy horses were also sold.

Spring training 1917 in Augusta opened with Griffith and Mike Martin complaining that they couldn't locate any ethyl or grain alcohol to rub down the players. The first waves of the prohibition laws were running through the South. They eventually found some jugs but were concerned that they might be seized at any moment.

The Nationals traveled to Bloomington, Illinois on May 22, 1917 for "Clark Griffith Day." His hometown was throwing a party in his honor. Griffith was supposed to pitch two innings against the local Triple-I League club but the game was washed out. The fun was not lost as former friends threw a banquet and roasted the manager. Stories were told well into the evening.

A reporter caught Griffith unprepared on July 1, 1917 and he admitted to throwing an emery ball during his heyday and even bragged of originating the pitch. The timing of the confession was odd considering he was about to become the most vocal opponent of the spitball and all other varieties of the shine ball. This was a different era and his priorities changed; his competitors were fairing better than his boys in throwing the trick pitches.[294]

Griffith's movement to ban the spitter stemmed mainly from the success of the White Sox pitchers in delivering wet balls, particularly the often-questioned and very successful Eddie Cicotte. Chicago was leading

---

[294] Griffith penned a forthright article in the July 1917 issue of *Baseball Magazine* in which he laid out his reasoning in calling for a ban on trick deliveries. In it he takes an honest look at his history in the matter and accepts responsibility for such. Clark Griffith, "Why the Spit Ball should be Abolished," *Baseball Magazine*, July 1917, p. 371

the American League virtually all summer. By mid-August, it appeared that only Boston had a chance to catch them. After White Sox pitcher Dave Danforth beaned Tris Speaker Griffith started openly lambasting the White Sox and calling for a ban on all freak deliveries. He continued to be vocal with the press and around the league and waged a one-man campaign with Ban Johnson and other executives to eliminate freak deliveries. Part of his impetus was the state of the game itself. He felt that pitchers during the Deadball Era had too great an advantage. As he noted, "Why encourage the stranglehold which the pitcher has on batting?"[295]

On August 28, Johnson issued the following order to his umpires: "You are directed to remove from the game a pitcher or player who discolors the ball with a foreign substance, such as, tobacco juice, licorice or oil, and his suspension for five days will automatically follow." The rule in truth wasn't strenuously enforced until the death of Ray Chapman in 1920.

The National League started following suit in February 1918. League president John Tener issued a statement warning young pitchers against basing their repertoire on trick deliveries and especially the spitball. Part of the impetus to ban the spitball stemmed from health concerns. With millions dying throughout the world from the Spanish Flu people were suddenly cognizant of what each other did with saliva and other bodily fluids. In 1920, only seventeen men were grandfathered to legally throw the spitball; all others were banned. Burleigh Grimes threw the last legal spitball in 1934.

Griffith's former west coast teammate Billy Sunday arrived in D.C. in early January 1918 for a six-week tour of his evangelical teachings. Griff caught his sermon on February 4. Clark previously heard on of his speeches in Baltimore. Cap Anson originally discovered Sunday at a firemen's skill tournament in Iowa. Anson claimed that Sunday was fastest man he ever saw and immediately assigned him to the major leagues without any lower classification experience. Not surprisingly, he struck out his first thirteen times at bat. Over eight seasons, Sunday proved little more than a spray hitter but at times he did shine on the base paths, as Anson predicted.

Undistinguished as a ballplayer, Sunday sobered up and quit the game at age 28 to take a job with the YMCA in Chicago. His pay cut exceeded $2,500 a year but he deemed the religious calling more powerful.

---

[295] Clark Griffith, "Why the Spit Ball should be Abolished," *Baseball Magazine*, July 1917, p. 371

The epiphany came to him while drinking on a street corner with teammates King Kelly, Ned Williamson and Silver Splint listening to a gospel service in 1887. Sunday became one of the nation's leading evangelists, as an ordained Presbyterian minister. His flamboyant sermons led the prohibitionist movement and decried science and liberalism.

Attendance in 1917 during the war was dismal, less than 90,000 for the season. The league average was 357,357. It's amazing the club survived. The Nats drew about 182,000 in 1918 much closer to the league average of 213,500. The institution of daylight savings for the first time on March 31 allowed Griffith to change his start times during the week from 3:15 or 3:30 to 4:15 or 4:30 without worrying about the game being called due to darkness. This way he was able to capture the government workers on their way home.

Tom Zachary joined the Senators in July 1919. He was that prized commodity, a lefthander who threw smoke. After serving in France during World War I with the Red Cross, Zachary went to the mound for Connie Mack in Philadelphia twice in 1918 under an assumed name, Walton, to protect his college eligibility. He is popularly known today as the man who gave up Babe Ruth's sixtieth home run in 1927.

In 1919, Joe Engel came across Bucky Harris playing in Buffalo and alerted Griffith. Clark first saw Harris playing for a Baltimore Shipyard club in 1918. Clark took off for Buffalo to watch the second baseman during a doubleheader. Harris went 6 for 6 and Griffith bought him on the spot for $2,500 on August 25. Harris came out of the Pennsylvania coal mines; he quit school at age thirteen to work in one. He also played amateur baseball, drawing the attention of local resident and Detroit Tigers' manager Hughie Jennings. Jennings found the ballplayer a spot in the minors in 1915.

From his first season in D.C., Griffith felt that a little added entertainment on the field would spark greater fan interest and thus increase the gate. Nick Altrock started clowning around, shadow boxing, in the coach's box while with Kansas City of the American Association in 1912. Club owner Patsy Tebeau, unappreciative of the antics, gave him his walking papers. Griffith didn't see it that way; he hired Altrock and let him work his magic with the crowd. At first, he started clowning to distract the opposing pitcher and was censured by the umpire. Eventually, Altrock fine-tuned his routine and gained the acceptance of Ban Johnson as long as he was entertaining the crowd and not trying to influence the game at hand.[296]

Utility player and fellow free spirit Germany Schaefer couldn't resist the temptation to join in on the fun. The two worked in tandem until Schaefer headed to the Federal League in 1915. That year, infielder Carl Sawyer took over for Schaefer for two seasons. Altrock worked alone from 1917-1919 until Al Schacht joined the routine in 1920. Altrock and Schacht perfected the routine, working together until 1935 when Schacht joined the Red Sox. The act was so popular that the pair performed on vaudeville and were regulars at the World Series and later the All-Star game, despite the fact that the men stopped speaking to each other after a tiff in 1927. The show had to go on for the sake of the Senators and for the cash. Altrock was reportedly making $180,000 a year during his heyday.[297]

The show in the coach's box consisted of a variety of mini acts which included: bowling, juggling, golf, wrestling, rowing, sliding, umpire and player mocking, imitating the action on the field, tight rope walking, shadow boxing and a host of other inventive pantomimes. The routine also included the use of props such as an oversized glove and top hat and tails. The rowing routine during rain delays was especially popular. Altrock continued to showcase his talents with the Senators beyond Griffith's passing.

---

[296] Peter Gordon, "Nick Altrock" biography at SABR's Biography Project
[297] Peter Gordon, "Nick Altrock" biography at SABR's Biography Project

CHAPTER TEN

NATIONAL TREASURE

Many consider Walter Johnson to be the premiere pitcher in major league history. He was certainly the backbone, the jewel of the Washington franchise. A cursory glance at the record book shows the man posting 417 victories and a career earned run average closer to 2.00 than 2.50. He tossed more shutouts than anyone in the history of the game, by twenty. What essentially makes a starting pitcher valuable to his teammates? If it's keeping his club in the game, than perhaps Walter Johnson is the most valuable pitcher the game has yet seen.

 Johnson was born in Kansas near the end of 1887, a few months before Clark Griffith made his pro debut. The Johnson family left their Kansas farm and settled in California in 1902 where Walter's father found a job in irrigation construction. Walter found a slot on the local Anaheim semipro club the Olinda Oil Wells for one game in July 1904 before joining the club in earnest the following spring. He was offered a job with the Tacoma club in the Northwestern League in 1906, shyly having to be talked into turning pro, and consequently venturing from home, by his parents.

 Johnson pitched in an exhibition game for Tacoma but was released without making it into a league game. Unfortunately, concerns over the horrendous San Francisco earthquake led in part to the Pacific Coast League folding. Expecting to pick up some quality PCL pitchers, Tacoma released the untested Johnson. Tacoma's manager even suggested that Johnson give up pitching. An ex-Olinda teammate suggested that

Johnson join him in Weiser, Idaho in the Southern Idaho League, a league that only played games on weekends and holidays. Officially, Johnson was an employee of the Bell Telephone Company who played ball for the local club and at times did some clerical work.

Back in California in July 1906, Johnson rejoined the Oil Wells in the new winter Southern California League. In the spring, he returned to Weiser. There, Johnson received offers from the Northwestern League and Pacific Coast League but rejected both. Senators' manager Joe Cantillon even wired on June 17 but was similarly turned down; apparently, the 19-year-old didn't feel he was ready to turn pro. Cantillon dispatched Clyde Blankenship to have a discussion with Johnson. After talking with his manager and parents, Johnson finally agreed to join Washington when Weiser's season finished at the end of July.

Johnson joined a truly awful team in August 1907. The Nationals didn't rise above sixth place until their twelfth year in the league. He won 25 games in 1910 and again in 1911 but no one else on the staff eclipsed thirteen victories. Clark Griffith took over the club in 1912 and gutted it. He rebuilt the club around the three men up the middle: 24-year-old Johnson, 25-year-old center fielder Clyde Milan and 31-year-old shortstop George McBride. It worked. Bob Groom chipped in twenty victories and Long Tom Hughes another thirteen and the club jumped into second place. They placed in the first division for much of the next two decades. The old adage about the Senators about being last in the American League, which sparked the musical *Damn Yankees* in 1955, doesn't pertain to the club from 1912 until after the collapse following the 1933 pennant. It is often overstated that Johnson pitched on some lousy teams. He may have but that changed by his fifth full season at age 24.

Johnson did at times have a fine supporting cast with Hall of Famers Sam Rice, Goose Goslin and Bucky Harris but no one other than Johnson won twenty games except for the first year Stan Coveleski came over from Cleveland in 1925 and Groom in 1912. Johnson was the quintessential number one starter, the stopper. He was the face of the ball club. Griffith announced to the sportswriters each of Johnson's expected start days in advance so they could relay the message to the fans and hopefully build the gate. It was Public Relations 101, but it kept the organization afloat.

After the club's breakout year in 1912, Griffith negotiated a $5,000 raise for his star pitcher to $12,000. No one in the game threw harder; as Johnson went, so did D.C. And so did Griffith's investment. The Federal

League burst onto the scene in 1914 and began offering extravagant contracts with sweet terms to established major league stars. The manager of the Chicago club, Joe Tinker, started hounding Johnson in early 1914. On May 24, he arrived in D.C. for an exhibition game. Tinker met with Johnson, offering a reported $25,000 per year. Chicago Whales owner Charles Weegham proudly boasted that Johnson would be wearing a Federal League jersey in 1915.

Representatives of the Brooklyn Feds came next. They made a similar offer on June 3. Griffith snapped to attention and sought Johnson's counsel. He offered either a five-year deal at $16,000 a season or a two-year contract at $18,000 a year. Johnson emerged from the meeting acknowledging his loyalty and friendship to Griffith, the Senators and Washington fans and expressing hope that a deal could be worked out so that he could stay in the American League. Griffith repeatedly tried to ink Johnson to a contract but the season ended with no such agreement in writing. On October 29, en route to a postseason exhibition contest Fielder Jones, manager of the St. Louis Feds, offered Johnson $20,000 a year through 1917 with $10,000 in cash up front.

Senators' president Ben Minor decided to take a hard line against Johnson, perhaps as some have said because the pitcher *slipped* from 36 to 28 wins and the club dropped a notch in the standings. His stance probably had more to do with the financial losses sparked by the Federal League war. The Senators were among the biggest losers financially in 1914.[298] Whatever the reason, Minor reneged on Griffith's initial offer and tried to steamroll the pitcher, expecting him to honor the reserve clause and maybe even sign for the same salary as 1914. Johnson still hadn't heard from the Senators in mid-November so he decided to write Griffith. On November 13, he sent a note requesting a three-year deal at $16,000 per annum plus a $6,000 signing bonus. The Senators didn't respond, nor did they to a second request.

Minor was holding out to get a feel for the Federal League. Would they fold before 1915? Federal League president James Gilmore already announced that the league would no longer throw big money at major league stars. Griffith, for his part, was holding intense conversations with the club's executives but he simply didn't have the votes to agree to Johnson's terms. He literally begged Minor not to take a

---

[298] Profits in 1914: Red Sox, $75,000; White Sox, $70,000; Tigers, $30,000; A's, $18,000; Browns,-$10,000; Senators, -$15,000; Yankees, -$20,000; Indians, -$80,000. Source: Dan Levitt's article "Ed Barrow, the Federal League and the Union League" in SABR's *The National Pastime*, 2008, p. 97

firm approach. Nevertheless, Minor mailed his offer on November 28. Johnson could have $12,500 for up to three years, end of discussion.

Johnson did not take it very well. Why should he sign for $12,500 when he could be financially secure after three seasons in the Federal League? Tinker stopped by Johnson's hometown Coffeyville, Kansas at the perfect time. Still seething, Johnson signed with Tinker after only twenty minutes of conversation on December 3. He received $17,500 a year through 1917 plus a $6,000 signing bonus. That same day Johnson received a letter from Griffith telling him to hold tight; he was negotiating with Minor for better terms. It was too late. Johnson was headed to Chicago for 1915.

The news hit Griffith like a punch in the gut. It didn't take a genius to figure out that the future of the franchise rested on Johnson's right arm. He won nearly 150 games over the past five seasons and he was only 27 years old. Clark worked day and night to build a winner since he took over the club in December 1911. He cultivated the community and personally put up $27,000 to buy into the club. He was the number one stockholder but today, December 3, 1914, he was helpless. More than anything else, the whole Johnson debacle drove him to find an opening to gain controlling interest in the club. From his perspective, he needed to get the stock for the sake of the franchise, and his investment. Looking around, he knew he was the only career baseball man in the boardroom. He had the vision and foresight. He'd just have to bide his time for now.

Griffith exploded. As he frequently did, Clark spouted off to the nearest reporter. Johnson betrayed Washington, the Senators and especially Griffith himself. There was going to be a lawsuit. Someone was going to pay. It was a typical response in a stressful situation and an understandable one. But, Griffith was smarter than his ranting; he'd find a way to get his star back.

As they had done since the formation of the league, Griffith, Ban Johnson and Charles Comiskey met to devise their strategy. Ban Johnson brokered a deal with Connie Mack sending Eddie Collins to the White Sox for $50,000 to bolster the American League's presence in Chicago to combat the Federal League. Griffith was more concerned about getting Johnson back; as he saw it, Johnson was the most valuable commodity in the American League. He contacted Pirates' manager Fred Clarke who owned a ranch in nearby Independence, Kansas, asking him to have a chat with Johnson. Clarke arrived in Coffeyville, insisting to speak with the entire Johnson family. He worked the room well, strumming the heartstrings and appealing to Johnson's sense of loyalty to Washington.

Walter was in tears by the end of the interaction. Walter and Clark met in Kansas City on December 19.

Minor still wouldn't relent on the salary issue so Griffith appealed to Johnson on every other issue but the money. Griffith promised to up the ante for 1916 but there was nothing he could do for 1915. He needed a year to work on Minor and the board. It worked. Johnson signed a $12,500 contract for one year. The Federal League was out of luck. Lawsuits were threatened through Opening Day but Johnson justified the move as one in accordance with the reserve clause.

One sticking point remained. Johnson accepted a $6,000 bonus from the Federal League and it was already spent to purchase a garage with his brother in Coffeyville. Griffith agreed to cover it. He first tried to sweet talk Ban Johnson into paying the money out of the league's emergency fund but that didn't work. Instead, Griffith worked a little magic and actually had Comiskey to pay off the debt. It was either that or Comiskey would have the great Walter Johnson pitching for another Chicago team. The White Sox owner just had to view it as a $56,000 purchase of Collins instead of $50,000.

Griffith even made good on his promise to negotiate better terms for the pitcher. Before the 1916 season, Johnson signed a five-year deal for $80,000. In the end, the whole affair strained relations all around. Johnson was humiliated. He gave a full account of the events to *Baseball Magazine* in which every sentence exuded his embarrassment. Griffith walked away from the mess realizing that he needed to gain control of the franchise. It was he who had the vision and he practically ran the club anyway. The rest were just part-time businessmen. The Senators didn't even have office space until Clark set up his own. He just needed some more cash and perhaps a partner or two and the club – and all it's decisions – would be his.

Day in and day out Johnson went to the mound for the Senators. He averaged 32 starts a year for the club and another seven in relief. He won the pitchers Triple Crown, wins, strikeouts and earned run average, three times: 1913, 1918 and 1923. Plus, he held on well past his prime, winning 163 games after turning thirty. He retired after the 1927 season and took a job managing for Newark in the International League. Johnson rejoined the Senators as manager in 1929, for $25,000 a year. The club did well during his four seasons, finishing in second in 1930 and in third the following two seasons and winning over ninety games each of the final three years. This was during the revival of the A's and the pennants flew in Philadelphia from 1929-1931. In 1933, he was named manager of the Cleveland Indians, managing there through 1935.

Johnson remained an icon around the D.C. area until his death in 1946.[299] He entered Republican politics and in 1936 hosted a rally for Presidential candidate Alf Landon at his Maryland farm. In 1938 he became the only Republican on the board of commissioners for Montgomery County, Maryland. Two years later, Johnson unsuccessfully ran for Congress from Maryland's 6th District.

From the moment Clark took over the club he and Johnson became lifelong friends. The Federal League incident only illustrates the strong bond they forged. Walter returned to the Senators for a lot less money and only a promise that Griff would make things better. As Johnson's grandson and biographer Henry W. Thomas penned, "A bond developed between Walter Johnson and Clark Griffith over the years that was part father-son relationship, part mutual professional admiration, and the rest genuine friendship."[300]

---

[299] In the early 1920s the Johnsons moved to Bethesda, Maryland, a D.C. suburb.
[300] Henry W. Thomas, *Walter Johnson*, 1995, p. 108

CHAPTER ELEVEN

GAINING CONTROL

Clark Griffith was always looking to the future. Shortly after acquiring a ten-percent stake in the Washington Nationals in December 1911, he was envisioning how to get control of the other 90%. When Clark acquired his initial stock, there was some speculation that he might also be named club president. The club's officers were never devoted to the game. They had other careers, like most other baseball magnates. Virtually all decisions were left to the field manager; however, he didn't control the purse strings or other essential stockholder concerns. As it turned out, Thomas Noyes maintained the position of president but he passed away within a year. Noyes' partner Ben Minor then took over the helm.

Griffith never overtly challenged his employers but he longed to have the final say on all matters. After almost losing Walter Johnson to the Federal League, Clark realized that he needed to get control of the club. For his part, Minor was a lawyer and wanted to focus on his practice. He maintained the club presidency at the behest of the stockholders. In 1916, Clark made his first push to gain control of the club. He enlisted 35-year-old local coffee manufacturer John H. Wilkins who agreed to lend financial support. However, Wilkins backed out when it became clear that the country was headed to war. Clark started making his move anyway. He sold a bunch of horse to be shipped overseas for the war effort. Then, he looked to unload his Montana ranch, finally selling towards the end of the war.

The Senators finished seventh in 1919. Griffith wanted to spend money to bring in some talent but that idea was a no go with the stockholders. The club was financially strapped - since before the war. Whispers in the boardroom questioned whether Griffith should even be maintained as field manager for 1920.

Connie Mack and Ben Shibe introduced Griffith to a 41-year-old grain exporter who became his partner for the next two-plus decades. William M. Richardson was an associate of Thomas Shibe, part owner of the Philadelphia Athletics, in the grain business. Richardson was a baseball fan but he was merely looking for an investment, not operational control of a ball club. Perfect! Griffith found his man.

In November 1919, the pair opened negotiations to buy the club. Richardson gave Griffith the okay to purchase as many shares as necessary. The club had 20,000 shares outstanding; Griffith already owned at least 2,000.[301] On December 13, the sale of the club was announced. Griffith and Richardson acquired 80% of the club at $15 a share, a dollar figure that matched what Griff paid for some shares back in 1911. They bought the shares of Noyes, Kauffmann, Rapley, Berry, Minor, Callahan, Kane, Walsh and some smaller stockholders.

Minor emerged from the meeting lauding Griffith. "I know of no better man than Griffith to assume control of the Washington Baseball Club…When Griffith came to Washington as manager in 1912, affairs were at a low in the club. He developed a team that proved the sensation of the league that year and since has put on the field a club that has been topped only by Boston [and Chicago] in the average standings."[302]

Now, Griffith had to personally come up with $83,000. He contacted the president of the Metropolitan National Bank, the club's depository. Griffith was granted the loan. In all, he put up some of his accrued cash and financed the rest through the institution. It was a sound investment. The ballpark itself was valued at $270,000. Richardson never even paid off his loan. The shares sat in a bank and he just used the dividend checks each year to pay down the balance. His heirs sold their 40% of the franchise for $550,000 in 1949. More important to Griffith, he was in complete control of the ball club. Richardson was given a formal title but he only popped up every now and again to attend social functions and essential meetings.

---

[301] He had purchased extra shares throughout the years when they became available.

[302] "Griff Man for Job, Ben Minor declares," *Washington Post*, December 14, 1919, p. 22

As soon as the sale was announced, Richardson firmly stated, "Mr. Griffith will be the active head of the club and will shape its policy." Not once did he veer from this. Richardson retained a title within the company but, other than ceremonial functions, he had little participation in the running of the club. At all times Griffith spoke for 80% of the club, which meant that his decisions were final. He wouldn't be challenged at the top for thirty years.

The Board of Directors of the Washington Baseball Club was cut from seven to three. Clark naturally assumed the presidency and Richardson was officially named as vice president, secretary and treasurer. To help run the club, Griffith brought in Edward B. Eynon, who served under various titles throughout Griffith's tenure with the Senators. Eynon was a renowned local golfer from the Columbia Country Club. Their paths crossed a few times since Griffith came to D.C. Eynon stopped by the ballpark and training camp from time to time with Edward Walsh, the club's secretary under Noyes and Minor. Eynon and Clark became good friends during the drive to sell Liberty Bonds during the World War I. Eynon was a Red Cross official and a supervisor of the Liberty drive. Griffith lent his support and often made stump speeches throughout the District promoting the sale of the bonds. The committee raised $27 million for the war effort.

Griffith picked the perfect time to buy the club, financially that is. Baseball was entering a new era; attendance was heartily rebounding after the war. The Black Sox Scandal was about to hit but that proved to be a mere bump in the road. Within a month, Red Sox owner Harry Frazee sold Babe Ruth to his drinking buddy Colonel Huston in New York. The Deadball Era officially ended with the outlawing of the spitball and new rules against scuffing the ball. As a result of the beaning death of Ray Chapman in 1920, umpires now replaced a ball after it became dirty or scuffed. No longer would the same beaten ball be used for countless innings. The new ball was also said to be a little livelier. Babe Ruth, permanently removed from his pitching duties upon joining the Yankees, began crushing the ball and fans came to see. In fact attendance was up all around; fans flocked to gates at all the parks. To capitalize on this newfound interest, some owners moved their fences in and later the foul poles were erected to better gauge long drives. Baseball strategy was never the same, the long ball had arrived. The Senators' average attendance from 1911-1920 of 238,000 jumped two-fold to 510,000 through the 1920s.

Between 1918 and '23, Frazee shipped the following men to New York: Ernie Shore, Duffy Lewis, Carl Mays, Ruth, Wally Schang, Waite

Hoyt, Sad Sam Jones, Joe Bush, Everett Scott, Joe Dugan, Herb Pennock and George Pipgras. Combine this with the destruction of the Boston and Chicago franchises and the sporadic showing of the Indians, Tigers and Browns throughout the decade and it is easy to see why New York was in an opportune position to shine throughout the decade. Griffith and Connie Mack hung in there as long as they could. From 1921-1933 the three shared all the pennants, seven for New York and three each for Philadelphia and Washington. The latter two franchises collapsed during the Depression and never recovered, at least in their original cities.

CHAPTER TWELVE

FAMILY MAN

Clark Griffith met his future wife in the summer of 1900 at a party in Chicago. Clark's acquaintance Mollie Long introduced him to Ann Robertson. Both Long and Robertson were cashiers at the grand, nine-story Marshall Field and Company department store on the northeast corner at the intersection of Washington and Wabash Streets. Ann lived a short walk from the store up State Street just off Lake Michigan with her mother, sister and brother. Ann, called Addie, was seven years younger than Clark, having been born in November 1876. A schoolteacher who had too many Anns in her class bestowed the nickname Addie on her. The Robertson family emigrated from Scotland in the early 1890s shortly before the World's Fair in 1893. Chicago attracted a great many Scottish immigrants during the 1890s. The trains from New York to the Windy City and surrounding areas were often full of new arrivals to the country.

Clark and Addie were married six months later on December 3, 1900 in Detroit. Why Detroit? Because, "We just wanted to get out of town," explained Clark.[303] The couple picked a random minister in Detroit and married. They later learned that same minister had married Clark's brother Earl in Helena, Montana a decade prior. Clark was 31 years old at the time of the marriage, Addie 24, and was in the midst of the American League upheaval. He was well on his way to securing a nice

---

[303] "The Clark Griffiths married 50 Years," *Washington Star*, December 3, 1950, page unknown

future for Miss Robertson and himself. In 1898, he purchased a ranch in Montana that helped finance his initial buy in of the Senators and later when he gained control of the franchise. He was making the National League maximum salary of $2,400 a year at the time, but was looking forward to boosting that in the new league. There was also a chance that he might attain part ownership in an American League club.

Addie had never seen a baseball game when she met Clark; however, she became a big fan and supporter. In fact, she became a sports enthusiast. Addie and her mother, sister and sister-in-law could often be found at the ballpark. In later years Senators' patrons affectionately called the Griffith matriarch "Aunt Addie." She could often be found sporting her trademark large, filly hats at Senator, Redskin and Georgetown football games. Addie "could fit into the fast social pace of Washington when she had to, but preferred the quiet evening before the huge fireplace in her living room."[304] She never did get used to the reporters criticizing her husband. Every now and again after a particularly upsetting article, she requested that the writer visit her at her box seat next to the Senators' dugout. When he arrived she'd chastise him and call him a "traitor," to the amusement of nearby, snickering fans.[305]

Addie inserted herself into her husband's day-to-day business only once. As she tells the story, "I'll never forget one time Clark wanted to release a pitcher when he was managing. I cried when he told me because I knew the pitcher's wife so well and knew that she was looking forward to a trip to New York with her husband. Because I cried, Clark kept the fellow around three months after he should have been released."[306]

The Griffith marriage lasted nearly fifty-five years until Clark's death. As Clark describes it, "I don't know of a couple who has had a happier married life. We're real pals, never had a fuss." Addie echoed the sentiment, "We've never had a squabble." She went on to describe her husband's thoughtfulness, "When the maid has a day off and I do the dishes, Clark wants to dry them. That's just a little thing but he does all the little things that count. He does them willingly, cheerfully, as if it's a

---

[304] "Mrs. Clark Griffith," October 23, 1957, un-cited article found in Griffith's Hall of Fame file

[305] "Mrs. Clark Griffith," October 23, 1957, un-cited article found in Griffith's Hall of Fame file

[306] "The Clark Griffiths married 50 Years," *Washington Star*, December 3, 1950, page unknown

privilege."³⁰⁷ Another of the secrets to a happy marriage was explained by Mrs. Griffith, "We've never lived beyond our means and I can't understand anybody who does. We've never bought anything without seeing our way clear to paying for it. Living that way eliminates so much worry. I've had everything I dreamed of as a girl but not at the cost of anxiety over finances."³⁰⁸

Clark kidded about providing for his wife, "She says I never take her anywhere. Shucks, since we've been married she's been hunting deep in Canada, spent a lot of time on a ranch in Montana, took a trip to Cuba and goes to Florida every year."³⁰⁹ He failed to mention that the purpose of many of those trips was baseball in nature.

Clark immediately took responsibility for Addie's entire family upon marriage. Addie's mother, Jane C., lived with the Griffiths until she passed away in October 1932. It was said that she hadn't missed a home ballgame since her daughter was married. Clark also took in his wife's sister, Jean. Though Clark and Addie never had children, they later informally adopted her brother's entire family. Addie also had a sister Christine who remained in Chicago.

The 1910 U.S. Census shows Griffith, Addie, Jean and Jane living in Hamilton County, Ohio while Griff was managing the Cincinnati Reds. They all relocated with him to New York after leaving Chicago. Jean worked for the Red Cross during World War I.

Clark helped Addie's brother Jim, a shortstop, get into professional baseball, finding him a slot with New Haven in May 1906.³¹⁰ However, not everyone could be a future Hall of Famer. Jim eventually moved to Montreal in 1906 or '07 when Griffith made him business manager of the Montreal Royals, an Eastern League club recently purchased by Frank Farrell, with Clark and Ed Barrow as minority shareholders. Jim eventually took a job with a local newspaper. He married, started a family and lived the rest of his abbreviated life in Montreal.

---

³⁰⁷ "The Clark Griffiths married 50 Years," *Washington Star*, December 3, 1950, page unknown

³⁰⁸ "The Clark Griffiths married 50 Years," *Washington Star*, December 3, 1950, page unknown

³⁰⁹ "The Clark Griffiths married 50 Years," *Washington Star*, December 3, 1950, page unknown

³¹⁰ *Sporting Life*, May 5, 1906, p. 3, misidentified as George Robertson

The Canadian Census gives an extraordinary amount of information. In 1911, the Robertsons were living at 535 Laurier in Montreal. Jim's wife Jane was born in Quebec in October 1883 and spoke English. They had one daughter, Mildred (Millie), who was born in October 1909. The family was Presbyterian. Jim was working sixty hours a week for a newspaper company making $600 a year.[311]

By 1922, Jim was ill, dying of cirrhosis of the liver, and found it difficult to maintain his job. Addie visited the family in Montreal and apparently didn't like the living arrangements and conditions of the household. With Clark's blessing, as he had a similar childhood experience, she brought two of the children home with her to Washington. Calvin Clark Robertson was born on December 1, 1911[312] and Thelma was born in 1913. Addie left the oldest daughter Millie to help rear the four younger boys, Bruce, born 1916, Sherrod (Sherry), born January 1, 1919 and twin brothers Jimmy and Billy born in 1921.

Calvin, 10, and Thelma, 9, never met Griffith but they all got along well and eventually the visit became permanent. Calvin attended Staunton Military Academy in Virginia and later George Washington University from 1932-1935. Calvin became the Nats' batboy in 1923 and held the job through two pennants and a world championship. In January 1935, Calvin and Thelma legally changed their names to Griffith; however, neither was officially adopted as many have reported. All the Robertson children called Griffith "Unk" or "Uncle," even Calvin and Thelma.

Clark and Addie purchased land and built a huge home in 1925 following the lucrative 1924 World Championship season. Located on the southwest corner of 16th and Decatur Streets at 4720 16th Street N.W. in D.C., it sat on Washington's diplomatic row.[313] At one time South Korean dictator Syngman Rhee was their neighbor. The Griffiths employed a live-in couple that took care of the cooking, cleaning and yard work. The Griffiths lived the rest of their lives in the house.

Jim Robertson passed away in 1923 at age 42. In November 1925, following another pennant-winning season, Clark and Addie brought the rest of the Robertson clan from Montreal and purchased and furnished a

---

[311] The 1911 Canadian Census even states that Jim Robertson held a $2,000 life insurance policy that cost $63.58 a year.

[312] Almost to the exact day that Clark made his first official decisions for the Washington franchise.

[313] "Demand growing for Moderately Priced Housing," *Washington Post*, May 31, 1925, p. R3

home for them in Takoma Park, Maryland, near Walter Reed Hospital, about ten minutes from the Griffith home. It was the first time Calvin and Thelma had seen their mother in nearly four years.

Virtually the entire Robertson family later worked for the Senators. It was indeed a baseball family. Millie, the oldest child, became Griffith's personal secretary in 1926. She could often be found at the ballpark and accompanying Addie during spring training. On September 27, 1934, she married Senators' manager Joe Cronin. They had three boys and a girl.

Thelma was a favorite of the reporters who often referred to her as a "pretty blonde." She replaced Millie as Griffith's private secretary in 1934 and kept the job until she married White Sox pitcher Joe Haynes on October 11, 1941. They first met at spring training in 1938 after Haynes was initially signed by the Nats as a free agent in early 1937. He was sold to Chicago in January 1941. In 1948, Griffith, wanting Thelma back home in D.C., traded for Haynes. He eventually became the club's vice president. Thelma assumed the title of vice president and treasurer after Clark's passing. The Haynes had a son named Bruce.

Bruce Robertson passed away at Griffith's home from rheumatic fever at age eleven on October 27, 1927. In time, Jimmy and Billy Robertson ran the concessions and maintenance at Griffith Stadium. Eventually, they oversaw all stadium operations.

Sherry Robertson signed with the Washington Senators out of the University of Maryland and joined the team in 1940, playing there through 1952. After leaving the field, Robertson joined the front office and became farm director in 1956, staying with the club after its move to Minnesota. He was named vice president in 1966. At the end of the 1970 season, October 23, he was killed in an automobile accident while on a hunting trip with Twins' officers and players. He lost control of his vehicle, swerved off the road and smacked a tree, sustaining massive head trauma.

Calvin was groomed nearly from the beginning to become Griffith's successor. Among his early jobs with the organization, Calvin was batboy, concession stand custodian, batting practice pitcher and locker room attendant. Calvin fell into perhaps the most enviable position of any young man growing up in America. He was Griffith's constant companion. He hung around in the office and was privy to the countless baseball discussions therein. Griffith was well liked and admired throughout the industry. Every baseball man in the country stopped by his office for a chat when they were in D.C. Calvin heard stories dating from the earliest days of the game.

More important, he learned the strategies of the game and how to run the business. In 1935, he was named general manager of the club's Charlotte franchise at age 24. Likewise, he transferred to Chattanooga in 1938 as president and general manager. He was quickly brought back to Washington as Griffith deemed the Chattanooga franchise in decline and didn't want to taint Calvin with its downfall. He was appointed head of concessions at Griffith Stadium and at this time became Clark's main confidant. He sat in on strategy meetings and acted as a sounding board as the Old Fox plotted the Senators' future. In this environment Calvin quickly gained a feel for club operations and personnel.

In 1944, Calvin was named vice president and became Griffith's foremost advisor in club affairs, his right-hand man so to speak. They spent the day together discussing field personnel and other matters. At night it was more of the same at the Griffith household. In mid-1954, Calvin was named executive vice president and assumed most of Clark's day-to-day duties. Calvin naturally took the company's top slot after his uncle's passing in 1955. Calvin married twice, to Natalie Niven and Belva Block, and had three children, Clark, Corinne and Clare with Natalie.

Two of Clark's sisters and his brother were still alive as of 1912. His last surviving sister Minnie, who married William G. Sheets in December 1896, passed away in Danville, Illinois on September 16, 1923. At one time, Sheets was a minority stockholder in the Senators. Earl Griffith moved to Montana at about the age of twenty in 1885. He met Verena Vaughn in Helena and they married on December 23, 1893. They lived in Craig, Montana until 1917 when Griffith sold off the ranch. Earl and Verena had three sons, Clark H., Shirley and Earl Jr., and three daughters, Jeannie, Mary and Jessie.[314] After leaving Montana, Earl and family moved to San Bernardino, California, near members of the Dillon family. In 1923, they moved across country to be with Clark. They lived in Tacoma Park, Maryland near the Robertson family until their death.

Clark's paternalism extended beyond his family to the men that worked for him and even complete strangers. Shirley Povich of the *Washington Post* later disclosed a tidbit about Griffith that he was asked to keep quiet at

---

[314] Clark, 6, and Mary, infant, were listed on the 1900 Census but neither appeared in the 1910 listing.

the time. After Griffith saw a photo of widow and her family in despair in the newspaper, he found a job for the mother and paid their housing costs for six months. He also kept loyal employees for life and took care of their families after their death. In 1938, longtime outfielder John Stone came down with tuberculosis and left the lineup in June. Griffith immediately wrote him a check for the entire season. He then threw a benefit game for his family the following month. When the proceeds fell short of paying off the family's mortgage on their Tennessee home, Griff wrote a check for the difference. To a lesser extent, Griffith helped rookie pitcher Red Anderson. When Anderson's father fell ill in 1941, the Nats owner sprung for a $160 airline ticket to send the pitcher home.[315]

Every Washington manager Griffith hired had previous played for him except Chuck Dressen in 1955 who came to the club at Calvin's behest. Griffith's clowns Nick Altrock and Al Schacht worked for him for decades. Mike Martin worked for Griffith for four decades, first as a trainer and later as a scout.

"Uncle Billy" Smith was a longtime friend of Griffith's as well. They began their relationship soon after Clark took over the Senators. Smith was managing Chattanooga of the Southern Association in 1912. Griffith decided to park his players there, using the club as his unofficial farm. This relationship continued through 1922 even as Smith moved to Atlanta, Richmond, back to Atlanta and onto Shreveport. Smith joined the Senators organization at the end of 1922, serving for nearly two decades as a scout, head concessionaire at Griffith Stadium, club treasurer and road secretary during spring training.

William A. Smith was born in Springfield, Ohio on September 12, 1871 to German-born parents. He began his professional career in the early 1890s as an outfielder with Elkhart, Indiana. He was soon recruited into managing in the minors, a job he did with various clubs from 1895 to 1922.[316] He won pennants with Macon from 1904-1905 and with Atlanta in 1907, '09 and 1913. He passed away on November 20, 1941 after a month-long battle with a liver ailment.

Joe Engel worked for the club for decades as a scout and farm director. John Morrissey was the head ticket manager since 1909, putting

---

[315] Arch Ward, "In the Wake of the News," *Chicago Tribune*, May 5, 1941, p. 19

[316] Smith's minor league managing career: Lynchburg, 1895-96; Norfolk, 1897; Knoxville and Ottumwa, Iowa, 1898; Davenport, 1899; Albany, 1900; Cortland/Waverly, New York, 1901; Terra Haute, 1902; Greenville, 1903; Macon, 1904-05; Atlanta, 1906-09; Buffalo, 1910; Chattanooga, 1911-12; Atlanta, 1913-15; Richmond, 1916-17; Atlanta (business manager), 1918; Shreveport, 1919-1922.

in 52 years by the time the expansion Senators left at the end of 1971. He was asked to relocate with the club in 1961 to Minnesota but declined. Even in the 1950s, Griffith had some of the same ticket sellers and gate tenders from as early as 1912.[317] Joe Fitzgerald worked for Griffith since the beginning in Washington. In 1912, he was the clubhouse boy. After his minor league career, from 1919-1927, Fitzgerald was a longtime bullpen catcher for the Senators. After that, he performed various functions for the boss such as acting as the Griffith's driver during spring training and for other functions. Griffith's will stipulated that Fitzgerald had a job with the Senators as long as the family owned the club.

Washington sportswriter Bob Addie made a courteous statement after Mr. Griffith's death, "Often, during the years I wrote about baseball, people would write me about what a cheapskate Clark Griffith was. I was urged to expose him as a penny-pinching miser with reckless disregard for the baseball fans of the city. But how could I? This was a man who carried more than 30 of his old teammates and opponents of the old days on his payroll. This was a man who gave to every charitable cause, who freely donated his stadium time and again."[318]

Edward Eynon served as Griffith's business manager and club and traveling secretary from late 1919 when he took over the club until their deaths in 1955. Eynon, known to baseball men as "The Judge," and Griffith were inseparable. It wasn't hard to recognize the pair, just follow the cigar smoke. Both had the ever-present cigar sticking out of their mouths. Eynon was a social guy who seemed to be born for the nation's capital. He practically grew up in a country club. These skills personified the D.C. atmosphere. A natural extension, one of his jobs with the Nats was to entertain and pander to the diplomatic community and the rest of government's elite. He was in charge of making arrangements for all Presidential, statesmen, ranking military and V.I.P. visits. His other primary job was just as important. It was said that he attended every game but never saw the end of any. He was squirreled away counting the receipts.

---

[317] Griffith kept stadium employees well past their primes. When the Redskins moved into Griffith Stadium, team owner George Preston Marshall offered to bring in professional ticket sellers because he was dissatisfied with the slowness of all the elderly gentlemen holding up the lines at football games. Clark wouldn't hear of it; he was committed to the pensioners. *Sporting News*, November 9, 1955

[318] Bob Addie, "Bob Addies's Column," *Washington Post*, October 29, 1955, p. 13

A D.C. native, Eynon was a top amateur golfer, winning tournaments throughout the Mid-Atlantic. He was a long hitter and champion of the Columbia Country Club and a founding member of the Burning Tree Country Club. Eynon tutored Griffith in golf in 1920, helping him refine his game. Though Griff played golf off and on since at least 1908, he didn't play tee it up regularly until he was 51 years old but he was still known to shoot in the 80s; some accounts say he broke eighty. Eynon and Griffith had a weekly foursome with Billy Smith, Nats' head concessionaire, and Charlie Bane, a local businessman, until Smith passed away in November 1941. Clark also played regularly with Calvin Griffith and Charlie O'Connell, a D.C. insurance man.[319] They usually played at the Columbia Country Club. Griffith was twice runner-up in the Senior Championship at his home course. The men also played tournaments at Congressional, throughout the Mid-Atlantic and in Florida during spring training throughout the 1920s, '30s and '40s. Griffith won a Tampa meet in February 1927, topping a field of 38.

Griffith teed it up with Presidents and golfing elites, such as, Walter Hagen, Bobby Jones and Gene Sarazen. Clark was a regular participant in the National Celebrities Tournament in Washington, driving off the first tee into his 80s. Jones was Griffith's lawyer in Atlanta during some legal troubles during his involvement with a local minor league club in 1929. Griffith also frequently golfed with Connie Mack and Judge Landis, among others. An Al Demaree article for the *Washington Post* recognized Griffith along with Nick Altrock, Jim Cooney, Dutch Leonard, Speed Martin, Carl Mays, Fred Merkle, Sam Rice, Eppa Rixey, Wilbert Robinson, Babe Ruth, Arnold Statz and Dazzy Vance as baseball's best golfers.[320] Old-timers Horace Allen, Sammy Byrd, Ty Cobb and Monte Ward could certainly be added to that list.

Clark also appreciated bowling; however, Sam Rice was the top bowler in the Senators' family. The baseball men often met on Thursday nights during the season. Clark's brother Earl also played every week. Of course, Clark had been hunting virtually since he was in diapers. He was known as one of the finest shots among his peers, even nailing a moving target on horseback. An unconfirmed story circulated that Griffith once traded a pitcher to Joe Cantillon for a bird dog. He also had the horse racing fever, spending countless hours and off days at the track.

---

[319] O'Connell and Griffith played together for over 25 years.

[320] Al Demaree, "Some Ball Players play Mean Golf," *Washington Post*, January 21, 1929, p. 10

Clark was often found at Redskin and Georgetown football games. Probably no man in Organized Baseball watched more Negro league games than Griffith. He also became heavily involved in boxing, wrestling and amateur and youth athletics around the District.

Starting in the early 1930s Clark hosted daily bridge and pinochle games at his office. Baseball men and reporters gathered to listen to the Senators' road games on the radio, playing cards, shooting the breeze and talking baseball. All were invited with the cast changing daily depending who was in town. Clark could be found, cigar in hand, laughing and joking with the boys. On an ambitious day he hopped from table to table maintaining a hand at each. He once joked that he traded for Bobo Newsom so often because he enjoyed playing him in pinochle.

Calvin was close at hand soaking it all in. He reveled in the company and relished his emerging role. The two left the office together for dinner at home with Addie, Thelma and family. After dinner, Clark typically smoked a Robert Burns' cigar, nipped a little Old Granddad and took a short nap. Then, Clark and Calvin met again, discussing baseball well into the night. Among Griff's favorite nighttime repasts was listening to the Lone Ranger radio show. As Joe Cronin put it, "You couldn't stir when that program came on the air."[321] He also loved the shoot-'em-up westerns of early television or on the occasional trip to the theater.

Mr. Griffith also loved to read in the evenings. Outside the typical interests of a baseball man, he was particularly fond of comic strips. His favorites were *Tarzan* and *American Adventure*. On the serious side he liked reading Mark Twain and any and all material relating to the life of Abraham Lincoln, a man he considered "our greatest American."[322]

Clark's office was a reflection of himself. Behind his desk, pictures of himself with every U.S. President since Wilson hung tossing out the ceremonial first pitch. Two hunting rifles were proudly displayed on the wall, one given to him by Al Spalding. A portrait of the Lone Ranger also clung to the wall, as well as a picture of the club's top star and Griffith's good friend Walter Johnson. A framed picture of Abraham Lincoln was displayed with an accompanying hand-written letter the President sent to

---

[321] Bob Broeg, "Griffith made Cronin part of Family affair in Baseball," *St. Louis Post-Dispatch*, November 3, 1968, p. B2

[322] "Clark Griffith says People are Wonderful," *Washington Star, Sunday Pictorial Magazine*, May 1, 1949, p. 4

a mother who lost five sons during the Civil War.[323] On his desk sat a simple yet poignant slogan, "Long Life: Sleep plenty, eat moderately and keep your conscience clean." He also had a slew of family photos displayed on his desk.

Stored in Clark's desk at the time of his death were numerous mementos of a long and exciting career in baseball.[324] Among the mundane items were his social security card, religious tracts and medals, honorary cards from various local organizations, dozens of clippings and pictures, a schedule from the 1897 season, letters dating back to 1880, autographed baseballs and a picture of the 1924 Senators. There was a loaded golf ball waiting to be slid on Joe Fitzgerald's tee. There was also hand-carved miniature furniture crafted by an employee at the ballpark that was a birthday gift.

Another golf ball bore the printed inscription "Mr. Vice President." At a recent celebrity golf tournament, Griffith walked on the first tee but forgot a ball. By this time, he was in his eighties and only ceremonially hit one ball and bowed out of the tournament. Richard Nixon flipped him a ball. There was also a silver bullet presented to Griffith on his birthday from The Lone Ranger.

Griffith also kept a scorecard that President Dwight D. Eisenhower filled out on Opening Day 1953 with big bold writing highlighting Mickey Vernon's game-winning home run against Allie Reynolds and the Yankees. It was signed, "For Clark Griffith, from his old friend, Dwight D. Eisenhower." Griffith also tucked away a rabbit's foot with a St. Christopher medal attached that was given to him by Mamie Eisenhower's mother, Minnie Doud, the same day.

There was a chunk of copper from his Montana farm. Two mini wooden bats carved from his Normal, Illinois boyhood home sat in one drawer. Another drawer held the three-year contract he signed on May 20, 1915 to manage the Senators. It called for a $10,000 salary to be paid over fourteen semi-monthly payments of $714.28.

The most interesting and amusing pieces were handwritten notes Griffith kept after many games from his youth. One in particular described a game that was forfeited to Louisville due to Clark's excessive

---

[323] "Clark Griffith says People are Wonderful," *Washington Star, Sunday Pictorial Magazine*, May 1, 1949, p. 4 – The letter written to Mrs. Lydia Bixby of Boston was the basis for the movie *Saving Private Ryan*.

[324] Desk contents described by Bob Addie in "Bob Addie's Column," *Washington Post*, November 24, 1955, p. 55

arguing. The simplicity of the note speaks volumes, "Game forfeited because of umpire's failure."

CHAPTER THIRTEEN

POLITICS OF THE GAME

A three-man board called the National Commission was formed in 1903 that administered major league baseball through the first two decades of the twentieth century. It effectively ended in February 1920 when Garry Herrmann, its nominal head, resigned following a no-confidence vote by National League owners. It was in essence toppled for two main reasons. First, there had to be a loser in each dispute. When the commission ruled against one team, giving rights of a player to a rival owner, hard feelings were harbored by the loser in the battle. The two most recent acrimonious cases involved Scott Perry and George Sisler. The resentments ran much deeper than mere player rights. The game brought together a diverse group of strong businessmen and personalities; they often clashed. The second major reason stemmed from the autocratic power wielded by American League president Ban Johnson.

  Johnson was the force behind the success of the American League. He amassed more power and more say in league operations than any National League president ever would. In the early years, he shifted monies and personnel around virtually at will. His fingers were in every pie. Typically, all financing matters and player transactions went through him. Managers were often hired and fired on his whim. Certainly, he controlled which potential buyers were ultimately accepted and wielded this power to his benefit. For his efforts, he was paid handsomely and, actually, became an investor in several franchises.

Johnson also had a way of alienating people. His tight relationship with Charles Comiskey disintegrated and others harbored resentments from Johnson's heavy-handedness. The initial tremors came as the first wave of American League owners sold out. No longer did club owners owe their strict allegiance to the American League president. They began to feel pushed around by him, a man they considered a caretaker of their investment, not its ultimate authority. When he voided the Yankees' acquisition of Carl Mays in 1919, club owners Jacob Ruppert and Cap Huston took him to court. Harry Frazee and Charles Comiskey leapt into the argument, siding with the Yankees. In the end, Johnson lost the battle, his power forever diminished.

Johnson was nothing if not spiteful; he made a disastrous attempt to have the Giants expel the Yankees from the Polo Grounds. He blatantly wanted the lease broken, a move detrimental to one of his clubs. The Yankees had played at the Polo Grounds since 1913 and continued to do so until Yankee Stadium opened in 1923. All hell broke loose. Ruppert and Huston charged the American League president with attempting to willfully damage their investment and force them from the league. Clearly, he stepped over the line in his efforts to get back at Ruppert and Huston; he was not above acting to the detriment of the league as a whole.

Griffith became a force in league politics during World War I. He was in a unique position residing in Washington D.C. near the nation's lawmakers and influential government personnel; however, it was the sheer force of his personality and his unrelenting will and promotion of the sport that cultivated them and established him as the unofficial ambassador of the game. His contributions will be examined later but he often took the point on many baseball issues, especially during the Depression and World War II when Judge Landis' staunch conservatism was scarcely welcomed by the White House.

In hindsight, it's clear that Major League Baseball entered 1920 under a cloud. Amid the challenge to Ban Johnson deeper ills were uncovered. Eight ballplayers conspired to throw the hallowed World Series in 1919. The Black Sox Scandal is the single darkest event in the history of American sports. It threatened the very core of the game, the public's confidence in the integrity of its matches. The fallout exposed the flaws in the system.

The Black Sox may have tainted the game in October 1919, but Griffith's former first baseman Hal Chase had been doing it for years. The byproduct of which led to the Series scandal. The fact that Chase routinely fixed games or at least tried to and got away with it added to a feeling of invincibility among the players. To boot, league officials routinely cleared Chase of any wrongdoings, often praising his sterling reputation when doing so. And, still other managers, like John McGraw, sought his presence on their rosters! In essence, many knew Chase was making additional cash with questionable play and saw that little was being done about it.

Some other players, a few even independent of Chase, had in one form or another benefited financially by appeasing gamblers. A lot of ballplayers spent their off hours in company with questionable characters either in a saloon, poll hall or elsewhere. Certainly, clean ballplayers knew this and drew their own conclusions. Rumors abound. Even if a player didn't know what was going on or how to get in on it, surely, it led at least to curiosity. Some even saw it as an opportunity to enhance their income. The temptation was present. In fact, notorious owner Harry Frazee openly permitted gambling at Fenway Park and gamblers even mobbed the field during a game in June 1917 trying to force a forfeit and victory for the opponent.

World War I forced the closing of racetracks. Gamblers sought other avenues of income. Ballplayers are notorious carousers and, as such, often found themselves in the company of like-minded individuals. It was only a matter of time before the two elements linked up. Gamblers have always befriended sports figures. With the tracks closed they had more time and devoted interest to do so. Similarly, with the doors shut in baseball after the Black Sox scandal, gamblers found their way to the upstart National Football League.

Baseball had an unwritten policy that it wanted to avoid negative press concerning these issues. Considering this, a player could have easily inferred that there was a well established "don't ask, don't tell" policy. If the corruption was present and no one brought it to light, why not take part and cash in?

Major League Baseball had a long history of incorporating gamblers and questionable politicians into its ownership ranks. In New York, Tammany Hall financed or otherwise gained influence in club operations from the beginning of the old National Association. As recently as 1914, a famed gambler, Frank Farrell, owned the Yankees. Oddly, or suspiciously, he shared ownership with former corrupt New York City police commissioner William Devery. Together, Devery and Ferrell, with Tim Sullivan, a future partner of Arnold Rothstein, controlled gambling in Manhattan during the 1890s. Likewise, Tammany cronies James Gaffney and John Carroll purchased the Boston Braves in 1912.[325]

Known gamblers, such as Rothstein, were frequent guests of management at the ballparks and often sat in the highly visible owners' boxes. Braves' owner Emil Fuchs was Rothstein's attorney and Giants' owner Charles Stoneham was a long-time business partner with the gambler. In turn, Rothstein was more than friendly with John McGraw. In fact, it was at McGraw's pool joint that Rothstein first gained fame after a marathon billiards contest in 1908.

This was the problem that particularly plagued Judge Landis in the early part of his tenure. Over the years, gamblers cultivated many strong relationships within the baseball industry, particularly in New York and Chicago. Al Capone could often be found shaking hands and joking with the players and officials in Chicago ballparks, even posing for a picture with Gabby Hartnett. It was only due to Landis' zero-tolerance of associating with gamblers and the fear of his wrath that broke the cycle. Along these lines, baseball found the perfect individual to lead it out of crisis.

Judge Landis became a national figure due to the important cases he ruled upon, mainly the Standard Oil antitrust case in which he forced John D. Rockefeller to travel to Chicago and appear before him. The Industrial Workers of the World, a union formed by socialists, anarchist and radicals, case during World War I also made national headlines as Landis sentenced I.W.W. secretary-treasurer Big Bill Haywood and 92 others to prison. Afterwards a bomb was exploded in the Federal Building, but Landis escaped injury. Landis also jailed Congressman Victor Berger for allegedly obstructing the nation's war preparations.

Baseball was a lifelong passion of Landis'. He played amateur and semi-pro ball in his hometown of Logansport, Indiana. Later, he worked and lived in Chicago, baseball's number-two-city and the hub of many crucial events in baseball history. He was often seen at the ballpark. The Federal League case brought Landis a great deal of appreciation and admiration from major league executives.

On January 5, 1915, the Federal League filed suit in federal court in Chicago, asking Judge Landis to declare illegal and void baseball's

---

[325] Gaffney, a partner in the New York City contracting firm Bradley, Gaffney & Steers, became interested in baseball ownership via his friendship with Griffith. The two became close during Griff's time with the Highlanders. *Sporting Life*, December 23, 1911, p. 7

National Commission and the National Agreement, the negotiated basic agreement that governed all of Organized Baseball. Landis was chosen, in part, because of the national attention he received in the Sherman Antitrust case against Standard Oil. The basic claim was that Major League Baseball was operating as an illegal monopoly and wielding that power. MLB, it was argued, had under its purview all but 300 of the approximate 10,000 professional ballplayers in the country. The Federal League wanted sweeping changes and rulings stating that the defendants are a monopoly, that the defendants have conspired against them and that all player contracts be declared null and void. Plus, they wanted compensation for such. Among the Federal League's filings is an affidavit by Miner Brown declaring that two players were traded for dogs.[326]

The case was presented on January 20 with Federal League attorneys strenuously claiming that the minor leagues and the players are oppressed by the monopolistic actions of MLB. Arguments were heard through the 23rd. Landis made a telling comment, as the *New York Times* puts it, "He characterized baseball as a national institution and warned both sides that it would not be well for anyone to strike a blow against it." Additionally, he was quoted as saying to a Federal League attorney, "Do you realize that a decision in this case may tear down the very foundations of the game, so loved by thousands, and do you realize that the decision might also seriously affect both parties?"[327]

On January 24, Landis began a long process of mulling the case over. Many within Organized Baseball hoped that he would find that the Sherman Antitrust laws didn't pertain to this case. Landis secretly hoped this himself but found the Federal League arguments compelling along these lines, causing him to repeatedly ask both parties to what end they felt the suit might lead. As this realization hit Landis, he retired to chambers and sat on the case. Later, he actively and indirectly[328] pushed

---

[326] Miner Brown submitted an affidavit claiming that Joe Cantillon, manager of Minneapolis of the American Association, traded a player for a bulldog. Brown also claimed that Roger Bresnahan, while manager of the Cardinals, traded a pitcher named Hooper to Richard Kinsella, manager of the Springfield, Ill. club of the Three-I League, for a bird dog.

[327] "Judge Landis takes Baseball Case under Advisement." *New York Times*, January 24, 1915, p. S1

[328] On April 27, 1915 the *New York Times* reported that Judge Landis held a conversation with his personal friend, Judge George Williams of St. Louis, asking him to intercede in securing a peace settlement between the parties. Williams then consulted with Phil Ball, owner of the St. Louis Federals, and Browns' owner Robert Hedges. Williams was currently and had been for a long time personal counsel to Hedges. Ball and Hedges both

the sides to settle the case so that he wouldn't be forced to rule on the matter. In the end, when the settlement occurred, Landis made statements along the lines that he considered the case a draw, finding weight in both arguments.

In December, an agreement was reached; however, the Federal League's Baltimore franchise left the meeting disgusted. They later filed separately and took the case to the United States Supreme Court. In October 1916 Landis headed an anti sports gambling crusade in Chicago. The following month he was mentioned for the first time as a potential head of the National Commission. On November 12, 1920, Landis was appointed as a one-man commission to act as the sole arbiter in major league disputes. The minor leagues soon endorse him as head of Organized Baseball as well.

Whispers of questionable conduct were heard throughout baseball history. Even National Commission chairman Garry Herrmann, the Cincinnati Reds' president and a politically questionable character, wagered $6,000 that Pittsburgh wouldn't win the pennant in 1906. To help his cause, Herrmann shipped outfielder Cy Seymour to the Giants. The previous summer Seymour led the league in hits, doubles, triples, RBI, batting average and slugging average.

It was accepted practice for one team's players to pay an inducement to another team's players for future or past victories over a pennant rival. Many variations of this took place and were uncovered by Judge Landis' investigations of the 1920s, particularly in the Ty Cobb/Tris Speaker affair. This practice personified the era. Players, en masse, thought nothing of the implications. Similar "incentives" can be traced as far back as an 1893 contest between Baltimore and Pittsburgh. Officially, inducements were not disallowed until Landis' ruling after an investigation of a 1917 case involving the Tigers and White Sox. The commissioner then expressed his reluctance to officially look into any further matters that occurred before his hiring, in essence giving amnesty for previous misdeeds.

Much of what we know about gambling and game-fixing scandals comes from players who were accused of malfeasance. When someone is charged, it sets of a chain reaction of accusations. The large majority of players never spoke publically on the issue. No one wants to be a rat. You have to live and travel with your peers day in and day out. Hence, no one

---

travel to Chicago to meet Landis in hopes of coming to some kind of agreement. "Judge Landis may end Baseball War," New York Times, April 27, 1915, p. 10

turned another player in. Only the fear of Landis changed that in the future.

This underlying current led in part to the disaster in October 1919. Griffith was never involved in the slightest with this activity. He employed Bill Burns, Hal Chase and Black Sox Chick Gandil but that was at the beginning of their careers. He worked for Tammany men in New York but that was a necessity; his focus stayed within the foul lines. Griffith was never a carouser and, thus, never stumbled into a compromising incident. Since he became a full-fledge owner in 1920, it was partially his mess to clean up. Actually, it was a benefit. Baseball was about to soar. The decisions made in 1920 and '21, the onslaught of Babe Ruth on-the-field and in the newspapers and prime economic conditions catapulted attendance and interest in the game to new heights.

Complicating matters, half the American League was in revolt against its president in 1920 and now the game's ruling body, the National Commission, was about to disband. The Yankees didn't relent; in fact, they broadened the lawsuits to include other American League officials. Ruppert wanted Ban Johnson out. Charles Comiskey of Chicago and Harry Frazee of Boston joined the Yankees in this sentiment.

The "Insurrectos", as they were named, attacked the validity of Johnson's twenty-year contract that he was awarded in 1910. But, they were only three. The Loyal 5 (Phil Ball of St. Louis, Griffith and Connie Mack, Frank Navin of Detroit and Jim Dunn of Cleveland) sat on the other side. At the winter meetings the Insurrectos were continually outvoted. Johnson kept up his defiance. However, many throughout baseball became irate with the American League president for blocking efforts to find a neutral party to head the National Commission.

Griffith allied with his old friend Johnson. Things became so bitter that the Yankees refused to trade with Washington in response to Griffith's backing. Clark took on the role of problem solver, trying to gain peace between the factions. In February 1920 peace, at least temporarily, won out. The Yankees got what they wanted, Carl Mays and a reduction of Johnson's powers. A two-man Board of Arbitration was established to review the American League president's fines and suspensions, effectively ending his autocratic rule. Both Ruppert and Griffith sat on this board.

During these meetings, Griffith won a personal long-standing battle. After years of preaching and campaigning, he finally gained a ban on the spitball and other freak deliveries on February 9. Knowing he was financially outgunned, Clark also pushed to limit the dollar sale of players to the preset waiver price. Clearly, this was a response to the sale of Babe

Ruth to New York the previous month. He never gained this concession. He made a similar proposal at the end of the 1930s to eliminate trades with the league's pennant winner, another obvious strike at the Yankees.

The end of 1920 brought another confrontational battle, this one over nominations to head the National Commission. Johnson knew this would completely usurp his powers. Consequently, he stonewalled nearly the entire year. The National League asserted itself on the issue; they wanted it resolved. On November 8, in Chicago the National League formally dissolved their alliance. The Insurrectos then seceded from the American League and joined a new twelve-team National League that was formed at least on paper. The first of the Loyal 5 to jump ship was offered the twelfth spot.

    National League executives sped off to Kansas City where the minor leagues were meeting to gain their support. Griffith was thrust into the role of peacemaker yet again. In Kansas City he jumped from meeting to meeting, trying to ease tensions and form a compromise that would maintain the status quo and save the two-league structure. He set a truce meeting with Charlie Ebbets of Brooklyn and held discussions with Garry Herrmann, bluffing him into believing that the Loyal 5 had the resolve and potential backers to establish a strong eight-team American League. Herrmann privately admitted that the National League really didn't want the Insurrectos and their troubles.

    All decided to return to Chicago for peace negotiations. The league presidents were excluded from the conversation. On November 12, Judge Landis was ushered in to replace the commission; baseball had its first commissioner. Griffith and ten other owners hopped a cab to formally offer the Chicago jurist the job. Landis smartly held out for the sweetest terms. Johnson waged several battles with the Judge, jockeying for power over the years. Johnson maintained his post for seven more years but the balance of power was forever shifted in 1920. The autocratic reign was over.

CHAPTER FOURTEEN

RIDING HIGH IN THE NATION'S CAPITAL

As soon as Griffith gained administrative control of the Senators, he contacted Harry Frazee in Boston who was seemingly auctioning off all his men except Harry Hooper. Washington was interested in Everett Scott and Braggo Roth. There was no way he could afford the asking price for Babe Ruth; it wasn't even a consideration. On January 20, the deal was made, Roth and Joe Shannon were headed to Washington. Griffith took another big step in D.C. history when he hired the club's first scout, Doc White, a popular pitcher and a native of the area. The Yankees had just made the extravagant deal for Ruth; the Roaring Twenties were off and running. The Ruth trade reverberated throughout the industry. Obviously, there was a ton of money to be had. The news hit just as Clark was mailing out the annual contracts to his players. Like every other owner in the majors, Griffith had a tougher time than usual inking the men to deals in early 1920.

Nineteen Twenty started off on a sour note. Utility infielder Joe Leonard fell ill while the club was in New York in late April. He was sent home for treatment but died on May 3 following appendix surgery. He was suffering from pneumonia as well; the surgery revealed that the appendix burst, causing gangrene. He was just 25 years old. In August a Carl Mays pitch killed Ray Chapman. As usual, Clark was quick to react and condemn an opponent. He sent the following telegram to Ban Johnson on August 17: "The American League should take immediate and drastic action regarding Mays and no alibi to be considered. You know this man and his methods. The public and players will act if you don't." It was harsh knee-jerk rhetoric and obviously sent at an emotional time. Saner heads would prevail.

Clark was overworked in 1920. He performed his usual duties managing the club, making trades and scouting. But, now he had all the administrative and financial details to oversee; the club was his and his alone. Personnel changes alone constituted a full-time job. So he made the smart move and turned over his field management duties to trusted lieutenant George McBride, who served as team captain and Griffith's right-hand man since he came to Washington. McBride hadn't appeared in over eighteen games since 1917. Since then he expanded his role to include coaching the infielders, base coaching and filling in as manager while Griff was away on scouting or administrative trips.[329]

McBride was the premier American League shortstop of his era. He led the league six times in double plays, five times in fielding average, four times in games, three times in putouts and once in assists and range. While the famed double play combination of Tinker to Evers to Chance only copped one double play crown between them,[330] McBride captured every one from 1908-1912 and again in '14. He was your typical good field, no hit shortstop. After sixteen years in the big leagues, his career batting average resided at a mere .218 and never did rise above .235. He posted the lowest career batting average and slugging average of all men with over 4,000 at bats.

Clark at all times maintained his general manager's role and authority of course. He suggested lineup changes, made trades and signed all the young talent; thus, plotting the course for each season. This was especially true during the championship seasons when he employed young, inexperienced field managers. Throughout his tenure in Washington, Griffith also was the club's primary press contact. He traveled with the club, watched all home games and oversaw training sessions both during the spring and throughout the season. He lent a hand here and there and never did relinquish his role as coach and mentor to his players. Along these lines he was known as "Teach" to generations of Washington ballplayers. His presence was felt daily throughout the organization. In essence he was the organization outside the field of play, probably more so than all but a few baseball magnates in history. He maintained administrative control over all essential club affairs until his death in 1955.

---

[329] Stephen Able, "George McBride" entry in *Deadball Stars of the American League*, 2006

[330] In fact, they only turned 56 double plays total in the pennant years 1906-10.

Griffith was a fundamental link to the fans. Often found among the spectators in the stands, Clark would talk baseball with anyone at anytime. His new role took him to countless banquets and charity events. Administratively, a lot changed with the club. For one, Clark became a huge benefactor for a slew of causes throughout the community. He lent the ballpark for countless causes and donor drives, for both the white and black communities. As Calvin Griffith became influential in club operations during the 1940s, he had numerous conversations with Griffith about at least charging a fee to cover cleaning costs. Clark wouldn't hear of it.

Griffith also embarked on improving the facility to accommodate more seating. To help offset this cost, he courted college football teams and boxing and wrestling promoters to hold their events at the expanded and renamed Clark Griffith Stadium. Nineteen Twenty also proved to be a pivotal year in the evolution of professional football and organized black baseball. Both eventually based clubs at Griffith Stadium and kept the Senators afloat financially during the Depression and for many years thereafter.

On July 27, 1921, the popular McBride was beaned in the temple during practice, suffering a concussion and lingering dizziness and fainting spells. Still in ill health, he resigned at the end of the year. The managerial job was turned over to first Clyde Milan and then Donie Bush for a year apiece. From 1920-1923, the club finished no higher than fourth, actually jumping from sixth place to fourth twice. But, there was definitely an upward swing in attendance, as there was throughout professional baseball.

In mid-1922, Griffith got into a war of words with Commissioner Landis. In wake of the Black Sox affair the Judge was making rounds to all the clubs warning the players about gambling and carousing and his wrath against such. Clark took it as a personal insult to his ballplayers, claiming that 98% of the men in baseball were honest and clean living. He refused to let the commissioner lecture to the Senators.

By the 1920s, one of the great builders in major league history, Ted Sullivan, was living in D.C. Griffith tapped his expertise and contacts, hiring him as a part-time scout. In May 1922, Sullivan took a trip to Europe looking to drum up excitement for a possible international exhibition tour featuring John McGraw's New York Giants and Griffith' Senators. Other international tours took place in 1874, 1888 and 1913. He traveled to Dublin, London and Paris but it was a no-go; the interest wasn't there.

In August 1923, Griffith finalized plans to expand seating at American League Park and make it more accommodating for football. The park was officially renamed after the club's president.

Taking the opportunity to back away from field responsibilities, Griffith set about building his championship clubs. The Senators already boasted such top talent as second baseman Bucky Harris, Walter Johnson, first baseman Joe Judge, right fielder Sam Rice and lefthanded pitcher Tom Zachary. On January 20, 1921, the Senators received lefthanded starter George Mogridge in a trade with the Yankees. He was a control pitcher and tossed the first no-hitter in Yankee history on April 24, 1917. Unbeknown to American League umpires, Mogridge threw a resin ball well after the spitball was banned. He hid the substance under the bill of his cap.

Scout Joe Engel picked up third baseman Ozzie Bluege from Peoria of the Three-I League for cash on August 27, 1921. Bluege was a rarity, a ballplayer that neither smoked nor drank. During the off-season, he worked, like his father, as an accountant for many prominent D.C. hotels and other businesses. Griffith, worried about his batting eye, ordered Bluege to stop doing so; however, the Senators didn't pay enough for him to quit. Another longtime employee, he worked for the organization until 1972 as a player, coach, manager, farm director and controller. Responding to a tip by Idaho Senator Herman Welker, Bluege was the one that signed a hard-hitting youngster named Harmon Killebrew.

Clark was golfing with a stockholder of the International League Orioles at the Suburban Country Club in Baltimore in September 1921 when he overheard that Jack Dunn was purchasing an outfielder from Joe Engel of Columbia in the South Atlantic League for $6,500. Griffith jumped on the phone with Engel and bought Goose Goslin from under Dunn for $7,000. Columbia had just run away with the pennant by 11.5 games. Goslin killed the ball, leading the league in batting, runs, hits and RBI. Seven thousand dollars was a steal for a twenty-year old that hit .390 with 131 runs batted in. Goslin, a New Jersey farm boy, was first discovered pitching semi-pro ball by minor league umpire Bill McGowan. Later, Goslin returned the favor, asking Griffith to help get McGowan promoted to the American League staff. The umpire worked in the league from 1925-1954, eventually gaining election to the Hall of Fame.

Griffith picked up top shortstop Roger Peckinpaugh in a three-way deal in January 1922. He was quietly building his championship club. Back in 1914, Peckinpaugh became the youngest ever manager at age 23, overseeing the final twenty games of the season for the Yankees. The Senators picked up catcher Muddy Ruel for $12,500 and center fielder Nemo Leibold in 1923. Ruel was the catcher when Carl Mays fatally beaned Ray Chapman. Another rarity, Ruel possessed a law degree from Washington University and later worked as an assistant to Commissioner Happy Chandler.

The Senators also added Allan Russell and Firpo Marberry to their roster in 1923. Both became key relievers for the club. Russell came over in a trade with the Red Sox in February 1923. He was one of the few remaining legal spitballers but his arm could no longer handle the strain of starting. Marberry, a purchase from Little Rock, became the game's first great relief pitcher; still, few realize that he posted a stellar 94-52 record as a starter. He was nicknamed for a resemblance to heavyweight contender Luis Firpo. A late starter, Marberry never pitched until he was 21 years old in 1920. After his playing career, he landed a job as an umpire in the American League in 1935.

Griffith needed a manager for 1924. He approached Ed Barrow multiple times to take the position but he was comfortable being the business manager of the World Champion Yankees. He also attempted but failed to trade with Charles Comiskey for Eddie Collins to take over the managerial reigns, a deal that involved Bucky Harris. George McBride was also asked to come out of retirement. The club president even briefly considered returning to the dugout himself. Finally, on February 9 he named 27-year old second baseman Harris to the post. Baseball men were a little stunned, some even questioning whether the Old Fox had gone senile, especially the club's veteran players. Harris was younger than all the Nat regulars save Goose Goslin and Ozzie Bluege.

Harris had been with the club since 1919; he was a solid player but no superstar. To name such a player with only four full seasons of experience to the position was unusual indeed; however, Griffith felt that he had a pennant winner and the "Boy Manager" was just the man to see to the crowning. Harris' playing skills quickly deteriorated after 1927, but he managed in the big leagues through 1956, picking up over 2,100 victories, three pennants, two world championships and a plaque in the Hall of Fame.

Harris also played professional basketball and it was with some difficulty that Griffith kept him away from the sport. Harris married Elizabeth Sutherland, the daughter of former U.S. Senator Howard Sutherland from West Virginia, one of Calvin Coolidge's administration officials. The President and First Lady, Grace, a huge baseball fan, attended the wedding in October 1926. Harris managed for Griffith in four decades over three separate occasions: 1924-1928, 1935-1942 and 1950-1954.

Prior to the 1924 season, the height of the right field wall at Griffith Stadium was raised to forty feet. On April 29, Clark won the release of his former second baseman Ray Morgan from a Baltimore jail. He was sentenced in February for attacking a patrolman. Griffith guaranteed his good behavior and hired Morgan as a scout.[331] He also hired his old pitching standout Jack Chesbro as third base coach; it was his first job in Organized Baseball since 1909. Chesbro was gone by June as Griffith rehired Al Schacht to team with fellow clown Nick Altrock. The two entertained the crowd for years to come.

The club sat in seventh place in mid-May but was solidly in first place after winning seventeen of 19 games just before July 4. The Senators went 18-7 during September to hold off the Yankees by two games. During the pennant run the club added righthanded swing pitcher Curley Ogden, and his perennial sore arm, off waivers from Connie Mack. Griffith also bought Earl McNeely from Sacramento of the Pacific Coast League for $35,000 and three other players to strengthen the outfield. McNeely arrived with a dislocated shoulder and Griffith held up payment, appealing to Commissioner Landis. The Judge agreed but McNeely started hitting so Griff paid up. In 43 games, the center fielder batted .330.

Interestingly, both league champions led the league in saves; times were changing. Unbelievable today, the pennant-winning Senators hit the fewest homers in the game in 1924, 22. This was the lively ball era? They also scored the third fewest runs. Obviously, pitching kept them in the pennant race; the mound staff gave up the fewest runs in all of baseball. Sam Rice led the league in hits and Goose Goslin the same in RBI. Babe Ruth captured pretty much every other offensive category. Walter Johnson led the league in wins, winning percentage, shutouts, strikeouts, fewest hits per inning, ERA and opponent batting average and on-base percentage. He was named the American League's Most Valuable Player. Reliever Firpo Marberry led in appearances and saves. Fellow reliever By Speece also proved integral as a late-inning replacement.

---

[331] "Clark Griffith wins release of Former Player from Jail," *New York Times*, April 30, 1924, p. 17

All hell broke loose just prior to the World Series. On September 27, 23-year-old, sophomore Giants outfielder Jimmy O'Connell approached Phillies shortstop Heinie Sand and offered him a bribe. Specifically, Sand was reportedly offered $500 to tank games to the Giants who were in a close pennant race with the Dodgers and Pirates. All three teams finished within three games of the flag; New York in the end won the pennant. Landis investigated and O'Connell confessed, naming coach Cozy Dolan as the instigator along with several other teammates including future Hall of Famers George Kelly, Ross Youngs and Frankie Frisch. Dolan was evasive under questioning. Landis permanently banned both Dolan and O'Connell on the eve of the World Series. The others were cleared. The Giants paid $75,000 to acquire O'Connell from San Francisco of the Pacific Coast League a mere two years earlier.[332]

A cry erupted throughout the baseball community calling for the removal of the Giants from the World Series or canceling the event altogether. Barney Dreyfuss and Ban Johnson, as part of their running feuds with John McGraw, among others supported the cancellation. Johnson even threatened legal action to stop the postseason matchup. This was Griffith's shining moment; he was irate, to put it mildly, with the American League president. Ending the storm, Landis ruled on October 2 that the World Series would go on as it always had.

Clark added seventeen rows of temporary seats in left field and some more in right center. The Senators won in seven games with Harris, Goose Goslin, Joe Judge, Tom Zachary and Roger Peckinpaugh leading the charge. Rightfully, Walter Johnson gained the final victory in the 12th inning when McNeely's grounder popped over third baseman Fred Lindstrom's head scoring Muddy Ruel. After eighteen seasons, Johnson had his world championship. Griffith reveled in the victory, calling it his greatest moment in the game. The fact that it came at the expense of two old foes, the Yankees and John McGraw, only made it sweeter. Clark lit up a cigar and let out a smile.

Ban Johnson intensified his rampage roundly criticizing Landis and even poking his head into Pacific Coast League affairs, further encroaching on the Judge's purview. The American League owners, united in support of Landis, issued a reprimand of Johnson and threatened his job. In Comiskey's words, "Shape up or ship out." Griffith had enough as well. What was Johnson doing trying to deprive him of a World Series

---

[332] This incident was never fully explained and leaves a lot to the imagination concerning just how many individuals were involved and to what extent.

appearance and the resulting financial windfall? The Judge was pleased; his chief rival was being smothered. Johnson kept at it and all but sealed his fate by calling for federal control of the game and remitting a spiteful telegram blaming Bucky Harris for losing the 1925 World Series. Johnson lost virtually all support; Griffith finally withdrew his support. It all ended in 1926. Johnson battled the Judge over a resin bag rule and lost, but the nail in his coffin stemmed from the Ty Cobb/Tris Speaker affair.

Out of the blue, Tigers player-manager Ty Cobb and Indians player-manager Tris Speaker turned in their resignations in late 1926. They were two of the finest players of the Deadball Era and two of the biggest names in the game. The sporting public was shocked and reporters suspected an underlying scandal. There was. In June, Ban Johnson paid $20,000 to former pitcher Dutch Leonard for two letters penned by Ty Cobb and Smokey Joe Wood. Supposedly, they implicated Cobb, Speaker, Wood and Leonard in a gambling scandal back in 1919. In consultation with other league officials, Johnson set about to push the two out of the game. Leonard and Wood were already retired.

Johnson must have been having a flashback to the old days if he believed he could unilaterally make these decisions without the Judge's consent. Landis commandeered the evidence and investigated. In the interim he released information for the press to mull over. Cobb and Speaker hired heavy-hitting lawyers and took their case to the media. Public opinion naturally weighed in favor of the superstars. In fact, Landis was vilified for publicizing the information prematurely. Cobb and Speaker were highly respected among the baseball public, two of the top-tier icons.

Landis delayed his decision, in part, to test the patience of Johnson. Another gambling case arose and Landis poured his full attention into conducting an investigation and interviewing witnesses. Meanwhile, Johnson was stewing. It was the beginning of the end for the American League president. Landis was very publicly usurping his power and humiliating him. Johnson popped off to the press that no matter what Landis decided Cobb and Speaker would never be allowed in the American League again. Landis hit the roof and called a meeting of the American League owners. Frustrated, Johnson felt the walls closing in. He went into an angry public tirade condemning Landis for everything supposedly wrong with the game since he took office. As mentioned, he even called for federal control of the game.

In essence, Johnson was forcing a showdown with Landis but he did not have the votes to do so. The owners met on January 23, 1927. Johnson came under immediate attack. Ultimately, they forced him to take time off due to "health reasons." He didn't return until Opening Day. On

January 27, Landis issued the ruling clearing the superstars and made a point of assuring that they re-signed with teams in the American League. Cobb joined Connie Mack in Philadelphia and Speaker signed with Griffith in Washington. Johnson fell out of favor with nearly every league executive. On July 8, the American League owners called a meeting under the pretext of discussing rule changes. Johnson must have known what was coming. He refused to attend but stayed nearby in the hotel. A debate ensued with Phil Ball of St. Louis the only real ally of Johnson. Three times the meeting broke up so Griffith, Ball and Jacob Ruppert could respectfully try to gain Johnson's resignation. Finally, Johnson slid it under the door. He left at the end of the season.

Griffith was feeling generous after the World Series. He gave Walter Johnson a raise to $20,000 and Harris a three-year deal at $30,000 a season. In December, the Senators picked up lefthanded pitcher Dutch Ruether off waivers from Brooklyn and future Hall of Fame spitballer Stanley Coveleski in a trade with Cleveland. The older pitchers were brought in to add stability to the staff. Forty-year-old Vern Gregg was added as well but that experiment failed.

The Senators beefed up their run production by 79 in 1925 and the pitchers still kept the bats quiet. Relief pitching proved integral yet again. The Nats won the pennant by 8.5 games over Philadelphia. Coveleski and Johnson each won twenty games for the Nats and Marberry again led in appearances and saves. Catcher Muddy Ruel led the league in virtually every fielding category. Coveleski led the league in ERA and Johnson had the lowest opponent batting average. Each was among the top-four in keeping men off base. Shortstop Roger Peckinpaugh was named the league's Most Valuable Player.

The World Series went to seven games again but Pittsburgh emerged the victor with two wins a piece by Ray Kremer and Vic Aldridge. Johnson also won two games but Coveleski dropped as many. Peckinpaugh had a horrendous series, committing eight errors including key miscues in Game 7. Leery of the Black Sox affair, Commissioner Landis had the shortstop followed by a detective after the series to make sure he wasn't under the influence of a gambler.

Griffith brought in Tris Speaker for a whopping $30,000 in 1927. The Red Sox approached the Senators in April seeking a trade for shortstop Buddy Myer. Clark didn't want to make the deal but Speaker convinced manager Bucky Harris to push for the deal. The Senators received Topper Rigney in return. Myer wasn't the best shortstop in the world but Griffith took a liking to him. He hit .281 with Boston in 1927 and .313 in '28. The boss wasn't please; it took five ballplayers to regain Myers' in a trade in December 1928. Joe Cronin was initially one of those five; luckily, the Red Sox chose Bobby Reeves instead. The incident was partly responsible for Harris' firing after the 1928 season. Myers, a graduate of Mississippi A&M, was originally purchased from New Orleans for $25,000. He converted to second base and manned that position in D.C. through 1941. A career .303-hitter, he won the batting crown in 1935 with a .349 mark.

After the 1927 season, Walter Johnson retired after twenty-one seasons. Two days later on October 17, Ban Johnson cleaned out his desk and said goodbye to his staff. In July 1928, Joe Engel told Griffith about a shortstop in Kansas City who was returned to the minors by Pittsburgh, who was rich on the left side of the infield with Pie Traynor and Glenn Wright. Kansas City was about to sell him to Wichita when Engel stepped in and offered $7,500 for Joe Cronin. The 21-year-old didn't even have a suit to wear to D.C.; he borrowed Engel's. Heading into Griffith's office, Engel introduced Cronin to Clark's secretary and adopted niece Millie. The scout forever took credit for introducing the future husband and wife.

Cronin was a San Francisco kid signed by Pirates' scout Joe Devine out of Sacred Heart College while playing semi-pro ball near Napa. Bucky Harris and Griffith argued throughout the 1928 season about the shortstop position. Griffith preferred Bobby Reeves at the position and ordered his manager to play him. Harris favored Cronin and began playing him at short on the road since Clark wasn't traveling with the club. Eventually, Harris proved right and Reeves was shipped to the Red Sox in the deal that brought Myers back to the Senators.

Late in 1928, Griffith contemplated buying the International League Baltimore Orioles. It would potentially be his first formal farm club. Jack Dunn, one of the most successful minor league owners and managers, just died of a heart attack while riding a horse during a dog show in Towson, Maryland on October 22. Dunn owned the club since 1909, purchasing it from Ned Hanlon for $70,000. Clark decided against the purchase and George Weiss stepped in to buy the franchise. Griffith also contemplated a purchase of Atlanta in 1929 before finally buying Chattanooga, his first official farm team.

On December 19, Bucky Harris was traded to the Detroit Tigers. He had slowed in the field and the Senators had just finished in fourth place, so Clark decided to make a move. Plus, teammates were complaining that Harris became too "heady" after his marriage to a diplomat's daughter. The District was ecstatic after Walter Johnson was named as the club's new manager.

In March 1929, Judge Landis declared Senators pitchers Guy Cantrell and Mel Simons free agents and fined the club $1,500 for "illegal" practices. It was one in a long list of battles Landis waged against the farming of ballplayers. Griffith was ticked, "It's just another of his Standard Oil Co. decisions. The decision is vindictive against the Washington club and unfortunately, as was the case in his joke $29,000,000 fine on Standard Oil Co., there is no supreme court to overrule him. But, Landis will not get away with this without a fight. The fact is he's getting too big for his job, and the first thing he knows he'll be out of it."[333] In 1938, Landis released 91 men from the Cardinals system for alleged farming abuses; two years later, 106 Tigers were granted free agency.

The club started slow in 1929; by July they were over twenty games out of first place. They then won only eight games in an extended 22-game road trip. The men were demoralized and fearing for their own jobs and that of their new skipper Walter Johnson. Griff did something he hadn't done since leaving the field manager's job; he addressed the entire team in the clubhouse. The message was in part a backing of Johnson and a kick in the pants for his men. The team didn't light the world on fire after the speech, but it certainly improved. At the end of the home stand, they stood at 34-51, 29 games out in sixth place. The Senators pulled to 71-81 by the end of the year, landing in fifth place. Hence, they posted a 37-30 record over the final two months or so of the year.

Griffith tried to purchase the Atlanta franchise of the Southern Association during the summer of 1929, even putting down $5,000 in good-faith money. The deal fell through, leaving a question mark about rights to certain players. In particular the clubs were fighting over pitcher Joe Giard. Landis summoned Griffith to Chicago to discuss the matter. On July 17, in Chicago Griff fell ill at 6:00 a.m. at the team's hotel and was taken to Mercy Hospital. At 2:00 p.m., he underwent an appendix operation. Edward Eynon, among others, rushed to his bedside. Gangrene developed but after two weeks resting in the hospital all was fine. Even from his sick bed, Griffith was administering the team. He flatly told reporters for all to hear, "I want to make it just as strong as possible, with no ifs, ands or buts about it, that I am perfectly satisfied with the manner in which Johnson is handling the team."

---

[333] "Griffith, angered by Fine, assails Landis hotly," *Washington Post*, March 17, 1929, M17

CHAPTER FIFTEEN

RELIEF PITCHING

Clark Griffith, the pitcher, won 24 games in relief against only nine losses. He led the league in relief wins in 1891, his rookie season, and again in 1901, the dawn of the American League. He also topped all in games finished in 1891, 1905 and '06. Today none of those totals would even register on the leader boards, but for the era 32 games finished in relief from 1905-1906 was significant. In fact, it changed the game.

When the Highlanders lost the 1904 pennant on Jack Chesbro's ninth inning wild pitch on October 10, Griffith came under some criticism for relying on two main starters too much during the season, especially from the club's ownership and local Tammany officials; however, criticism being what it is, Griffith would have been roundly praised if the club won that game. It was true that Chesbro and Jack Powell put up a lot of innings that season, starting 96 games between them and finishing 86. Highlander pitchers finished 80% of the games they started in 1904. With Griffith as the main reliever, the figure dropped to 58% in 1905 and 64% in 1906. In comparison Chesbro notched 48 complete games in 1904 but only matched that total between 1905 and '06. When manager Griffith relieved his starter in 42% of the games in 1905, no other manager topped 27% and the majors averaged only 20%. The marks were similar in 1906, Griffith's 36% to the majors' 22%. In no uncertain terms the new strategy was a revolution; it was a clear break from tradition. Griffith pulled his starter 64 times in 1905. The previous high was 38.[334]

The Highlanders still pulled their starter the most in 1907 with 38% compared to the overall 25%. The idea caught on in 1908. Griffith still yanked his starter the most, 42% of the time, but he wasn't far ahead of some others like National Leaguers Joe Kelley, John McGraw, John McCloskey and Fred Clarke. In all, major league managers began to adopt the strategy, replacing their starters in 32% of the games. In 1910 the National League became the overwhelming leader in fewest complete games, 695 to 856. American League managers did not fully jump on board until 1913. By the Senators' championship season of 1924, the average number of complete games was less than 50%. As historian John Thorn stated in *The Relief Pitcher*, Griffith "was the first manager to make full use of his bullpen." Plus, he was the ace out of the pen. The development of the bullpen stands as Clark Griffith's most significant strategic contribution to the game.

Griffith continued to rely heavily on the bullpen. In the early to mid 1920s, John McGraw of the Giants and Griffith showed that the skillful use of relief specialists could indeed win pennants and even world championships. Allan Russell, Firpo Marberry and Jack Russell proved instrumental in each of the Senators' pennant victories. Washington's first full-time reliever was Russell, a righthander who relied heavily on the spitball from his first year in the majors in 1915 with the Yankees. In 1920 while with the Red Sox, Russell suffered a blood clot in his brain and nearly died after a beaning. He was paralyzed on his right side for five weeks. After an ineffective 1922 campaign, Boston sold him to Jack Dunn in Baltimore who then turned around and made a profit by peddling him to Griffith. Russell came over in 1923 and relieved 114 times through three seasons, two pennants and a world championship. He was the first man in major league history to relieve in 200 games.

The first truly great fireman in major league history was Firpo Marberry. Marberry, a big, strong Texas farm boy, predominantly threw a heavy fastball. He was plucked from a Little Rock, Arkansas club near the end of 1923 by Griffith. In his first full season in the majors in 1924, Marberry set the single season record with fifteen saves, helping the Senators to the world championship in the process. The following year, he became the first man to relieve fifty times in a season. From 1925-1926 he relieved 114 times, amassing 37 saves. Again, the figures wouldn't

---

[334] Brooklyn, 1900

register by today's standards, but they were unheard of at the time. Marberry was the first to accrue 300 relief appearances and to notch 100 saves. He led the league six times in games and five times in saves. As Mr. Thorn commented, "Fred Marberry was without question the dominant relief pitcher of his day."[335]

The Senators crossed up their opponents with 73 relief appearances by Russell and Marberry in 1924 and another 85 the following year. From 1927-1928, Washington utilized the game's first extensive lefty/righty bullpen combination. Marberry and the southpaw Garland Braxton made 185 relief appearances, posting 34 saves. After Walter Johnson became the club's manager in 1929, Marberry was used as both a starter and reliever through 1932. He amassed 88 starts, 93 relief appearances, 58 wins and 32 saves, leading the league twice in the latter category. In 1933, he was shipped to Detroit, registering 31 victories during their pennant run in 1934. His arm went bad the following season. After six games in 1936 with the Giants and Senators, Marberry's major league career was over. He finished with 148 victories, 53 of them in relief, and 101 saves.

Clark Griffith was a starting pitcher by trade, like all pitchers who began their careers in the nineteenth century. His relief totals prior to 1905 were really no different than many other starters who were called upon at times to finish games for teammates. There was little systematic planning to the process unless the manager was occasionally babying a sore starter. In 1905, Griffith decided to preserve the right arms of Jack Powell and, especially, Jack Chesbro. Since Griffith was himself the wildcard on the staff and at the end of his mound career, he chose to fill the void; hence, Griffith the manager and the pitcher were breaking new ground simultaneously.

During the Giants' pennant runs from 1921-1924, John McGraw tapped Slim Sallee, Claude Jonnard, Red Causey and Virgil Barnes as relief specialists. Griffith did the same to cop two pennants and a world championship in the mid 1920s. The Senators boasted the first great reliever and were the first to extensively utilize both lefty and righty firemen in the same season.

---

[335] John Thorn, *The Relief Pitcher*, 1979

CHAPTER SIXTEEN

GREAT DEPRESSION

The Great Depression of the 1930s affected every individual and business in the country, threatening many with bankruptcy. Make no mistake, baseball has always been a business; it had to cope. Three forces prevented the formation of an organized and forward-looking action plan: sentimentalism, conservative club ownership and a crotchety commissioner. Luckily, the game's innate strength pulled it into relative financial stability, at least at the major league level, well before the rest of the economy.

Clark Griffith grew up in the game. It was virtually all he knew since he was in high school. He was by nature sentimental and conservative when it came to his passion, baseball. As such, Clark was slow to adopt many innovations and at times he stood in the way of progress and progressive thinking. His initial approach to change was usually to rail against it until it could be proven an asset. As such, he was among the biggest initial opponents of nighttime baseball, the All-Star Game, football in the District and other issues; however, he became among the loudest supporters of each after a complete analysis of the subject.

Griffith was something that Kenesaw Landis was not, and never would be, a businessman. Landis took a huge salary for merely making decisions and passing judgments on others' actions. Griffith and the other owners, though invested in the Judge, found a way to make progressive ideas work. This was essential as belts tightened during the 1930s. For example, Landis stood in way of the farm system and night baseball. The businessmen came to see these as significant measures to control costs and generate revenue. Those facts may have been lost on the commissioner, but they were essential to the men who ran the individual clubs, the real caretakers of the game.

Innovation was the key. In fact, it had to be. Everyone saw the minor collapsing team by team and league by league. Recreation dollars were tight. If the adage about having to spend money to make money is true, than surely this was a scary proposition in the 1930s. Baseball would be forced to tweak the system from within. Entrepreneurs rose to the top; they made an impact. Hence, many of the advances of the day were proposed and forged by men like Arch Ward, Gus Greenlee, William Bramham, Frank Shaughnessy, Larry MacPhail and two Cooperstown residents, rather than that staid, conservative hierarchy of old.

Griffith and the other owners focused on the bottom line. On the whole major league baseball was too strong to be held back. It was still charging hard from its most popular decade to date and its most popular player, Babe Ruth, was still regularly parking the ball in the outfield bleachers. The game recovered for the most part by the mid-1930s, well before the rest of the economy. But, it didn't thrive. Like the country as a whole, baseball excelled after 1945.

More so than today, each franchise had to fend for itself. Actually, Major League Baseball is a single unit. On the surface, each team contends against the other on the field for the superior nine. Financially, they rely on each other to be successful. This is unique to sports. Some franchises did well during the decade; others floundered. No club shifted its territory until 1953 even though advances in transportation and population shifts may have made it wise to do so earlier.

In the standings and in the ledger books, the Yankees, Giants, Cubs, Tigers and Cardinals did well. The A's did well for a while in the standings but Connie Mack sold his best players for mega-bucks after his club slipped in wins and at the gate. Profitable Sunday baseball was not legalized in Philadelphia until November 1933, too late to save Mack from dismantling a second dynasty. The Red Sox also shined after millionaire Tom Yawkey purchased the franchise in 1933, four days after collecting his inheritance. After spending $1 million to buy the club and $1.5 million to refurbish Fenway Park, Yawkey shelled out another million to buy Lefty Grove, Joe Cronin, Lyn Lary, Moose Solters, Bill Werber, George Pipgras, Rick Ferrell, Carl Reynolds, Wes Ferrell and Jimmie Foxx, among others.

The Senators won a pennant during the decade; however, the organization collapsed in the standings after that and never consistently contended for first place until they relocated to Minnesota. Profits were up and down throughout the decade but paled in comparison to the 1920s. The club was able to stay afloat because of rental fees collected from boxing, wrestling, various Negro league clubs, college football and the Redskins at Griffith Stadium. The value of the rental fees to Griffith and his club cannot be overstated. They were his lifeline during the troubled times.

The Browns, Phillies, Pirates and Braves barely eked out a living during this time. It's amazing that a club or two, especially the Browns, just didn't collapse. Major league attendance during the downturn (in millions):

1929	9.6	1932	7.0	1935	7.3	1938	9.0
1930	10.1	1933	6.1	1936	8.1	1939	9.0
1931	8.5	1934	7.0	1937	8.9	1940	9.8

Each team took a varying piece of the pie (average through the 1930s, in 1,000s):

American League		National League	
Boston	482	Boston	390
Chicago	411	Brooklyn	656
Cleveland	494	Chicago	879
Detroit	734	Cincinnati	445
New York	909	New York	752
Philadelphia	409	Philadelphia	229
St. Louis	118	Pittsburgh	372
Washington	414	St. Louis	405

One way the government sought to stabilize itself during the Depression was to increase taxes on the sporting industry. Assessments were levied on ticket prices, up to 20% of face value. Cutting costs was the key for each club. Only one stadium was built during the 1930s and '40s, Municipal Stadium in Cleveland in 1931. As expected, renovations and maintenance expenditures were often postponed during the trying times.

The players without a collective bargaining agreement bore the brunt of the downturn. Average salaries fell from $7,500 in 1929 to $6,000 in 1933. Babe Ruth, history's all-time gate attraction, took a sizable, involuntary reduction in salary. Commissioner Landis even took a pay cut to show solidarity. The owners cut the roster size in 1931 from 25 to 23 to save on manpower costs. Moreover, some further capitalized by naming one man as player-manager at a single salary. Many players, black and white, supplemented their income by playing exhibition games after the season or over the winter on the west coast or in Mexico, Cuba, Venezuela or other warm-weather areas.

Concerning the lower classifications, many major league executives held off expanding into a comprehensive farm system while times were tough even though they understood the benefits as highlighted by the Cardinals and Yankees' successes. This was a duel-edged sword. The other clubs didn't have the expense of a comprehensive farm system but they had higher per player acquisition costs. The Cardinals, for one, funded their system by selling off their excess players to other major and minor league clubs. In essence the rest of the league paid for the Cardinals to train their talent; plus, they were only able to purchase the men St. Louis decided it didn't need. This was a unique position that the others couldn't capitalize on because they waited too long to develop a farm; it was financially prohibitive to start one during the Depression.

The minor league clubs and leagues that did survive owe their gratitude to foresighted National Association president William Bramham, night baseball, major league cash infusions and to their own ingenuity. Each minor league team adapted or failed. Many teams and even entire leagues simply disbanded. Larry MacPhail drew a blueprint for success when he courted the St. Louis Cardinals and convinced them to purchase his Columbus franchise. With the cash he marketed his team through such untried stunts as night baseball.[336] His mediocre club flourished at the gate. MacPhail was even so bold as to build one of the few new stadiums

---

[336] Night baseball was not a new idea. Games had been played under artificial lights since September 2, 1880, at Nantasket Beach in Hull, Massachusetts, a scant year after Thomas Edison invented the incandescent lamp. Various Negro league, minor league and college teams all predate the majors, using a crude lighting system to attract after-work crowds. Al Spalding installed lights at Chicago's Lakefront Park in 1883 but no National League contests were played under the stars. Likewise, the Brooklyn Federal League franchise installed light towers at Washington Park for the upcoming 1916 season, but the league folded prior to Opening Day.

of the era. Many lower leagues decreased their ticket prices and enacted a tiered playoff system, called the Shaughnessy Plan, to entice frequent fan visits.

Similarly, Negro league clubs survived by ingenuity and perseverance because the majority of the population, white Americans, took little notice. Ridiculously, one of the strongest teams in the history of the game, the Pittsburgh Crawfords of the prewar era, gained few admirers outside the black community. The top black clubs that did survive owe more to Gus Greenlee and his friends' depression-proof gambling cash than any other factor. Such interests heavily seeded the reformed Negro National League in 1933.

The highly successful All-Star Game was the brainchild of *Chicago Tribune* sports editor Arch Ward. In 1933, he noticed that all teams were scheduled an off day on July 6. The date coincided with the World's Fair held in Chicago that year. Ward proposed an exhibition between the stars of each league. The idea took off from there. Profits were initially funneled to retired, needy ballplayers. It was at first established as a one-time event; however, the following year, the Giants demanded that the National League be able to host a similar affair at the Polo Grounds.

A major breakthrough came for Boston in 1929 and for the Pirates, A's and Phillies in 1933 with the repeal of the Blue Laws in their states that prohibited Sunday contests. All franchises now enjoyed profitable Sunday gates. The Sunday doubleheader became the financial savior of the industry.

The loudspeaker was first introduced at the Polo Grounds in 1929. By 1932, uniform numbers became standard throughout the majors. Each advance made the game more fan-friendly and marketable. Baseball has often always failed to maximize its marketing potential. It was always *the* game, the bread and butter of the newspaper industry. Club executives never developed a full marketing plan; the newspaper gave them all the copy they could ever ask for. Consequently, club owners took care of the reporters, covering their expenses and giving then expensive gifts at the holidays. There was rarely a need to look at marketing as a whole since there wasn't as yet a national media, rather there were sixteen mini game plans, all based in local markets.

Baseball has always been a nostalgic game, more so than other sports. It became ingrained as such with the opening of the National Baseball Hall of Fame in 1939. Two Cooperstown, New York residents, Stephen Clark and Alexander Cleland, were seeking to promote their tiny community. They focused on the Mills' report which named hometown hero Abner Doubleday as the father of the game. The pair started a tiny museum to house game-used items and other memorabilia and planned a celebration to honor the 100th anniversary of Doubleday's invention. National League president Ford Frick took the idea and ran with it, aiding in the creation of a formal hall of fame and having sportswriters vote in its members. Griffith was among the first to offer donations for the project, back in 1935. He also offered his assistance with the accumulation of historical facts.[337]

Underappreciated, radio was also a major impetus in the rebirth of the sport. The first broadcast of a major league game took place on August 5, 1921 by a Pittsburgh station that showcased the Pirates versus the Phillies with Harold Arlin on the mike. Radio broadcasting expanded during the 1930s. The first World Series aired was the New York contest in 1922. In 1925, Wrigley offered the broadcasting rights to Cubs games for free. Others followed but the Boston, Chicago, Philadelphia and St. Louis owners agreed not to air away games since they'd conflict with their cross-town rival who would be at home at the time. New York magnates in collusion refused to send any games over the airwaves.

Powell Crosley and Larry MacPhail brought radio broadcasting to Cincinnati and New York, respectively. By the end of the 1930s, radio broadcasts were a staple throughout the industry. In 1935, Landis negotiated baseball's first broadcasting contract. RCA and Columbia paid $400,000 to air four World Series. Fans who couldn't afford a radio often found businesses or friends who shared. Others lived vicariously through the numerous editions of local newspapers. Baseball, cinema and an occasional prize fight were the nation's diversions during the hard times.

Eventually, night baseball became a staple in the industry, but not right away. It had its detractors including Landis and Phillip Wrigley, who fought it until his death. It is obvious today that night games would draw a larger crowd. After a while, it was obvious then, too. Sentiment prevented many from jumping on the bandwagon. Griffith had a checkered history with the idea, first hating it, speaking against it at every turn; however, he converted after recognizing its economic potential. He became the leading proponent for the innovation, pressuring Landis and National League opponents to expand its use.

In November 1935, after MacPhail brought the first night game to the major leagues, Griffith reluctantly agreed to vote for the innovation but he swore that he would never put up lights in his park. To him,

---

[337] Letter dated June 5, 1935 from Griffith to Alexander Cleland, Griffith file at the National Baseball Hall of Fame

"Night baseball is just a step above dog racing." As late as 1939 he was quoted as saying, "This game wasn't meant to be played at night. It was meant to be played in the Lord's broad sunlight, just as it has been for 100 years. There's more to a ball game than just a ball game. There's fresh air, sunshine and everything that goes to make a fine afternoon."[338]

Griffith changed his tune about night games during the war. He was being crushed financially and needed a lifeline. He petitioned Landis for more night games. When that didn't work, he prompted President Roosevelt and his administration to do his bidding for him. As a result, the Senators were granted more night games each year than any other club. Eventually everyone installed lights, even the Cubs.[339]

---

[338] Shirley Povich, "This Morning with Shirley Povich," *Washington Post*, May 18, 1939, p. 19

[339] The following parks installed lights:

1935	Cincinnati	Crosley Field
1938	Brooklyn	Ebbets Field
1939	Philadelphia	Shibe Park
	- Both the A's and Phillies	
	Cleveland	Municipal Stadium
	Chicago	Comiskey Park
1940	New York	Polo Grounds
	St. Louis	Sportsman's Park
	- Both the Browns and Cardinals	
	Pittsburgh	Forbes Field
1941	Washington	Griffith Park

The remaining franchises had to delay night baseball until after the war. The first night contest took place on June 15, 1935 in Cincinnati, drawing a healthy 20,422 fans. Innovator MacPhail brought the lights to the majors. He is also responsible for the second team, the Dodgers, hosting evening ball. Connie Mack initiated the first night game in the American League on May 16, 1939 with 15,109 spectators in attendance.

CHAPTER SEVENTEEN

ONE LAST PENNANT

The major news out of the Senators' spring training camp in 1930 revolved around Goose Goslin's holdout. After he finally did sign, an irate Griffith shipped him off to the Browns for two key members of the 1933 pennant winner, pitcher General Crowder, who won 83 games for the Senators in his first three-plus seasons, and Hall of Fame left fielder Heinie Manush. The deal proved an even bigger coup when Griffith reacquired Goslin with Fred Schulte, a top defensive center fielder, and Lefty Stewart at the end of 1932.

Manush, a lifetime .330-hitter, began his career in Canada in 1921. He soon joined the Tigers, playing in the same outfield as Hall of Famers Ty Cobb and Harry Heilmann. On the last day of the 1926 season, Manush went 6 for 9 to top Babe Ruth for the batting crown and ruin the slugger's best shot at the Triple Crown. A Cobb disciple, Manush demanded out of the organization after his manager was forced out. In 1933 Manush became the first man ejected from a World Series game after he yanked umpire Charlie Moran's bow tie and let it snap back. After leaving the majors in 1939, he played seven more seasons in the minors until the end of World War II.

A few days after the Goslin deal Washington acquired troubled first baseman Art Shires from the White Sox. Shires was a pain in the neck for baseball administrators during his brief four-year career. He was tough, loud and walked around boastfully calling himself "Art the Great." The first baseman did manage to hit .291 in 290 games from 1928-1932 when he wasn't fighting. In late 1929, the 21-year-old from Texas was cash poor so he started boxing professionally. At the time he was serving a suspension from the White Sox for getting drunk and punching manager Lena Blackburne in the eye, something he did twice that year.

The brawler's first fight was against a competitor named Dan Daly who later confessed to tanking the match. Soon, Shires found that he could make more money promoting bouts with other sporting celebrities than by playing baseball. Art the Great fought George Trafton, the rugged Chicago Bears center, Cleveland Indians pitcher Tony Faeth and Boston Braves catcher Al Spohrer. Cubs' owner William Wrigley canceled a proposed bout with star Hack Wilson. In all, the heavyweight amassed a 5-2 record in seven matches. Judge Landis feared that Shires' associations might lead to gambling, or probably already had. He was already banned from boxing in 32 states for allegedly participating in the rigged bout with Daly. In late 1930, Landis gave Shires an ultimatum to choose either baseball or boxing. Shires left baseball but returned in '32 with the Boston Braves. Shires also had a brief career as a pro wrestler. He later managed for Griffith at Harrisburg.

The Senators also purchased Joe Kuhel in 1930. They paid $65,000 for the slick-fielding first baseman from Kansas City of the International League. The July 4 doubleheader in D.C. proved why Griffith respected and appreciated Babe Ruth; over 35,000 fans showed up to see the games versus the Yankees. The Senators won 94 games in 1930 with five pitchers winning at least fifteen games; however, the Philadelphia A's took the pennant by eight games.

On August 1, Hazel Johnson, wife of manager Walter Johnson, passed away at Georgetown University Hospital, leaving five young children in their father's care. The contest was postponed that day. Tragedy struck the Senators organization later that year as well. An automobile killed Joe Engel's son Bryant, 9, after he ran into the street on November 17. Engel, a longtime Griffith employee, was the president of the club's Chattanooga franchise; he was going through a messy divorce at the time. The following April, Griffith's old teammate and colleague Jimmy McAleer committed suicide by gunshot at his home in Youngstown, Ohio.

Nineteen-Thirty was a shock to many within the baseball industry, particularly pitchers. Statistically, the season was an anomaly. The National League batting average shot to .304, over twenty points higher than just two years prior. The league ERA reached 4.98, nearly a point higher than 1928. Both figures dropped significantly in 1931. The numbers rose in the American League as well, but much less dramatically. The Senators were the only club in the majors with an ERA under 4.00,

3.97. The Central, New York-Pennsylvania and Pacific Coast Leagues and the American and Southern Associations all also had aggregate batting averages over .300.

A new practice, the Senators players were issued numbers on their uniforms in 1930, a year after the Yankees restarted the initiative.[340] By the mid 1930s all clubs would be donning them. On August 22, the Baltimore Black Sox and Philadelphia Hilldales met at Griffith Stadium. The Negro leagues soon setup permanent residence in D.C., generating valuable rental revenue for the Senators that helped carry them through the lean years. The Senators won 92 games in 1931, but that was only good for third place behind the strong A's and Yankees teams.

On July 4, 1932, the Senators Carl Reynolds slammed into Yankees catcher Bill Dickey during a rundown, knocking the ball loose. Dickey rose and punched Reynolds in the jaw, breaking it. Griffith was livid, petitioning American League president Will Harridge for a severe penalty. Dickey was fined $1,000 and suspended for thirty days. It was definitely a severe penalty for the time but it held up, sparking a lot of yelping from New York and a running feud with the Senators owner. The Senators won 32 of their last 42 games in 1932, giving a glimpse of the pennant-winning club to come.

It wasn't enough to save Walter Johnson's job. The decision was already made to replace him at the end of the season. Johnson, like Clyde Milan before him, was routinely criticized for being too soft on the players and not instilling enough fire in the men. That's hard to see; he was at the helm for four years, winning over ninety games each of the final three seasons. The Senators just came up against one of the few teams in baseball history to win over 100 games a season for three consecutive years, the A's.[341] Plus, the Yankees ran away with the pennant in 1932, posting 107 victories. The American League was just too tough. Washington won more games than any National League club since 1930.

Once again, Griffith considered coming out of retirement to assume the field leader's job after letting Johnson go. Instead he hired 26-year-old Joe Cronin a week later. Griffith went with a young guy at the helm again. Why not? It worked before. Upon assuming the position, Cronin

---

[340] The Indians briefly wore numbers on their sleeves in 1916 and '17. The Cardinals did as well in 1923.

[341] Prior to the increase to a 162-game season, only the A's, 1929-31, and Cardinals, 1942-44, won 100 games three years in a row. The Cubs from 1906-10 and the Yankees from 1936-39 should also be noted for runs broken up by a 99-victory season.

approached the boss with a list of three pitchers he wanted; the two went to the winter meetings in December with a plan. They acquired pitchers Earl Whitehill, Jack Russell, Lefty Stewart and outfielders Goose Goslin and Fred Schulte. After a 46-98 record from 1926-1932, Russell was converted to a full-time reliever by the Nats and posted twelve wins and thirteen saves in 1933.

Cronin walked away from the winter meetings in awe of the internal workings of the game. He was particularly impressed that Griffith plucked Goslin, Schulte and Stewart from the Browns. He was also amused that after the six hour trade meeting with St. Louis owner Phil Ball that ended at 2 a.m. Griffith kept at it. As Cronin describes, "On the way down in the elevator Mr. Griffith offered to buy back from Ball the pitcher he'd just traded him, Brown."[342]

In January, they picked up catcher Luke Sewell. Sewell, one of the few men to catch in the major leagues in twenty seasons, secretly helped the young Cronin manage his pitching staff. By casually throwing dirt around behind home plate, Sewell was signaling Cronin at shortstop to either warm-up a new pitcher or to bring in a new one. Later, Cronin was branded as a manager unable to develop a pitching staff and for his inefficient use of it. Without Sewell this became evident after he took over Boston. Sewell later managed the St. Louis Browns to their only pennant in 1944. He also started the practice of having the infield dragged after the fifth inning. After retirement, Sewell was chairman of Richard Nixon's Ohio campaign in 1972.

Goslin, Ozzie Bluege and Sam Rice were the only constants on the three Senators pennant-winning clubs. Six of the eight regulars hit over .295 in 1933 with Kuhel, Myer, Cronin and Manush topping .300. Kuhel and Cronin knocked in over 100 base runners each. General Crowder posted 24 victories and saved another four games. The recently acquired trio of Whitehill, Stewart and Russell posted 49 wins and 14 saves. Monte Weaver added another ten victories. The Senators finished with a 99-53-record, seven games up on the Yankees. Unfortunately, the Giants managed by Bill Terry defeated the Nats in five games in October. The only Senators win came in Game 3, a shutout by Whitehill.

Oddly, in 1933, Griffith visited the notorious gangster Al Capone at Atlanta Penitentiary. To some it seems Capone was merely seen as a businessman. Throughout the season Cronin frequently clashed with

---

[342] Bob Broeg, "Griffith made Cronin part of Family affair in Baseball," *St. Louis Post-Dispatch*, November 3, 1968, p. B2

Goslin and Crowder. The two were soon shipped off. The Senators also released the 43-year-old Sam Rice, an all-time favorite in D.C, in January 1934. He was one of Griffith's favorites as well, partially because he annually signed a blank contract and let the owner fill in the salary figure. He retired at the end of the year with 2,987 hits. Rice didn't even know how many hits he had nor was 3,000 a magical number at the time. Griffith later offered to allow Rice to come back to accrue the thirteen hits, but the ballplayer declined; he was out of shape by then.

The Senators' owner raised some eyebrows in 1934 when he signed House of David pitcher Allen Benson. The House of David was a Hebrew communal colony located at Benton Harbor, Michigan. King Benjamin Purnell originally established it in 1903. The group became famous for its barnstorming baseball club with its fully bearded members and for a 1920s scandal in which the founder was charged with taking advantage of over one hundred underage girls within the colony. The House of David clubs became extremely popular and at times boasted some big names: Pete Alexander, Satchel Paige, Dizzy Dean and Babe Didrikson. Benson was signed by one of Griffith's top scouts, Joe Cambria, after he saw him strike out twelve Harrisburg Senators of the New York-Pennsylvania League. Griffith, a showman, wanted the novelty of promoting the only bearded player in the majors; however, Benson flopped after two games. Clark claimed that he was too thin to be effective in the majors.

The Senators took a nosedive in 1934 and for the most part remained near the bottom of the standings throughout the rest of their stay in Washington. After the season, the wealthy owner of the Boston Red Sox, Tom Yawkey, pursued a deal for Joe Cronin. Despite the pennant-winning drive, the Senators didn't make any money in 1933; in fact, the ledger books showed a loss of $500 and more debt was racked up in '34. Griffith was under some financial pressure when he was contacted by the Red Sox; he owed $125,000 to a D.C. bank. Yawkey's men initiated the bidding but Griffith wasn't receptive at first, as Cronin was highly valued both professionally and personally. Nevertheless, Clark and Edward Eynon took a trip to Boston on October 26 to confer with the Boston owner. At the time, Cronin was on his honeymoon, traveling through the Panama Canal headed to San Francisco to introduce his new bride, Griffith's niece Millie, to his family.

Yawkey and his general manager Eddie Collins offered a lot of money for the Senators 28-year-old manager and shortstop, a lot of money. Cash wasn't enough; the savvy Griffith demanded that shortstop Lyn Lary be thrown in any potential deal. Yawkey balked at first because he had recently paid the Yankees $35,000 for Lary. After further negotiations, he agreed at the last minute, just before the Washington executives were scheduled to return home. The Red Sox agreed to send Lary and $225,000 to the Senators for Cronin. Griffith tentatively agreed, pending a conversation with his new nephew-in-law.

When he returned to Washington, Griffith called the west coast and talked with Cronin, leaving the final decision up to his manager. Cronin figured that it was an incredible sum for the Senators to pass up and he relayed his consent. As he noted, "I told him 'Better take it, Unk, because I didn't think I had a constitution strong enough to play, manage and be in the boss' family, too."[343] To ease the pain of relocating, Griffith worked out a five-year contract for Cronin that would make him a rich man. Yawkey was in the middle of buying up some of the biggest names in the game, money was no object. The deal was a good one for Cronin as well; he was headed to a perennial pennant contender, leaving a team that wasn't and being well compensated for his efforts.

At the time of Cronin's sale, Babe Ruth was making noise about quitting the game altogether if he wasn't handed the reigns of a major league club. Reports suggested that Griffith offered Babe Ruth the manager's job at $15,000 a year and a cut of the gate. Ruth wanted $30,000. The two couldn't agree.[344] Ruth was supposedly all but given the manager's position in Detroit in 1933 as well but he was too busy traveling to Hawaii to bother returning a call from Tigers' owner Frank Navin. Navin, ticked off at Ruth's indifference, hired Mickey Cochrane who in turn rewarded him with a pennant in 1934. Griffith decided to bring back Bucky Harris for his second stint as the Nats' manager. In 1936, Joe Cambria offered Ruth the manager's position with his Albany club, which had a working agreement with the Senators.[345] Speculation arose that Ruth would potentially be one step from the Senators job, a coveted major league managerial slot. But, Ruth declined that offer as well, refusing an assignment with a minor league club.

---

[343] Bob Broeg, "Griffith made Cronin part of Family affair in Baseball," *St. Louis Post-Dispatch*, November 3, 1968, p. B2

[344] "Clark Griffith after Manager for Senators," *Christian Science Monitor*, October 27, 1934, p. 6

[345] "Ruth considering Albany's Offer," *New York Times*, November 29, 1936, p. S7

The Senators completely flopped at the gate in 1935, drawing only 255,011 fans, their lowest mark since 1919 and over 200,000 below the league average. That year, Griffith battled Judge Landis over the right to offer bleacher seats to children at 25 cents. The Senators were doing it since 1933 but Landis claimed it was against the league bylaws. Griffith eventually won the argument in 1936. Clark was truly fearful that his club might not survive the Depression. In order to survive he developed a plan to cut costs and raise revenue. Cutting costs, the Senators soon divested from the Chattanooga franchise and focused on acquiring cheap Cuban talent. On the revenue side Griff set out to attract some renters to his park. Thankfully, the Homestead Grays and Redskins soon took him up on his offer.

In December 1935, Griffith met with Joe Carr at the winter baseball meetings.[346] Carr was president of the Columbus franchise in the American Association. He was also the commissioner of the National Football League. Griff was trying to lure a NFL franchise to D.C. to play at Griffith Stadium. He'd seen the potential for profitable football rental revenue while leasing his park to the local George Washington University team. After nailing down an agreement for full use of the park with Griffith, George Preston Marshall announced in December 1936 that he was bringing his Boston Redskins to the nation's capital. Marshall was well known throughout the District, as he made his fortune in area after inheriting his father's chain of laundries.

In August 1938, Griffith expressed some frustration that the local sports reporters were taking a great deal of interest in the Redskins during their training camp, taking press away from the Senators. Unreasonably, Griffith threatened to lock the football team out of Griffith Stadium if the local papers didn't stop covering football during the baseball season. He brought in a competitor. The Senators were now the worst major professional team in D.C., behind the Redskins and the Homestead Grays. At the time, Sammy Baugh was playing shortstop in the American Association and International League, hitting an even .200. Originally signed by Rogers Hornsby, he was merely one of hundreds of Branch Rickey's farmhands. On the gridiron, "Slingin' Sammy" revolutionized the game. Baugh was an All-American at Texas Christian University in 1935 and '36 before joining the Redskins the following year. As a rookie, Baugh led the Skins to the NFL championship and again in 1942. They were perennial contenders through World War II. By the end of his career sixteen years later, he held every passing mark in the game. His presence was a two-edge sword for Griffith. On one side, he took press away from

---

[346] "Griffith eyes Pro Eleven in Capital," *Washington Post*, December 3, 1935, 19

the Senators; however, the Redskins rose in the standings, which meant a good deal of cash for their landlord.

The Griffith family enjoyed football games; they caught many at Griffith Stadium over the years. On December 11, 1938, Griffith and Cronin took a train to New York to watch the NFL Championship Game between the Giants and Packers. Some of the best baseball in America was being played in the Negro leagues during the 1930s until after the war. The Homestead Grays and Washington Elite Giants boasted some of the biggest names in the game: Buck Leonard, Josh Gibson, Vic Harris, Cool Papa Bell, Biz Mackey and Sammy T. Hughes. Griff happily invited the clubs to play at his stadium. He enjoyed watching the contests as well.

Also in 1935 Griffith tweaked his all-time all-star team:[347]

Catcher	Buck Ewing
1st Baseman	George Sisler, previously chose Charles Comiskey
2nd Baseman	Nap Lajoie, previously chose Eddie Collins
Shortstop	Hans Wagner, previously chose Herman Long
3rd Baseman	Home Run Baker, previously chose Jimmy Collins
Left Fielder	Babe Ruth, previously chose Bill Lange
Center Fielder	Tris Speaker
Right Fielder	Ty Cobb
Pitcher	Walter Johnson.

This concept of an all-time team fit in with an idea brewing in upper state New York. In June, Griffith became one of the first contributors to a baseball museum that was being proposed by businessmen in Cooperstown. He sent a portrait of the game's supposed founder Major General Abner Doubleday that he secured from friends at the U.S. War Department. He also shipped prints of U.S. Presidents tossing out the ceremonial first pitch at Griffith Stadium. By the end of 1935, National League president Ford Frick latched onto the idea and began calling the project a hall of fame.

In October 1937, Yankees owner Jacob Ruppert laughed at all Griffith's trade proposals. He joked, "What are you talking about? I give away better

---

[347] "Griffith, on his 66th Birthday, picks his All-Time All Star Team," *Washington Post*, November 21, 1935, p. 21

ballplayers then you got."[348] Griffith received a little justice for that comment in 1939. He led the drive to eliminate trading options for pennant winners. As of December 7, pennant winners were forbid from acquiring players within their own league except through the waiver system. The resolution passed 7-0 at the American League meeting; the National League did not adopt the rule. It was a clear stab at the Yankees who won the last four World Championships. Considering that traditionally few inter-league trades occurred, the rule had the potential to be problematic for pennant winners.

Griffith also proposed that a team could only own one franchise at each minor league level above Class-D. It was another slap at the affluent Yankees. The American League rejected the proposal. The Yankees had a fine team in 1940 regardless of any short-lived restrictions.

---

[348] Irving Vaughn, "Yanks' Owner laughs at Deal with Senators," *Chicago Tribune*, October 10, 1937, p. B4

CHAPTER EIGHTEEN

FARM SYSTEM

The National League was originally formed before the 1876 season. The following year the first two loosely defined minor leagues were assembled. They organized, in part, to combat the National League's penchant for barnstorming through their territories without regard for local scheduling, thus "robbing" the locals of their fan base; plus, the National League teams had no qualms about raiding local rosters for their best talent. Today, we view all other leagues as inferior and subservient to the majors. Back in the early years that wasn't necessarily the case. By Griffith's time, the concepts of major and minor leagues and of Organized Baseball were pretty well defined.

He entered the minors in the late 1880s, settling in the majors in 1893. This was a turbulent time in baseball history. It saw the rise and fall of the Players League and the merger of the National League and American Association. A relative calm existed within the structure of Organized Baseball throughout Griff's time with the Chicago Cubs until the American League flexed its muscles at the beginning of 1901, which obviously Griffith was partially responsible for.

The American League refused to renew their membership within the National Agreement in 1900 and the National League tossed it aside as well in 1901. Each league then signed any and all available talent, thus threatening the established minor leagues. In response, the minors formed their own governing body called the National Association. Like the concept of Organized Baseball, this essentially formed a monopoly. The benefits were simply too hard to ignore: an enforceable reserve clause; salary limits; promise of enhanced profits and controllable expenses; greater control over operations in general. Plus, the National Association offered a central body to settle disputes without the costly legal expenses that would otherwise be incurred.

Finally, tensions between the two major leagues eased in 1903 and a new National Agreement was inked in October. The agreement formally recognized the National and American Leagues as the leaders of the structure known as Organized Baseball. The minor leagues, under the administration of the National Association, accepted this inferior status and sacrificed their independence to gain security and a promise of financial stability. The agreement also outlined the basic structure for farming and drafting of ballplayers. The minors subdivided into classifications, A, B, C and D, which were typically separations based on levels of talent. Class-A minor leagues had a higher number of roster spots than Class-B, paid higher salaries and had the right to draft from the lower classifications and so on down the line to B, C and D.

Nothing is that simple. It took time and purpose to legitimately establish tiers of talent. Eventually, the demarcation took place and the system stands as we know it today. At that time, the structure wasn't as organized. It took Branch Rickey's system of scouting, recruiting, classify, training and advancing personnel to set rigid boundaries within the National Association. It should be noted that some clubs and leagues remained outside Organized Baseball, refusing for various reasons to sign the National Agreement. They were called "outlaws."[349]

Clark Griffith operated within the system as baseball men had for decades. During his first two decades in charge of clubs, he virtually oversaw all personnel decisions, except in Chicago and Cincinnati for five years, where Charles Comiskey and Garry Herrmann, respectively, were very involved. He practically built an entirely new franchise in New York for 1903. Like all managers, he had tentacles throughout the nation eying talent. Countless others remitted letters and telegrams touting potential prospects. Just one man, Griffith couldn't be everywhere nor did he have the financing to send a staff of scouts to follow up on every tip. At times he left his club to personally make scouting trips or sent others to do so, such as, coaches, players or associates. Players and managers at all levels

---

[349] The early Pacific Coast League, formed in 1903, was perhaps the most successful. The Negro leagues were never invited to join the conglomerate. Nor would they have been welcomed if they had applied.

and sportswriters and umpires also proved helpful. Basically anyone with any connection to the game was pumped for information on young ballplayers. Mix this with the entrepreneur spirit of minor league owners in both promoting their own talent and hoping to cash in on such and one has a general idea how clubs filled their rosters.

Griffith eventually employed seasoned scouts like Ted Sullivan, Joe Engel and Joe Cambria to scour the bushes for him, but that was years, even decades, away. There was no farm system to pull from to fill weaknesses or replace injured players. Baseball men had to network. As such, Clark knew virtually everyone throughout the industry. He met them at meetings, played with or against them, hunted with them, met them through associates or at least heard of them. Like any smart businessman, Griffith traveled extensively watching games and conversing with fans, reporters and baseball men. Plus, at times men simply came to him. They wanted something, either to share information or to sell him a player.

Like everyone in the industry, Griffith got burned at times, purchasing sub par players. Eventually, he developed a few profitable relationships that proved lucrative over the years for both parties. Griffith claimed that old-timers like Mack and himself worked together on trades. If one needed a player, they'd get a deal done regardless of whether it was an imbalanced transaction. They just made it up with the other the next time. Another way to find seasoned ballplayers was to maintain contacts at various universities and colleges. Here was a great source of talent that had shown some measure of success. Plus, there was no one to purchase the player from; the acquisition cost was minimal.

Word of mouth was the major source of information. Tidbits were picked up in newspapers but for the most part it was simple conversation that turned an eye to young talent. Men did favors for each other because they knew one day they'd need the same. Reporters played an integral role linking the various networks, as did fans, community members and thousands throughout the country in small towns and out of the way communities. Ballplayers were also pumped for information on teammates and opponents as they advanced through the professional system.

Griffith heard about a specific ballplayer and kept notes on him. This was almost a job in and of itself. He often sent someone to check on a hot tip or he simply went himself. Many times these trips led to interest in an entirely new youngster. There were no forty-man rosters to pluck from. Creativity came into play. The National Agreement of 1903 officially banned the farming of players. It was an early attempt to counter the influence of richer clubs. Otherwise, a few might have significant reserves of talent at minimal cost ready to join the parent club on a moment's notice. Thus, Major league baseball men latched onto optioning a player. They purchased a man and kept him on a minor league roster until he was needed. By 1912, the National Commission started to limit the number of these reserve players. Eventually, major league clubs began to financially support a minor league franchise or to merely purchase them outright. These working agreements exponentially increased a parent club's reserve of talent. From here, it is obvious to see how an organization could develop a network of clubs, classify them by talent level and then train their personnel in various methods of the game and move them along progressively so that they would have the required seasoning when they received the call to join the parent club. This was precisely the system Branch Rickey built in St. Louis and later Brooklyn.

The players in such a system had little say. They were bound to a specific club or organization within the professional baseball monopoly by the reserve clause. There was no jumping between clubs seeking the best deal possible. Organized Baseball closed that loophole. Other than by the grace of an owner the only way a player could negotiate a better deal, if they felt they were being exploited, was to brand himself as a problem and a troublemaker. A player had to hold out or otherwise cause friction. It was virtually his only leverage. This was a bold move though and it was often done in the face of heavy criticism by management, the media and even the fans. The deck was truly stacked against the individual ballplayer.

This was exactly what Griffith did before he hopped to the White Sox in 1901. He railed against the strong arm of management and, consequently, was branded as a troublemaker. Fortunately for him, Ban Johnson's league upset the balance between management and labor. Many players capitalized. Other than brief respites during the Federal League uprising in the 1910s and a minimal shockwave by the Mexican League after World War II, the players as a whole gained little influence until Marvin Miller spoke for them in the 1970s and '80s. Commissioners may have at times sided with a player but they were no friends to labor despite the rhetoric otherwise. They were empowered by the men who financed the industry to oversee disputes and help guide policy.

Player acquisition fees could be stiff. Sure major league teams could draft players at a reasonable fee but that was only an available option at the end of the minor league season. During the season, the costs could be dear. In April 1915, Griffith openly declared that he was forever done with buying players; they cost too much and the Washington board of directors wasn't easily cajoled for the extra cash. He planned to solely develop ballplayers, signing them when they were very young at minimal cost.[350] It's clear by his declaration that he fully understood the same benefits that Branch Rickey soon realized. Unfortunately, the Senators didn't have the money and/or the wherewithal to see the plan through.

By November 1918, the minors were fighting strong to eliminate the drafting system whereby major league clubs could select talent at a preset fee, always too low a figure as far as minor league executives were concerned. They were also demanding an end to the practice of farming players. Both issues in the mind of minor league officials were an unfair restraint of trade. The profit potential was being drastically held down. Of course, the majors saw it differently; they felt they couldn't afford to pay top dollar on a player by player basis. In January 1919, the relationship dissolved; the majors and minors split out of the acrimony. The draft was cancelled; all players must be purchased on the open market for cash.

Since Griffith took over the Senators in 1912, he was using his friend Joe Cantillon's Minneapolis Millers as an unofficial farm club. He also had a farming relationship with his cousin Frank Dillon in Los Angeles as well as minor league manager Billy Smith. The Senators parked players with Smith from 1912-1922 through the managers various stops in the minors: Chattanooga, 1912; Atlanta, 1913-1915 and 1918; Richmond, 1916-1917; Shreveport, 1919-1922. Like the rest of baseball, these relationships were strained in 1919. At the time, Griffith only had one player assigned to Minneapolis, Carl Sawyer and he wasn't likely to be used at the major league level again. Going into Opening Day, the Senators owned a total of 21 players, all of whom were on the major league roster. There was no one in reserve.[351] This left the club vulnerable and in a poor position financially; if Griffith needed a man during the season, it would cost dearly.

After a season at odds, the majors and minors resumed their formal ties; however, the draft was not restored until January 1921. Even then, a league could opt out of the drafting system. Five leagues did including all of the Class-AA leagues, the highest contemporary ranking. It wasn't until the end of 1924 that all the Class-AA leagues fell in line allowing drafting, optioning and recalling of players.

---

[350] "Griffith's new Departure," *Boston Herald*, April 24, 1915, page unknown

[351] J.V. Fitzgerald, "Minneapolis 'Farm" now in Disfavor," *Washington Post*, February 16, 1919, p. 22

This was the era in which Rickey decided to invest in minor league holdings in earnest.[352] The Cardinals couldn't afford to pay market fees; they needed an edge. By 1925, they accrued five affiliates. The following year they won their first National League pennant. During the 1930s, St. Louis owned or had working agreements with perhaps as many as forty organizations and was a perennial pennant contender. The Yankees followed their lead, investing heavily in young talent. The entire concept threatened many within the industry, especially the cash-poor, small market clubs like the Senators. For one, few teams believed they could financially follow in their footsteps. After the St. Louis and New York farm systems matured, it was obvious that the others were well behind the curve. The Senators surely were. It was a large reason for their failures after 1933.

On the Senators end, Joe Engel began running into brick walls in 1929 while trying to secure talent for his boss. As the *Washington Post* explained, "Scout Joe Engel has run into one disappointment after another in his efforts to dig up 'ivory' for the Nationals. He has run down tip after tip, only to find that, either because of 'chain store' ownership or working agreements, the player he sought already was tied up…even college players…"[353] Entire leagues were soon being spoken for via direct ownership of all their clubs or through working agreements. This wasn't just happening in a few leagues in professional baseball; Griffith's American and National League rivals were establishing roots throughout the nation. As a consequence, he railed against the farm system and all of its supposed evils, even while he was trying to buy into the idea. The Nats had a working relationship with Birmingham during the 1920s, but that was only a cursory relationship. By the end of the decade, it was obvious that a successful major league club needed more, direct ownership of a minor league franchise.

Griffith made his first serious attempt to acquire a farm club in 1929. He agreed to purchase the Atlanta club of the Southern Association for $650,000. Putting $5,000 down, he was to take over the club on June 14. The Senators called off the deal at the last minute after being warned by Southern Association president John Martin that the other league clubs would not approve the deal. They were fearful of direct control of their franchises by major league executives. Atlanta president Rell Spiller threatened to sue Griffith for fulfillment of the contract. Words were

---

[352] Rickey's interest in an extensive farm system actually dates as far back as 1913 in his discussions with St. Louis Browns owner Robert Hedges.

[353] Frank H. Young, "Source of New Talent is Problem," *Washington Post*, June 23, 1929, p. M15

exchanged and lawsuits threatened. Famed golfer Bobby Jones acted as Griffith's lawyer in the affair. In the end, Griffith couldn't be held liable considering that Spiller couldn't gain the necessary votes to win league approval of the deal.

Unable to enter the Southern Association through the front door, Griffith had longtime scout and trusted ally Joe Engel purchase the Chattanooga Lookouts in November 1929. Engel's loan to purchase the club was backed by Griffith and the Senators. The other Southern Association owners were very leery about having major league ownership of one of their clubs as demonstrated by the Atlanta incident. Consequently, Engel was formally admitted to the league but denied a seat on the league's board. As the *Washington Post* put it, "In refusing to accept Engel as a director of the league...The directors went on record as condemning and strongly opposing major league ownership of a Southern [Association] club."[354] They didn't want to give him a vote in league matters.

The Senators actually had a working relationship with the Lookouts since 1927.[355] Immediately after Engel's purchase of the Lookouts, Griffith moved his training camp to Chattanooga and broadened his transactions with the club. The relationship only intensified. Eventually, it became clear to all that Griffith, not Engel, actually owned the Lookouts. Engel oversaw the club through 1936 until Calvin Griffith replaced him.

On March 26, 1932, Engel, known as the "Barnum of Baseball," signed 17-year-old pitcher Jackie Mitchell. She may have been the first woman of the twentieth century to sign a professional contract in Organized Baseball. Hall of Famer Dazzy Vance trained Mitchell, a lefty. In a publicity stunt on April 2, she struck out a chuckling Babe Ruth and Lou Gehrig. Engel planned to use her in regular league games but the next day Judge Landis overturned her contract claiming that Organized Baseball was "too strenuous" for women to play.

Throughout the 1930s, the Senators developed working relationships with a few clubs. Griffith was never ecstatic about it, feeling that he put more money into his subsidiaries than he got out. As he noted, "About the only exceptional players we ever developed at Chattanooga are Buddy Lewis and Cecil Travis. In my opinion, interest in the minors would be much

---

[354] "Engel denied Directorship in League," *Washington Post*, November 19, 1929, p. 17

[355] Based on the shifting of men from one club to the other

keener if they worked independently, but these smaller clubs needed help during the Depression and there was the fact, too, that competition among rich clubs for players to be developed on farms reached a point where everybody went into the chain system on some scale or another. My honest opinion is that baseball in general would be far better off without farms…But, we can't get away from them now. Because the rich major league clubs have built up extensive systems, the other clubs are forced to maintain what farms they can for protection. I don't believe the game will ever outgrow them."[356]

In 1937, Griffith sold the Class-A1 Lookouts and purchased the Charlotte Hornets, placing Engel in charge of the club. Griffith tried to explain his reasoning in regard to farm club ownership. "I own only one minor league club, Charlotte in the Class-B Piedmont League. That looks bad. But here's what you newspaper fellows don't realize. Class-B leagues today are far stronger than before the development of the farm system. Today there's little difference between Class-B and Class-A or A1, even AA. In fact, my Class-B team at Charlotte in '38 was far better than Class-A Springfield this year [1939]. Here's the reason. The Yanks, Cards, Red Sox, Reds, Dodgers and other clubs own a flock of players. They can place just so many on their Double-A teams. The others, even though they can play Double-A ball, are shipped to A, A1 or even B. Consequently, the lower leagues are correspondingly stronger…Now I don't own any Double-A ball clubs, but that doesn't prove I don't own Double-A players. This season I moved three youngsters up from Charlotte – Haynes, Estalella and Bloodworth. All three made good."[357]

Since Griffith didn't own a slew of affiliates, he relied on his scouts to find the best talent available. There was one proviso and all his scouts were well aware. Yes, they were hired to mine the nuggets, find the best young talent, but they were also expected to save money. In way this seems contradictory or at least difficult. The Senators, with one of the lowest population bases to pull from, were indeed frugal; the entire organization would just have to work harder and with greater efficiency. However, the margin for error of this method of operation was very low.

---

[356] "Griff Bewails Farms," un-cited newspaper article dated June 17, 1937 located in Griffith's Hall of Fame file

[357] Jack Smith, aka Jimmy Powers, "Old Fashioned Fox," New York Daily News, October 25, 1939, page unknown

The Senators paid over $200,000 for young talent in 1930 alone.[358] That was a lot of money for the club, even in a profitable year. Griffith ventured into minor league ownership, in part, to lessen these costs on a per player basis. He wasn't entirely successful along those lines; farm clubs needed a good deal of support, especially during the Depression. Mr. Griffith was successful in working with his main scouts Joe Engel, Mike Martin and Joe Cambria in this regard. The Griffith-Cambria relationship was unique in professional baseball; perhaps there was never one like it in all of American sports.

---

[358] $201,400, over half of which went for Joe Kuhel ($69,000) and Carl Fischer ($39,000), "Nats Expend $201,400 for Talent during 1930, Stockholders are told," *Washington Post*, January 7, 1931, p. 13

CHAPTER NINETEEN

FERTILE CUBAN SANDLOTS

Cincinnati manager Clark Griffith worked the first two Cubans, Armando Marsans and Rafael Almeida, in major league history into his lineup in 1911. Two years later, he inked Merito Acosta and Jack Calvo to contracts with his Senators. He also sought unsuccessfully to reacquire Marsans and Almeida. For welcoming Cuban ballplayers into major league baseball, Clark became a hero to the sporting community on the island. The Cuban community wished to honor him for this but the scheduling never panned out; it was years before he actually made it to Cuba. His goodwill and reputation paved the way for a breakthrough in international signings, especially after he gained control of the franchise. The Senators brought up 33 Cuban players from 1920-1955. The rest of the majors could only boast twenty in total. Plus, the Senators organization signed many more from the island nation and even supported the Havana Cubans of the Florida International League from 1946-1953. When Mr. Griffith made his only trip to Cuba in 1946, he was mobbed by well-wishers. Few in the baseball-frenzy country exceeded his status as an icon of the American game.

Baseball was played as early as the 1860s on Cuba, initially brought to the island by American sailors. For a time, it was outlawed during the country's struggle for independence from Spain. Specifically, on October 1, 1868, baseball was declared illegal by the colonial head of the country, Francisco de Lersundi, as an "anti-Spanish game with insurrection tendencies, opposed to the language and favored the lack of affection to Spain." The first formal clubs and league weren't formed until 1878.

Esteban Bellan, a light-skinned Cuban native, played in the National Association. Not considered a major league by many, the National Association was a forerunner of the National League nonetheless. He attended Fordham University in New York before joining the Troy Haymakers in 1871.[359] In the winter of 1878, Bellan helped form the Habana Base Ball Club, the first documented baseball club in Latin America. Like Japan and other locales in Latin America, baseball became a national obsession in Cuba.

The Senators only signed two of those 33 Cuban ballplayers prior to 1935 when Griffith initially sent Joe Cambria to the area. Cambria was born in 1890 in Messina, Italy and immigrated to the United States with his family as an infant, growing up in Boston. He played semi-pro ball and joined his first professional club in 1910, Newport of the Rhode Island State League. A broken leg in 1912 ended his career. He later served in World War I, drifted to Baltimore and started the successful Bugle Coat & Apron Service Company. In December 1929, he purchased his first ball club, the near-bankrupt Hagerstown, Maryland, Hubs of the Blue Ridge League, for just enough cash to cover outstanding debts.

In 1932, he purchased the Baltimore Black Sox, expanded his park, Bugle Field, and entered the club in the new Negro National League the following year. The club lost money and he divested from the team at the end of the season. Cambria also owned a local semi-pro club and sponsored boy's baseball teams. On a trip to watch his nephew Calvin play ball on one of those boy's teams, Clark Griffith met Cambria. At the time, Cambria was having financial trouble and needed $1,500 to keep his teams afloat. Griffith lent him the cash and they struck up a friendship that soon led to a business relationship and a lifelong bond.

Through the rest of the decade, Cambria bought and sold over a dozen minor league clubs in Martinsburg, WV, Youngstown, OH, Albany, NY, Harrisburg and Lancaster, PA, Trenton, NJ, Greenville, SC, Salisbury, MD, Orlando and St. Augustine, FL and other spots. He sold the laundry business in 1938 to concentrate solely on baseball. With each

---

[359] At age 13, Esteban and his older brother Domingo came to the United States in 1863 to begin school in September at St. John's College, later renamed Fordham University, in Bronx, New York. St. John's, the first catholic institution of higher learning in the northeastern U.S, was a popular site for wealthy Cuban families to send their children during the turmoil of seeking independence from Spain.

of his clubs Cambria established a working agreement with the Senators; he was committed to Mr. Griffith. Though the two never signed a formal contract, the first option on any ballplayer was always reserved for Washington.

Cambria supplied the Senators with talent for two decades. When Griffith needed a ballplayer, he called Cambia or Joe Engel and a man was soon headed to D.C. The Griffith/Cambria relationship was one of the most unique in sports history. Cambria lived frugally, but he always had investments on the side. His loyalty to Griffith was such that he turned down significantly higher offers for Mickey Vernon and George Case among others and turned them over to the Senators for considerably less cash. Such a relationship didn't exist anywhere else in sports. For example, other major league executives were willing to pay $10,000 for Case but Cambria sold him to Griffith for $1,000 and a promise to make up the difference if Case made good. In fact, most of the players came to Griffith in this manner. His outlays were few and secured by the fact that the ballplayer had to prove himself before money was forked over. Cambria took part in this relationship willingly; he was committed to the betterment of Mr. Griffith and the Senators. In essence, he believed that he served a higher purpose; as such, financial benefits were secondary.

In return, the Senators handled much of Cambria's administrative concerns and provided valued advice. More than once, Griffith interceded between Commissioner Landis and Cambria to smooth over issues and minimize fines and other penalties. Landis, a farm system foe, could be overbearing; a wheeler-dealer like Cambria needed a man like Griffith running interference for him. Overall, Cambria did well financially. He only bought talent cheaply, mostly high schoolers or young semi-pro players. If a young man showed a glimmer of hope, Cambria sold him to Griffith or another club if the Senators passed. He also made money buying and selling clubs. For instance, he purchased the Albany franchise for $7,500 and sold it years later to the New York Giants for $52,000.

Cambria signed the following Americans that made the majors: Allen Benson, George Case, Webbo Clarke, Joe Cleary, Gil Coan, Frank Compos, Reese Diggs, Cal Ermer, Lou Grasmick, Bill Hart, Joe Haynes, Joe Krakauskas, Ed Leip, Mickey Livingston, Ed Lyons, Paul Masterson, Walt Masterson, Hugh Mulcahy, George Myatt, Russ Peters, Babe Phelps, Jake Powell, Ray Prim, Hal Quick, Pete Runnels, Sandy Ullrich, Mickey Vernon, Johnny Welaj, Taffy Wright, Early Wynn and Eddie Yost. Cambria never paid much for talent, including his American finds. He once stated, "You could pay more for a hat than I paid for Vernon, Yost, Case and Masterson." He went even further, "I never gave anybody a nickel bonus. I don't believe in making a boy a financial success before he starts." Cambria signed most players for his clubs and the Senators out of high school for little or no bonus. He scouted and signed many of his players from semi-pro clubs and the low minors, including independent clubs. He'd brag about landing a player for the price of a meal or even an ice cream cone. This fit in nicely with the slim farm budget the Senators had under Clark Griffith.

In early 1941 Commissioner Landis issued an edict prohibiting scouts from owning minor league franchises. Cambria sold all his baseball assets and became Griffith's primary scout. He proved one of the most successful in history. Since Griffith's budget was typically meager, Cambria scoured semi-pro clubs and the low minors for players. Eventually, he traveled to Puerto Rico, Mexico and Panama looking for cheap labor. His biggest splash came in Cuba.[360]

Griffith and Cambria started signing Cuban players in 1932, purchasing Ysmael "Mulo" Morales from Alex Pompez. Morales joined Albany the following season. Bobby Estalella joined the club in 1934 and made the parent club's roster the following year. Cambria's All-Star squad in Baltimore in 1934 also contained several Cubans. By 1936, Cambria brought eight Cubans to Albany's training camp. One, Tomas de la Cruz, was also picked up from Pompez. Cambria though started to make his own trips to the island to gain connections and scout players.

The island proved a windfall for the Senators; for example, Pascual was signed for just $175. Cambria's status in Cuba was such that Pascual turned down a $4,000 offer from the Dodgers to sign with Washington.[361] The scout typically offered the young Cuban players about $75 a month and then put them on a plane headed for Key West. They'd catch a bus to their final destination.

Cambria's interest in Latin players developed during his ownership of a Negro league franchise. The Black Sox played with and against Latin talent. It was obvious the men could play and perhaps they could be had cheaply. Considering Griffith's history with signing Cuban talent, a plan evolved.

For years, Cambria was Clark Griffith's chief source of labor, the only full-time scout for much of the time. By 1938, Cambria worked more or less full-time for the Senators. He was perhaps the most productive in

---

[360] Cambria had played in Cuba in 1911.

[361] Per Fresco Thompson, Bob Addie, "Vernon NO shrinking Violet: Bob Addie's Column," *Washington Post*, March 26, 1961, p. C1

seeking and landing talent of all scouts in history – sheer numbers, no exaggeration. By that time, he spent much of his time stationed/living in Havana. He divided his time between Cuba, his other baseball interests and his Baltimore home. He virtually relocated to Havana in the early 1940s.

Numerous signings followed, well over 400. The Cuban presence was, in essence, the core of Senators during the war years, helping to revive the club. Since they were exempt from the military draft, Griffith invited as many as possible to spring training. With the influx of talent the Senators jumped to second place in 1943 and '45.

Cambria's lasting fame in baseball circles stems from his mining of Cuban talent. Some in the United States would call it "Ivory Hunting." Per the *Hartford Courant*, "They poke a lot of fun at Uncle Joe. They say he chases his prospects up trees and lassos them, or smokes them out of their caves; that every time a young fellow in Cuba hits the ball out of the infield he hears about it." One sportswriter in Cuba, Jess Losada of *Carteles*, referred to him as "The Christopher Columbus of Baseball," a barb denoting his thirst for and taking of the island's treasures.

He signed the following Latin ballplayers that made the majors: Luis Aloma, Ossie Alvarez, Vincente Amor, Julio Becquer, Alex Carrasquel, Jorge Comellas, Sandy Consuegra, Yo-Yo Davalillo, Juan Delis, Bobby Estralella, Angel Fleitas, Mike Forniecas, Ramon Garcia, Preston Gomez, Vince Gonzalez, Mike Guerra, Evelio Hernandez, Connie Marrero, Marty Martinez, Rogelio Martinez, Willie Miranda, Rene Monteagudo, Julio Moreno, Cholly Naranjo, Tony Oliva, Baby Ortiz, Roberto Ortiz, Reggie Otero, Camilio Pasqual, Carlos Pasqual, Carlos Paula, Pedro Ramos, Armando Roche, Freddy Rodriquez, Raul Sanchez, Luis Suarez, Gil Torres, Roy Valdes, Jose Valdivielso, Zoilo Versalles, Adrian Zabala and Jose Zardon. In all, Cambria signed hundreds of Cuban prospects. He typically signed between ten and twenty a year to professional contracts. Cambria's influence was felt throughout Latin America. Carrasquel was the first ballplayer from Venezuela in Organized Baseball. Likewise, Cambria sent the first Nicaraguan to a major league camp, Gilberto Hooker in 1956 with Washington.

Cambria became a fixture in Havana. He merged his Italian with scattered Spanish phrases to speak "Pidgin." He cut a stereotypical figure wearing baggy pants, and an un-tucked, full-length shirt with fake pearl buttons. The "fat little Italian" with a cigar in his mouth could be found everyday patrolling Gran Stadium, the high schools or wherever young men played ball. Cambria also invested in the community, purchasing the three necessities, an apartment building, a bar and a minor league franchise, the Havana Cubans of the Florida International League.

The Senators signings at first became a boom to the Cuban League, instilling pride in local talent and sparking interest in the league. All the talent on the island flowed towards Havana so naturally Cambria set up stakes there. Eventually, he decided to branch out and secure amateur talent closer to their homes. He signed a lot of teenagers. In doing so he was blamed for bringing about the demise of the amateur leagues. With so many young men inked to professional contracts, the amateur leagues base of talent was shrinking considerably.

Not without cause, many in Cuba resented Cambria and his tactics. He signed players cheap and, as noted, he signed a lot of them. They were often required to sign blank contracts, to be filled in by Cambria at a later time. The men were then sent to the United States to play in the pro leagues. This not only stripped the island of talent but, considering that most of the Senator's farm teams were in the south, these young men ran into American racism. For these reasons, Cambria was derided as an "Ivory Hunter" or unflatteringly called the "Christopher Columbus of baseball."

Eventually, baseball men in Cuba rebelled against Cambria. One of the most vocal was local sportswriter Jess Losada. To combat Cambria's mass signings, Losada and the Cuban government invited the Cincinnati Reds to the island to set up shop. Cambria no longer had the island to himself. Both interests operated in Cuba until Fidel Castro's revolution killed off all relations with the United States. Cambria and Castro, a big baseball fan, were actually pretty tight. During the government's transition, Castro guaranteed Cambria's safety and declared that everyone show him respect. At times Castro's forces even sent men to guard Cambria.

The Reds fielded a Triple-A team called the Havana Sugar Kings in the International League from 1954-1960. Much of the roster was filled with local talent, such as, longtime major league pitchers Orlando Pena and Mike Cuellar and infielders Leo Cardenas and Cookie Rojas. With the communist revolution on the island in 1959 political pressure mounted on the International League. In July bullets were fired in political celebration outside the stadium that nicked a coach and a player on the field as they landed. The visiting club left the country as soon as possible and league officials forced the relocation of most of the club's remaining home games to the road. Finally, the International League abruptly relocated the franchise to New Jersey on July 8, 1960. The club was on the road in Miami at the time. Several Cuban players and their manager immediately resigned and returned home. Others, like Pena, stayed in the United States to pursue their careers. The Cuban talent pipeline was dead.

Cambria stayed with the Senators organization after Clark Griffith's death and relocated with the club to Minnesota. At the time of his passing in 1962 at age 72, he had scouted in Cuba for over 25 years. Cambria frequently lamented about his fondness for Griffith and his loyalty to the organization. He often relayed his wishes to be buried in a Senators uniform. In fact, at a press conference in Minnesota, Calvin Griffith joked that Cambria would now have to be buried in a Twins jersey. At the time, Cambria played along with the joke. When Calvin left the room, Cambria turned to the reporters and reiterated that, "I haven't changed my mind. I still want to go out in a Washington uniform. Washington was Mr. Griffith's club."

CHAPTER TWENTY

ROLE IN INTEGRATION

Clark Griffith was at the forefront of the integration issue throughout his time in the game during the 20th century. He played an integral role in all the major events. Some point to the fact that he railed against Branch Rickey for tampering with Negro league players. The fact is Rickey completely ignored Negro league contracts and held the black leagues themselves in low regard. Griffith held the established Negro leagues in high regard. As no other man in Organized Baseball, he conversed with Negro league executives and benefactors concerning their trials and tribulations as businessmen, especially Cum Posey. Thus, he understood their challenges and priorities. As such, when major league executives swooped in and began stripping the league of its talent, often with little regard for legal contracts, Griffith spoke up. It wasn't integration in and of itself that he was railing against. How could it be? As Rickey acknowledged, Griffith long ago integrated the major leagues.

There is no historical account of any overt racial incident outside normal bench jockeying ploys in Clark Griffith's career nor is there any hint that he harbored any derogatory feelings toward anyone which is unusual for a man born in 1869 and grew to be friends with Cap Anson, a staunch segregationist. Clark was born in Vernon County, Missouri, which had a history of pro-slavery feelings; however, it was a vastly different community in the 1870s. The Griffiths were one of a number of Northern families that moved to the area after the Civil War. They were from

Abraham Lincoln's home state and quite naturally adopted his ideals. Griffith himself hailed Lincoln and his goals as the American ideal.

Clark had few opportunities to play against black players after he reached the majors. Organized Baseball was virtually segregated by the time he arrived and there was no way Anson was going to allow one of his men to play with or against an African-American. Later, Griffith was respected and genuinely liked by black sportswriter Sam Lacy, Negro league executives and players, all of who had many dealings with the Senators owner. No man in Organized Baseball saw more Negro league games than Clark. No one at the top level of Organized Baseball was as accessible and willing to lend assistance.

At the turn of the century, Griffith and John McGraw gave a black player, Charlie Grant, a tryout. It was Griffith's first days as a major league manager. The first time he was actually in charge. McGraw of the Baltimore Orioles was the one that needed men to fill out his roster. Griffith took over the American League's reigning championship club and added enough solid personnel before camp to cop another pennant as the league ascended to the major league level. McGraw wanted Grant for his roster; Griffith pitched and hit to him for his colleague.

Shortly after taking over the Yankees, Griffith tried out Luis Bustamante, an infielder with the All-Cubans, a black team.[362] Clark commented that Bustamante was "too chocolate," which in the vernacular of the time meant that no matter how well he played, he'd never be accepted by the league.

What eventually set Clark Griffith apart from his counterparts in the game was his embrace of Cuban players; in essence, he opened international markets. More than one of these men had dark skin. Griffith brought the following Cubans to the majors:[363]

1911 Armando Marsans, Rafael Almeida

---

[362] Bustamante is a member of the Cuban Baseball Hall of Fame.

[363] An unfortunate side effect of hiring Cuban players was the hope it gave black American players that integration was forthcoming. This wouldn't happen for decades. An example of this is a quote from the *Chicago Defender*, a black newspaper, on July 8, 1911 about blackball's great Pete Hill: "…if that boy Hill keeps up the rough stuff, he will be passing for a Cuban next year or playing on Clark Griffith's Cincinnati Reds." The "rough stuff" is referring to his hitting and fielding exploits. J.H. Wright, "American or Chicago Giants Which?," *Chicago Defender*, July 8, 1911, p. 1

1913 Merito Calvo, Jack Calvo

1920 Jose Acosta, Ricardo Torres

1935 Roberto Estalella

1937 Mike Guerra

1938 Rene Monteagudo

1940 Gilberto Torres

1941 Roberto Ortiz

1944 Preston Gomez, Baby Ortiz, Luis Suarez, Santiago Ullrich, Roy Valdes

1945 Armando Roche, Jose Zardon

1948 Angel Fleitas, Moin Garcia, Enrique Gonzalez

1950 Sandy Consuegra, Connie Marrero, Lim Martinez, Julio Moreno, Carlos Pascual

1951 Cisco Campos, Willie Miranda

1952 Mike Fornieles, Raul Sanchez

1954 Carlos Paula, Camilio Pascuel

1955 Julio Becquer, Juan Delis, Vince Gonzalez, Pedro Ramos, Jose Valdivielso

The Senators/Twins brought another half dozen Cuban ballplayers to the majors in the years immediately following Mr. Griffith's death, including stars Zoilo Versalles and Tony Oliva. Hundreds of Cuban ballplayers were signed by the Senators' organization itself; naturally, many never made it out of the minors. When Branch Rickey signed Jackie Robinson in 1945, whispers throughout Organized Baseball scoffed and said that Clark Griffith had long ago integrated the game. The only difference being that Griffith's men spoke Spanish.

 To American mores it was acceptable to pass a dark-skinned player off as white as long as he spoke Spanish with a strong accent. Griffith fully realized the implications of what he was doing by hiring Cuban ballplayers. He also was fully aware that he was placing dark-skinned ballplayers on his roster. However, he may not have realized he was doing anything particularly radical; he just needed some ballplayers, preferably cheap ones. Few realize it even today. Griffith's hiring of Cuban ballplayers was a clear divergence from major league baseball's historical methods of operation. Just because there was no great backlash or to-do in the national press, doesn't alter the fact that Griffith openly and without apology integrated the game over a decade before Jackie Robinson took the field. Bobby Estalella, added to Washington's roster in 1935, was clearly of African ancestry. Even if one disputes the argument that Griffith integrated the game, he did something just as radical. He opened the first productive international talent market for major league baseball. Conversely, he opened major league baseball to the international community.

Whether or not major league officials publicly called Griffith on the carpet for integrating the game, the black community and certainly the Hispanic community knew it to be the truth. As an *Atlanta Daily World*, an African-American newspaper, reporter noted during spring training in 1939, "A preview of what will happen to colored ballplayers when and if they are admitted to the big leagues is given in the story written from the Washington baseball club training camp, where owner Clark Griffith is giving tryouts to several Cubans."[364]

Black teams were a big draw in the District. Just in the same manner that Griffith coaxed the Redskins to the area, he welcomed the Homestead Grays and other black clubs to Griffith Stadium. This was a mutually beneficial relationship; obviously, if the Senators made money, so did the Grays.

Washington D.C. was a segregated city; and one heavily populated by African-Americans. Griffith Stadium itself sat in the middle of a black community. Actually, it grew to be that way; that wasn't the case when the site was first developed for the American Association back in 1891. The club was first located at the end of a trolley line in a white suburb. By the 1930s, the Senators had one of the strongest black fan bases in the majors, especially considering its relative market size to New York, Philadelphia and Chicago.[365] There were no signs at Griffith stadium but custom dictated segregated seating, as it did at Sportsman's Park in St. Louis,[366] the majors only other formally segregated city. African-Americans sat in the right field pavilion or left field bleachers during Senators contests.

---

[364] "Darkskinned Cubans will face Colorphobia in Major Leagues," *Atlanta Daily World*, April 4, 1939, p. 5

[365] 1940 African American population: New York 458,000, Chicago 278,000, Philadelphia 251,000, D.C. 187,000, Baltimore 166,000 and Detroit 149,000.

[366] Both the Cardinals and Browns played at Sportsman's Park.

A reporter for the *Atlanta Daily World* toured Griffith Stadium in 1939. He noted how devoted black fans were, despite viewing a perennially poor team. He was impressed with the hiring practices of Mr. Griffith, noting, "Wandering through the improved ballpark, a favorable impression is gathered when the large number of colored workmen busy in the park is noted. Negroes at the stands selling refreshments: Negro ground attendants which they do not have in New York: colored maids in the rest rooms and wherever you turn there is a smiling colored man or woman ready and willing to assist. This is in direct contract to parks in New York, for instance, where few Negroes are employed…Yep. Washington is a swell baseball town and whether the team leads the league or whether it is at the bottom of the scrap pile, loyal colored fans still turn their footsteps toward the Senators' home when that team is entertaining."[367]

Like every community a few incidents over the years sparked controversy. From October 5-8, 1920, Senators first baseman Joe Judge organized interracial exhibition games between the Brooklyn Royal Giants and a team of white all-stars. They were not the first such contests but they would be the last despite potential profits. The Royal Giants took three out of four games. During one contest, Washington outfielder Frank Brower punched a black umpire in the face. Not wanted any such trouble again Griffith banned interracial games from the stadium for over two decades. Similarly, Senators pitcher Bill McAfee slugged a black fan on the road in Cleveland in 1933.[368] He was roundly booed upon his return to D.C. and was eventually shuffled to St. Louis.

Local backlash ensued after Senators radio announcer Arch McDonald, a Southerner, remarked on the air, "They are funny things, these colored baseball games…" Popular sportswriter Sam Lacy was particularly incensed.[369] The biggest incident gaining national attention involved Jake Powell of the Yankees in 1938. Powell was originally a Washington farm product and well known to Senators fans. During a pre-game radio interview in July in Chicago Powell responded to a question about what he did during the off-season. He said that he was a cop in Dayton, Ohio who spent his time "cracking niggers over the head." Commissioner Landis immediately suspended him for ten days.[370] Powell

---

[367] "D.C. Colored Fans take their Ball Seriously," *Atlanta Daily World*, May 1, 1939, p. 5

[368] "McAfee punches Heckler in Jaw, Indians Protest," *Washington Post*, June 28, 1933, p. 15

[369] Brad Snyder, *Beyond the Shadow of the Senators*, 2004, page 59

[370] "Powell suspended for Radio Remark," *New York Times*, July 31, 1938, p. 63

required a police escort when the Yankees came to D.C. in August. Black fans showered him with bottles in his first game back from suspension.[371] Griffith exacerbated the issue when he announced later that he was interested in reacquiring Powell, which he ultimately did in 1943.

Griffith Stadium was built in 1911 but wasn't fully utilized until Clark took over the team in 1920. Black teams started using the facility regularly in the mid 1930s but the Washington Potomacs in 1924 and Washington Pilots in 1932 predated this era. The Washington Elite Giants also called Griffith Stadium home from 1936 until the club relocated to Baltimore the following year due to lack of support. The local Black Senators and semi-pro Royal Giants used the stadium briefly in 1938 and 1939, respectively. From the beginning Griff watched the games and was accessible to blackball officials and players. In 1932 he had a long chat with a *Pittsburgh Courier*, an African-American newspaper, reporter while watching a Pilots-Pittsburgh Crawfords game. Clark particularly admired Mule Suttles, claiming that watching him was "worth anybody's money."[372]

The first truly successful black team in Washington was the Homestead Grays from 1937-1948. The club originated near Pittsburgh but eventually found their permanent residence in the nation's capital. They became extremely popular in the late 1930s, just as the Senators were floundering in the standings.

The Homestead Grays were a good team and boasted some great talent. By 1937, Griffith regularly sat in his box seat watching their games. In fact he saw virtually every game from 1942-1943 and numerous games during the other years. He was impressed with the quality of play and admired the skills of many of the black athletes, particularly Josh Gibson and Buck Leonard. He also respected the black businessmen who ran the game, particularly Grays' owner Cum Posey, who had Griff's ear. Clark went out of his way to accommodate the Grays and Posey. In 1943, when scheduling problems were forcing the playing of the entire Negro League World Series out west, Griffith rearranged the Senators' schedule so two games could be played in the east.[373] He was also the first major league

---

[371] "Powell survives Bottle Barrage as Yanks rout Senators," *New York Times*, August 17, 1938, p. 14

[372] "Washington Senators Owner sees bright Future for Negro Leagues," *Pittsburgh Courier*, September 3, 1932, p. A5

[373] Cum Posey, "Posey's Points," *Pittsburgh Courier*, September 18, 1943, p. 17 and Cum Posey, "Posey's Points," *Pittsburgh Courier* October 2, 1943, p. 16

owner to allow black clubs to use his lights for night games, from the first year the system was installed in 1942.[374]

Due to his amicable personality and his obvious accessibility, Griffith became the de facto liaison between the Negro leagues and Organized Baseball. Certainly, Commissioner Landis wasn't approachable on these matters. *Baltimore Afro-American* reporter Sam Lacy, a political force in black baseball, continually lobbied Griffith to integrate the Senators. The pair held numerous conversations concerning the future of both leagues. For a long time they had a good rapport.

Griffith was straddling both worlds. Much of counseling Griffith gave and actions in an intermediary role were well accepted and won praise. He wasn't progressive on the issue of integration, save the hiring of Latin ballplayers. Combine this with the fact that D.C. was a segregated city and that rental revenues from black teams were essential to the financial health of the Senators, Griffith didn't formally integrate the club until very late. In truth, it was much too late. Naturally, he gained heat for his inaction and duplicity, whether actual or imagined. Lacy became put off by his conversations with Griffith that seemingly led nowhere. The majors were a slow-moving monopoly; they did things at their own pace.

As time wore on and no black man wore a Senators' uniform until September 1954 relations became strained and embittered at times. Whatever shortcomings Griffith had they paled in comparison to local Redskins owner George Preston Marshall, a staunch racist; however, baseball was king of sports and professional football.

Black fans were encouraged with the acceptance of Bobby Estalella, 1935, and Alex Carrasquel, 1939, in the major leagues. Both were widely considered to be black by both black and white spectators. There was no unwritten rule about Latin ballplayers in the majors, so Griffith signed all he could. Whatever admonishments or difficulties he had with other league executives concerning the issue are lost to closed-door meetings and behind-the-back whispers. The issue was a bone of contention for sportswriters on both sides of the fence. And, Griffith didn't tiptoe around the issue; he poured it on, signing as many Latin players as he could.

Naturally, the black press and public became livid that the major leagues brought up a man with one arm, Pete Gray, a man with one leg, Bert Shepard, about fifteen players under age 18 and numerous foreign-born players during World War II, but wouldn't even consider a black

---

[374] John R. Clark, "Wylie Ave.," *Pittsburgh Courier*, November 12, 1955, p. B19

man. African-Americans were expected to fight and die for a country that treated them as second class citizens. Sam Lacy and Wendell Smith of the *Pittsburgh Courier Journal* were especially bitter. As Smith wrote, "Mr. Griffith would give Washington fans dark players from other lands, but never an American Negro." Another bone of contention was money. The Senators were making upwards of $100,000 a year on park rentals to the Homestead Grays plus more for various exhibition contests and all-star games. Griffith was also paying the Latin ballplayers less than the white players.

As noted, Griffith put himself in the middle of the controversy. To his credit, few other men in Organized Baseball made themselves accessible. They skirted controversy and often refused to be quoted. Often, they simply waved the black leagues aside, claiming they were nothing more than an extension of the rackets. They rarely if ever held a meeting with Negro league officials and sportswriters about the subject of integration. Perhaps, they had some underlying motives they wished to conceal. Perhaps, they just wanted others to deal with the difficulties.

Sam Lacy wrote Commissioner Landis in November 1937 requesting an audience to discuss the integration issue. He failed to reply so Lacy contracted Griffith in December. The pair held a two and a half hour meeting. Landis didn't want to be involved. Griffith gave some advice that was endorsed by Lacy at the time but eventually wore on him, believing that he was being handled or pushed aside. Griffith didn't close the door to the idea of African-Americans joining the majors but he offered pointers that reflected the mood of the men within Organized Baseball.

In a nutshell Griffith suggested that the Negro leagues clean house and strengthen their leagues. Gamblers were heavily involved in the Negro National League and this offended Landis to no end. He also presented two long-standing arguments which, in part, were perhaps arguments designed to keep the status quo. He feared for the demise of the Negro leagues if black men were allowed into Organized Baseball and that he was concerned for the safety of the individual that actually did break the color barrier. Both arguments were later seen as age-old methods to placate the issue, especially the latter. The demise of the Negro leagues was a legitimate concern. Many of Griffith's contacts in black baseball were club owners and executives. These weren't the people pushing for integration. They knew as well as anyone the potential damage that could be done to their league and, of course, their investment. It was the black community as a whole and sportswriters voicing the opinion that pushed for integration. In the end, Negro league executives didn't stand in the way of integration but they surely weren't welcoming it with open arms. Jackie Robinson jumping his Kansas City Monarch club and playing in the Dodgers' organization surely wasn't beneficial to the financial backers of the Negro American League.

Lacy left the meeting with renewed vigor and belief that the Negro leagues needed to tighten its ranks and correct some real or imagined problems. In actuality, the problem was with all of America and the fervent desire for or the complacent acceptance of racial segregation. Griffith was really in a bad situation and would have been best served keeping out of it like every other baseball man. But, he was a mediator, a facilitator and one to work to try to bring all sides together.

Plus, Griffith honestly believed in the integrity of the Negro leagues. Time and again he expressed strong support for the organization, long before his verbal battles with Branch Rickey. Few others eloquently expressed a similar positive message. No one, outside William Benswanger in Pittsburgh, ever went to more than a handful of games. None clapped as often and enjoyed as many contests as Clark Griffith. He was a fan of baseball, not a social reformer. Moreover, Griffith was just one of sixteen owners; he didn't speak for everyone. The man that did, Landis, shunned the controversy. It is hardly detrimental to Griffith for offering sound advice on a difficult issue in a situation that he really didn't control. No one else even listened to the concerns of Negro league executives, certainly not Branch Rickey; he merely lurked on the outskirts and raided the league of its players without even considering compensation. He knew that Negro league executives wouldn't sue over breach of contract since that would put them in a poor position in the black community. Thus, Rickey felt a measure of immunity in his actions. In truth, the Dodgers weren't a poor organization. They could have easily paid a fair price for Rickey and others. Bill Veeck, a man with far less financial wherewithal, negotiated a deal for Larry Doby.

In 1942, Brooklyn Dodgers manager Leo Durocher remarked that he'd employ black players "if they weren't barred by the owners." Judge Landis, on the defensive, declared that there was no such ban, "either by rule, agreement or subterfuge." Asked what he thought, Griffith advised the Negro leagues to strengthen so that one day they could join Organized Baseball and compete en masse, possibly challenging the major leagues. He was quoted in the *Pittsburgh Courier*, "My idea is that the Negro leagues should be developed to the place where they will also assume a commanding place in the baseball world. The drawing power of Negro baseball is increasing and it should increase even more rapidly if the colored leagues are improved. Then they, too, can pay their stars big salaries. Then when the Negro leagues are developed properly, some day the top teams could play our top clubs for the world championship and thus have a chance to prove their caliber."[375]

After the Monarchs drew a large crowd on June 26, 1942, Griffith openly talked about purchasing Josh Gibson. Also in June, the United Federal Workers petitioned Landis and Griffith on behalf of Negro league players for inclusion in Organized Baseball. On December 3, 1943, Sam Lacy and Paul Robeson, a national black political figure, addressed the major league owners on the segregation issue. Afterwards Griffith was quoted in the *Baltimore Afro-American*, "My opinion now is the same as it was then, and that is that; colored players should have their own league and white players have theirs."[376] No denying that statement; Griffith was part of the establishment.

Branch Rickey announced the signing of Jackie Robinson just after the World Series in 1945. Griffith's immediate response was, "Eventually I hope the Negroes will have their own league under the administrative group that governs all baseball. I hope to own a club in such a league." Then, he brought up the compensation issue, "The only question that occurs to me is whether organized ball has the right to sign a player from the Negro league. That is a well-established league and Organized Baseball shouldn't take their players. The Negro league is entitled to full recognition as a full-fledged baseball organization."[377]

The comments sparked a verbal back and forth between Rickey and Griffith in the press. Rickey justified his pilfering of Robinson because the Negro leagues were nothing more than a "racket." Hence, they deserved no recognition. Griffith also drew the ire of Sam Lacy who didn't want anything standing in the way of Robinson actually making the big leagues; however, Lacy didn't seem to have any derogatory comments for J.L. Wilkinson's cries of protest along the same lines, "We had money invested in Jackie. They got a $100,000 player from us for nothing." Rickey also scoffed at Griffith as already employing black ballplayers, "Mr. Griffith initiated the practice of bringing Negroes into baseball under the guise of Cubans. I investigated the Negro organizations and have found out they are not leagues, not even organizations. Negro baseball is in the zone of a racket, and Mr. Griffith knows this very well."

---

[375] Chester L. Washington, "Judge Landis' Okay spurs Interest in annual East-West Classic," *Pittsburgh Courier*, July 25, 1942, p. 16

[376] Ralph Matthews, "Clark Griffith won't budge on use of Colored Players," *Baltimore Afro-American*, December 11, 1943, p. 1

[377] "Club Heads give Views," *New York Times*, October 24, 1945, page 17

Much has been made of the Griffith-Rickey exchanges in 1945. The contention was really prompted by Cum Posey and other club owners who sought out Griffith in response to Rickey's invasion on their territory. In early 1945 to cover his intentions of scouting a black player, Rickey announced his backing of the United States League, a new black league. The USL, led by deposed Negro National League president Gus Greenlee, was a direct threat to the established black leagues, charging into direct competition for talent, attendance and financial survival. The first barbs in the press between Griffith and Rickey were actually over this issue. Griffith was speaking on behalf of Posey, Effa Manley and others. Rickey's threat to the established leagues was even greater after his intentions became clear with the announcement of Robinson's signing. Naturally the first reaction of Posey and the others, voiced through Griffith, was a combative one. The leagues were fighting not only for respect for their contractual rights, but for their very survival.[378]

Regardless of the animosity between the pair, Rickey ran into much harsher rebukes by his colleagues. Griffith's initial opposition was of a constructive nature. That wasn't necessarily the case with many of the other major league owners. In response to Robinson's signing and other changes within the game, the majors formed an advisory committee in 1946; it was headed by Larry MacPhail and included: Ford Frick, National League president; William Harridge, American League president; Sam Breadon, St. Louis Cardinals owner; Phillip Wrigley, Chicago Cubs owner; Tom Yawkey, Boston Red Sox owner. Nineteen Forty-Six was a turbulent time with the surge of talent returning from the war, efforts at unionization, Mexican League encroachment, swelling of the minors from twelve to over forty leagues and, of course, the signing of Jackie Robinson which was widely debated throughout the country.

MacPhail's committee met in July and August and presented its recommendations on August 27 at the Waldorf Hotel in New York. The committee was firmly against integration. The report even warned Rickey about going ahead with his plans. Basically, the report focused on the tired old excuses against integration: that most Negro leaguers are not qualified to play in the majors; that these men have not gone through Organized Baseball's formal minor league system; that existing Negro league contracts need to be honored; that the income from renting stadiums to the Negro leagues was sorely needed; that integration may make the major league's white clientele uncomfortable. The owners, as a

---

[378] "Rickey's Stand on Negro Loop challenged by Washington Boss," *Atlanta Daily World*, May 24, 1945 p. 5 and "Griffith takes Lead for Loops," *New York Amsterdam News*, November 17, 1945, p. 1

whole, deemed the report too strongly worded for public consumption. They collected and destroyed all copies, at least they thought so.[379] However, a vote was taken, 15-1 against integration. Obviously, the opposing vote was the Dodgers. Regardless of the opposition by his colleagues, Rickey had the support of Commissioner Happy Chandler and proceeded.

The questions began to mount as time wore on and still the Senators didn't field an American black player. Protestors started to show up at Griffith Stadium in the early 1950s as they did in other parks. In the vernacular of the day Griffith referred to them as a "committee of communists." Defiant, he wasn't going to be pushed around. In April 1953 he commented, "Nobody is going to stampede me into signing Negro players merely for the sake of satisfying certain pressure groups." Griffith didn't pull any punches; in fact, the harder he was questioned, the harder he fought back. He was determined that the first black Senator be a great one. After all the delaying and railing against his detractors, Griffith finally added a black player seven and a half years after Jackie Robinson first appeared on a major league diamond. It happened more with a thud than any great fanfare. After hitting .290 with Charlotte in the Sally League, Carlos Paula, a dark-skinned Cuban, was anticlimactically brought up as the club's first official black player in September 1954, playing left field and going 2 for 5 on the 6th. It would be another five years before every major league club employed a black player. The Red Sox were the final holdout. The Detroit Tigers of 1961 were the last team to field an African-American on its everyday roster.

---

[379] The existence of the report was first exposed by Rickey in February 1948. "Dodger President reveals Secret Committee Report," *Christian Science Monitor*, February 17, 1948, p. 12

CHAPTER TWENTY-ONE

FINANCING ON A SHOESTRING

Like Charles Comiskey, Frank Navin and Connie Mack, Clark Griffith was among the last of the dinosaurs that derived the bulk of his income through his ball club. Unlike those three, Griffith's club resided in the least populated city in the American League and by far the sparsest populated metropolitan area.[380] If he was going to make a go at it and succeed in the nation's capital, Griff would have to do it on a shoestring budget. If that meant aggressive bargaining techniques with his ballplayers, than so be it. If that meant he would at times be called a cheapskate or other such derogatory term, well that's how it would have to be. He couldn't draw the crowds or the cash like his rivals in New York, Chicago, Boston or Philadelphia. That was where the money was. D.C. was a small market, the smallest, and the Senators were run with a small market mentality.

The club needed a steady hand, a man with a vision and the fortitude to stick to a plan. He had to compete year in and year out against clubs with far greater resources. Financially, the deck was stacked against the club before the season even began. Part of the Senators' personality

---

[380] City and metropolitan area populations in 1914 (in 1000s): New York, 2,615 and 6,475; Chicago, 2,185 and 2,447; Philadelphia, 1,549 and 1,972; St. Louis, 687 and 829; Boston, 671 and 1,520; Cleveland, 561 and 613; Detroit, 466 and 501; Washington, 331 and 368. Source: Dan Levitt's article "Ed Barrow, the Federal League and the Union League" in SABR's *The National Pastime*, 2008, p. 97

was defined by being the American League club with the fewest resources. The following traits, in some way, can be tied to this: tight payroll and talent-purchasing budget; aggressive local marketing; anti-farming stance; entertainers in the coaching boxes; strong reliance on stadium rental fees; utilization of cheap Cuban labor; anti-New York stance; favored night game schedule.

In late 1919, Griffith put everything he had into the Senators. Financially speaking, he walked into the most expensive era, to date, in major league history. This was made abundantly clear a few weeks later when the Yankees announced the purchase of Babe Ruth for a whopping $125,000 plus a $300,000 loan. The outrageous sum paid for Ruth in January 1920 sparked an upward trend in salaries as players realized their economic potential. The market certainly changed, both on the plus side and on the minus side. About the same time minor league executives suspended the draft. Now, major league clubs were forced to purchase each minor league player outright. Thus, the cost of talent soared for the major leagues. Fortunately, Ruth came through, helping to spark unprecedented interest in the game. Consequently, the 1920s proved to be the period with the most potential for profit as well. Griffith grabbed his share with pennants in 1924 and '25.

    Not surprisingly, in order to make a profit a club had to limit its costs. The most significant expenditures stemmed from spring training, ballpark maintenance and upkeep, farm system, player acquisition and payroll expenses. The Nationals' profitability depended on how well Griffith could control these factors. Spring training was pretty much always a bust; rarely did the club cover these expenses with revenue from exhibition games. Before the season even started, the Nats were operating in the red. The club spent a considerable amount of money, $672,000, from 1920-1924 to put a second deck on the grandstand, convert the bleachers to concrete and add seating and other amenities to the renamed Griffith Stadium. In 1939, the club spent another $75,000 on improvements. Two years later, Griffith spent $230,000 on a 1,140,000-watt lighting system, obtaining a $125,000 interest-free loan from the American League to do so.

    The Senators never developed an extensive farm system but they did feel the sting of rising player acquisition costs and spiraling salaries. The Nats spent $450,000 buying players from 1920-1924 to build their first pennant winners in D.C. Griffith spent even more than that in the early 1930s to build his last pennant winner. Specifically, the Nats paid $154,500 in 1929 and $201,400 in 1930 for talent. The outlays dropped off dramatically by the mid 1930s for a couple of reasons. During the pennant run in 1933, the Senators lost money. Griffith had to find a better way to field a major league team; acquisition costs were sapping all profits. He soon developed a working arrangement with Joe Cambria. Griffith helped with the initial costs and continued expenses and administration of the minor league teams that Cambria owned. In return the Senators received first crack at the talent. As a result, acquisition costs dropped to about $100,000 in 1936 and all the way down to $49,500 in 1944. The Senators placed second in the American League in 1943 and '45 despite spending relatively little to fill their roster.

In November 1929, the Senators purchased the Chattanooga Lookouts of the Class-A Southern Association, their top farm club for years. Later, they acquired the Charlotte franchise in the Class-B Piedmont League. Griffith also had working agreements with a number of other clubs, many of which belonged to Cambria. Though acquisition fees did fall off, the Senators had significant outlays to maintain their farm system, as small as it was. Certainly acquiring cheap Latin talent helped keep costs down. However, the Senators never had a productive farm system. They rarely competed in the standings after 1933. During Griffith's first 22 seasons in Washington the club finished in the first division sixteen times. Over the next 22 seasons, they cracked the first division only four times, three of those were between 1943 and '46. Obviously, the Senators didn't, or couldn't, compete year in and year out after the Depression. Due to Griffith's reluctance or inability to spend, the Senators were often comprised of other teams' leftovers. They were forced to draft from the other clubs and explore the otherwise untapped market in Cuba.

Salary figures for field personnel fluctuated from year to year. In 1929, the major league roster cost $231,618 in salaries, $187,059 in 1933. Payroll for 1939 equaled $165,849, but started to rise again to $192,190 in 1943 and especially after the war. Nineteen Forty-Six personnel costs equaled $356,631; two years later, the figure was $380,000. In 1950 the players made $304,959.

An often-overlooked expense was the upkeep major league owners were expected to grant reporters. They provided transportation and room and board for the sportswriters. A generous financial gift was also provided at the holidays. The Senators spent a good deal on community relations as well. Griffith Stadium was lent to various organizations and for numerous functions free of charge. More so than any other park. The black community held many functions, religious and otherwise, at Griffith Stadium. Clark wouldn't even charge a cleaning fee to many charitable causes. Being a governmental hub, numerous civic and religious organizations and government agencies were granted free use of the park for a wide range of fundraising causes, especially during the war. Clark personally spent a large chunk of his life at various banquets, government affairs, charity drives and amateur sports functions.

The Senators' revenue came from attendance, advertising, concessions, broadcasting, player sales and park rental fees. Griffith couldn't have bought a baseball team at a better time in history; attendance took off in 1920 and never again fell to 1919's level of 243,000. However, the Senators themselves fell below the league average every year except 1925, 1930-1931, 1933 and 1943, sometimes significantly so. From 1901-1960, the Senators only drew over one million customers once, in 1946, and didn't hit a half million until the championship year of 1924. The stadium's largest crowd, 38,701, saw Walter Johnson pitch Game 4 of the 1925 World Series. The low occurred on September 7, 1951 when only 460 patrons occupied seats near the end of another poor season in the standings.

The phenomenon known as Babe Ruth helped spur an attendance boom during the 1920s. Not only did the Yankees consistently draw more than anyone at their home park but they were the biggest draw on the road as well. Every club owner looked forward to Ruth and the Yankees coming to town. Recreation dollars loosened considerably during the 1920s; in fact, an attendance boom started immediately following World War I. The increased fan fervor and attraction of the long ball sparked a good deal of ballpark construction and modifications.

Sunday baseball also spurred attendance in D.C. As conciliation to soldiers and governmental employees in Washington, the D.C. Board of Commissioners permitted Sunday baseball in a vote on May 14, 1918. The Senators wasted no time; they asked the Indians to travel to town on their off day on May 19 to squeeze in a game. Fifteen thousand fans showed up. The Nats and Doc Ayers won 1-0 in twelve innings. Ayers allowed only seven hits and scored the only run. Sunday baseball was a hit. Working his potential fan base, Griffith gave season passes to Washington clergy to entice Sunday turnouts.

Prior to 1918, the Senators made many one-day hops on Sundays to capture a piece of the big payday; many times they took a train to Cleveland for a game. Connie Mack and the Athletics made many such trips to D.C. prior to legal Sunday baseball in Philadelphia in 1934. In 1932 alone they trekked to Washington six times for profitable contests.

Night baseball proved to be a major boon to weekday attendance in the District. Griffith was hesitant at first but after he saw the economic potential of night baseball, he became its leading proponent. The first night game in D.C was held in 1941; at the time each team was permitted seven a year. Griffith petitioned the league for more and eventually used his unique status in the nation's capital to gain twenty-one night games a year for the Senators. In 1943, all limitations were removed.

Washington D.C. was an itinerant government town; many residents were only temporary, hailing from other parts of the country. Hence, the Senators were not the team they grew up adoring. Some were only interesting in going to Griffith Stadium when their favorite team came to town. Consequently, many cheered for the opposition. Naturally it became particularly hard to attract new fans to Griffith Stadium after the collapse in the standings in the mid 1930s. The Senators tried to spur attendance with showmanship. Griffith always had his clowns, Germany Schaefer, Carl Sawyer, Nick Altrock and Al Schacht, entertaining the crowd during batting practice and during lulls in the game. The Senators nearly always boasted a couple players who were born locally to keep fans interested. The club fielded the major's only bearded player and even a one-legged pitcher.

Like many ballparks, Griffith Stadium was plastered with signage. Advertising revenue was crucial to covering the team's expenses. One famous photo of Josh Gibson rounding third at the park shows at least twenty-three separate advertisers. The list included Shah & Shah Jewelers, Yellow Cab, *Washington Post*, Coke, Dr. Pepper, Mike Martin's Liniment, Squirt, Wilson Sports Equipment, 7Up and Baker Lumber and Millwork. Beer was never sold at Griffith Stadium but there were plenty of beer and cigarette billboards throughout the park. A 50-foot National Bohemian beer bottle stood above the right center field scoreboard.

By the mid 1920s, road games were regularly aired over the radio in D.C. In 1934 Griffith hired Arch McDonald on the recommendation of Joe Engel to recreate road games for radio broadcasts. In a poll by *The Sporting News* in 1933, McDonald won the title of America's favorite broadcaster, the first such Announcer of the Year award.[381] Amazingly, he won the award while working in the minor leagues in Chattanooga, Tennessee.[382] McDonald called Senators games through 1956, save one season with the Yankees in 1939.

In 1937, the Senators received $20,000 in local radio revenue, far below the $75,000 commanded in Chicago. Baseball had a love/hate relationship with radio and television in the beginning. Revenues were traditionally tied to attendance so many in the baseball industry feared that

---

[381] He won again in 1942.

[382] This may have involved some ballot box stuffing by Joe Engel.

broadcasting might keep people at home instead of bringing them in. Most executives only aired their road games. Griffith was no exception. When attendance dipped in 1939, he cut back on radio broadcasting. Washington became one of the first clubs to televise its home games in 1938. Today, it's understood that broadcasting actually drives attendance, as it attracts many new fans as well as piquing the interest of those already enthralled with the sport.

By the 1950s, revenue from radio and television was becoming substantial, life-altering so to speak. In 1950, the Senators received $125,000 from Liggett & Myers Tobacco Company for the rights to televise all games. Cutting back from 1951-1952, the Christian Heurich Brewing Company paid to advertise just 21 games each year. Arrow Beer Company paid $90,000 to air just thirty games in 1953. Calvin Griffith then negotiated a breakthrough deal with National Bohemian for $250,000. Another deal with Chesterfield brought in $150,000. The Senators eventually lost a good chunk of their broadcast revenue after the St. Louis Browns relocated to Baltimore, less than fifty miles from the nation's capital.

The Redskins of the National Football League played at Griffith Stadium from 1937-1960. During the war, Griffith was making about $100,000 a year from football rentals and a percentage of the concessions. Howard University, Georgetown, Army, Marines, Naval Academy and other local colleges played both baseball and football at Griffith Stadium as well. High schools did drill competitions and other events at the park. Griffith Stadium also hosted concerts, such as, Louis Armstrong. The All-American Girls Professional Baseball League played exhibition contests at Griffith Stadium. Professional wrestling matches took place at the stadium as well as boxing after it became legal in the District in 1934. Joe Louis defended the world championship at Griffith Stadium on May 23, 1941 against Buddy Baer. Ezzard Charles also fought in Washington.

The Washington Potamacs were the first black team to consistently utilize Griffith Stadium from 1923-1924. The Senators charged 25% of the gross profits and all the concession dollars. The Potamacs moved to Delaware because they couldn't make a profit in D.C. Cum Posey, a 2006 Hall of Fame Inductee, had his Homestead Grays split their time between D.C. and Pittsburgh's Forbes Field. In 1940, the Grays established Washington as its permanent home base. They'd play Sunday doubleheaders at Griffith Stadium in front of 3,000-4,000 fans. The Senators ticket manager, Jim Morrissey, handled ticketing, publicity and promotion for the Grays games. The Senators cut included 20% of the gross profit, a rental fee and expenses for ticket sales, ushers and clean up.

A increase in the African-American population in D.C. from 187,000 in 1940 to 281,000 in 1950 made a strong base for the Grays to draw from. Attendance dipped in 1941, to about 1,500-3,000 per game, but took off in mid 1942. The boom took place for several reasons. First, the Grays decided to hire their own public relations guy to specifically attract black fans. Second, Clark Griffith lifted the ban on interracial games, which were a strong draw for black clubs. Last, heralded Satchel Paige made a couple starts at the park. At the end of the season the Grays played the Kansas City Monarchs in the World Series on scattered dates throughout September. The Monarchs won in five games. World Series games were also played at Griffith Stadium from 1943-1945.

In 1942, the Grays drew 127,690 fans for an average of 11,608 for each of the eleven home dates. The Senators averaged less than half that. The Senators probably made around $60,000 off the Grays in 1942. The Grays drew 225,000 fans on 26 dates in 1943. The Senators made over $100,000 off the Grays that year. The Grays proved such a strong draw that Clark Griffith rescheduled a Senators game to accommodate the Negro League World Series in 1943. Whispers around the league even suggested that Griffith was a part owner of the Grays.

The Grays were an extremely strong draw in Washington through the war and beyond and a profitable one for the Senators. Understanding this, it is easy to see Griffith's reluctance to integrate, which would potentially lead to the decimation of the Grays. The Grays also hosted the All-Star Classic in 1946, three days before the East-West Game. It attracted over 15,000 fans, netting $7,500 for the Senators.

According to the report submitted to the United States House Committee on the Judiciary in 1951, the Senators profits and dividends were:

	PROFITS	DIVIDENDS
1920-1924	$626,356	$100,000[383]
1925-1929	$577,712	$80,000[384]
1930-1934	$-28,288	$0.00[385]
1935-1939	$55,797	$60,000

---

[383] 1920-21 dividends unknown

[384] 1926-28 dividends unknown

[385] 1931 dividends unknown

1940-1944	$224,417	$20,000[386]
1945-1949	$1,279,779	$200,000[387]
1950-1954		$160,000[388]

It must be kept in mind that many of the Senators' administrative staff and officers were members of Griffith family. The club provided a nice income for the Griffith/Robertson clan. The dividends were paid to the club's stockholders. Mr. Griffith owned about 40% of the franchise.

The Senators survived the lean years because of the business opportunities Clark was able to capitalize on; it wasn't the gate at Senators games that kept the company afloat during the Depression. With profits during the 1930s at less than $30,000 many would have at least considered relocating the club. His relationship with United States government officials kept the team in D.C. Because of these ties, Major League Baseball was also interested in keeping a team in the nation's capital. After Clark's death, the club's weaknesses financially became glaringly apparent. It had already lost the lucrative revenue from the Negro leagues; plus, the Redskins were looking for their own venue. The relocation of the Browns into nearby Baltimore solidified the need to move the club. Calvin Griffith took this initiative in 1961, relocating the team to Minnesota.

---

[386] 1940-43 dividends unknown

[387] 1946 dividends unknown

[388] 1952-54 dividends unknown

CHAPTER TWENTY-TWO

...*LAST IN THE AMERICAN LEAGUE*

The adage proclaiming the Washington franchise to be a perennial last place club stems from the 1903-11 seasons when the team finished at the bottom four times and in seventh place the other five seasons. After Griffith took over the club, the team didn't fall to the bottom of the standings again until 1944. That 1944 season was sandwiched between two second-place finishes. During the Old Fox's tenure, the club finished in first 3 times, second 5 times, third 6 times, fourth 6 times, fifth 6 times, sixth 7 times, seventh 8 times and eighth 3 times. Exceedingly poor clubs, save the war years of 1943 and '45 and the postwar, marked the 1940s and '50s.

The 1940s were filled with strife within the game. Obviously, the war completely uprooted the entire nation, not just baseball. Strictly within the game, troubles arose due to integration, unionization, encroachment by the Mexican League, flooding of talent after the war ended, Landis' continued assault on the farm system and the death of the first commissioner.

Griffith entered the 1940s rethinking his whole game plan. Attendance was down in 1939 and the team lost a lot of money supporting its farm clubs and spent $75,000 updating its park. Heretofore a discarded idea, Clark changed his thinking and sought an estimate for installing lights at Griffith Stadium to draw on potentially lucrative night games.[389]

In late January 1940, Landis sent a stern 3,000-word letter to all major league owners recommending the dissolution of their farm systems.[390] His letter came shortly after his edict which granted free agency to 91 members of the Detroit Tigers and fined the organization an unprecedented sum of money. In general, Griff welcomed the blast on the farm system; he had been railing against it for years. Clark was practical. He recognized that the Class-C and Class-D clubs were the "life's blood of American baseball" and needed direct financial support in order to survive. As he put it, "I agree with Commissioner Landis that the manner in which some farm clubs are run can be, and is, an evil. But until Landis can advance some concrete proposal that will allow the Class-D leagues to flourish, I'll fight to the last breath…Class-D leagues are always in need of help. One or two clubs in a Class-D league might make money some years, but there isn't a Class-D league in the country that will balance the slate when an audit is made at the end of a season."[391] In hindsight, the farm system was engrained within the game; it wasn't going anywhere. Landis and Griffith could bluster all they wanted.

In April 1941, Griffith returned to Bloomington, Illinois for the first time in twenty years. He attended a dedication for a plaque honoring Hoss Radbourn.[392] On August 15, 1941, the Senators were up 6-3 in the eighth inning with Boston at bat and one out at Griffith Stadium. Joe Cronin was on first with Ted Williams at bat. Rain started pouring, causing a 45-minute delay. However, the game couldn't be continued because of the muddy field. The Senators were awarded the victory, but Red Sox manager Cronin protested because the Washington grounds crew made no attempt to cover the field. Eight days later, American League president William Harridge upheld Cronin's protest and awarded the game to Boston via forfeit.

In the ninth inning of the first game of a doubleheader on September 29, 1943 at Griffith Stadium, Senators third baseman Sherry

---

[389] "Night Baseball considered by Griffith of Senators," *New York Times*, January 20, 1940, p. 20

[390] John Drebinger, "Baseball divided on Landis Method of curbing Farms," *New York Times*, January 28, 1940, p. S1

[391] "Griffith concedes Reform Need but will Fight Landis Methods," *New York Times*, February 6, 1940, p. 29

[392] "Bloomington pays Tribute to Old Hoss Today," *Chicago Tribune*, May 1, 1941, p. 31

Robertson fielded a batted ball by the Indians Ken Keltner. He threw to first, blasting the ball well over Mickey Vernon's head. It soared into the stands fracturing the skull of a 32-year-old fan named Clarence Stagemyer; he died several hours later. The coroner ruled the death accidental.[393]

In 1943, *The Sporting News* named Griffith Major League Executive of the Year for helping the team rise from seventh place to second and for his efforts with the Baseball Equipment Fund during the war. In the mid 1940s, mainly 1944 and '45, the Senators put forth one of the most unique starting rotations in the game's history. Four of the team's main pitchers were knuckleballers: Roger Wolff; Dutch Leonard; Johnny Niggerling; Mickey Haefner.

Griffith took his first airplane trip in 1944, to attend the All-Star game at Forbes Field in Pittsburgh. Rip Sewell uncorked two eephus pitches to George McQuinn in the eighth inning that day to the delight of the crowd.

On April 20, 1944, former Senator Elmer Gedeon was killed over St. Pol, France. Gedeon, a multi-sport star at the University of Michigan, appeared in five games in the outfield for the club in September 1939 before being drafted in early 1941. He was one of two major leaguers killed in action during World War II, the other being Harry O'Neill who had a cup of coffee with the Athletics in 1939 as well. Gedeon, a pilot, was shot down while on a bombing mission to destroy a German construction site. Washington minor league prospect Jimmie Trimble was also killed in action. Griffith signed Trimble, a high school pitcher, in May 1943 at a tryout camp for $5,000 and a four-year scholarship to Duke University. Trimble was a local boy, growing up in Chevy Chase, Maryland. In early 1944 he enlisted in the Marines. On February 28, 1945, he was killed when Japanese soldiers stormed his foxhole on Iwo Jima.

Cecil Travis was a popular shortstop-third baseman for the Washington Senators. In 1941, he led the league in hits with 218 while slugging .520, belting 101 RBI and scoring 106 times. He finished second in batting race to Ted Williams with a .359 average. The following January, Travis enlisted in the Army just weeks after Pearl Harbor. He returned to the majors at age 31 after the war but was never the same. His feet froze during the Battle of the Bulge, later necessitating an operation and forever limiting his mobility in the infield. He also hadn't played regularly in four years and was terribly out of baseball shape. Travis batted

---

[393] "Wild Throw Fatal to Fan," *New York Times*, October 1, 1943, p. 22

a mere .252 and then .216 before retiring in 1947. Griffith immediately hired him on as a scout.

Fighter pilot Bert Shepard was shot down over France in May 1944, necessitating the amputation of his right leg below the knee. Captured by the Germans, he was liberated from a prison camp, Stalag IX-C, in October. He was then fitted for an artificial limb. Shepard, a former minor league pitcher, believed that he could still be effective on the mound; thus, he began practicing daily. Still recovering at Walter Reed Hospital in D.C. in early 1945, Shepard met Under Secretary of War Robert Patterson, an acquaintance of the Senators' owner. Patterson contacted Griffith and asked him to give Shepard a tryout. Griff signed him to a contract as a pitching coach at the end of March, also having him pitch in a War Relief Fund game in July. On August 4, 1945, Shepard was inserted into his only major league game, allowing just one run in 5.1 innings. Shepard continued in the minors, even playing first base, through 1955. In 1949, remarkably, he stole five bases.

On November 25, 1944, Commissioner Landis passed away at age 78. Some within the industry wanted to limit the authority of the next commissioner. To them, Landis held too much power. Griffith didn't see it that way. To quote, "You can search the record books but you will not find an instance in which he abused the authority vested in him or which he assumed. His successor should go into office on the same basis as Landis operated."[394] Clark did want to hire someone from outside the game.

That person ended up being Happy Chandler, a United States Senator from Kentucky. Griffith and Chandler were well acquainted. Chandler was a frequent visitor at Griffith Stadium during his time in D.C. and the two struck up a friendship during the many social functions held in the city. Chandler was a strong backer of keeping baseball going during the war, which endeared him to many within the industry. Those two factors and his friendship with Yankees owner Larry MacPhail landed Chandler the commissioner's post on April 25, 1945 by a unanimous vote. Two days later, he made his first appearance at a ballpark as commissioner, Griffith Stadium. Chandler maintained both jobs until leaving the Senate in November 1945. During Chandler's first year at the helm, Branch Rickey signed the first acknowledged African-American of the 20th century, Jackie Robinson, a players union took foothold and the

---

[394] "Griffith Asks Quick Choice," *New York Times*, December 10, 1944, page S2

Mexican League sent officials to the United States enticing major leaguers to jump their contracts.

The 1945 American League pennant race was a tight one. The Senators and Tigers were within a game or two of each other through much of the stretch run in August and September. For the season Washington led the majors with a 2.92 ERA. The pennant winners, Tigers and Cubs, were the only other clubs under 3.00. Griff's knuckleballers won sixty games for the Nationals. On offense the Senators topped the Tigers in batting, but perhaps the difference was in the power department. In the cavernous Griffith Stadium the Senators led the league in triples but only knocked one dinger at home, by Joe Kuhel on September 7. In total the club only hit 27 homers to Detroit's 77.

Perhaps the difference in the race was the significant amount of doubleheaders Washington players endured near the end of the season. The men were worn out after playing sixteen doubleheaders from August 19 until the end of the season.[395] The doubleheaders and a nearly three-week road trip in September were designed to allow the Redskins practice time at Griffith Stadium. Going into the final day of the season, September 23, another doubleheader, the Nats trailed the Tigers by 1.5 games. Detroit lost 5-0 to the Browns, but the Senators dropped a heartbreaker 4-3 to the A's in the twelfth inning. The season was over for the Senators; in October the Tigers defeated the Cubs in the World Series in seven games.

Nineteen Hundred Forty-Six brought a great deal of turmoil within major league baseball. Athletes, both young and old, came flooding into professional baseball after their release from military service. Though not significant in numbers, this was also the first year black men officially reentered Organized Baseball. Rosters were expanded to handle the inflow. There seemed to be a shortage in every aspect of American life as tens of thousands men and women returned home with cash in their pockets. Ten Senators slept in the clubhouse during April and May due to the postwar housing shortage.

There just weren't enough jobs in professional baseball to accommodate all the men who sought to fill them. This was especially troublesome for returning professionals that were supposedly guaranteed

---

[395] The Senators played doubleheaders at the end of the 1945 season on: August 19, 20, 22, 25, 26, 29, 31 and September 2, 3, 5, 6, 9, 10, 15, 16, 23.

their old jobs within the G.I. Bill of Rights. Lawsuits were filed throughout baseball by returning GIs that found their roster spots in jeopardy or nonexistent. Along these lines, the Senators were responsible for returning 36-year-old outfielder Bruce Campbell, who spent 38 months in the service. In April, the club released him with the standard fifteen days of pay, far short of the $9,000 he was due for the year.[396] Campbell caught on with Buffalo of the International League but was released in July. In a similar case in June, a federal judge in Seattle ruled that the local club had to pay Al Niemic a full year's salary. Consequently, Campbell filed a complaint with the Selective Service Board and then pursued the case in the courts. Griffith settled the case on August 1. He offered to pay the difference between the $9,000 figure and Campbell's salary in 1946 from Buffalo and Minneapolis, who he reported to shortly after the settlement.[397]

Complicating affairs at 1946 training camps, Jorge Pasquel of the Mexican League started throwing around money tampering with men under contract to major league clubs. Pasquel, a shipping magnate, caused a stir through American ball. He claimed to have virtually unlimited financial resources to lure top-notch big leaguers and create a third major league South of the Border. Mexico, like the U.S., was experiencing a postwar boon; plus, their oil fields were producing, pumping vital cash into the economy. Pasquel felt that recreational dollars would soon flow towards Mexican baseball. After all, the country had strongly supported bullfighting and soccer for decades.

Potentially, the majors were ripe for turnover. Every training camp was stocked three to four deep at each position with the return of professionals from military service after World War II. Even those who posted twenty-win seasons or won batting titles or home run crowns during the war were unsure of their status with the return of guys like Greenberg, Feller, DiMaggio and Williams. The Mexican League was already extremely successful - since the 1930s - in raiding Negro league rosters and even lured some fringe major leaguers.

Danny Gardella and Luis Olmo were the first to grab the money. Then, Pasquel contacted Bob Feller, Hank Greenberg and Stan Musial. Musial, for one, was offered a suitcase full of cash. All three turned him

---

[396] The $9,000 figure comes from Campbell's salary in 1942, his last year in the majors before being drafted.

[397] Al Costello, "Griffith decides to Settle Campbell Case out of Court, Will pay Salary Difference," *Washington Post*, August 2, 1946, p. 12

down but major league executives were sufficiently concerned that Commissioner Happy Chandler threatened all contract jumpers with a five-year suspension. In the end, only seven established major leaguers signed on; in total, 27 Americans made the trip. The two biggest names Mickey Owen and Vern Stephens quickly headed north after experiencing the unattractive living conditions. Eventually, the money dried up after the Mexican presidential elections and the remaining American players were left to fend for themselves. American owners now had the upper hand and ignored the returnees, that is, until lawsuits were filed challenging the reserve clause and the game's monopoly status. Only one jumper, Sal Maglie, went on to post a significant big league career.

Gardella was one of eighteen big leaguers to jump to the Mexican League in 1946. For doing so, he faced a five-year suspension from the big leagues and no guarantee of being accepted back. He sued on the basis that he was bound only by the reserve clause not a signed contract. He asked for $300,000 for the conspiracy to keep him out of Organized Baseball. On their end, Major League Baseball did not relish the thought of a court challenge to the reserve clause or a review of their monopoly practices. Gardella initially lost in federal court in Manhattan but won on appeal. Baseball's brass shied away from having the U.S. Supreme Court scrutinize them under federal antitrust laws and settled the case. Gardella received perhaps as much as $60,000 and all the jumpers were given amnesty in mid-1949. It was the first widely successful challenge to the reserve clause.

Griffith took his Senators to Havana during spring training in 1946. Hundreds of well-wishers met him at the airport. March 10 was designated as "Clark Griffith Day" in Havana. He was given a gold medal for his part in the advancement of Cuban ballplayers before a crowd of 8,000 at Tropical Stadium. Griffith used the spotlight to rail against the Mexican League, aggressively calling for Cuban assistance putting "the outlaw Mexican League out of business."[398] Happy Chandler was also on hand to hopefully organize forces against the Mexican League's encroachment. On March 17, Griffith, still in Havana, announced tentative plans to form an international baseball congress that could in theory help settle disputes in the future. The idea sprung from a meeting between Griffith, Cuban sports director Luis Rodriquez and Jorge Pasquel's brother Bernando.[399] To further solidify his ties to the island,

---

[398] "Cuban Gold Medal to Clark Griffith," *New York Times*, March 11, 1946, p. 20

[399] "Griff gets Cordial with Mexican Boss," *Washington Post*, March 18, 1946, p. 10

Griffith purchase 1/5 of the Havana franchise of the Florida International League.

Out of the turmoil of early 1946 emerged a new players union, the American Baseball Guild led by Robert Murphy. Griffith became the first baseball official to speak publicly against the union. On April 21, he gave an earful to reporters. His tirade centered on four main principles: the sanctity of the reserve clause; impracticality of collective bargaining; uselessness of a union in baseball; implication that a 'free market' already existed that was doing its job by raising salaries to their proper levels. Today, much of his thinking has been rebuffed as fallacy but at the time it was firmly believed by many in the game, even a good percentage of the players as well.

On April 29, the union took its first concerted effort, filing an unfair labor practices charge against Griffith and the Senators for his outburst eight days earlier. Specifically, Murphy charged that Griffith made "statements derogatory to the American Baseball Guild…did counsel and urge the players against joining the guild; and, further, did make statements calculated to intimidate and coerce the players on the club from exercising their rights to self-organization." In reply, Griffith branded the charges "ridiculous." Yes, he had defended the reserve clause in his communication with his players but made no concerted effort to attack the union.[400] Nothing came of the charges, a flimsy effort to gain recognition and publicity for the cause. Baseball with its legal monopoly status indeed held great power over its employees. Naturally, baseball officials felt a strong need to uphold its historical dominance. It was another thirty years before the reserve clause was substantially curtailed and collective bargaining showed its true effectiveness.

For the August 20, 1946 game at Griffith Stadium, Clark contacted the Aberdeen, Maryland Army Ordinance Plant to rent a photoelectric cell device, a primitive speed gun. He wanted to put on a pre-game show to calculate just how fast Bob Feller actually threw. For the promotional cost of only $500, Griffith lured 30,000 to the park to see Feller set a world's record by throwing a pitch at 98.6 miles per hour.[401]

Griffith was inducted into the National Baseball Hall of Fame in 1946. Hard to believe by today's standards, he never even attended the

---

[400] "Charges filed by Baseball Guild against Nats' Griffith," *Washington Post*, April 30, 1946, p. 1

[401] "World Record for Bob Feller," *Christian Science Monitor*, August 21, 1946, p. 12

ceremonies; in fact, only one of the fifteen inductees did, Ed Walsh. Griff didn't attend future ceremonies either. In 1968, he was inducted as well into the Missouri Sports Hall of Fame.

In November 1947, the Senators traded Jerry Priddy to the Browns for infielder and future longtime soap opera actor Johnny Berardino who wanted to negotiate with his new club through his agent. Griffith wouldn't hear of it. Berardino threatened to retire to pursue an acting career, which led to the voiding of the trade.

Ever the showman, Griffith put on perhaps his most comical display on April 4, 1948. In Orlando, Florida the 78-year-old Griffith raced 85-year-old Connie Mack on the base paths. The men started at third base dressed in three-piece suits and took off for home. The newspaper headline the next day declared it a, "Dead Heat Tie."[402]

On November 14, 1948, Griffith made the worse trade of his long career, a deal pushed for by Calvin Griffith. He shipped Mickey Vernon and Early Wynn to the Indians for Eddie Robinson, Ed Klieman and Joe Haynes. The special attraction of the trade for the Griffiths was the return of Haynes family to D.C. Haynes was married to Calvin's sister and Clark's niece Thelma.

In January 1950, the Nats longtime equipment manager Frank Baxter passed away. He first joined the club as a bat boy during Griffith's first year with the club, 1912. Mike Martin gave him the job after seeing Baxter work diligently cleaning up the park. At the time neighborhood kids swept the ballpark each morning to gain free admittance to the park for an afternoon game. He was promoted to assistant trainer and then equipment manager by Griffith, joining the club full-time in 1923.[403]

Bucky Harris returned in 1950 for his third stint as Senators manager. He spent the previous season managing San Diego in the Pacific Coast League after being fired by the Yankees and being replaced by Casey Stengel. He used his knowledge of the Yankees' system to work skillful trades for Bob Porterfield, Fred Sanford, Tom Ferrick, Jackie Jensen and Spec Shea.

On April 16, 1950, two Senators farm hands were killed in an auto crash. Ralph Fraser, 20, and Bert Roseberry, also 20, were driving

---

[402] "Even a Snail could Win this Race," *Chicago Tribune*, April 5, 1948, p. B1

[403] "Frank Baxter dies, joined Nats in 1912," *Washington Post*, January 5, 1950, p. 18

just south of Emporia, Virginia. They were members of Griffith's Class-D franchise of that city.[404]

During spring training on March 30, 1952 in Orlando, a scary incident happened at the Hotel Angebilt. Addie Griffith was in the room by herself while Clark was at the park. She turned to notice a man in the room; luckily, he fled when she screamed. Security nabbed the individual, William S. Loucks, 27. He was caught with a sack full of Addie's jewelry and cash, total value $13,000.[405]

The Senators finished with a .500 record in 1953 despite having the American League batting champion, Mickey Vernon, on the roster and the league leader in victories and shutouts, Porterfield. Porterfield also won *The Sporting News* AL Pitcher of the Year award. In 1954 Griffith tapped the Orioles for one of the club's top all-time power hitters, Roy Sievers. In six seasons with the club he knocked 180 dingers and drove in 574 runners. Sievers was eventually sold to the Indians for $150,000 and two players.

A seemingly insignificant rule change took effect in 1954. It was customary for years for ballplayers to leave their gloves on the field between innings. They put them outside the foul lines and even on the field of play. Amazingly, this caused little trouble over the decades.[406] The change may have stemmed from the July 12, 1952 game between the White Sox and Senators. Washington was trailing 1-0 in the fifth inning when White Sox shortstop Sam Dente, making a play on a ball hit by Jim Busby, tripped over Pete Runnels' glove which was laying in short left field. He was charged with an error which would have been the third out. The Senators then scored twice to take the lead and eventual win. The *Washington Post* headline the next day read, "Boot by Dente Helps Nats Plenty Over Chisox, 2-1."

Another rule change that had a dramatic effect in the future can be attributed to the Senators in the 1950s. Griffith was typically pressed for cash as owner of the Senators, especially during the 1950s. He took a dislike to his players "wasting" pine tar by slopping it all over their bats. He pushed for the rule that curtailed its use. The ruling formally prohibited foreign substances on bats above eighteen inches from the bottom. Billy Martin cited this rule in dramatic fashion after a George Brett home run in 1983.

---

[404] "Crash Kills 3; 2 Victims Nats' Rookies," *Washington Post*, April 17, 1950, p. 1

[405] "Mrs. Griffith foils Theft," *New York Times*, March 31, 1952, p. 21

[406] Though, a hit deflecting off a glove influenced the outcome of a game late in the pennant race in 1905.

On June 19, 1954, the Senators landed one of the greatest power hitters of all-time, Harmon Killebrew. Griffith was alerted to Killebrew by Herman Welker, a Republican Senator from Idaho, who knew the kid, a resident of Payette, Idaho, since he was six years old. Griffith was at the park on day shooting the breeze with Welker and others when he mentioned the need for an infielder. Welker offered up the Killebrew tidbit. As simple as that, the club found their cleanup hitter of the future.

Killebrew was playing semi-pro ball in the Idaho-Oregon Border League at the time. The Nats' farm director Ossie Bluege took a weekend trip to see the youngster. Over three games, Bluege saw him go 12 for 12 with four homers and three triples. One of the home runs soared over the wall at the 435' sign. Bluege didn't trust the posting, so he measured it himself; it proved correct.

Killebrew was no secret. The Senators needed to outbid twelve other clubs and use their connection to Senator Welker to land the 17-year-old. Killebrew was intent on playing both baseball and football at the University of Oregon[407] but the Senators' offer was too tempting.[408] They paid an estimated $50,000[409] for the club's first bonus baby. As Bluege put it, "I've always been opposed to bonus players, but I've got to admit this youngster impressed me." After Bluege reported back to Mr. Griffith, the Senators manager declare, "Get him at all cost. The sky is the limit."[410] Killebrew became the face of the franchise for nearly two decades, though his biggest contributions were made in Minnesota.

As happened at various times through history, baseball came under fire during the 1950s for its business practices, particularly relating to its monopoly status and antitrust exemption. Lawsuits were pending by individuals, teams and even complete leagues.[411] Legislative bills were also introduced against Organized Baseball. This caught the eye of monopoly foes Senator Estes Kefauver of Tennessee and Representative Emmanuel

---

[407] His brother's alma mater

[408] Jim Rosengren, "108 Questions: Interview with Harmon Killebrew," *108 Magazine*, Spring 2007, p. 92

[409] Though, figures between $25,000 and $50,000 have been bandied about.

[410] "Senators pay $50,000 to First Bonus Player," *New York Time*, June 20, 1954, p. S3 and Bob Addie, "Bluege sees .847 Hitter get 12 for 12," *Washington Post*, June 20, 1954, p. C2

[411] One of the big issues at the time was the Pacific Coast League's push to become a major.

Celler of Brooklyn; they led the charge. Hearings were held before a U.S. House of Representatives judiciary committee on monopoly power, chaired by Celler, in July, August and October 1951. Naturally, this was done to great fanfare and publicity. Dozens of baseball men testified, including executives, managers, players and umpires.

One of the main focuses was the reserve clause. Griffith testified on October 15. Like many others in the industry including the players, he declared the absolute necessity of the reserve clause, "Otherwise it would spoil he whole setup." He acknowledged the fact that he jumped the clause to join the American League. For all its smoke, pomp and circumstance, the investigation and subsequent report, known as the Celler Report[412] issued in 1952, led to no great conclusions or recommendations. Basically, it told baseball to fix its own problems and suggested that Congress should back off. It did however expose the first well-documented look into the highly secretive finances of Major League Baseball. It included figures on attendance, expenditures, salaries, income and profit and loss statements.

By the end of 1950, a small but strong group of owners were pushing for the ouster of Commissioner Happy Chandler. Leading the charge were Del Webb and Dan Topping of the Yankees and Fred Saigh[413] of the Cardinals. That winter, the majors held their winter meetings in St. Petersburg. Calvin Griffith attended, representing the Senators. Though it wasn't on the agenda, Chandler's contract came up in discussions. His contract was due to expire in May 1952 but he'd been promised an extension.[414] On the contrary, the anti-Chandler gang tried to oust him from his position at the meeting; however, they needed a unanimous vote since the issue wasn't on the original agenda.

Calvin, in long distance consultation with Clark, stood as the lone opposition to the commissioner's ouster. The vote of 15-1 was not enough to fire Chandler. The opposition refused to drop the issue. In the end all voted for the resolution that stated, "It is the unanimous vote announcing that a new commissioner be selected and elected as soon as possible." Though he agreed, Griffith did so only after demanding that

---

[412] The report was named after Representative Emmanuel Celler, a Democrat from Brooklyn. The report is actually titled *Study of Monopoly Power: Organized Baseball in the House of Representatives*. Celler would open another investigation into baseball's antitrust exemption in 1957, presumably in response to the loss of the Dodgers.

[413] Pronounced "Sigh"

[414] The vote was 7-9 against renewing his contract.

the potential list of "new" commissioners could also include Chandler's name.⁴¹⁵

The deck was clearly stacked against Chandler. Still, he vowed to keep his job "until the last second of my term of office." He did so despite a report that he was offered a $100,000 benefits package if he resigned. The leagues met separately in February but they in essence vowed to remove Chandler prior to the next combined meetings in July. Chandler's main proponents were Griffith in the American League and Phil Wrigley of the Cubs in the National League. His foes were gaining momentum.

On March 2, 1951, Chandler flew to Orlando to meet with Clark Griffith to develop a strategy for the showdown that was coming in the middle of the month. The leagues scheduled a meeting for March 12 with the election or rejection of Chandler on the formal agenda. Griffith was hopeful of accruing the votes for reelection and made a prolonged speech in his favor, but in the end the vote was 9-7 against his reelection. Therefore, he was a lame duck but was not forced out of office. His contract didn't expire for fourteen months. They wanted him out, one way or another nonetheless. If he didn't offer his resignation, they were prepared to eliminate the office altogether. In April he gave his settlement terms.⁴¹⁶ In June, they were accepted and he resigned in July. In September his replacement, Ford Frick, was elected after a list of 500 was pared down.

---

⁴¹⁵ "Attempt was made to buy Chandler off but Griffith's Lone Vote blocked Move," *Washington Post*, December 14, 1950, p. B6

⁴¹⁶ The terms included the paying of his $65,000 annual salary through April 30, 1952 and release from any responsibility in the numerous lawsuits pending against MLB.

CHAPTER TWENTY-THREE

STATESMAN

In March 1916, Pancho Villa ordered Mexican raiders to cross the border and attack points in Columbus, New Mexico. The raid sparked a great deal of ethnocentric pride and fervent nationalism among Americans. Clark Griffith was one of them, as well as many other baseball men. At spring training at the University of Virginia in Charlottesville that year, Griff received a telegram from the National Security League, a popular nationalist, militaristic, nonpartisan organization. The NSL had over 50,000 members in 150+ chapters throughout the country.[417] It wanted to know, "Please find out how the boys in your club stand on the question of adequate preparedness for national defense. Wire result with your opinion. We hope your club is solid for America first on this question." Clark responded, "First, last and always. Players and myself for preparedness. Can take my team to Mexico, whip Villa, and guarantee to open the season at the Polo Grounds."[418]

The importance is not in the message or the reply, but in the effect it had on Griffith. With the Villa incursion and the war raging in Europe, he began to think ahead. Were Americans really prepared? How could he, a 46-year-old man, help? Was baseball ready for the potential effects on the game? The idea came to him one day while speaking with

---

[417] John Whiteclay Chambers II, *To Raise an Army*, 1987

[418] "College Pitcher added to Nationals' Staff," *Washington Post*, March 12, 1916, p. S1

his men in the spring of 1916. Major league ballplayers could practice military techniques and tactics. He then made the proposal to his men and other American League executives. Captain Huston of the Yankees, in particular, loved the idea. He approached his contacts in the War Department to sell them on the idea; Griffith sold the idea to those within baseball.

Jake Ruppert and Huston purchased the New York Yankees at the turn of 1915, infusing needed cash and enthusiasm into the game. Huston, a Buffalo native, took up his father's trade of civil engineering, finding work as such in Cincinnati. During the aftermath of the Spanish-American War, he led a group of volunteer engineers to Cuba in service of the American government. After his commission ended, he remained, forming an engineering and construction company. By 1914, he made a fortune building sewer systems and dredging Havana Harbor.

Ban Johnson endorsed the military drill plan in 1917, hoping it would buy the game some goodwill in the nation's capital in the upcoming year. Men within the game feared the impending military draft and possible truncation of the baseball season. American League clubs were required to perform military-style drills and training for an hour a day during training camp. Actual drill sergeants were employed to lead the men. To ease the adjustment and gain enthusiasm, Johnson offered a $500 prize to the best drilled group and another $100 to that club's instructor.[419] The ballplayers in tandem performed marching and close-order drills with a baseball bat at their right shoulder instead of a rifle.

The drilling and marching began to wear on the athletes by the middle of March. The Dodgers, Tigers and Indians ceased the training altogether. On April 6, five days before Opening Day, the United States declared war on Germany, which naturally renewed interest in the drilling. Many clubs put on displays on Opening Day for their home audiences. The St. Louis Browns won the prize money. In D.C. on April 20, Assistant Secretary of the Navy Franklin D. Roosevelt led a group of soldiers from Fort Myers and the marching Nationals and Athletics' squads in a flag raising ceremony. Many clubs kept drilling into the season, throughout the summer. Charles Comiskey even bought his men khaki uniforms and rifles.[420]

---

[419] "Second Griff Band entertains for Georgia Practice Field," *Washington Post*, March 7, 1917, p. 8

[420] "C. Milan and Foster are too Ill to Play," *Washington Post*, August 24, 1917, p. 8

As an important figure in the nation's capital Griffith became heavily involved in fundraising efforts to help finance the war. He organized benefit games for the Red Cross and other war-related causes. On June 30, 1917, he umpired the annual Congressional baseball game. Clark also made plans to tour southern military camps and send two major league clubs to France at the end of the season.[421] Griffith was a member of the Commercial Club in D.C. He toured numerous times with the group selling Liberty Bonds. The club sent two trucks throughout the city. The first displayed buglers and a piano with a pianist, a singer and an emcee hawking the benefits of purchasing the bonds. The second truck showcased Griffith, city golf champion Edward Eynon and other local celebrities. Clark entertained the crowd with baseball stories while pushing the bonds.[422] He did one better than all other baseball officials across the nation. He went out many days at 4 pm leading the two vehicles to movie theaters, newspaper offices or any place that crowds formed to encourage all to buy war bonds.

Baseball officials as a group stepped up their fundraising efforts in 1918 after being threatened with the truncation of their season. They promised 10% of the revenue from the 1918 World Series to war fund coffers. The main feather in baseball's cap was another brainchild of Griffith's, the Bat and Ball Fund. Few, if any other, private fundraising drives attracted as much national attention. It was another way Griff help protect the interest of the game, highlighting baseball's morale-boosting potential. The success of the funding drive for the Bat and Ball fund led to its revival in the 1940s, during the Second World War.

Griffith came up with the idea in early 1917 of creating a fund for supplying baseball equipment to servicemen at home and abroad. To finance the project he asked every man, women and child in the country to donate 25 cents. He wanted all baseball fans to remit their quarter and then send out four chain letters asking for the same; hopefully this system would prompt all Americans to contribute to the effort. In May, he began soliciting newspapers, businesses and government officials throughout the country. The drive gained immediate attention on May 22 when President Woodrow Wilson endorsed the plan and remitted his quarter. The letter to Griffith, from Wilson's private secretary Joseph P. Tumulty read, "My

---

[421] "Baseballs to Ordway," *Washington Post*, August 6, 1917, the plans never came to fruition, p. 10

[422] "Washington's Liberty Loan Total reaches $15,000,000," *Washington Post*, October 26, 1917, p. 2

Dear Mr. Griffith: The President directs me to acknowledge the receipt of your letter of May 7 and to say that it affords him pleasure to contribute 25 cents toward the fund for the purchase of baseball paraphernalia to be presented to the soldiers of the several training camps to be established throughout the country. I, too, am glad to have a share in this fine movement and enclose a quarter herewith."[423]

Griffith dubbed the project the Bat and Ball Fund. After the Presidential endorsement the quarters started flooding into Griffith Stadium. Within a relatively short time he amassed thousands of dollars. In June he put his first shipment together. It cost $7,524.50 or a little over 38,000 quarters. He purchased the equipment and sent it to France on an American steamer, the *Kansan*. Unfortunately, a German U-boat sank the ship on July 11, 1917.[424] When word of the loss reached the baseball men on July 17, Griffith renewed his efforts, even more determined. Clark immediately received nearly a $1,000 in donations from Vice President Thomas Marshall, Ban Johnson and several newspaper companies. National League president also John Tener promised to appeal to his league's owners for help as well.[425]

Individual clubs, both major and minor league, throughout the country began Clark Griffith Days, fundraising drives. The events were undertaken with a great deal of fanfare. Bands played and drilling competitions took place while soldiers roamed the stands with collection plates. Typically, local newspapermen, business and community leaders either donated funds or led funding efforts to add to the kitty. For example, $400 was raised in Pittsburgh and $741 in Chicago. Columbus, Ohio mailed Griff a check for $2,200 and Binghamton, New York contributed $2,507 by the end of the baseball season.[426]

During the first week of August, the fund recovered enough, allowing Griffith to send packets to Camp Ordway, Fort Meyer, Quantico, Virginia and other locales. At the end of the season Griff promised to tour the camps throughout the country to judge for himself their needs.[427] He also placed orders for new equipment to be sent to France. Each baseball set cost about $30 and contained a catcher's mask,

---

[423] I.E. Sanborn, "War Aid from Baseball," *Chicago Tribune*, May 23, 1917, p. 13

[424] "Griffith's Gift of Baseballs sunk," *Washington Post*, July 17, 1917, p. 2

[425] "Griffith starts Second Baseball Fund so Sammies may play Game," *Washington Post*, July 18, 1917, p. 2

[426] "Binghamton boosts rising Bat and Ball Funs by over $2,500," *Washington Post*, September 12, 1917, p. 8

[427] "Baseball for Armies," *Washington Post*, August 6, 1917, p. 3

catcher's mitt, chest protector, first baseman's mitt, three bats, twelve balls, three bases and pegs, a rule book and 125 scorecards. Griffith also sent about 500 copies of *The Sporting News* to France for the servicemen.

Fundraising efforts went on throughout 1917 and '18. The White Sox and Giants remitted 1% of their World Series shares to the fund. In September General John Pershing, head of American forces in Europe, sent Griffith a personal thank you note for the equipment. He even threw in a little plug for the sport saying that playing baseball helped his men learn how to toss grenades.

Griff put an order for $30,000 worth of merchandise on September 26 to go to National Guard camps. It was the largest order ever placed for baseball equipment.[428] In October, Griffith worked out a deal with the Spalding, Wilson, Reach and Western House sporting goods companies for supplying equipment. They extended him a $20,000 line of credit so he could ship the goods immediately. They even agreed to accept Liberty Bonds as payment.[429]

The efforts continued hard into 1918; it was almost a second job for Griffith. Actually, it was more so. He needed to hire help. The National League finally came around in December 1917, deciding to organize fundraising efforts for the fund. The fund took another financial hit when a bank in Gary, Indiana failed, taking with it $1,350 of the funds' assets.[430] The Baseball Fraternity, the extinct players union led by Dave Fultz, emptied its coffers in 1918. Its accounts were closed and fed to the Bat and Ball Fund, over $2,000.[431]

The last hurrah for the fund occurred in February 1919. Griff's old teammate Bill Lange went to France as an emissary for the YMCA. He was sent to coach soldier teams for the YMCA and to possibly establish, in the wake of American presence in Europe, an international baseball league. The league was to include England, Belgium, France and possibly Italy. Lange also looked into the potential for a tour by major league clubs to Europe in the fall. Clark seized the opportunity and entrusted Lange with $40,000 of baseball equipment to be distribute to

---

[428] "Griffith lets $30,000 Contract to supply Soldiers in U.S. with baseball Equipment," *Washington Post*, September 27, 1917, p. 10

[429] "Griffith sells Liberty Bonds," *Washington Post*, October 27, 1917, p. 8

[430] "Bank Failure costs Griffith Fund $1,350," *Washington Post*, August 28, 1918, p. 8

[431] "Baseball Fraternity gives $1,117 to War Fund," *Washington Post*, October 27, 1918, p. 20

the troops.[432] Lange returned in August dejected from his inability to spread baseball to the Europeans.[433]

In all, about 3,100 kits were distributed from 1917-1919 at a cost of about $95,000. *Baseball Magazine* and *The Sporting News* subscriptions were also doled out; in fact, the fund purchased over 150,000 copies of *The Sporting News*. Over $100,000 was raised and spent by Griffith for the Bat and Ball Fund during World War I.

Griffith nearly spent all the goodwill he mustered through the Bat and Ball Fund and Liberty Bond drives leading the charge for exemption of ballplayers from the military draft. On May 23, 1918, Secretary of War Newton D. Baker issued the "Work or Fight" order. In essence, able-bodied men of draft age were expected to serve their country or to maintain employment in a war-related industry. Baseball men feared this for well over a year. Ban Johnson and others in the game were previously seeking deferments for players on a case-by-case basis. Sparking some hope, New York Yankees pitcher Happy Finneran even successfully argued in early 1918 that he would be unable to find employment after serving in the military since his only marketable skill was playing ball. Washington catcher Eddie Ainsmith appealed to his draft board claiming that he should be exempt from the draft due to a similar argument. He was rejected in July and ordered to find useful employment or be designated as Class-A1 for draft purposes.

By this time baseball men were seeking a clarification to the "work or fight" rule. Griffith personally appealed to the local draft board on Ainsmith's behalf; though there were already baseball appeals making their way up to Baker for final judgment, the Ainsmith case reached the Secretary of War first. Griffith made the formal appeal on July 13; he was hoping to receive the same deferments that were granted actors as entertainers. It was the first official brief filed by Organized Baseball on the subject. He basically presented three points. First, he argued that the skills learned by professional baseball players were not easily transferable into other lines of work; second and consequently, ballplayers were ill equipped for employment in a war-related industry. Finally, Griff stressed that baseball was essential to the morale of the country; thus, wholesale drafting of its players would cause undue harm to the nation.

---

[432] "Plan World-Wide League," New York Times, January 19, 1919, p. 27

[433] "To teach Lads Baseball," *New York Times*, August 26, 1919, p. 8

In ruling on the Ainsmith case on July 19, Baker formally declared that baseball was a non-essential occupation. Baker rejected Griffith's first two points out of hand; however, the third point about the essential function of baseball was taken seriously and addressed with President Wilson. To Baker, these were serious times and sacrifices were required; baseball should in no way be given preferential treatment.

Baseball men were sent into a panic. Ban Johnson, reacting hastily, declared that the season would end in two days. He then recanted in the face of opposition within the game. On July 20, Griffith and club president Ben Minor met with Baker and the Provost Marshall of the Army, General Enoch Crowder, who oversaw the drafting of the Selective Service Act. They hoped their personal familiarity with the men would gain favor for the sport. At the meeting Griffith and Minor were advised of the specifics of the ruling and the government's position in the matter. The pair made no formal request at that time. Other baseball officials contacted Washington insiders as well, including National League president John Tener, a former governor of Pennsylvania and U.S. congressman. Baseball officials then met en masse and drew up a brief which appealed to Crowder to postpone the implementation of the draft against baseball personnel. Major league officials feared that only about sixty men would remain if the government demanded immediate compliance. Pending a new ruling, word out of Washington was hopeful that baseball's request would be granted. Griffith and Minor continued their courting of government officials including the President himself.

On July 26, Baker, under advice from politicians, ruled that he wouldn't enforce the "work or fight" rule against baseball until September 1. Baseball was left to work out the details of their season. Johnson unilaterally decided that the game should end on August 20. On August 3, American League officials met and decided to overrule Johnson. Griffith, Charles Comiskey and Harry Frazee led the charge and were in agreement with National League owners. They decided to continue the season through Labor Day and then play the World Series. In rebuking Johnson, the men told reporters that Johnson is "through spending our money. From now on the club owners are going to run the American League. His rule of ruin policy is shelved."[434]

In all, 144 American and 103 National Leaguers went into the armed forces during World War I. The 1918 and '19 seasons were shortened; attendance was significantly down in 1918, the lowest mark since 1902, severely curtailing profits. More importantly, seven major

---

[434] "Owners overrule Johnson Closing Plan," *Chicago Tribune*, August 4, 1918, p. A1

leaguers and at least four minor leaguers died while in service. WWI ended up having little effect on baseball as a whole in comparison to the Second World War. To highlight, by January 1945, 5,400 of the 5,800 professional ballplayers in Organized Baseball in 1941 were in the service; over fifty were killed.

Without a doubt the quality of play on the field on major league diamonds was diminished during WWII. How much so is left to conjecture. League champions and statistical leaders are questioned to this day. Lou Boudreau in his book, *Lou Boudreau: Covering All the Bases*, states "It was still called "major league" baseball, but I'd have to say the caliber of the game...was Triple-A, at best, maybe only Double-A." To baseball historians, the most significant telltale factor of on-the-field play during the war is fact that St. Louis won the American League pennant in 1944. One of the true second-tier franchises in sports history, the Browns were able to put it together for one year while the brightest major league stars were overseas. They finished higher than fourth a mere six times since their inception and only once in consecutive years. Sadly, the Browns had only risen into the first division nine times since 1901. When the regulars returned in 1946, the Browns naturally sunk to the bottom of the standings. They didn't compete for the pennant again until 1960, long after moving to Baltimore.

Some important advances were spurred by the war. Teams, Washington especially, increased the signing of Latin American players in part because they weren't subject to the military draft. A proliferation of night games and radio broadcasts also occurred. As a result of contract disagreements by some service returnees, the first semi-effective player and umpire unions developed after the war. The most significant headway was in the area of racial integration. Throughout the service, African-American men played with white men. It became apparent to many that if African-Americans were expected to fight beside white men than why should they be excluded in other areas? Of course, this did not happen overnight in baseball and, in fact, difficulties continued for decades.

Since its inception, All-Star Game profits were funneled to a relief fund benefiting retired, indigent ballplayers. In 1941, the profits were sent to the USO, United Service Organizations, to buy athletic equipment for servicemen. Four days after the Japanese bombed Pearl Harbor, baseball executives established the World War II version of the Bat and Ball Fund, renamed the Baseball Equipment Fund. Once again, Clark Griffith took charge with Ford Frick assisting from the National League. Each league contributed $2,000 and $20,000 was borrowed from a discretionary fund administered by Commissioner Landis.[435] The Baseball Writers Association of American also chipped in a $1,000. More importantly, baseball decided to donate all the proceeds from the 1942 All-Star Game to the fund, not just the profits. All sixteen clubs picked up the cost of the event.[436]

With $25,000 in hand, Griffith immediately contacted Captain Frederick Weston of the Army morale division and several sporting goods companies. All the equipment during WWII was distributed among the military camps at the discretion of the joint Army and Navy Committee on Welfare and Recreation. Griffith obtained a discounted price for the equipment from the Louisville Bat Manufacturing Company and the Goldsmith, Spalding and Wilson sporting goods companies. On December 30, he placed his first order for 18,000 baseballs and 4,500 bats. There were two types of kits during WWII: Kit-A included a dozen baseballs and three bats; Kit-B contained the catcher's gear, a mitt, mask, chest protector and shin guards.[437]

The 1942 All-Star game on July 6 netted $89,314.58 for the war effort, $50,000 of which was allotted to the equipment fund. There was also an all-star game in Cleveland on July 7 that guaranteed $100,000 for the war effort, $42,548 to the fund. This game pitted stars from the service versus ballplayers still in the league. Over 62,000 fans showed up to see Bob Feller start the game for the service team. He ended up losing 5-0. Baseball raised another $73,576 during a Brooklyn-New York charity game.

In December 1942, MLB allotted another $25,000 to the equipment fund. They also decided to hold sixteen relief games, one by each team, in 1946 and donate all the proceeds from the All-Star Game again. In total for the year baseball, from the majors down through amateur efforts, donated over $1.3 million to the war effort.[438] Professional baseball in total raised $133,359 for the equipment fund. In 1942, Griffith sent 4,659 Kit As and 647 Kit-Bs to servicemen. He sent

---

[435] The $20,000 was borrowed against the 1942 All-Star Game proceeds.

[436] John Drebinger, "Ott pays $50,000 for First Baseman," *New York Times*, December 12, 1941, p. 36

[437] "1,500 Baseball Orders made for Service Men," *Washington Post* December 31, 1941, p. 19

[438] "Sports thrived during 1942as Part of War Effort," *New York Times*, December 20, 1942, p. S1 efforts within the horse racing industry by far raised the most money in sports, over $3 million.

another 267 dozen balls to various organizations. The sporting goods were shipped to over 900 different locations in the United States, England, Iceland, Canal Zone and the Caribbean. To end the year, Griffith ordered another 3,000 Kit-As and 400 Kit-Bs.[439]

The 1943 All-Star Game at Shibe Park made $65,174 for the equipment fund plus another $25,000 from Gillette for the radio sponsorship rights.[440] By 1943, some of the equipment made its way into American prisoners' hands in Europe and Japan via the War Prisoners Aid program. The 1944 All-Star Game's proceeds were also funneled into the war effort; however, the following year's game was cancelled at the request of the Office of Defense Transportation.

Through 1944, Major League Baseball raised $2.6 million for the war effort.[441] The minor leagues during that time amassed over $7,000,000.[442] The Baseball Equipment Fund spent $328,000.34 by the end of the war.[443] So much sporting equipment was purchased by the military during the war that civilians had a hard time buying any themselves. The military purchased 90% of the sporting goods made in the country, a cost of $38,000,000 a year.[444] In April 1946, Clark cleared the Baseball Equipment Fund accounts by donating the last $8,330.77 to the National Baseball Hall of Fame.[445]

After the Reds and Phillies played on June 18, 1909, an exhibition game between amateur clubs was played at the Cincinnati ballpark, the Palace of the Fans. Griffith attended along with members of both major league squads and about 3,000 other fans. Five temporary 100-foot light towers were erected for the contest. Clark's initial response to night baseball was optimistic, "I don't believe night ball is destined to rival the daylight

---

[439] "Majors to send 36,000 Balls, 9,000 Bats and catching Equipment to Men in Service," *New York Times*, December 27, 1942, p. S1

[440] James, P. Dawson, "$115,174 realized for Bat-Ball Fund," *New York Times*, July 14, 1943, p. 24

[441] "Major Loops have raised Millions for War Relief," *Dunkirk Evening Observer*, Dunkirk, New York, February 8, 1945, p. 14, $2,630,460 in total: $1,053,951 in 1942, $725,104 in 1943, $851,405 in 1944

[442] "$7,000,000 by Minors given to War Agencies," *New York Times*, January 21, 1945, p. 54

[443] *Abilene Reporter*, May 10, 1946, p. 10

[444] "Civilians won't get Sports Equipment for quite a while," *Washington Post*, August 27, 1944, p. M7

[445] per a thank you letter to Griffith from the Hall of Fame, located in Griffith's Hall of Fame file

article, but I will say I was much surprised at the ease with which the game was played under tonight. Under improved lighting it will grow more popular."[446]

He wasn't as judicious in his comments about baseball under the lights in the 1930s. In fact, he was downright antagonistic after Larry MacPhail orchestrated the first night game in major league history in 1935. In 1939, he started to change his mind. On May 16, he attended the first American League night game, at Shibe Park in Philadelphia. Though unimpressed with the power of current lighting systems, he grudgingly saw night baseball as inevitable. "I won't have night ball in my own ballpark because it isn't good enough yet. But in the years to come, they'll perfect it. No doubt about that…there's no stopping it."[447] The minor leagues were playing nearly 70% of their games at night by 1939.[448] In 1939 and '40 the Senators drew less than 400,000 each year, averaging less than 4,500 and 5,000 fans, respectively, a game. Average attendance for night games in 1940 were 2, 3 even 4 times as much as the average games in each city that had a lighting system.[449] That changed Griff's mind; in January 1940, he asked for bids on putting a lighting system in Griffith Stadium.

The system was installed at Griffith Stadium for the 1941 season at a cost of $230,000, $125,000 of which was financed through an interest-free loan from the American League. Eight towers were raised containing a total of 764 light bulbs, 1,140,000 watts. The first major league night game in D.C. took place on May 28, with 25,000 in attendance. The Nats lost, but 25,000 fans on a Wednesday night was hard to ignore. At the time, clubs were only allotted seven evening games a year. That simply wasn't enough. Griffith figured at that rate it would take at least three years just to break even on the lighting system. By the end of the year, America was at war. Griffith knew this would change the whole complexion of the city, the nation's capital, a government town. On December 11, the same day that the Baseball Equipment Fund was created, Griffith took his argument to the baseball winter meetings. He wanted unlimited night games during the work week; after all, major league baseball had been making concessions to capture government workers in Washington as far back as the nineteenth century by pushing back starting times to 4:30 pm. Clark convinced the American League to

---

[446] David Pietrusza, *Lights On!*, 1997

[447] Bob Considine, "On the Line with Considine," *Washington Post*, May 17, 1939, p. 19

[448] William M. Mead, *Baseball Goes to War*, 1998, p. 37

[449] *Sporting News*, September 1940, as found on baseball-almanac.com

side with him but the National League opposed the idea. Commissioner Landis cast the deciding vote, against expanding night baseball.[450]

Griffith wasn't to be denied; he worked the back channels, getting President Franklin Roosevelt to put a plug in for him in January 1942. Within the famed "Green Light" letter, which urged the continuation of the game during the war, Griffith managed to get the following passage attached: "And, incidentally, I hope that night games can be extended because it gives an opportunity to the day shift to see a game occasionally."[451] With the President endorsing night baseball what

---

[450] John Drebinger, "Ott pays $50,000 for First Baseman," *New York Times*, December 12, 1941, p. 36

[451] The Green Light Letter, addressed to Judge Landis and dated January 15, 1942, in its entirety:

My dear Judge:--

Thank you for yours of January fourteenth. As you will, of course, realize the final decision about the baseball season must rest with you and the Baseball club owners -- so what I am going to say is solely a personal and not an official point of view.

I honestly feel that it would be best for the country to keep baseball going. There will be fewer people unemployed and everybody will work longer hours and harder than ever before.

And that means that they ought to have a chance for recreation and for taking their minds off their work even more than before.

Baseball provides a recreation which does not last over two hours or two hours and a half, and which can be got for very little cost. And, incidentally, I hope that night games can be extended because it gives an opportunity to the day shift to see a game occasionally.

As to the players themselves, I know you agree with me that the individual players who are active military or naval age should go, without question, into the services. Even if the actual quality to the teams is lowered by the greater use of older players, this will not dampen the popularity of the sport. Of course, if an individual has some particular aptitude in a trade or profession, he ought to serve the Government. That, however, is a matter which I know you can handle with complete justice.

Here is another way of looking at it -- if 300 teams use 5,000 or 6,000 players, these players are a definite recreational asset to at least 20,000,000 of the fellow citizens -- and that in my judgment is thoroughly worthwhile.

With every best wish,

Very sincerely yours,

Franklin D. Roosevelt

could Landis do? He backed off his stance against night games, granting each club 14 a year. Washington was permitted twenty-one.

Griffith was soon looking for more. On July 6, 1942, Landis again cast the deciding vote that denied Washington's request to play every weekday game in the evening. Griff continued to fight. In March 1943, he wrote to Stephen Early, the first White House press secretary, noting that unlimited night games in the capital "would be in the best interest of war workers in Washington." In July, the National League and Landis finally relented. On the 13th, the Senators were granted unlimited night games except on Sundays and holidays when they weren't needed. The following July all teams were granted the same.

Night games proved a boon for Griffith and the Senators, as well as the league itself. The average attendance for the 91 night games in the American League in 1943 was 9,667[452], as compared to the average for the other games, 5,355[453]. The average for 35 night games in D.C. was 8,935[454], with a figure of 6,390[455] for the other 41 games. In 1944, the American League averaged 9,987[456] paying customers in its 133 contests under the stars. The other daytime contests averaged 7,140[457]. The figures for the Nats aren't as dramatic, 7,065[458] in 44 night games to 6,496[459]. Still, it's clear that a market existed for an evening at the ballpark. The owners who hadn't installed lights prior to the war soon did so after it ended, except the Wrigley family, which held out into the 1980s.

The attack at Pearl Harbor shook baseball men to their core, not just tapping their nationalistic fervor but threatening their investment as well. When the United States formally entered the Second World War in December 1941, many assumed that the upcoming baseball season would

---

[452] 879,704 / 91 = 9,667, night attendance according to "A.L. saw big Gain in Night Baseball," *New York Times*, December 3, 1944, p. S2

[453] 2,816,865 / 526 = 5,355, remaining attendance and games in the AL in 1943

[454] 312,717 / 35 = 8,935, night attendance according to "A.L. saw big Gain in Night Baseball," *New York Times*, December 3, 1944, p. S2

[455] 261,977 / 41 = 6,390, remaining attendance and games for Washington in 1943

[456] 1,328,310 / 133 = 9,987, night attendance according to "A.L. saw big Gain in Night Baseball," *New York Times*, December 3, 1944, p. S2

[457] 3,469,848 / 486 = 7,140, remaining attendance and games in the AL in 1944

[458] 310,879 / 44 = 7,065, night attendance according to "A.L. saw big Gain in Night Baseball," *New York Times*, December 3, 1944, p. S2

[459] 214,356 / 33 = 6,496, remaining attendance and games for Washington in 1944

be curtailed, if not cancelled altogether. After all, the game employed some of the finest athletes in the country, men at the peak of their physical prowess, men that were needed and expected to fight for their country. The last thing baseball executives wanted was to appear unpatriotic, but hey they wanted the game to go on.

The investors in the game wanted to know where baseball stood. They needed clarification and hopefully assurances that the 1942 season would go on. Commissioner Landis seemed to be the man to lead the charge. After all, he stood at the head of Organized Baseball. But, there was a problem; Landis was a staunch conservative and had long ago alienated the Roosevelt Administration with his outspoken rebukes. His wasn't a welcomed face at the White House. Besides, Landis firmly believed that the war effort was of much greater concern than mere baseball. He was not about to ask for any special favors for the game.

Clark Griffith was one of the leading figures in D.C. for thirty years. His name was synonymous with the town, more so than many within the government itself. He was baseball's statesman; the Washington insider who was familiar with the men and women that made up the various government and military agencies. He was the best man to present the game's agenda to the nation's leaders. After all, he had been doing so since before the First World War. Griffith and Roosevelt were well acquainted. Roosevelt was a visitor at Griffith Stadium since Clark's earliest days in D.C. By 1942, Roosevelt had held the office of President for nearly a decade. Griffith called on him every year at the White House to present the President and First Lady with their season's pass, as he had done with every President since 1912. During those years in office, Roosevelt attended ten games at Griffith Stadium. Furthermore, Roosevelt was an ardent baseball fan. He made small wagers on Senators games with staff members. To get a heads-up on the ballplayers and the condition of the teams, he often called Griffith during the season to help his betting odds.

Griffith did his bidding in private as Landis would never have approved. He despised Roosevelt. Clark held conversations with General Lewis Hershey, head of the Selective Service System, and others about approaching President Roosevelt on the issue. His biggest ally came from St. Louis. Browns owner Don Barnes introduced Griffith to Robert E. Hannagan, a rising star in the Democratic Party.

Hennegan, born in 1903, played minor league baseball and professional football. After graduating law school, he held various political offices in St. Louis as a confidant of Mayor Bernard Dickmann. In 1940 he managed Harry Truman's successful reelection campaign to the U.S. Senate. In 1942 at age 38, he was chairman of the Democratic city committee of St. Louis. Hannegan was also involved in local sports and maintained friendships with Cardinals owner Sam Breadon and Browns owners Barnes and Bill DeWitt Sr. Shortly after the Green Light letter, Roosevelt named Hannegan as a collector for the Internal Revenue Service and then commissioner of the IRS. In 1944, he became chairman of the Democratic National Committee and later U.S. Postmaster General. That year, Hannegan urged a reluctant Truman to accept the vice-presidential slot on the Roosevelt ticket. Three years later, he purchased the Cardinals from Breadon and served as club president until shortly before his death in 1949.[460]

After meeting with Griffith, Hannegan approached the President. Griffith then had Landis remit a letter to the White House inquiring about what course it felt baseball should take in the upcoming year.[461] The result was the Green Light letter that urged the game to proceed. Baseball breathed a huge sigh of relief. Play ball!

The section of the letter about night games came as a surprise to both Griffith and Hennegan; it was not a major part of their push. They were pleasantly surprised.[462] Others within the industry weren't as pleased by this development, particularly Landis and National League opponents to night baseball. But, why dwell on it? The letter from the President was a blessing. Griffith was a little displeased himself that the letter didn't allude to possible draft exemptions for ballplayers. But, that clearly wasn't going to happen. Griff put a good spin on it: "The Washington club expects every man, star or rookie, to do his duty."[463]

The Green Light letter became a bone of contention by many in the government as the war dragged on. They wished the President hadn't sent it. The country was facing its biggest crisis and hardy young men were playing baseball for money. To some, it seemed an inconsistency. Griffith, for his part, tried to get Roosevelt to issue a similar letter in 1943, but the White House deemed it unwise to do so.

---

[460] Robert Sobel, "Robert E. Hannegan," *Biographical Directory of the U.S. Executive Branch: 1774-1989*, 1990

[461] Handwritten letter, just enough words illegible to prevent reproducing - basically just an inquiry letter asking what should be done with spring training approaching for 16 major league and 320 minor league clubs

[462] Hannegan's friend Don Barnes was also in favor of night game and stressed such to Hannegan.

[463] Shirley Povich, "This Morning with Shirley Povich," *Washington Post*, January 17, 1942, p. 17

Baseball performed a juggling act over the next four seasons, 1942-1945. Rosters were constantly in flux as established players entered the service and younger, or perhaps older, players took their place. To the benefit of the game, those players assigned to winter war-related employment were often permitted to leave those jobs in time for spring training. Older players were at times brought back to the majors during the war. For example, catcher Paul Richards left the majors in 1934 but retuned during the talent shortage in 1943. Sig Jakucki had been out of the majors since 1936 before the Browns brought him back in 1944; he posted 13 wins during their pennant drive. Jimmie Foxx retired after the 1942 season but returned for the Cubs and Phillies, even pitching in nine games. Paul Schrieber was a batting practice pitcher for the Yankees. He was activated in 1945 even though he last pitched in the majors 22 years earlier. Other men who returned to the majors during the war after long absences include Pepper Martin, Babe Herman, Ben Chapman, Debs Garms, Joe Vosmik, Hod Lisenbee and Clyde Sukeforth.

The Tigers signed forty-year-old, career minor leaguer Chuck Hostetler in 1944. The oldest rookie in major league history, at that point, was playing for a semi-pro club. The majors also tapped the other end of the spectrum, playing fourteen boys under age eighteen.[464] Another, Chris Haughey played one major league game, on his 18th birthday.

[464]	Joe Nuxhall	15 years old
	Carl Scheib	16 years old
	Tommy Brown	16 years old
	Putsy Caballero	16 years old
	Rogers McKee	16 years old
	Eddie Yost	17 years old
	Granny Hamner	17 years old
	Eddie Miksis	17 years old
	Erv Palica	17 years old
	Cass Michaels	17 years old
	Charlie Osgood	17 years old
	Art Houtteman	17 years old
	Roy Jarvis	17 years old
	Gene Patton	17 years old

Each major league club dedicated an executive during the war to oversee the draft eligibility for each player and make efforts to gain each a deferment. Griffith had a leg up here. He regularly lunched with General Lewis Hershey, head of the Selective Service. He actually obtained deferments for Buddy Lewis and Cecil Travis in the spring of 1941; they didn't join the war-effort until the baseball season was over. Clark also mitigated his troubles by employing draft-ineligible Cuban players during the war. The draft seemed to hurt the Senators less than most in that they jumped to second place in both 1943 and '45.

In reality, the draft hit everyone hard. It actually began on October 16, 1940 when all males between the ages of 21 and 36 were required to register. Only five major leaguers, most famously Hank Greenberg, were chosen in the initial lottery. Before Pearl Harbor, less than two hundred professional ballplayers, almost all in the minor leagues, missed any playing time. By 1944, 340 major leaguers and about 3,500 professional ballplayers in total were in the service. Of the 5,800 men on professional rosters in 1941, only four hundred of them remained civilians.

Transportation and travel during the war were crucial issues. The Director of the Office of Defense Transportation, Joseph B. Eastman, provided major league officials with guidelines concerning these issues. For example, in May 1942 Eastman requested that baseball officials in each state coordinate with local transit companies to determine the best start times for games. Eastman was concerned that rush hour times in certain communities had changed due to the war effort. In short, businesses were altering their schedules during the war causing greater traffic during times that may now conflict with ballgame traffic. In D.C., Griffith was "glad to cooperate with defense people." He already recognized the altered patterns and was considering a change from his normal 3:15 pm start times during the work week.[465]

In November, Eastman remitted another letter to baseball executives. He asked Organized Baseball to consider curtailing spring training travel and limiting railroad travel as much as possible for the duration of the war. Specifically, Eastman requested that baseball "select training sites as near as possible to each team's home city where climatic conditions would be suitable." Major league executives discussed this at the winter meeting in early December, but were unclear of the specifics of

---

[465] "Shift in Baseball Starting Time proposed to ease Rush Hour Jam," *New York Times*, May 22, 1942, p. 28

Eastman's request. Actually, they were reluctant to believe that they were being asked to abandon their warm-weather camps. Griffith therefore was selected to meet with Eastman to coordinate plans for the upcoming year.[466] They met on the 14th.

Griffith reported back to American League president Will Harridge that Eastman strongly urged that clubs forgo their annual treks to California, Florida and Texas. Specifically, "Eastman suggested that clubs which might have picked camps in those three states have alternate sites in mind" before he made a formal ruling in February based on "military camp conditions and troop movements in those states."[467] The ODT also wanted baseball to curtail their travel in the upcoming season. Griffith's news shook up the industry, especially since exhibition schedules had already been hashed out. The National League in particular took a shot at the messenger, claiming that Griffith was never selected by them to conduct such hearings.

Consequently, Commissioner Landis was forced to intercede and meet with Eastman. The results were the same. On January 5, 1943, Landis announced that the season would be pushed back a week, that spring training would be held within a "sharply defined area" and that the majors would jockey its schedule to eliminate one road trip around the league each season for each club.[468] For example, the Senators trained in College Park, Maryland, the Yankees in New Jersey and the Athletics at Wilmington, Delaware and Frederick, Maryland through the end of the war.

The new restrictions especially threatened the Negro leagues and other black baseball clubs because the ODT also banned the use of private buses by ball clubs as of March 15, 1943. The restrictions further limited the availability of gas, oil and tires. Negro league officials asked Griffith to intercede on their behalf. On March 6, Griffith, Cum Posey, Negro National League secretary, and J.B. Martin, Negro American League president, met with Eastman and three of his associates at Griffith Stadium. Martin argued that bus travel was the only feasible option for day-to-day travel, since "most small town have no accommodations for Negroes." In effect the banning of bus travel would put black baseball out

---

[466] "Griffith to consult ODT Chief within Week," *New York Times*, December 12, 1942, p. 23

[467] "ODT Ruling due by Feb. 7," *New York Times*, December 15, 1942, p. 34

[468] "Majors postpone Start of Baseball Season to April 21 and Close to Oct. 3," *New York Times*, January 6, 1943, p. 20

of business. They offered to cut there travel in half and to rides trains whenever possible. Martin left the meeting in high spirits. "I feel much relieved and believe we will be able to operate this season. While not being able to schedule as many league games as heretofore, there will be more exhibition games with larger attendance and the East vs. West Game as usual."[469]

The travel restrictions forced the Senators to reconsider their commitment to the Charlotte franchise of the Piedmont League. In fact, the league itself was on the fence about closing for the duration of the war. Griffith originally purchased the Charlotte Hornets back in 1937. On January 24, 1943, at his office Griff held a lunch meeting with league owners. The league decided to continue on despite the ODT restrictions but Griffith opted out. He suspended operations of the Charlotte club; the city never did rejoin the league. Instead, he converted his ball field there into a camp for soldiers on weekend leave from boot camp.

Griffith in truth reconsidered his entire commitment to the farm system. From 1937-1941, the Senators owned or held working agreements with between five and ten clubs each season. After 1942, the club maintained connections with only Chattanooga and Williamsport through the end of the war.

Griffith enjoyed a relationship with every U.S. President and the First Family from Teddy Roosevelt to Dwight Eisenhower. In fact, he cultivated these relationships, personally and professionally. With great fanfare he went to the White House at the beginning of each year to present the President and First Lady with their season's pass. On the wall in his office sat photos of Presidents throwing out the ceremonial first pitch. The practice actually began in 1910 when Griffith was still with Cincinnati, but Clark was the one who actively encouraged each President to show up for the game to kick the season off. He was successful despite the pressing requirements of the President's job and struggles getting American League president Ban Johnson to schedule the Senators at home to open every season. Ceremonial Presidential first pitches kicked off the Senators' season every year except 1912, 1914, 1917-1920, 1926,

---

[469] "Martin believes Negro Leagues will operate," *Chicago Defender*, March 20, 1943, p. 21

1939 and 1942-1945.[470] Sitting Presidents visited Griffith Stadium 62 times during Griffith's reign.[471]

Griffith took his Highlanders to the White House to meet Teddy Roosevelt in May 1908. Roosevelt was not a big baseball fan; his main interest in the game stemmed through his sons' love of it. William H. Taft grew up loving the game. He played amateur ball around Cincinnati growing up. Clark later told exaggerated stories that Taft was almost good enough to make the majors. Taft's brother Charles for a time owned the Chicago Cubs. Griffith first met William Taft on May 4, 1910 in St. Louis. His Reds were playing the Cardinals at Robison Field. The President left in the second inning with the Cards up 5-0 and went across town to Sportsman's Park III to catch part of the Browns-Indians game.

Woodrow Wilson was a huge baseball fan, even playing in college. He dubbed a room in his home "The Dugout." He'd go there to read baseball and discuss it with anyone interested. During his terms in office, Wilson poured over the sports section with aides on a daily basis, examining box scores, recaps and events related to the game. In 1913, he caught three consecutive games in April versus the Red Sox. Though not in D.C., Wilson was the first sitting President to attend the World Series, in 1915 in Philadelphia. Politically, Wilson felt it unwise to attend ballgames during the war, he was glad to have an excuse to attend one in May 1918, a Red Cross benefit game. After he fell ill, Wilson sat in the back seat of a car and watched games from behind the bullpen at Griffith Stadium.

Warren Harding was a big baseball fan as well. He owned parts of two minor league clubs in his hometown of Marion, Ohio, a Class-C Ohio-Pennsylvania League club in 1907 and a Class-D franchise in the Ohio State League in 1911. On February 8, 1922, the American League owners were in D.C. holding preseason meetings. Griffith organized a trip to the White House for the group to meet the President. That day, Griffith extended his customary invitation to Opening Day. Harding replied, "If I am alive, I will be there with my scorecard and pencil."[472]

---

[470] Ban Johnson refused to give special consideration to the Senators to attract the President to the park for the ceremonial first pitch. Through Johnson's reign as American League president, Washington opened on the road half the time (which would be expected by any club), in 1914. '16-17, '20, '23 and '25. Over the next thirty years, the club opened at home except in 1934, '39, '45, '47 and '51.

[471] Taft 2 games, Wilson 10, Harding 4, Coolidge 10, Hoover 6, FDR 10, Truman 16 and Ike 4

[472] "Rumored that Majors will 'Freeze Out' Belligerents," *Washington Post*, February 9, 1922, p. 16

The Coolidge family was torn when it came to baseball. The President didn't much care for the game, but he used it for his political benefit; he dutifully attended most Opening Days. On October 1, 1924, he hosted the pennant-winning Senators on the White House lawn, giving a long-winded speech in front of nearly 100,000 fans. On the campaign trail that October, he also attended three World Series games. He would have seen all four in D.C. but Game #2 was on a Sunday, sparking religious objections. Grace Coolidge on the other hand loved the game; she probably attended more games than every President combined. She grew up loving the game, working as official scorekeeper for her alma mater Vassar College. She stayed to the end of every game she attended, always keeping score. The American League gave her a lifetime pass with a choice of World Series seats every year.

Herbert Hoover loved the game as well. He attended a World Series game in Philadelphia every year during the A's pennant run from 1929-1931. He also sat through quite a few games at Griffith Stadium before becoming President, including a 1924 World Series contest.[473]

Naturally, Franklin Roosevelt had many opportunities to attend ballgames as President, since he was in office so long. He attended a World Series game in D.C. in 1933 and one in New York in 1936. He was also the first sitting President to attend an All-Star Game, in 1937 at Griffith Stadium. On the campaign trail Roosevelt was present on October 1, 1932, Game #3 of the World Series, and saw Babe Ruth's heralded called shot. He also attended every Opening Day, save 1939 when the Senators opened on the road, until the war started. Griffith traveled to the White House each year during the war to present the President with his pass and to put a plug in for the sport, informing him of the game's fundraising efforts. Clark later admitted to advising the President to skip the games as the war demanded his full attention.

Harry Truman and Clark Griffith got along like two peas in a pod. Their temperaments were similar as well as their backgrounds. Both were from Missouri. Griffith even actively campaigned for Truman in 1948. Truman was always a baseball fan, but he grew up a Browns fan. Realizing the significance of the Presidents absence from the ballpark during the war, he caught a game at Griffith Stadium a mere six days after the formal Japanese surrender in September 1945. On August 17, 1948 Truman appeared at a ceremony for Griffith at the stadium. It was the first attendance at a night game by a sitting President.

---

[473] One such game took place on May 22, 1922, where he sat with President Harding and General Pershing.

Dwight Eisenhower was a big sports fan, especially of baseball during his life. He grew up idolizing Honus Wagner; however, by the time he was elected President, he became obsessed with golf to the point he believed any attention to other sports (or even the duties of his office) was a cutting into his golf time. He kicked off his presidency with a little controversy in the sports world, deciding to skip Opening Day 1953 to play golf. The game was postpones due to rain, so the President decided to mend fences and attend the rescheduled date. The Eisenhower and Griffith families got along well. On June 5, 1953, the new President used his position to bring some sporting heroes to lunch at the White House. He was especially thrilled with the appearance of golfer Gene Sarazen, but he also enjoyed the company of Griffith, a few Senators, Lefty Grove, Tris Speaker, Joe DiMaggio and Rocky Marciano.

Naturally, Griffith held friendships and associations with numerous other government and military officials. He was a regular at the annual Congressional baseball game, occasionally umpiring the contest and donating the use of Griffith Stadium for the event and uniforms or other items. Likewise, he was a supporter of the U.S. Government League, which put him in contact with J. Edgar Hoover, who was on the board of directors, and others.

In May 1924, Griffith let the U.S. Olympic Committee use the ballpark for an exhibition benefit. President Coolidge attended, seeing the Senators take on the Quantico Marine baseball team. The event raised money to send Olympians to France to compete. In September 1924, he donated the use of the ballpark for a combined concert by the Army, Navy and Marines to help raise $40,000 to equip every D.C. hospital with radios. The event happened just in time for sick and injured fans to listen to the Senators' first World Series.

Griffith developed strong friendships with baseball enthusiasts and frequent Griffith Stadium visitors Edward Douglass White and Fred M. Vinson, Chief Justices of the Supreme Court, and Vice Presidents James Sherman and Richard Nixon. Franklin Roosevelt's Vice President John Nance Garner was also a huge baseball fan who idolized power-hitting, White Sox first baseman Zeke Bonura. He kept lobbying Griffith to trade for him. The Senators owner finally relented, acquiring Bonura in March 1938 for Joe Kuhel. Bonura rewarded both Griffith and Garner with a fine season at the plate, though he was notoriously poor in the field. On Opening Day Bonura homered and then ran over to Garner's box and gave him a hug.

CHAPTER TWENTY-FOUR

CHALLENGE AT THE TOP

William M. Richardson, co-owner of the Senators since 1919, passed away on June 10, 1942. He held the title of vice president for years but was never active in the day-to-day affairs of the club. His job as president of the National Portland Cement Company took up much of his time. He occasionally attended winter meetings and various ceremonies throughout the years with Griffith or his friend Tom Shibe; however, he kept his word and never interfered with Griffith's administration of the club. Richardson never even directly paid his bank loan to purchase the club; he merely let his stock sit at the First National Bank of Philadelphia and collected the dividends off his investment. The club proved quite profitable, at times paying it largest stockholders, Griffith and Richardson, a substantial yearly bonus.

Richardson had no wife or sons to pass the business to;[474] his interest in the club fell to his twin brother, George. George M. Richardson lived in Pitman, New Jersey, working like his brother in Philadelphia in the cement and export businesses. Also like his brother, George had little to do with the administration of the club, despite holding the title of vice president. When Calvin Griffith was named vice president, George was happy to accept the title of treasurer. George passed away in August 1948, leaving his shares in the Nats to his son

---

[474] His wife Florence passed away at their Atlantic City, New Jersey home on February 27, 1934. He did have a daughter named Mary.

William E., who assumed the treasurer's title with a salary of $10,000 per year.

Griffith always assumed that he had an understanding with the Richardson family that he had an option to purchase their shares whenever they decided to divest from the club. That proved not to be the case. The Richardson family actively put their shares in the franchise up for sale in 1949, after putting feelers out since 1945. After hearing this, Griffith made several attempts to come to terms with the family. He already owned 45% of the club, needing only 1,044 shares to gain a controlling interest.[475] In fact, he believed he was still negotiating when a loud, obnoxious individual entered the Senators offices on December 21, 1949.

After William and George Richardson's deaths, the family, which owned 40% of the club, took the stance that they were no longer obligated to allow Griffith to match any bids for the stock because he purchased small lots as they became available over the years which gave him a greater percentage of the club than they owned. In July 1949, they entered serious negotiations to sell out. Richardson never actually paid off his original loan. At one point it was collateralized at $402,000, which prompted the bank to push for its liquidation. The collateralized pledges were eventually whittled down to $150,000 by the time of the sale.

Behind the scenes, John James Jachym[476] was interested in purchasing the Richardson shares. Jachym, a 31-year-old resident of Jamestown, New York, became interested in baseball as a scout for Branch Rickey in the Cardinals' system. He also operated one of the club's baseball schools. After World War II, he purchased the Jamestown Falcons of the PONY (Pennsylvania, Ontario, New York) League for $35,000, selling out to the Detroit Tigers in 1947 for $50,000 and becoming an assistant farm director. In 1940, he graduated with a degree in journalism from the University of Missouri. He worked as a reporter before enlisting in the Marines in 1941. Jachym fought at New Guinea, New Britain and Guadalcanal, earning the rank of captain and a Silver Star.[477]

After the Senators' venture, Jachym made quite the name for himself in the areas of sports, philanthropy and business. In sports he was

---

[475] A percentage of stock was in Calvin and Thelma Griffith's names.

[476] Pronounced "Yo·kum"

[477] Arlingtoncemetery.net

a lifelong friend of Pete Rozelle and held close friendships with Rickey, Vince Lombardi and Paul Brown. Jachym later acted as an advisor or principal in the sale of baseball's Brooklyn Dodgers, Milwaukee Braves, New York Yankees, football's Baltimore Colts, Chicago Cardinals, Los Angeles Rams, Washington Redskins and the Montreal Canadians and Chicago Bulls. His main involvement was in the PGA, where his association last for 37 years. He sat on the PGA advisory committee and was later named chairman and served as official American observer at eighteen Ryder Cup competitions. In 1994, he was elected an honorary member of the PGA.[478] In the 1950s Jachym went into investment banking, specializing in mergers and acquisitions. At one time he brokered the largest business transaction in Chicago history to date.[479]

In November 1949, Jachym found his financial godsend and main investor in the Senators' deal, Hugh A. Grant. Grant was a 38-year-old millionaire from Bradford, Pennsylvanian. He founded the Grant & Mohan Oil Company in 1934, selling out in 1948. After that, his fortune increased as he collected extensive royalty checks from South Pennsylvania and Texaco Oil companies. Grant became a big name in harness racing, as one of the sport's prominent owners. While attempting to purchase into the Senators, he guaranteed Commissioner Happy Chandler that he'd divest from his horse racing and breeding interests.

Jachym headed the seven-man syndicate that approached the Richardson family. Grant's name was kept out of the negotiations but his $400,000 was the bulk of the group's financing. The Richardsons sold their 7,851[480] shares to the Jachym group for $70 a share, $549,570 on December 16, 1949[481]. The deal was signed at the law offices of Joseph W. Henderson in Philadelphia. The initial plan was to keep the deal secret until April 3, 1950 but word leaked out. Griffith reportedly offered the Richardsons $72 a share just a short time after the family committed to Jachym.

The other bidders included a group headed by Louis E. Wolfson. The Wolfson group of Miami millionaires recently purchased the Capital Transit Company. Another group included George Preston Marshall, Leo Deorsey and H. Gabriel Murphy was also interested. A Philadelphia

---

[478] As of 2008, the list of Honorary Members of the PGA included only nine individuals, including three Presidents, Gary Player and Bob Hope.

[479] Arlingtoncemetery.net

[480] 19,400 shares outstanding

[481] The highest bid before the Jachym group entered the bidding was $65 a share.

syndicate headed by a realtor named Schlee also offered a bid. The most interesting bidder was Bill Veeck. Veeck quickly realized that he and Griffith wouldn't mix well so he backed off.

Jachym walked into the Senators offices on Friday, December 21 without previously announcing himself. No one knew who he was. Griffith had never met him. Jachym was shown to Calvin Griffith's office where he produced the papers that identified him as the purchaser of the Richardson stock. Calvin's jaw dropped; he was in shock. Jachym was led to Mr. Griffith's office for an introduction. Clark was stunned but gracious. He became miffed when Jachym refused to divulge the identity of his financial backers. Internally, Griffith was irate. The situation and irked him, as did Jachym's personality; Griffith instantly disliked the intruder. The dislike turned to detest after Griff discovered that Jachym had secretly contacted the Yankees in early December about a trade for first baseman Dick Kryhoski, second baseman Snuffy Stirnweiss and pitcher Don Johnson.

Griffith never needed a majority of the stock to run the club. He always had the Richardson backing which sealed his decision-making authority. Suddenly, the stock of the smaller minority shareholders came into play. Interests other than Griffith and Jachym owned about 15% of the company. Clark immediately went on the defensive, fearing the loss of control of his franchise. Luckily, the largest minor shareholder was Woody Young,[482] a Washington tobacco merchant and longtime Griffith friend and ally.

Jachym quickly realized the error in his approach. Both he and Grant announced publicly that they weren't trying to usurp Griffith and take control of the club. They insisted that they had no intention of acquiring a majority of the stock. It was too late. Griffith was circling the wagons and amassing his votes for the upcoming stockholders meeting to be held in early January. Tensions rose as discussion of Jachym's potential position within the company was bantered about. Griffith was adamant that Jachym be excluded from not only an active position in the company but from the board of directors as well. Commissioner Chandler stepped in and even went to bat for Jachym but Griffith was having none of it.

Jachym on the other hand took the offensive, declaring that he wanted to be very active in running the club, as demonstrated by the trade attempt with the Yankees, and insisted on an office and responsibilities.

---

[482] E. Wootton Young

In a heated exchange with a reporter he made the fatal mistake of offending Grant, the moneyman. Jachym took offense to the suggestion by the reporter that he was just a front man and erred in his choice of words concerning his power within the syndicate. With all the negative press and animosity by the Senators officials Grant declared that out of respect for Griffith he wouldn't press for a title for Jachym.

The stockholders met on January 3. Griffith, 80, was once again unanimously elected president and Jachym was given the cold shoulder. Despite contending that he wasn't trying to usurp Griffith,[483] he wasn't granted an office, a title or a place on the board. He wasn't even given the shareholders' customary season's pass.[484] Calvin was again elected vice president. Young was elected treasurer to replace William E. Richardson. Jachym's attorney Frederick J. Ball was elected to the board and named assistant secretary. Edward Eynon held the other slot on the board and was once again named secretary.

Jachym departed in a huff, threatening legal action. It was a huge disappointment. He viewed himself as a baseball man but was just ousted from the club. Defeated and dejected, the Jachym group soon agreed to sell their shares to H. Gabriel Murphy, a D.C. insurance man. The sale couldn't officially take place until later in the year because of capital gains laws.

Griffith and Murphy were well acquainted with each other and had a good working relationship if not a friendship. Murphy was involved with athletics at Georgetown University for years. He often negotiated rental fees with the Senators owner for use of Griffith Stadium for Georgetown football games. Murphy officially purchased the club on June 23, 1950 for $620,000. The Jachym group made about $85,000 on the deal, which included $15,702 of dividends granted at the beginning of the year.

Griffith and Murphy worked out a deal early in the year. On July 15, Griffith officially became the majority stockholder of the Washington Senators.[485] Murphy sold him the last 500 shares he needed to take him over the top. Griffith now controlled 52% of the club, 48% from the

---

[483] Jachym was cordial and polite during the meeting and had actually garnered some friendships among the stockholders.

[484] He was however given two Opening Day tickets.

[485] In actuality Murphy was the single largest individual stockholder. The Robertson children, Calvin, Thelma, James and Billy, owned some of the Griffith stock.

Griffith-family portfolio and Young's 4%. In exchange Murphy was granted an option to purchase the Griffith shares if they chose to sell prior to 1960.[486] Murphy was named second vice president and elected to the board. Most importantly, Mr. Griffith would oversee the club until his death.

---

[486] And vice versa

CHAPTER TWENTY-FIVE

CHANGING OF THE GUARD

By 1940, Clark Griffith was 70 years old but he was still running the club as he always had. He was the general manager, chief media liaison, administrative decision maker and at times on-the-field instructor. Though he rarely traveled with the club anymore, Griffith saw every home game and also attended Redskins and Grays games at his stadium. Even during the Senators away games, he held court at his Griffith Stadium office and listened to the game on the radio with team personnel, sportswriters or any number of local or out-of-town visitors. Soon, he brought Calvin Griffith, who was learning the administrative end of the business with one of the team's farm clubs, into the Nat's front office to gradually assume the duties of the aging president.

In April 1935, Calvin Griffith was named business manager and secretary-treasurer of the Chattanooga Lookouts at age 23 while still at George Washington University. Joe Engel was the club's president. In 1937, Calvin replaced Engel after Mr. Griffith reassigned the latter back to a scouting role, but Engel soon took over the Charlotte farm club. Calvin also became the club's field manager. The club was operating at a loss, so Clark soon pulled Calvin out so he wouldn't be associated with a sinking ship. In August, the Senators sold out for $125,000. Calvin then took over the Charlotte Hornets as president and field manager, again replacing Engel. He remained with the Hornets as both president and field manager through 1941, capturing the pennant in 1938.

After leaving Charlotte, Engel severed his direct employment relationship with the Senators to take control of the Chattanooga franchise. He didn't have the $125,000 to purchase the club from Griffith, so he issued stock and allowed local fans to purchase shares. The club would later rejoin the Senators' organization via a working agreement. Engel oversaw the Lookouts until the club folded in 1965. Engel then started scouting for the Minnesota Twins, the relocated Washington franchise.

In 1942, Calvin rejoined Clark in D.C. For two years, he held the position of assistant secretary of the Nationals, overseeing concessions at Griffith Stadium and acting as traveling secretary. In January 1944, Calvin was elected vice president of the club. Gradually he began taking over the duties of the elder Mr. Griffith. Specifically, he attended league meetings in place of the team's president and assumed a much greater role in the organization, especially in the areas of player trades and media contracts, television and radio.

By the 1950s, Calvin was making his imprint on the club. He remodeled the stadium, increasing capacity, and started to move the fences in to assist the club's power hitters. Charlie Dressen, the first manager from outside the organization, was also hired. In December 1953, he was elected to the newly created position of executive vice president in recognition of his role in the company as de facto president concerning day-to-day decision-making. By this time, Clark was 84 years old, the oldest executive in the game.[487] Both Griffiths conversed on a daily basis concerning club affairs. At times they clashed, particularly in response to the proposed new club in Baltimore.[488] There was no mistaking however that on grandiose league matters Mr. Griffith was still in charge of mapping the direction. All major decisions involving the club were still subject to his final approval until his death.

The identity and image of the Senators' organization and that of Clark Griffith were intertwined, more so than any such relationship in sports at the time other than Connie Mack in Philadelphia. It was inevitable that he started paring back his duties. For those who noticed, the gradual shift of

---

[487] After Connie Mack's retirement in the early 1950s

[488] Calvin did not want the St. Louis Browns to transfer to nearby Baltimore. He voted for the transfer though under orders from Clark. Mr. Griffith believed that the rivalry with Baltimore would eventually help spark a revival of the Washington franchise. Calvin though understood that the financial situation in the nation's capital would perhaps only get bleaker.

power to Calvin was natural. After all, that's how businesses had been run since before Adam Smith. A close observer may have noticed a small but significant change in April 1952 that essentially signaled the end of the Clark Griffith era of club management.

Since the first moment in December 1911 that Griffith assumed responsibility for the club, he was the go-to guy. He was accessible to the fans and media, and of course the entire baseball community. He made every significant decision and informed the public through the media on a daily basis. If Walter Johnson was due to pitch on a particular day, Griffith told the sportswriters who got word to the fans. If the club or league needed to make any change, no matter how large or small, Mr. Griffith was the one quoted in the *Washington Post* or *Washington Star* about its significance. He was the organization and all learned about it through him.

In April 1952, the Senators hired a professional director of public relations, the last team to do so.[489] Never in years past had anyone even considered such a thing; it simply wasn't needed. The idea came from Calvin but it was really in response to Clark's withdrawal from the day-to-day affairs. *Washington Post* reporter Shirley Povich for one missed the old days. As he noted, "It's a break from tradition…But in late seasons, Griffith withdrew from the press-agentry business, turned it over to office aides who had neither his charm to charm his listeners nor his truculence in defending the Washington athletes…Griffith fronted for his whole ball team, saw no need for a professional public relations man. Out in Chicago, tycoon Phil K. Wrigley might have recoiled at the thought of phoning a sports editor and demanding more space or better treatment for his Chicago Cubs, but Mr. Griffith was never reluctant. He viewed his Washington team as a civic enterprise, never quite understood that it might be regarded as something else. He has also been the most accessible club owner in the league…Griffith was always available to talk about his club"[490]

The Old Fox no longer pulled all the strings. The difference in the character of the team became evident to Povich in October 1949 while the club was in the process of one of its worst season's in history. On September 30, 1949 while the club was in the process of losing its 103rd game of the season, the Senators issued a meek statement to the

---

[489] The new director of public relations was Howie Williams. Shirley Povich, "This Morning with Shirley Povich," *Washington Post*, April 14, 1952, p. 8

[490] Shirley Povich, "This Morning with Shirley Povich," *Washington Post*, April 14, 1952, p. 8

effect that it had just purchased outfielder Irv Noren from the Hollywood Stars. Povich didn't find out until two days later, and with considerable digging, that Noran was purchased for $70,000.[491] Plus, the fact that he had just hit nearly 30 home runs and batted .330 and won the Pacific Coast League MVP award. At the end of a horrible season, without Mr. Griffith's input, no one in the organization felt the need to boost the public's confidence for 1950 by announcing an exciting revelation; the signing of a potential superstar. As Povich put it, "When the Nats, sorely in need of some favorable notice, got something to brag about; they had no lungs."[492]

Clark Griffith's was a remarkably health man. He never pursued any of the great vices with gusto, as many within the baseball industry did. He did smoke cigars later in life but he drank little. He ate moderately and he held a good night's sleep at a premium. For this, he was rewarded with a relatively graceful decline. He had well-publicized sporadic problems throughout the years, such as an appendix operation in 1929. The problems intensified around age 80. On April 24, 1950, he supposedly missed his first home game since joining the club due in 1912 to a severe cold.[493] In December 1950, Mr. Griffith underwent a hernia operation, spending much of the month in bed. On January 5, 1951, he collapsed in Orlando while touring his spring training site. He collapsed again in June but soon bounced back. In his later years Griffith suffered from lumbago, lower back pain. His back bothered him since the late 1930s. By the 1950s, it was a constant problem and in all likelihood the root of his withdrawal from day-to-day operations of the franchise. It sapped his strength, the discomfort keeping him away from the office.

In September 1955, Griffith developed neuritis, a localized inflammation in his back, which caused a good deal of pain and tenderness. He remained uncomfortable and house ridden during September and October.[494] He failed to attend the World Series for the first time since its inception. On Wednesday, October 19, he was taken to Georgetown University Hospital "for complete rest" per personal

---

[491] Retrosheet.org lists the price as $50,000.

[492] Shirley Povich, "This Morning with Shirley Povich," *Washington Post*, April 14, 1952, p. 8

[493] Though, he may have missed a home game due to the appendix operation.

[494] September 27, 1955, a Tuesday, marked Griffith's last appearance at his office.

physician and club doctor Dr. George A. Resta.[495] Griff was also suffering from stomach discomfort. Resta described his condition as "painful but not serious."[496]

In the afternoon of the 22nd, Clark suffered a massive stomach hemorrhage unrelated to the neuritis. He was placed on the critical list and given blood transfusions. Mr. Griffith's condition improved steadily throughout the next two days as the transfusions were continued until the bleeding stopped on the 24th. His blood pressure rose and his pulse strengthened. He was still listed as critical. Resta was guarded in his prognosis, mainly due to his patient's age. As he put it, "The age factor is heavily against Mr. Griffith's chances for survival."[497]

On the night of the 24th, Griff developed congestion in his left lung that prompted the doctors to place him in an oxygen tank. Resta commented that the congestion "must be expected in a man of Mr. Griffith's age. All I can say is that his chances of recovery are as good now as they were before. It is natural in these cases that congestion might follow. One lung is involved and Mr. Griffith is being given oxygen." Clark was awake and in seemingly good spirits. At this point, the family was restricted from the room. Griffith was "getting progressively better" throughout the day on October 26 and 27.

He fell asleep around 7:30 pm on the 27th for the last time. Just after 8:00 pm he suffered a sudden relapse and died in his sixth floor room at 8:40 pm. Calvin was at his bedside. Calvin, seemingly trying to console Senators' fans lamented, "Mr. Griffith led a wonderful life and had a peaceful death. No man could ask for more…The old man lived an exciting life and he loved every minute of it." He left a wife, Ann, of nearly 55 years, six nieces and nephews and 13 grandkids or grand nieces and nephews, depending on how one wants to view it. Mr. Griffith lived just short of his 86th birthday, 67 of those years were spent in professional baseball.

Condolences poured in from all over the country from fans, the baseball community and from Presidents. Well wishes were received from the

---

[495] Resta was the Senators' physician from at least 1950 until the time the expansion Senators left for Texas in 1972. He was also the team doctor for the Washington Redskins through 1974.

[496] "Clark Griffith in Hospital to rest from Neuritis Attack," *Washington Post*, October 20, 1955, p. 21

[497] Shirley Povich, "Washington Team's President rallied after Hope was given up Week Ago," *Washington Post*, October 28, 1955, p. 1

three living Presidents, Hoover, Truman and Eisenhower, Mrs. Eisenhower and her mother Mr. Doud, South Korean President Syngman Rhee, Vice President Richard Nixon, former Vice President John Nance Garner, numerous congressmen such as Representative Carroll Kearns of Pennsylvania and Senator Herman Welker of Idaho, Ty Cobb, Ted Williams, Ford Frick, Rocky Marciano, manager Julio Sanquily from Havana, umpire Bill McGowan, Bruce Beemer (The Lone Ranger) and hundreds of baseball men and their families and thousands of fans. Nick Altrock summed up the sentiments for many that knew the Senators boss well, "When I heard that Mr. Griffith died, I cried like a baby."

Griffith's body was laid out at S.H. Hines Funeral Home at 2901 14th Street on Saturday and Sunday, October 29 and 30. Thousands of admirers, fans, friends and mourners filed past the body, getting a last look at the Washington baseball icon. Services were held at the Elks Lodge of D.C. on the latter evening. The funeral took place at 11:00 am on Monday morning of October 31. Over 700 people packed the Hamline Methodist Church at 16th and Allison Streets. It was the largest gathering of baseball celebrities since the death of Babe Ruth in 1948. Among those attending were Jack Bentley, Charlie Berry, Eddie Brannick, Walter Briggs, Jim Busby, Ellis Clary, Charles Comiskey III, Joe Cronin, Bill DeWitt, Charlie Dressen, Al Evans, Ed Fisher, Warren Giles, Roy Hamey, Will Harridge, Bucky Harris, Cal Hubbard, Arnold Johnson, Frank Lane, Walt Masterson, Clarence Miles, George Myatt, Walter O'Malley, Gabe Paul, Bob Porterfield, John Quinn, Paul Richards, Branch Rickey, Pants Rowland, Muddy Ruel, Frank Shea, Chuck Stobbs, Horace Stoneman, Tom Umphlett, Mickey Vernon, Eddie Yost and a deluge of Griffith Stadium employees and numerous other fans, government officials and baseball insiders.

Among the notable absent were Commissioner Ford Frick, Edward Eynon and Connie Mack. Frick was in Japan. Eynon was ill himself. Many of the baseball men visiting D.C. stopped by Eynon's residence to pay their respects. He passed away on November 7 at age 74, shortly after celebrating his 50th wedding anniversary. Mack, nearly 93 years old, was not initially told of Griffith's passing. He was laid up in bed after fracturing his hip. His doctor and family feared that he'd insist on attending the funeral and he was not well enough to do so. Mr. Mack passed away a few months later on February 8, 1956.

Reverend J. Artley Leatherman, pastor of the Hamline Church, and Reverend Dr. Edward Latch of the Metropolitan Memorial Methodist Church gave the eulogies. October 31 was a sunny day; over one hundred cars filled the processional that led to Fort Lincoln Cemetery in

Brentwood, Maryland.[498] The path along the way was lined with fans, well-wishers, school children and fireman paying their last respects. A Masonic ceremony was held alongside the Griffith family mausoleum. The Masonic pallbearers included Phil Howser, business manager of the Charlotte Hornets, James Ritchie, superintendent at Griffith Stadium, and former ballplayers Ossie Bluege, Nats' farm director, Bill Werber, a local insurance agent, Bill Jurges, a local businessman, George Case and Sam Rice.

On November 1, Calvin was elected president of the Senators at age 43. To show solidarity within the franchise, Gabriel Murphy nominated him for president. Joe Haynes, the former Thelma Griffith's husband, was named roving minor league pitching instructor. Sherry Robertson was named assistant farm director. Bill Robertson assumed the position of supervisor of Griffith Stadium personnel and maintenance. Jim Robertson continued as director of concessions. The other club directors were maintained: Woody Young, vice president; Edward Eynon, secretary; John Powell, the club's attorney and assistant secretary; Murphy, treasurer. Eynon soon passed away, which slotted Powell into the secretary position. Haynes was elected vice president by the end of the year to settle any potential family rift.

Mr. Griffith turned over a debt-free Senators franchise and ballpark valued at approximately $4,000,000.[499] The coffers only had a $25,000 balance. After the attempted coup by John Jachym, Clark rewrote his will, dated July 20, 1950, to make sure the club remained under family control after his death. On November 11, 1951, he added a voting-trust codicil to help ease the inevitable inheritance taxes that plagued baseball families in other cities and ensure that Calvin took over the club.[500]

---

[498] Other ballplayers buried at Fort Lincoln Cemetery include Tom Brown, former teammate, Fred Buckingham, Don Casey, Ed Fuller, Charlie Gooch, former senator, Joe Haynes, former Senator and son-in-law, Charlie Luskey and Frank Watt. Calvin Griffith, Fritz Pollard, Ralph Wiley and several former U.S. Congressmen and Senators were also interred there.

[499] S. Oliver Goldman, Financial Editor, "Nats' Stock Jumps, Stirs Speculation," *Washington Post*, October 6, 1955, p. 26 - based on the fact that nearly $2.5 million was recently paid for 79% of the St. Louis Browns club. The Browns did not own their own ballpark.

[500] "Clark Griffith leaves Bulk of his Nats' Stock to Widow," *Washington Post*, November 5, 1955, p. 12 - most recently, the families of Jacob Ruppert, Yankees, and Walter Briggs, Tigers, faced tax difficulties.

The Griffith family owned 48% of the club.[501] At death Mr. Griffith owned 4,432 shares in the club, about 22% of the outstanding 19,400 shares. He bequeathed 1,500 shares to his wife Ann "to do with as she sees fit" and 50 shares each to Bill, Sherry and Jim Robertson. The rest of the shares were placed into a voting trust[502] that upon the death of Ann would revert to her sister-in-law Jean Robertson and Calvin and Thelma. When Griffith and Richardson acquired control of the franchise in 1919, they paid $15 a share. Just a month before Clark's death, an offer was made for the club at $125 a share.[503] Ann and Calvin were named executors of the estate. In addition to the above, Clark also bequeathed $13,000 to friends and relatives.[504] The estate was estimated at approximately $250,000 in negotiable stock, real estate and other holdings.[505]

In December 1955, Major League Baseball voted to devote the 1956 All-Star Game to the memory of Clark Griffith. The contest, to be called the Clark Griffith Memorial Game, was already set for D.C. Ceremonies honoring Griff were held.

On August 6, 1956, a memorial dedicated to Clark was unveiled at his stadium before a game versus the Yankees. The monument consisted of four sides. One side was a bust of the Senators' owner; the other sides listed his achievements. It cost $7,000, all of which was donated by the public. On hand for the dedication was the commissioner, both league presidents, Vice President Richard Nixon, Secretary of State John Foster Dulles and Attorney General Herbert Brownell.

A plaque was dedicated to Mr. Griffith on March 23, 1968 at the club's longtime spring training facility in Orlando, Tinker Field. It resides there today. Over 900 seats from Griffith Stadium were moved to Tinker Field.

---

[501] Gabriel Murphy was actually the largest individual stockholder with 39% of the club.

[502] For the first five years, only Ann and Calvin had votes.

[503] S. Oliver Goldman, Financial Editor, "Nats' Stock Jumps, Stirs Speculation," *Washington Post*, October 6, 1955, p. 26

[504] Cash disbursements included: Edward Eynon, $5,000; Earl Griffith Jr., nephew, $500; Jean Robertson, sister-in-law, $2,000; Marie Wise, former employee, $500; Mildred Cronin, $1,000; Shirley Griffith, nephew, $1,000; Virginia Sheets Neil, niece, $1,000; Jessie Griffith, niece, $1,000; James Ritchie, nephew-in-law, $1,000.

[505] The residence at 4720 16th Street was valued at $70,000.

Addie Griffith passed away at home after having a heart attack while watching television early Monday morning on October 14, 1957 at age 82. She had just attended a Redskins' game.[506]

Not long after the death of Mr. Griffith, Calvin began making plans to relocate the franchise. In 1956, he was already discussing a move to the west coast, perhaps Los Angeles or another part of California. After much ado and years of financial stress, the Senators moved to Minnesota in 1961.

---

[506] The bulk of her $244,590.02-estate passed to her sister-in-law Jeanne C. Robertson. Mrs. Robertson passed away in February 1958. Thelma Robertson Griffith Haynes passed away in October 1995. Calvin Robertson Griffith passed away in October 1999.

APPENDIX

CHRONOLOGY OF SELECTED EVENTS

November 20, 1869	Birth at Clear Creek, Missouri
February 1872	Death of father
Circa 1880	Family relocation to Bloomington, Illinois
1887	Beginning of a career, semi-pro and pro ball
May 2, 1888	First game in Organized Baseball
July 1888	Traded to Milwaukee Brewers
July 8, 1888	Pitches first game for Milwaukee
Winter 1888-1889	Attended Classes at Illinois Wesleyan College
March 1891	Jumped Milwaukee for St. Louis of the AA
April 11, 1891	Major league debut with St. Louis Browns
July 1891	Released by St. Louis
August 3, 1891	Debut with Boston Reds of American Association
September 21, 1891	Released by Boston
Winter 1891-1892	Roping cattle and playing ball in Helena
April 1892	Debut with Tacoma of Pacific Northwest League

August 21, 1892	Collapse of Pacific Northwest League
September 1892	Debut with Missoula of Montana State League
1893	Pitching distance stretched to 60'6"
January 1893	Signs with Oakland of the California League
March 1893	Debut with Oakland
August 13, 1893	Collapse of California League
September 7, 1893	Debut with Chicago Colts of the National League
September 14, 1893	First National League victory
October 23, 1893	Returns to California to play winter ball
August 25, 1894	"Pitches" Washington Monument
May 20, 1895	Places five hits, one of few pitchers to do so
July 31, 1895	First open defiance of Cap Anson
Winter 1896-1897	Attended law classes at Northwestern University
Spring 1897	First sparks of unionizing movement
August 13, 1897	First major league shutout
October 3, 1897	Cap Anson's final games with Colts
Winter 1897-1898	Attended law classes at Northwestern University
Winter 1898-1899	Purchased a ranch in Craig, Montana
June 10, 1900	First formal meeting in unionizing effort
October 13, 1900	American League capitulates to players union
December 3, 1900	Married Ann Robertson
December 1900	Union rebuffed by National League officials
January 1901	Forms Clark Griffith Company
February-March 1901	Travels extensively to sign talent for AL
March 1901	Acknowledges allegiance with Chicago White Sox
April 24, 1901	Manages first-ever AL game and victory
May 23, 1901	Walked Nap Lajoie with the bases loaded
September 1901	White Sox win first American League pennant
October 1901	First efforts to establish a New York franchise

July 17, 1902	AL assumes control of the Baltimore Orioles
August 28, 1902	Announced as New York manager for 1903
January 11, 1903	Major Leagues enter into a truce
March 11, 1903	Baltimore Orioles sold to New York interests
March 18, 1903	Blasting for ballpark in New York begins
June 16, 1903	Pitches first shutout in Yankees history
November 1903	Attempted to purchase the Detroit Tigers
October 10, 1904	NY loses pennant to BOS on final day of season
1905	First to consistently use the squeeze play
1905-1906	First manager to extensively utilize a bullpen
February 27, 1906	Buys into Montreal of the Eastern League
August 2, 1906	First-known double-switch
May 5, 1908	First visit to White House
June 24, 1908	Griffith and Highlanders part ways
December 11, 1908	Signs with Cincinnati Reds
Winter 1909-1910	Builds a pitching and batting device
March 17, 1911	Fire, American League Park in D.C.
July 4, 1911	First two Cubans on a major league roster
October 30, 1911	Joins Washington club
December 1911	Completely revamps Washington's roster
June 18, 1912	First real excitement in Washington AL history
August 13, 1913	Offers $100,000 for Ty Cobb
October 7, 1914	Last day as active ballplayer
December 3, 1914	Walter Johnson signs with the Federal League
Spring 1916	Proposed military drilling by baseball men
February 1917	Sold Montana ranch
May 1917	Initiated the Bat and Ball Fund
May 14, 1918	Sunday baseball becomes legal in D.C.
December 13, 1919	Gained controlling interest in Washington
January 20, 1920	Announcement of the Babe Ruth deal
October 2, 1920	In uniform for the last time

November 12, 1920	Commissioner Landis is appointed
1922	Brought Calvin and Thelma into household
October 1924	Senators won world championship
1925	Purchased a home on Diplomats' Row in D.C.
November 1925	Brought rest of Robertson clan to D.C. area
October 15, 1927	Walter Johnson retired
October 17, 1927	Last day of Ban Johnson's baseball career
July 17, 1929	Underwent appendix operation
November 1929	Purchased first formal farm club, Chattanooga
1934	Griffith first sends Joe Cambria to Cuba
December 1936	Redskins move into Griffith Stadium
1940	Grays designate D.C. as its permanent base
May 28, 1941	First night game at Griffith Stadium
December 1941	Initiated the Baseball Equipment Fund
January 1942	Franklin Roosevelt issues the 'Green Light' letter
July 13, 1943	Senators finally granted unlimited night games
January 1944	Calvin Griffith named club's vice president
July 1944	Griffith takes his first airplane ride
November 25, 1944	Commissioner Landis passes away
March 10, 1946	"Clark Griffith Day" in Havana
1946	Elected to the National Baseball Hall of Fame
December 1949	Outsiders purchase into Senators
October 15, 1951	Testified before the U.S. Congress
December 1953	Calvin Griffith named club's executive VP
April 15, 1954	Baltimore joins the American League
October 19, 1955	Admitted to Georgetown Hospital
October 27, 1955	Death at Georgetown Hospital
November 1, 1955	Calvin Griffith elected club president
1961	Washington franchise relocated to Minnesota

BIBLIOGRAPHY

Alexander, Charles C. *John McGraw*. New York: Viking Penguin Inc., 1988.

Alexander, Charles C. *Our Game: An American Baseball History*. New York: Henry Holt and Company, Inc., 1991.

Alexander, Charles C. *Breaking the Slump: Baseball in the Depression Era*. New York: Columbia University Press, 2002.

Axelson, G. W. *Commy: The Life Story of Charles A. Comiskey*. Jefferson, North Carolina: McFarland & Company, Inc., Publishers, 2003.

Bevis, Charlie. *Sunday Baseball: The Major Leagues' Struggle to Play Baseball on the Lord's Day, 1876-1934*. Jefferson, North Carolina: McFarland & Company, Inc., Publishers, 2003.

Bryant, Howard. *Juicing the Game: Drugs, Power, and the Fight for the Soul of Major League Baseball*. New York: Penguin Group, 2005.

Browning, Reed. *Baseball's Greatest Season: 1924*. Boston: University of Massachusetts Press, 2003.

Bowman, John and Joel Zoss. *Diamonds in the Rough: The Untold History of Baseball*. Chicago: Contemporary Books, 1996.

Boxerman, Burton A. and Benita W. Boxerman. *Ebbets to Veeck to Busch: Eight Owners Who Shaped Baseball*. Jefferson, North Carolina: McFarland & Company, Inc., Publishers, 2003.

Burgos Jr., Adrain. *Playing America's Game: Baseball, Latinos, and the Color Line*. Berkeley, California: University of California Press, 2007.

Burk, Robert F. *Never Just a Game: Players, Owners, and American Baseball to 1920*. Chapel Hill, North Carolina: The University of North Carolina Press, 1994.

Casway, Jerrold. *Ed Delahanty in the Emerald Age of Baseball*. Notre Dame, Indiana: University of Notre Dame Press, 2004.

Deford, Frank. *The Old Ball Game: How John McGraw, Christy Mathewson, and the New York Giants created Modern Baseball*. New York: Atlantic Monthly Press, 2005.

Deveaux, Tom. *The Washington Senators, 1901-1971*. Jefferson, North Carolina: McFarland & Company, Inc., Publishers, 2001.

Dewey, Donald and Nicholas Acocella. *The New Biographical History of Baseball*. Chicago: Triumph Books, 2002.

Dewey, Donald. *The 10th Man: The Fan in Baseball History*. New York: Carroll & Graf Publishers, 2004.

Dewey, Donald and Nicholas Acocella. *Total Ballclubs: The Ultimate Book of Baseball Teams*. Wilmington, Delaware: Sports Media Publishing, Inc., 2005.

DiSalvatore, Bryan. *A Clever Base-Ballist: The Life and Times of John Montgomery Ward*. New York: Patheon Books, 1999.

Evans, David A. *Late in the Game* from *The National Pastime* No. 22. Cleveland, Ohio: Society for American Baseball Research, 2002.

Everybody's Magazine. California: University of California, 1911.

Felber, Bill. *A Game of Brawl: The Orioles, the Beaneaters and the Battle for the 1897 Pennant*. Lincoln, Nebraska: University of Nebraska Press, 2007.

Fleitz, David L. *Cap Anson: The Grand Old Man of Baseball*. Jefferson, North Carolina: McFarland and Company, Inc., 2005.

Gentile, Derek. *The Complete Chicago Cubs: The Total Encyclopedia of the Team*. New York: Black Dog & Leventhal, 2004.

Ginsburg, Daniel E. *The Fix Is In: A History of Baseball Gambling and Game-Fixing Scandals*. Jefferson, North Carolina: McFarland and Company, Inc., 1995.

Gonzalez Echevarria, Roberto. *The Pride of Havana: A History of Cuban Baseball*. New York: Oxford University Press, 1999.

Hirshberg, Charles. *ESPN25*. New York: Hypersion, 2004.

Ivor-Campbell, Frederick, Robert L. Tiemann and Mark Rucker. *Baseball's First Stars*. Cleveland: The Society for American Baseball Research, 1996.

James, Bill. *The New Bill James Historical Baseball Abstract*. New York: The Free Press, 2001.

James, Bill and Rob Neyer. *The Neyer/James Guide to Pitchers: An Historical Compendium of Pitching, Pitchers, and Pitches*. New York: Simon and Schuster, 2004.

Johnson, Lloyd and Miles Wolff. *The Encyclopedia of Minor League Baseball, Second Edition*. Durham, North Carolina: Baseball America, Inc., 1997.

Johnson, Walter. "Why I Signed with the Federal League." *Baseball Magazine*, April, 1915, No. 6, pp. 53-62.

Jones, David. *Deadball Stars of the American League*. Dulles, Virginia: Potomac Books, Inc., 2006.

Kavanagh, Jack. *Ol' Pete: The Grover Cleveland Alexander Story*. South Bend, Indiana: Diamond Communications, Inc., 1996.

Kavanagh, Jack. *Walter Johnson: A Life*. South Bend, Indiana: Diamond Communications, 1996.

Kerr, Jon. *Calvin: Baseball's Last Dinosaur*. William C. Brown Publishers, 1990.

Koppett, Leonard. *Koppett's Concise History of Major League Baseball*. Philadelphia: Temple University Press, 1998.

Lamster, Mark. *Spalding's World Tour: The Epic Adventure That Took Baseball Around the Globe and Made it America's Game*. New York: Public Affairs, 2006.

Lanctot, Neil. *Negro League Baseball: The Rise and Ruin of a Black Institution*. Philadelphia: University of Pennsylvania Press, 2004.

Levy, Alan H. *Joe McCarthy: Architect of the Yankee Dynasty*. Jefferson, North Carolina: McFarland & Company, Inc., Publishers, 2005.

Lieb, Frederick G. *The Baltimore Orioles: The History of a Colorful Team in Baltimore and St. Louis*. Carbondale: Southern Illinois University Press, 1955.

Light, Jonathan Fraser. *The Cultural Encyclopedia of Baseball*. Jefferson, North Carolina: McFarland & Company, Inc., 1997.

Lowry, Philip J. *Green Cathedrals: The Ultimate Celebration of All 271 Major League and Negro League Ballpark Past and Present.* Reading, Massachusetts: Addison-Wesley Publishing Co., Inc., 1992.

Marquis. *Who Was Who in America, Volume 3, 1951-60.* Chicago: The A. N. Marquis Company, 1963.

Mead, William B. and Paul Dickson. *Baseball The Presidents' Game.* New York: Walker and Company, 1997.

Mead, William B. *Baseball Goes to War: Stars Don Khaki, 4-Fs Vie for Pennant.* Washington D.C.: Broadcast Interview Source, Inc., 1998.

McKenna, Brian. *Early Exits: The Premature Endings of Baseball Careers.* Lantham, Maryland: Scarecrow Press, 2006.

McKenna, Brian, "Charlie Grant," SABR Biography Project

McKenna, Brian, "Hoss Radbourn," SABR Biography Project

McKenna, Brian, "Joe Cambria," SABR Biography Project

McKenna, Brian, "Norris O'Neill," SABR Biography Project

McKenna, Brian, "Steve Bellan," SABR Biography Project

Miller, James Edward. *The Baseball Business: Pursuing Pennants and Profits in Baltimore.* Chapel Hill, North Carolina: The University of North Carolina Press, 1990.

Morris, Peter. *A Game of Inches: The Stories Behind the Innovations That Shaped Baseball, The Game on the Field.* Chicago, Ivan R. Dee, 2006.

Morris, Peter. *A Game of Inches: The Stories Behind the Innovations That Shaped Baseball, The Game Behind the Scenes.* Chicago, Ivan R. Dee, 2006.

Morris, Peter. Level *Playing Fields: How the Groundskeeping Murphy Brothers Shaped Baseball.* Nebraska: University of Nebraska Press, 2007.

Murdock, Eugene C. *Ban Johnson: Czar of Baseball.* Westport, Connecticut: Greenwood Press, 1982.

Nelson, Kevin. *The Golden Game: The Story of California Baseball.* San Francisco: California Historical Society Press, 2004.

Oleksak, Michael M. and Mary Adams Oleksak. *Latin Americans and the Grand Old Game.* Grand Rapids, Michigan: Masters Press, 1991.

Pietrusza, David. *Lights On!: The Wild Century-Long Saga of Night Baseball.* Lanham, Maryland: The Scarecrow Press, Inc., 1997.

Pietrusza, David. *Judge and Jury: The Life and Times of Judge Kenesaw Mountain Landis.* South Bend, Indiana: Diamond Communications, Inc., 1998.

Podoll, Brian A. *The Minor League Milwaukee Brewers 1859-1952.* Jefferson, North Carolina: McFarland & Company, Inc., Publishers, 2003.

Povich, Shirley. *The Washington Senators: An Informal History.* New York: G.P. Putnam's Sons, 1954.

Povich, Shirley. *All Those Mornings…At the Post.* New York: Public Affairs, 2005.

Reidenbaugh, Lowell. *Take Me Out to the Ball Park.* St. Louis: *The* Sporting News Publishing Co., 1983.

Reisler, Jim. *A Great Day in Cooperstown: The Improbable Birth of Baseball's Hall of Fame*. New York: Carroll & Graf Publishers, 2006.

Riley, James A. *The Biographical Encyclopedia of the Negro Baseball Leagues*. New York: Carroll and Graf Publishers, 1994.

Rothe, Anna. *Current Biography: Who's News and Why 1950*. New York: The H. W. Wilson Company, 1951.

Schlossberg, Dan. *The New Baseball Catalog*. New York: Jonathan David Publishers, Inc., 1998.

Seymour, Harold. *Baseball: The Early Years*. New York: Oxford University Press, 1960.

Seymour, Harlod. *Baseball: The Golden Age*. New York: Oxford University Press, 1971.

Shatzkin, Mike and Jim Carlton. *The Ballplayers: Baseball's Ultimate Biographical Reference*. New York: Arbor House, 1990.

Skinner, David. *Havana and Key West: Jose Mendez and the Great Scoreless Streak of 1908. The National Pastime #24*. Cleveland: SABR, 2004.

Snyder, Brad. *Beyond the Shadow of the Senator: The Untold Story of the Homestead Grays and the Integration of Baseball*. Chicago: Contemporary Books, 2003.

Sobel, Robert. *Biographical Directory of the U.S. Executive Branch: 1774-1989*. Westport, Connecticut: Greenwood Press, 1990.

Society for American Baseball Research. *The SABR Baseball List and Record Book*. New York: SABR, 2007.

Solomon, Burt. *Where They Ain't: The Fabled Life and Untimely Death of the Original Baltimore Orioles. The Team that Gave Birth to Modern Baseball.* New York: Doubleday Books, 1999.

Solomon, Burt. *The Baseball Timeline.* New York: DK Publishing, Inc., 2001.

Sowell, Mike. *The Pitch That Killed: Carl Mays, Ray Chapman and the Pennant Race of 1920.* New York: MacMillan Publishing Company, 1989.

Sowell, Mike. *July 2, 1903: The Mysterious Death of Hall-of-Famer Big Ed Delahanty.* New York: MacMillan Publishing Company, 1992.

Spalding, John E. *Always on Sunday: The California Baseball League, 1886 to 1915.* Manhattan, Kansas: Ag Press, 1992.

Spatz, Lyle. *Bad Bill Dahlen.* Jefferson, North Carolina: McFarland and Company, Inc., 2004.

Stark, Benton. *The Year They Called Off the World Series.* New York: Avery Publishing Group Inc., 1991.

Stout, Glenn. *Yankees Century: 100 Years of New York Yankees Baseball.* New York: Houghton Mifflin Company, 2002.

Sullivan, Dean A. *Early Innings: A Documentary History of Baseball, 1825-1908.* Lincoln, Nebraska: University of Nebraska Press, 1995.

Sullivan, Dean A. *Middle Innings: A Documentary History of Baseball, 1900-1948.* Lincoln, Nebraska: University of Nebraska Press, 1998.

Thomas, Henry W. *Walter Johnson: Baseball's Big Train.* Washington D.C.: Phenom Press, 1995.

Thorn, John. *The Relief Pitcher: Baseball's New Hero*. New York: E.P. Dutton, 1979.

Thorn, John, Phil Birnbaum, Bill Deane, Rob Neyer, Alan Schwarz, Donald Dewey, Nicholas Acocella and Peter Wayner. *Total Baseball: The Ultimate Baseball Encyclopedia, Eighth Edition*. Wilmington, Delaware: Sport Classic Books, 2004.

Tiemann, Robert L. and Mark Rucker. *Nineteenth Century Stars*. Cleveland: Society for American Baseball Research, 1989.

Tofel, Richard J. *A Legend in the Making: The New York Yankees in 1939*. Chicago: Ivan R. Dee, 2002.

Tygiel, Jules. *Past Time: Baseball as History*. Oxford: Oxford University Press, 2000.

Voigt, David Quentin. *American Baseball: From the Commissioners to Continental Expansion, Volume II*. University Park, Pennsylvania: The Pennsylvania State University Press, 1992.

Werber, Bill and C. Paul Rogers III. *Memories of a Ballplayer: Bill Werber and Baseball in the 1930s*. Cleveland: The Society for American Baseball Research, 2001.

Wilson, Nick C. *Early Latino Ballplayers in the United States: Major, Minor and Negro Leagues, 1901-1949*. Jefferson, North Carolina: McFarland & Company, Inc., Publishers, 2005.

Zimbalist, Andrew. *In the Best Interest of Baseball?: The Revolutionary Reign of Bud Selig*. Hoboken, New Jersey: John Wiley & Sons, 2006.

CONTEMPORARY NEWSPAPERS and MAGAZINES

108 Magazine

Abilene Reporter, Texas

Atchison Champion, Atchison, Kansas
Atlanta Constitution
Atlanta Daily World
Baltimore Afro-American
Baltimore Sun
Baseball Magazine
Boston Globe
Boston Herald
Brooklyn Eagle
Chicago Daily Tribune
Chicago Defender
Cincinnati Enquirer
Daily Inter Ocean, Chicago, Illinois
Daily Picayune, New Orleans
Daily Review, Decatur, Illinois
Decatur Daily Republican, Illinois
Decatur Republican, Illinois
Denver Evening Post
Dunkirk Evening Observer, Dunkirk, New York
Hartford Courant
Knoxville News Sentinel
Lincoln Evening News
Los Angeles Times
Milwaukee Daily Journal
Milwaukee Daily News
Milwaukee Sentinel
Morning Oregonian, Portland
New York Amsterdam News
New York Daily News
New York Evening Telegram
New York Times

North American, Philadelphia

Outing Magazine

The Pantagraph, Bloomington, Illinois

Pittsburgh Courier

Sandusky Star, Ohio

Sporting Life

The Sporting News

St. Louis Globe-Democrat

St. Louis Post-Dispatch

St. Louis Sporting Times

St. Paul Daily News

Steubenville Herald, Ohio

Washington Post

Washington Star

Weekly Herald Dispatch, Decatur, Illinois

Yenowine's Illustrated News, Milwaukee, Wisconsin

WEB SITES

alookatcook.com

ancestry.com

arlingtoncemetery.net

baseball-almanac.com

baseballlibrary.com

davidpietrusza.com

findagrave.com

fortunecity.com

maurybrown.com

minorleagueresearcher.blogspot.com

nevamo.com

normal.org

nyc.gov

paperofrecord.com

proquest.com

retrosheet.org

roadsidephotos.sabr.org/baseball/bbblog.htm

sabrwebs.com/minors

usmo.com

wikipedia.org

worldgolf.com

MISCELLANEOUS

Clark Griffith's file at the National Baseball Hall of Fame, pulled July 2008

Harmony Lodge No. 17 F.A.A.M. Bulletin, April 1945

Society for American Baseball Research, Biography Project

INTERVIEW

Clark Griffith II, a one-hour phone conversation on February 6, 2006

SPECIAL THANKS:

Thanks to Marc Blau for his insight into Tacoma baseball and his connections there.

Thanks also to Jim Price for his experience with Tacoma and Montana baseball history and his patience with my numerous approaches for his insight.

I am perpetually awed over the courteousness and insight of the men and women who frequent Baseball-Fever.com, my daily source of baseball history communication.

Thanks to Tom Swift, author of *Chief Bender's Burden*, for an email exchange and his insight into Clark Griffith and Chief Bender's relationship.

SELECT INDEX

Ainsmith, Eddie, 296
Almeida, Rafael, 156-159
Altizer, Dave, 155
Altrock, Nick, 167-168, 171-172, 180-181, 198
Anson, Cap, 26-28, 54, 62, 65-69, 89-90
Baker, Newton D., 296-299
Bancroft, Frank, 155-156
Bellan, Esteban, 252
Bescher, Bob, 153-154
Bluege, Ozzie, 215-216, 288
Brush, John, 79, 93, 99, 128-130, 152
Buffington, Charlie, 36, 71
Callahan, Nixey, 81
Campbell, Bruce, 283
Cambria, Joe, 251-257
Cantillon, Joe, 49-50, 58-59
Celler, Emmanuel, 288-289
Chandler, Happy, 282-284, 289-290
Chase, Hal, 136-138, 141, 148-149, 205-206
Chesbro, Jack, 223
Cobb, Ty, 120-121, 123, 141, 156, 172-173, 209
Coolidge, Calvin, 311
Coolidge, Grace, 311
Comiskey, Charles, 50-51, 93, 100-101, 113, 156, 205

Crowder, General Enoch, 297

Cronin, Joe, 196, 201, 221

Dahlen, Bill, 61-62, 65, 66, 79, 80, 82

Davis, George, 110, 117, 129

Delahanty, Ed, 53-54

De Oro, Alfredo, 143

Dickey, Bill, 235

Dillon, Pop, 11, 141, 160, 246

Dunn, Jack, 172, 174, 215

Eastman, Joseph B., 307

Eisenhower, Dwight, 312

Elberfeld, Kid, 123, 128-129, 145

Emslie, Bob, 69

Engel, Joe, 172, 175, 180, 198, 215, 221, 234, 247-248, 253, 319-320

Eynon, Edward, 8, 190, 199-200, 222, 237, 293, 317, 324

Farrell, Frank, 125-128, 131, 133-135, 138, 141-142, 145, 148, 194, 206

Fitzgerald, Joe, 199

Freedman, Andrew, 70, 82, 108, 110, 115-119, 125-126

Fultz, Dave, 120-122, 295

Gardella, Danny, 283-284

Garvin, Ned, 113, 139

Gedeon, Elmer, 280

Gieschen, Louis, 47-48

Gilmore, Jim, 174

Glade, Fred, 146-148

Gompers, Samuel, 90-91

Goslin, Goose, 183, 215-218, 233, 236-237

Grant, Charlie, 102-103

Grant, Frank, 26

Griffith, Calvin, 200, 214, 248, 257, 275, 277, 286, 289, 313, 316, 319-321

Hannegan, Robert E., 304-305

Harding, Warren, 310

Harris, Bucky, 180, 183, 215-216, 219-221, 238, 286

Hart, Jim, 20, 52, 63, 66-67, 69-70, 83-84, 89-90, 94, 98, 102, 134

Herrmann, Garry, 96, 98-99, 129, 149-153, 157-158, 160, 164, 204, 209, 211, 243

Hoover, Herbert, 311

Howell, Harry, 120-121, 131, 148

Hoy, Dummy, 33-34

Hurst, Tim, 54, 80, 142-143

Hutchison, Bill, 22, 60, 62, 68, 71, 84

Irwin, Arthur, 35-36

Jachym, James J., 314-317

Johnson, Ban, 49-50, 56, 68, 89-96, 99, 101, 105-106, 108, 112, 115, 120, 127, 129-131, 134-137, 143-144, 150-153, 156, 161-164, 172, 176-179, 181, 185-186, 204-205, 210-212, 218-221, 245, 292, 294-297, 309

Johnson, Walter, 11, 50, 85, 145, 166-167, 170-176, 182-188, 201, 215, 217-218, 220-222, 225, 234-235, 272, 321

Joss, Addie, 75-76, 111

Landis, Judge, 99, 137, 174, 200, 205, 207-211, 214, 217-220, 222, 226-227, 229, 231-232, 234

Killebrew, Harmon, 215, 288

Kilpatrick, Charles, 42

Kittridge, Mal, 57, 65, 70, 90

Lacy, Sam, 259, 262, 264-265, 267

Lajoie, Napoleon, 76, 98, 104, 109, 120-121, 129

Lange, Bill, 39, 53, 55, 61, 64, 66, 69-70, 81-82, 90, 173, 240, 295-296

Marberry, Firpo, 216-217, 220, 224-225

Marsans, Armando, 156-160, 172, 251

Martin, Mike, 155, 168, 178, 198, 250, 274, 286

McBride, George, 167, 177, 183, 213-214, 216

McGraw, John, 74, 79, 83, 90, 97, 101-103, 105, 107-109, 117-118, 120, 124, 128-130, 134, 137, 143, 150, 153, 164, 176-177, 206-207, 214, 218, 224-225, 259

McNabb, Edgar, 39, 55, 57-58

Milan, Clyde, 145, 167, 183, 214, 235

Minor, Benjamin, 145, 184-185, 188, 297

Moran, Bill, 35

Morgan, Ray, 172, 217

Mullane, Tony, 42, 111

Murphy, H. Gabriel, 315-318

Murphy, Robert, 285

Navin, Frank, 161, 172, 210, 238, 270

Nichols, Kid, 25, 57, 61, 64, 68, 70-71, 81, 83, 132

Noyes, Thomas, 161-166, 169-170, 188-190

O'Connell, Jimmy, 137, 218

O'Connor, Jack, 119-121

O'Neil, Dan, 157

O'Neill, Norris, 50-51, 55, 144

O'Neill, Tip, 33-34

Pasquel, Jorge, 283-284

Posey, Cum, 308

Povich, Shirley, 4, 7, 197

Powell, Jake, 253, 262-263

Radbourn, Hoss, 15, 18-20, 30, 32, 71, 74, 76, 157, 279

Rice, Sam, 176, 200, 215, 217, 236-237

Richardson, George, 313-314

Richardson, William M., 189-190, 313-314, 326

Rickey, Branch, 145, 148, 239, 243-246, 258-260, 266-267, 281, 314, 324

Robertson, Sherry, 196

Roosevelt, Franklin, 302, 304-305, 309-312

Rothstein, Arnold, 206-207

Rusie, Amos, 64, 68, 70-71, 73, 82, 88, 90, 116-117, 173

Ruth, Babe, 174, 180, 190, 200, 210, 212, 217, 227, 229, 233-234, 238, 248, 295, 311, 324

Schaefer, Germany, 168, 181, 274

Schriver, Pop, 62

Selbach, Kip, 74-75

Shepard, Bert, 264, 281

Shugart, Frank, 100, 106-107, 110

Smith, Billy, 200, 246

Smith, Pacer, 17-18

Speaker, Tris, 167, 175-176, 179, 209, 219-220

Stovey, George, 26

Sunday, Billy, 179-180

Sutton, Ezra, 23-24

Travis, Cecil, 248, 280-281, 307

Truman, Harry, 304-305, 311, 324

Tweed, Boss, 116

Von der Ahe, Chris, 15, 31-32, 35, 37, 90

Waddell, Rube, 83-84, 97, 113, 133, 135, 142

Wagner, Honus, 79, 98, 128, 153, 312

Ward, Monte, 4, 117, 132, 200

Weyhing, Gus, 54, 68, 72

Wilson, Woodrow, 293-294

Works, Bill, 39-41, 44, 46

Yawkey, Tom, 227, 237-238, 268

Young, Cy, 37, 35, 70, 74, 81, 85, 109, 112, 120, 132, 173

Zachary, Tom, 180, 215, 218

Zimmer, Chief, 92-95

Printed in Great Britain
by Amazon